EYES OFF THE PRIZE

As World War II drew to a close and the world awakened to the horror wrought by white supremacists in Nazi Germany, African American leaders, led by the NAACP, sensed the opportunity to launch an offensive against the conditions of segregation and inequality in the United States. The "prize" they sought was not civil rights, it was human rights. Only the human rights lexicon, shaped by the Holocaust and articulated by the United Nations, contained the language and the moral power to address not only the political and legal inequality, but also the education, health care, housing, and employment needs that haunted the black community. The NAACP understood this and wielded its influence and resources to take its human rights agenda before the United Nations. But the onset of the Cold War and rising anti-communism allowed powerful Southerners to cast those rights as Soviet-inspired and a threat to the American "way of life." Enemies and friends excoriated the movement, and the NAACP retreated to a narrow civil rights agenda that was easier to maintain politically. Thus, the Civil Rights Movement was launched with neither the language nor the mission it needed to truly achieve black equality.

Carol Anderson is an Assistant Professor of History at the University of Missouri–Columbia. Her research on African Americans, the United Nations, and human rights has received generous financial support from the American Council of Learned Societies, the Ford Foundation, and the Eisenhower World Affairs Institute. She has received multiple awards for teaching and is a recipient of the William T. Kemper Fellowship for Teaching Excellence.

EYES OFF THE PRIZE

The United Nations and the African American Struggle for Human Rights, 1944–1955

CAROL ANDERSON

University of Missouri–Columbia

CAMBRIDGE UNIVERSITY PRESS
Cambridge, New York, Melbourne, Madrid, Cape Town,
Singapore, São Paulo, Delhi, Tokyo, Mexico City

Cambridge University Press
32 Avenue of the Americas, New York, NY 10013-2473, USA

www.cambridge.org
Information on this title: www.cambridge.org/9780521531580

First published 2003
8th printing 2011

A catalog record for this publication is available from the British Library.

Library of Congress Cataloging in Publication Data

Anderson, Carol (Carol Elaine)
Eyes off the prize : African Americans, the United Nations, and the struggle for human rights, 1944-1945 / Carol Anderson.
p. cm.
Includes bibliographical references and index.
ISBN 0-521-82431-1 – ISBN 0-521-53158-6 (pbk.)
1. African Americans – Civil rights. 2. Human rights – United States – History – 20th century. 3. African Americans – History – 1877-1964. 4. Civil rights movements – United States – History – 20th century. 5. United Nations – United States. I. Title.
E185.61 A543 2003
323.1′196073–dc21 2002031554

ISBN 978-0-521-82431-6 Hardback
ISBN 978-0-521-53158-0 Paperback

Dedicated to
Mommy, Daddy, and Little Dave
I miss you.

Contents

Acknowledgments

The writing of this book could have easily been the subject of a book itself. I thank all of those who gave me the strength, support, and sense of humor to get through it. First and foremost, I thank my parents, George and Beth Anderson, who although they died before the book was completed, gave me the inner peace I needed to carry on. And then, there are my sons, Aaron and Drew, whose wry sense of humor always helped me keep things in perspective. I thank my brothers, Earl, David, and Wendell, for making me believe that I could do anything. But, then again, high-stakes, winner-takes-your-dignity pinochle with K.D., Jimi Hendrix, full throttle, at 6 A.M., and going 100 mph down Main Street in a '64 midnight blue Chevy Malibu will do that for you. I honor and thank my neighbors for life, Charles (Is Said) and Anita Lyons, who gave me a village whether I was right across the street or a thousand miles away. I sincerely thank Wendy O'Donnell, who was always there for me even when I didn't know I needed it. Thanks for "kidnaping" me, for being "not nice," and being there regardless. No one does it better. A special thank you to my best friend, Yolanda Comedy, who was my rock when the earth crumbled beneath my feet. Yolanda had the wisdom and compassion to handle all of the phone calls at three in the morning, whether it was about yet another death in the family, the Biblical flood that wiped out almost an entire floor of my house, including my home office, or the... (well, as I said, that would be another book in and of itself).

Through it all, I have been fortunate to have incredible colleagues at the University of Missouri–Columbia, at Ohio State University, and throughout the country, who have read chapters, helped revise grant proposals, and shared sources. Your insights, whether I was able to incorporate them or not, always pushed me to think deeper and further about what I was saying. Thank you Kwame Alford, Rowland Brucken, Robert Collins, Mary Dudziak, Cary Fraser, Cheryl Greenberg, Patrick Hadley, Patrick Hill, Michael Hogan, Mary Ann Heiss, Abdullahi Ibrahim,

Ruth Iyob, Franklin Knight, Michael Krenn, Paul Pierpaoli, Brenda Gayle Plummer, Lewis Randolph, Linda Reeder, Jonathan Rosenberg, Marshall Stevenson, Jr., Arvarh Strickland, William Walker, Garry Walters, Steven Watts, Robert Weems, Jr., George White, Jr., LeeAnn Whites, Laura Wexler, Elisse Wright, and the anonymous reviewers who provided wonderful suggestions for taking the manuscript "to the next level." I also must thank two amazing undergraduate research assistants, Jamenda Moss-Briscoe and Vernon Mitchell, Jr., who could ferret out even the most obscure sources quickly and with ease. Of course, none of this would have been possible without the expertise of the archivists and librarians, such as Dennis Bilger, Liz Safly, JoEllen El-Bashir, Lynn Bassanese, Robert Parks, Nancy Snedeker, Geoffrey Swindell, William Stoltz, Connie May, Albert King, Fred Bauman, and Kia Campbell, whom I thank profusely.

I am also indebted to the Ford Foundation, the American Council for Learned Societies, the Eisenhower World Affairs Institute, the Mississippi Humanities Council, the Research Board of the University of Missouri System, the Research Council of the University of Missouri–Columbia, the Council on Inter-institutional Cooperation, and Ohio State University for generous research and fellowship support.

Finally, I thank Lewis Bateman and Alia Winters at Cambridge University Press for having the vision to take this project on and move it forward with such skill and alacrity.

I know that what I am asking is impossible. But in our time, as in every time, the impossible is the least that one can demand – and one is, after all, emboldened by the spectacle of human history in general, and American Negro history in particular, for it testifies to nothing less than the perpetual achievement of the impossible.

James Baldwin
The Fire Next Time

Introduction

The Struggle for Black Equality

> *There is not even a common language when the term "equality" is used. Negro and white have a fundamentally different definition. Negroes have proceeded from a premise that equality means what it says.... But most whites in America... proceed from a premise that equality is a loose expression for improvement. White America is not even psychologically organized to close the gap—essentially it seeks only to retain it.*
>
> Rev. Dr. Martin Luther King, Jr.[1]

How could all of the blood, all of the courage, and all of the martyrs of the Civil Rights Movement still leave in its wake a nation where schools are more segregated than ever, where more than half of all black children live in poverty, and where the life expectancy of African Americans has actually *declined*? And how could a movement with so much promise still leave more than six million African Americans trapped and dying in the "underclass"?[2] The answer lies, I believe, not so much in the well-documented struggle for civil rights, but in the little known, but infinitely more important, struggle for human rights. For too long, civil rights has been heralded as the "prize" for black equality.[3] Yet, those rights, no

1. Martin Luther King, Jr., *Where Do We Go From Here: Chaos or Community* (New York: Harper & Row, 1967), 8.
2. Gary Orfield, Susan E. Eaton, et al., *Dismantling Desegregation: The Quiet Reversal of Brown v. Board of Education* (New York: New Press, 1996); Deborah L. Cohen, "Half of Black, Hispanic Children May Be Poor by 2010," *Education Week*, 3 November 1993; Jessie Carney Smith and Robert L. Johns, eds., *Statistical Record of Black America* (New York: Gale Research, Inc., 1995); William J. Wilson, *The Truly Disadvantaged: The Inner City, the Underclass, and Public Policy* (Chicago: University of Chicago Press, 1987).
3. Juan Williams, *Eyes on the Prize: America's Civil Rights Years, 1954–1965*, with an introduction by Julian Bond (New York: Viking Penguin, 1987); Clayborne Carson, Vincent Harding et al. eds., *The Eyes on the Prize Civil Rights Reader: Documents, Speeches and Firsthand Accounts from the Black Freedom Struggle* (New York: Viking Penguin, 1991); *Eyes on the Prize: America's Civil Rights Years, 1954–1965*, Vol. 4, *No*

matter how bitterly fought for, could only speak to the overt political and legal discrimination that African Americans faced. Human rights, on the other hand, especially as articulated by the United Nations (UN) and influenced by the moral shock of the Holocaust, had the language and philosophical power to address not only the political and legal inequality that African Americans endured, but also the education, health care, housing, and employment needs that haunted the black community.

In fact, toward the end of the Second World War, the African American leadership, led by the National Association for the Advancement of Colored People (NAACP), had already decided that only human rights could repair the damage that more than three centuries of slavery, Jim Crow, and racism had done to the African American community. Civil rights, no matter how noble, could only maintain the gap. The NAACP, therefore, marshaled its resources – including a war chest of more than one million dollars, nearly 500,000 members, and access to power brokers throughout the world – to make human rights *the* standard for equality. Although there were other African American organizations contributing to this effort, including the black Left, none of them had the credibility, the money, and the influence to make human rights the agenda in the struggle for black equality.[4] Only the NAACP could do that. Yet, even with all its clout and prestige, the Association recognized that it could not singlehandedly alter the trajectory of America's sordid racial history.

The NAACP, therefore, forged important, but ultimately flawed, alliances with Eleanor Roosevelt and Harry S Truman to aid in the struggle for African Americans' human rights. Yet, whereas Roosevelt and Truman were clearly committed to some measure of civil rights, they were both unable and unprepared to fight for a world that embraced full equality for African Americans. Truman was emphatic. "'I wish to make clear,'" he told a group of black Democrats, "'that I am not appealing for social equality for the Negro. The Negro himself knows better than that, and the highest type of Negro leaders say quite frankly that they prefer the society of their own people. Negroes want justice, not social equality.'"[5]

Easy Walk (1961–1963), produced and directed by James DeVinney and Callie Crossely, Blackside, Inc., 1987, videocassette.

4. For works that suggest a much more important role for the black Left see, Penny M. Von Eschen, *Race Against Empire: Black Americans and Anticolonialism, 1937–1957* (Ithaca, New York, and London: Cornell University Press, 1997); Gerald Horne, *Communist Front? The Civil Rights Congress, 1946–1956* (London and Toronto: Associated University Presses, 1988).
5. Quoted in, Harry S. Ashmore, *Civil Rights and Wrongs: A Memoir of Race and Politics, 1944–1994* (New York: Pantheon Books, 1994), 57.

With this narrow philosophical framework, Truman set out to implement his vision of equality for the black community. He issued executive orders to desegregate the federal bureaucracy and the military. He commissioned a study on the status of civil rights in the United States. He also had the Justice Department support a range of desegregation cases winding through the court system. And although this was an impressive start, especially compared with the sluggish civil rights efforts of Franklin Roosevelt and Dwight Eisenhower, Truman's efforts did not even come close to what needed to be done. Instead, it becomes evident that he often engaged in the politics of symbolic equality – executive orders issued with little or no funding to finance the endeavor; powerless commissions created to once again study "the Negro problem" and give the aura of action; and directives issued from on high with no enforcement mechanism and no serious repercussions for noncompliance.

Similarly, although scholars and admirers speak glowingly about Eleanor Roosevelt's unstinting support for African American equality, she, too, was one of the masters of symbolic equality.[6] The stories of her battles to allow Marian Anderson to sing at the Lincoln Memorial, coupled with her act of racial defiance in a Southern Jim Crow theater, cemented Roosevelt's reputation as "a friend of the Negro." A closer examination of her actions in the UN and the repercussions of those actions for the black community, however, reveal a very different story. Thus, in her role as chair of the UN Commission on Human Rights, although she sympathized with the plight of African Americans, she was even more responsive to the public relations exigencies of the Cold War, which called for sanitizing and camouflaging the reality of America's Jim Crow democracy. She, therefore, joined with Texas Senator Tom Connally and others in an attempt to thwart a complaint to the UN charging South Africa with racial discrimination and systematic human rights violations. Roosevelt, Connally, and the other members of the U.S. delegation voiced strong concerns that, if the complaint succeeded, it would set a dangerous precedent that could ultimately lead to the United Nations investigating the condition of "negroes in Alabama."[7]

6. See, for example, Allida M. Black, *Casting Her Own Shadow: Eleanor Roosevelt and the Shaping of Postwar Liberalism* (New York: Columbia University Press, 1996); A. Glenn Mower, Jr., *The United States, the United Nations, and Human Rights: The Eleanor Roosevelt and Jimmy Carter Eras*, Studies in Human Rights, ed. George W. Shepherd, Jr., no. 4 (Westport, Connecticut: Greenwood Press, 1979); Alpha Kappa Alpha Sorority, Inc.: National History, http://www.uca.edu/org/aka/nationalhistory.htm. Accessed May 18, 2002.

7. Minutes of the Tenth Meeting of the General Assembly Delegation, October 28, 1946, US/A/M/(CHR)/10, Box 60, File "US/A/M/(CHR)/1-32," *Records of the U.S. Mission*

Roosevelt also used her chairmanship and influence to manipulate the human rights treaties in ways that would shield the United States from UN scrutiny and assuage the powerful Southern Democrats, who "were afraid" that the UN's treaties just "might affect the Colored question." After all, the senators from Georgia and Texas railed, those treaties were nothing more than a "back-door method of enacting federal anti-lynching legislation."[8] Mrs. Roosevelt, therefore, fought for the insertion of a clause in the Covenant on Human Rights that would allow states that were in a federal system, such as Georgia, to disregard the treaty completely. Mrs. Roosevelt explained the benefits of this federal–state clause to a skeptical Southern audience as she promised that, even with a Covenant on Human Rights, the federal government would never interfere in "murder cases," investigate concerns over "fair trials," or insist on "the right to education." In essence, Eleanor Roosevelt had just assured the Dixiecrats that the sacred troika of lynching, Southern Justice, and Jim Crow schools would remain untouched, even with an international treaty to safeguard human rights.[9] Obviously, then, although the United States was willing to use the rhetoric of human rights to bludgeon the Soviet Union and play the politics of moral outrage that the Holocaust engendered, the federal government, even the liberals, steadfastly refused to make human rights a viable force in the United States or in international practice.[10]

to the United Nations, Record Group 84 (hereafter *RG 84*); Minutes of the Eleventh Meeting of the United States General Assembly Delegation, October 28, 1946, US/A/M/(CHR)/11, ibid.; Minutes of the Fifteenth Meeting of the General Assembly Delegation, November 12, 1946, US/A/M/(CHR)/15, ibid.; Minutes of the Tenth Meeting of the United States Delegation to the Third Regular Session of the General Assembly, October 5, 1948, US(P) A/M/(CHR)/10, Box 60, File "US(P)/A/M/ (CHR)/1-34," ibid.

8. Memorandum from Ralph E. Becker [to Senator Thomas C. Hennings, Jr.], January 22, 1954, Folder 4772, *Papers of Thomas C. Hennings, Jr.*, Western Historical Manuscript Collection, University of Missouri–Columbia, Columbia, Missouri (hereafter *Hennings Papers*); Fisher to Rusk, memo, January 19, 1950, Box 8, File "Genocide (folder 1 of 2)," Lot File 55D429, *General Records of the Department of State, Record Group 59* (hereafter *RG 59*).
9. "Statement to the Press by Mrs. Franklin D. Roosevelt on the 'Federal State' Clause of the Covenant on Human Rights," press release, June 6, 1952, Box 4588, File "Human Rights Commission, undated," *Papers of Eleanor Roosevelt,* Franklin D. Roosevelt Presidential Library, Hyde Park, New York (hereafter *Roosevelt Papers*); Lowell Limpus, "UN Pact Won't Clash with States' Rights, Says Mrs. Roosevelt," June 9, 1952, found in Box 626, File "UN Secur. Council 'Commission on Human Rt. of the Econ. & Soc. Coun.,'" *Republican National Committee Newspaper Clippings,* Dwight D. Eisenhower Presidential Library, Abilene, Kansas (hereafter *RNC*); Walter White to Jacob Javits, March 6, 1952, Box 117, File "Bills: McCarran Bill—General—1950–52," *Papers of the National Association for the Advancement of Colored People,* Library of Congress, Washington, D.C. (hereafter *Papers of the NAACP*).
10. David P. Forsythe, "Human Rights in U.S. Foreign Policy: Retrospect and Prospect," *Political Science Quarterly* 105:3 (Autumn 1990), 435–54; Louis Henkin, "U.S.

The international struggle for African Americans' human rights thus became entangled in the entrenched power of the Southern Democrats and the shallowness of white liberal commitment to black equality. The struggle was ultimately destroyed, however, by the Cold War and the anti-Communist witch hunts, which compromised the integrity of the black leadership, twisted the definition of human rights into the hammer and sickle, and forced the NAACP to take its eyes off the prize of human rights.

Mary Dudziak, Michael Krenn, and Thomas Borstlemann have ably demonstrated how the Cold War muddied U.S. foreign policy and compelled the federal government to make several grudging but key concessions on the civil rights front to quell mounting international criticism.[11] The Cold War, however, affected much more than the federal government's half-hearted, but necessary, response to black inequality.

The Cold War also systematically eliminated human rights as a viable option for the mainstream African American leadership. During the McCarthy era, human rights and the United Nations became synonymous with the Kremlin and the Soviet-led subversion of American democracy. The Southern Democrats and isolationist Republicans joined together and denounced rights, such as housing and health care, as foreign to all liberty-loving Americans and inspired by the scourge of Marxist dogma. Although the right wing's anti-Communist fulminations were to be expected, elements of those basic sentiments were shared across the ideological spectrum. Eleanor Roosevelt, for example, also made the political distinction between the revered political and legal rights emanating from Western thought, such as the right to free speech, and the untried, untested, and unwashed economic and social rights that seemed so dear to the Soviets and other communists. Truman and his advisors agreed and tried desperately to rein in or at least neutralize the UN's human

Ratification of Human Rights Conventions: The Ghost of Senator Bricker," *American Journal of International Law* 89:2 (April 1995), 341–50; Dorothy Q. Thomas, "We Are Not the World: U.S. Activism and Human Rights in the Twenty-First Century," *Signs: Journal of Women in Culture and Society* 25:4 (2000), 1121–24; Sandy Vogelgesang, "Diplomacy of Human Rights," *International Studies Quarterly* 23:2 (June 1979), 230–35.

11. Mary L. Dudziak, *Cold War Civil Rights: Race and the Image of American Democracy*, Politics and Society in Twentieth-Century America, eds. William Chafe, Gary Gerstle, and Linda Gordon (Princeton, New Jersey and Oxford: Princeton University Press, 2000); idem, "Desegregation as a Cold War Imperative" *Stanford Law Review* 41:1 (November 1988), 61–120; Michael L. Krenn, *Black Diplomacy: African Americans and the State Department, 1945–1969* (Armonk, New York: M. E. Sharpe, 1999); Thomas Borstlemann, *The Cold War and the Color Line: American Race Relations in the Global Arena* (Cambridge, Massachusetts and London: Harvard University Press, 2001).

rights initiatives and to supplant the international community's expansive definition of human rights with one that included only a small number of political and legal rights.

As bad as this situation was, it got decisively worse when the Eisenhower administration came to power in 1953. With no firm commitment to either the UN, human rights, or African Americans and pressured by the right wing to jettison all of the covenants on human rights or risk the Damocles' sword of the Bricker Amendment, which would have turned the president into a mere figurehead, Eisenhower and his secretary of state, John Foster Dulles, eagerly announced that the United States had decided to abandon the human rights declarations and treaties altogether, because, in addition to being impractical, those treaties harbored communistic ideas and were a direct threat to the basic liberties protected by the Constitution.

With the presidents, the Senate, and even some liberals identifying the economic and social rights provisions of the UN's treaties as a "Soviet Trojan Horse," the foundation for true black equality was now roundly repudiated as subversive, communistic, and even treasonous.[12] The NAACP was caught. To push further for human rights was to risk all of the dangers that being labeled a "communist front" entailed. Moreover, because a fight for human rights exposed the depths of America's flawed democracy to the world, it also served as a ready-made propaganda weapon for the Kremlin, which, when wielded, would then only reaffirm the insidious allegations about the NAACP's communist bent. On the other hand, to jettison human rights was to leave the black community with only the hope of civil rights, which the NAACP's own analysis made clear was not enough to rectify the destruction that centuries of human rights violations had caused. As wholly inadequate as civil rights may have been, however, they carried the protection of being firmly rooted in American tradition and the Bill of Rights.

The NAACP clearly stood at the proverbial crossroads. Pressured by the image-conscious demands of the Cold War; hounded by white liberal allies to turn toward more traditional, pragmatic goals; thrown off course by internal dissension and power plays; distracted by battles with the Communist Party, USA; chastened by the telling example that the U.S. government was making of the black Left; and hopeful that its legal strategy would be more than enough to bring about equality, the NAACP opted to reincarnate itself as an "American organization" and retreat from the struggle for human rights.

12. Quoted in, Rowland Brucken, "A Most Uncertain Crusade: The United States, Human Rights and the United Nations, 1941–1954," (Ph.D. diss., Ohio State University, 1999), 233.

The results were devastating. The fight for black equality was now limited to the narrowly confined, traditional arena of political rights and the "Soviet-tainted" goal of economic and social rights – even though essential for true black equality – was overtly removed from the NAACP's agenda. And because the African American Left was destroyed by its own strategic blunders and the McCarthy witch hunts, there was no countervailing force, no matter how small, to balance the NAACP's forced retreat. The remaining black leadership could therefore only envision a civil rights, not a human rights, movement and would soon discover that blacks in the northern slums could not be freed by hymns, protest marches, or Supreme Court decisions. This would be one of the most tragic, but not yet explored, legacies of the Cold War. Until now.

1

Beyond Civil Rights

The NAACP, the United Nations, and Redefining the Struggle for Black Equality

Power concedes nothing without a demand. It never did and it never will.
Frederick Douglass[1]

War loomed. This time, however, African Americans were determined that there would be no repeat performance of the First World War's broken promises. As they well knew, and as Walter White, executive secretary of the NAACP, reminded them, their only "reward" for postponing the fight for equality in 1917 was to be "lynched and even burned at the stake" in 1919. Hardened by the "bitter green" memories of that betrayal, White vowed that during the Second World War, African Americans would not back down "one iota" from their demands for full equality.[2] That trenchant spirit led labor leader A. Philip Randolph to announce that "'American democracy is a failure. It is a miserable failure.'"[3] Instead of constitutional rights and guarantees, Randolph asserted that African Americans were flogged by Jim Crow and lynching; disfranchised by poll taxes and white primaries; suffocated by "goodwill and a white God"; and

1. Frederick Douglass, *Two Speeches by Frederick Douglass: One on West India Emancipation Delivered at Canandaigua, Aug. 4th, and the Other on the Dred Scott Decision, Delivered in New York, on the Occasion of the Anniversary of the American Abolition Society, May 1857* (Rochester, New York: C. P. Dewey, [1857?]), 22.
2. "Fight for Liberties Here While Fighting Dictators Abroad, Says N.A.A.C.P.," December 12, 1941, Part 1, Reel 14, *Papers of the NAACP: 1909–1950* (Washington, DC: University Publications of America, 1982), microfilm (hereafter *NAACP*); "Address by Walter White, Secretary, at the Closing Session of the Thirty-First Annual Conference of the National Association for the Advancement of Colored People," June 23, 1940, *The Papers of Eleanor Roosevelt, 1933–1945*, Reel 19 (Frederick, Maryland: University Publications of America), microfilm (hereafter *Roosevelt)*; Minutes of the Meeting of the Board of Directors, December 8, 1941, Part 1, Reel 3, *NAACP*.
3. Quoted in, Roi Ottley, *New World-A-Coming*, The American Negro: His History and Life Series, ed. William Loren Katz (Cambridge, Massachusetts: Riverside Press, 1943; reprint New York: Arno Press and the *New York Times*, 1968), 252 (page numbers refer to reprint edition).

impoverished by "charity," when all they wanted was equality – social, political, religious, and economic equality.[4]

For the black leadership, America's "limited and racial and divisible democracy" became all the more intolerable as the United States prepared to wage war against the Nazis and the doctrine of white supremacy.[5] It was simply incomprehensible to Walter White how the United States could "fight a war for freedom" with a Jim Crow army.[6] Nor could he find any rational, sane reason why U.S. military officers would tell "the British ... that all Negroes have tails, that they are savage, diseased, illiterate and will rape their women" and not expect black soldiers to become "embittered" and question who the real "enemy" was. "It is tragic," White noted, "that the Civil War should be fought again while we are fighting a World War to save civilization."[7]

The arsenal of democracy's "whites only" hiring policy inspired similar disgust. An NAACP report noted that, "as late as the summer of 1942, only three percent of the people working in war industries were colored. Only when there was virtually no one else to hire" and "almost every other labor source was exhausted" were African Americans even considered.[8] As a result, of 29,215 defense contract employees in the New York area, "only 142 were Negroes." In St. Louis, with a population of more than 100,000 African Americans, 56 defense factories "employed an average of three Negroes" each.[9]

During the First World War, for the sake of unity, African Americans would tacitly agree to "close ranks," set aside their "special grievances," and quietly endure this type of blatant discrimination.[10] The Second World War, however, evoked a very different response. Harlem's

4. Call to "We Are Americans, Too" Congress, enclosure, A. Philip Randolph to Rayford Logan, March 17, 1943, Box 181-7, Folder 1, *Rayford Logan Papers*, Manuscript Division, Moorland-Spingarn Research Center, Howard University, Washington, DC (hereafter *Logan Papers-MSRC*).
5. A. Philip Randolph quoted in, Ottley, *New World-A-Coming*, 252.
6. Walter White to Arthur Spingarn, March 23, 1945, Box 94-8, Folder 181, *Arthur B. Spingarn Papers*, Manuscript Division, Moorland-Springarn Research Center, Howard University, Washington, DC (hereafter *Spingarn Papers*).
7. "Observations and Recommendation of Walter White on Racial Relations in the ETO [European Theater of Operations]." February 11, 1944, Reel 19, *Roosevelt*.
8. "Factual Supplement: A Program for Progress in Race Relations: NAACP Legal Defense and Educational Fund, Inc.," enclosure of copy of proposal to the Ford Foundation, Walter White to Eleanor Roosevelt, June 25, 1951, Box 3338, File "NAACP, 1951," *Roosevelt Papers*.
9. Ottley, *New World-A-Coming*, 289–90.
10. David Levering Lewis, *W. E. B. Du Bois: Biography of a Race, 1868–1919* (New York: Henry Holt and Company, Inc., 1993), 556; Charles Young to Arthur B. Spingarn, November 5, 1917, Box 94-8, Folder 189 *Spingarn Papers*.

Photo 1.1. The leadership of the NAACP (l to r): Roy Wilkins, Walter White, and Thurgood Marshall.
Visual Materials from the NAACP Records, Library of Congress.

Amsterdam-Star News reported that, unlike the First World War, "'now the Negro is showing a 'democratic upsurge rebellion,' bordering on open hostility.'"[11] "Discontent and bitterness," Walter White asserted, "were growing like wildfire among Negroes all over the country."[12]

One White House official warned his colleagues about this firestorm of black resentment. Philleo Nash, an aide in the Office of War Information, remarked that during the last war, African Americans "did not attempt... to bargain for economic improvement" and for that display of loyalty they "were hit harder" than anyone else by the Depression. To make matters worse, the economic devastation in the black community had been "accompanied by the rise of white supremacy movements in both North and South." As a result, the docile, patriotic Negro had vanished. For this war, Nash warned, "Negroes are in a militant and demanding mood."[13]

11. Quoted in Ottley, *New World-A-Coming*, 289.
12. Ibid., 292.
13. Philleo Nash to Jonathan Daniels, memo, December 16, 1943, Box 29, File "OWI-Files Alphabetical File-Race Tension-Jonathan Daniels File-Memoranda Nash to Daniels: 1942–45," *Papers of Philleo Nash*, Harry S Truman Presidential Library, Independence,

A. Philip Randolph, in fact, threatened to march 100,000 African Americans directly in front of the White House unless President Franklin Roosevelt issued an executive order prohibiting discrimination by defense contractors.[14] Even under the threat of imprisonment for sedition, the black press carried Randolph's defiant message and refused to print the "patriotic" stories that the War Department insisted on.[15] Instead, at the NAACP's national convention, *Oklahoma Black Dispatch* editor Roscoe Dunjee challenged the American government to come up with something more original than the idea that African Americans were supposed to fight Hitler's army with only "a mop and a broom."[16] Black government official Robert Weaver echoed that sentiment when he intoned that, "'We cannot stop tanks with squads of janitors. We cannot blast the enemy with buckets of charwomen.'"[17]

The black leadership was "so determined" to break Jim Crow that even "friend of the Negro," First Lady Eleanor Roosevelt, was ignored.[18] At the urging of her husband, she tried to persuade Randolph that it would be a "grave mistake," one that could lose friends, embolden enemies, and set back all of the "progress" African Americans had made to date if the march occurred.[19] The black leadership politely thanked her and continued to plan its peaceful assault on the White House. One editorial in the *Chicago Defender* asserted that:

> If the "March on Washington" does nothing else, it will convince white America that the American black man has decided henceforth and forever to abandon the timid role of Uncle-Tomism in his struggle for social justice, no matter what the sacrifice. On to Washington.[20]

Indeed, Walter White cut short the NAACP's national convention so that its attendees could march en masse down Pennsylvania Avenue.[21]

Missouri (hereafter *Nash Papers*); "Attachment No. I: Factors affecting Negro attitudes towards the war," fragment of report, Box 55, File "WH Files-Minorities-Negro Attitudes Toward War," ibid.

14. Walter White, *A Man Called White: The Autobiography of Walter White* (New York: The Viking Press, 1948), 191–92.
15. Earnest L. Perry, Jr., "Voice of Consciousness: The Negro Newspaper Publishers Association During World War II," (Ph.D. diss., University of Missouri–Columbia, 1998), 60–81.
16. "Weak Links in the Chain of Democracy: Keynote Address of Roscoe Dunjee," June 24, 1941, Part 1, Reel 10, *NAACP*.
17. Quoted in Ottley, *New World-A-Coming*, 289.
18. Ibid., 292.
19. Eleanor Roosevelt to A. Philip Randolph, June 10, 1941, Reel 15, *Roosevelt*.
20. Quoted in Perry, "Voice of Consciousness," 66.
21. "NAACP Conference Cut Short to Favor March for Jobs," June 20, 1941, Part 1, Reel 10, *NAACP*. Randolph called off the march after President Roosevelt signed E.O. 8802 establishing a Fair Employment Practices Committee (FEPC).

The NAACP also intensified its offensive against another one of the main pillars of black inequality, Jim Crow education. After almost 50 years of legalized segregation and African Americans being shunted away in the worst schools in the United States, it was clear that whites had readily embraced the "separate" component of the *Plessy v. Ferguson* decision. It was the concept of "equal," however, that seemed to elude them. Thus, although the federal government estimated that in 1941 it would take the equivalent, in 1998 dollars, of more than $632 million to equalize the black school system in the United States, a wartime poll showed that 85 percent of whites were convinced that African Americans "had the same chance" as they did "to get a good education."[22] Because no state, no matter how rabidly segregationist, could truly afford a "separate but equal" school system, the NAACP decided to break Jim Crow by making the states confront the full financial ramifications of the *Plessy* decision.[23]

Similarly, Walter White decided that the NAACP and black voters were going to have to make it very "expensive" for lawmakers to continue to ignore the brutal reality of lynching.[24] Black people had already paid the ultimate price. In one week alone – in Mississippi – there were three lynchings.[25] Later, in Liberty, Mississippi, a 62-year-old minister was bludgeoned and his tongue cut out because he was a "smart nigger" who had hired a lawyer to protect his oil-rich land from local whites.[26] Of course, the bloodshed was not confined to America's most notorious state.[27] On a Sunday morning in 1942, Cleo Wright was pulled out of a jail in Sikeston,

22. "National Opinion Research Center: University of Denver, Final Tabulation," May 1944, attachment to Philleo Nash to Jonathan Daniels, memo, July 21, 1944, Box 29, File "OWI-Files Alphabetical File-Race Tension-Jonathan Daniels File-Research," *Nash Papers*; Bureau of Labor Statistics Data, Consumer Price Index-All Urban Consumers, September 28, 1998. In 1941, the U.S. Office of Education estimated that it would take $43 million to equalize schools. Using the CPI for September 1998, that estimate equals $632 million.
23. Richard Kluger, *Simple Justice* (New York: Vintage Books, 1977); "Educational Attainment of the Population 25 Years Old and Over in the United States: 1940 (Bureau of Census)," n.d., Box 168, File "Census Bureau, 1940–53," *Papers of the NAACP*; Emery M. Foster to Walter White, December 2, 1941, Box B173, File "Statistics: Education of Negroes, 1941," *Papers of the NAACP-Legal*.
24. Walter White to Arthur Spingarn, April 23, 1940, Box 62, File "Anti-Lynching: Barkley, Alben, 1940," *Papers of the NAACP*.
25. "Mississippi Mob Lynches a Slayer," October 18, 1942, *New York Times* found in Box 408, File "Lynching: Lynching Record, 1940–45," ibid.; "2 Negro Boys Lynched," October 13, 1942, *New York Times* found in ibid.
26. "Preacher Slain; Tongue Cut Out," June 24, 1944, *New Orleans Informer and Sentinel* found in Box 408, File "Lynching: Liberty, Mississippi, 1944," ibid.; Edward R. Dudley to Paul M. Kattenburg, November 10, 1944, ibid.
27. For Mississippi's reputation see, David M. Oshinsky, *'Worse Than Slavery': Parchman Farm and the Ordeal of Jim Crow Justice* (New York: Free Press, 1996), 1–107.

Missouri, dragged through the black neighborhood, drenched in gasoline, and torched for traumatic effect.[28] In Florida, a 14-year-old was killed, and his father forced to watch, because the boy had sent a white girl a Christmas card.[29] This violence was no aberration. By September 1940, the NAACP was investigating 11 possible lynchings.[30] Of course, for all of these murders, no one was ever brought to justice. Walter White angrily observed that, "as long as human beings are shot, hanged, and roasted to death ... without the federal government lifting a finger to do anything about it," America's little "Sunday school lectures to other nations" did nothing more than expose this "hypocritical thing called democracy."[31]

Still, the Senate remained unaffected and dawdled over a federal anti-lynching bill. Disgusted, White gave an interview to the *Louisville Defender*, in which he described Senate Majority Leader Alben Barkley's (D-KY) ineptitude in moving the bill through the Senate. Barkley was outraged. He denounced White's actions as "contemptible" and expressed his "considerable resentment" that the head of the NAACP would act so irresponsibly. White, who was determined to "raise so much hell" about the senator's incompetence, would "blast back" that the Kentuckian had no idea what resentment really was. Try being an African American and watching what should be basic legislation being "kicked about in the Senate" for years. Try watching the "complete failure of the Senate leadership," which has neither the "moral courage" nor the "determination to put up any effective resistance" to the "cocksure" Southerners, just crumble on an issue in which black lives hang in the balance. "It is this situation," White declared, that has caused "widespread resentment which," by the way, was "steadily growing."[32]

28. For the "rationale" behind and description of the Cleo Wright lynching see, "An Informal Report on Attitudes in Southeast Missouri Relative to the Lynching of Cleo Wright, Negro," January 25, 1942, Box 42, File "Internal Security File: Treasury File-NAACP Misc. (folder 2 of 2)," *Papers of Stephen J. Spingarn*, Harry S Truman Presidential Library, Independence, Missouri (hereafter *SJSpingarn Papers*). Also see, Dominic J. Capeci, Jr., *The Lynching of Cleo Wright* (Lexington: University of Kentucky Press, 1998).
29. Elbert C. Robinson to Walter White, January 4, 1944, Box 408, File "Lynching Live Oak, Florida, 1944," *Papers of the NAACP*; Harry T. Moore to Roy Wilkins, March 25, 1944, ibid.
30. Walter White to Robert F. Wagner, September 24, 1940, Part 7, Series B, Reel 33, *NAACP*.
31. Address by Walter White, Secretary, at the Closing Session of the Thirty-First Annual Conference of the National Association for the Advancement of Colored People, June 23, 1940, Reel 19, *Roosevelt*; NAACP Calls on Senate to Bring Up Anti-Lynch Bill before Adjournment, September 27, 1940, Part 7, Series B, Reel 33, *NAACP*.
32. Walter White to Alben Barkley, April 23, 1940, Box 62, File "Anti-Lynching: Barkley, Alben, 1940," *Papers of the NAACP*; Walter White to Arthur Spingarn, April 23, 1940, ibid.; Walter White to P. B. Young, May 3, 1940, ibid.

Unmoved, Barkley told the NAACP leadership that he simply would not fight for an anti-lynching law because such "controversial legislation" would "interfere with national defense." Barkley knew from first-hand experience that the Southerners would hold all other legislation hostage while they filibustered against the anti-lynching bill.[33] White, however, argued that the point was not to let a handful of rogue legislators hijack the Senate's agenda, but to change the rules on cloture to allow a simple majority vote, instead of two-thirds, to end a filibuster. He said that Barkley, "like most southern white men ... believed that Negroes could be soft-soaped" into shutting up and going meekly into a corner. Well, not this time. National defense or no, "war or no war, we've got to keep fighting."[34] The NAACP's special counsel, Thurgood Marshall, who was also disgusted with these "weak senators," agreed. He laid out for Barkley the cold, brutal facts of the most recent lynchings in South Carolina, Florida, and Tennessee, and then declared that in a nation starved for military personnel, begging for factory workers, and striving for international credibility, it had to be painfully obvious that the "Anti-Lynching Bill is just as important as portions of the National Defense Program."[35]

Indeed, African Americans were openly questioning whether this was a nation worth dying for. One "black editor bitterly commented, 'Remember Pearl Harbor ... and Sikeston, Missouri.'"[36] A. Philip Randolph sneered at the thought of fighting for democracy in Burma while African Americans burned in Birmingham.[37] In a 1942 conference with Lord Halifax of Great Britain, Walter White noted that many African Americans "were so despondent and so skeptical that white people could ever practice democracy [that] they find difficulty in differentiating between the prejudices of Nazi Germany and that which, for example, Negroes encounter in Mississippi."[38] Howard University professor

33. Alben Barkley to Roy Wilkins, August 6, 1940, ibid.; *The Congressional Record*, August 11, 1937 (Washington, DC: 1938), 8695–96.
34. Walter White to P. B. Young, May 3, 1940, Box 62, File "Anti-Lynching: Barkley, Alben, 1940," *Papers of the NAACP*; Walter White to Charles T. Brackins, May 16, 1940, ibid.
35. Thurgood Marshall to Alben Barkley, August 7, 1940, ibid.
36. Quoted in, Lorenzo J. Greene, Gary R. Kremer, and Antonio F. Holland, *Missouri's Black Heritage*, 2nd ed., revised by Gary R. Kremer and Antonio F. Holland (Columbia: University of Missouri Press, 1993), 159.
37. A. Philip Randolph, quoted in Ottley, *New World A-Coming*, 252.
38. Johnpeter Horst Grill and Robert L. Jenkins, "The Nazis and the American South in the 1930s: A Mirror Image?" *Journal of Southern History* 58:4 (November 1992): 688–90; Confidential Office Memorandum on conversation with Lord Halifax by the Secretary at the residence of Mr. Thomas W. Lamont, April 24, 1942, Box 204, File "Conference with Lord Halifax, 1942–43," *Papers of the NAACP*.

Rayford Logan, therefore, scoffed at the notion that America was fighting to preserve democracy and countered that, "It might not be a bad idea to have some democracy to defend."[39]

It was not, however, just the African American leadership that was bristling at "this hypocritical thing called democracy." In a letter to the *Pittsburgh Courier*, a young black man, who was dreading service in a Jim Crow army, asked whether "the kind of America I know" is even "worth defending" and whether he should risk life and limb just to "live half-American."[40] Harry Carpenter, a black Philadelphia truck driver, had a very straightforward answer. Believing it absurd for a black man to be in the army fighting for a democracy that never fought for him, Carpenter angrily yelled out at one African American soldier, "You're a crazy nigger wearing that uniform – you're only out fighting for white trash. This is a white man's Government and war and it's no damned good."[41] Then, remembering the horrible violence that black veterans faced after the First World War, Carpenter taunted the soldier. "When the war is over, the white folks will be kicking you niggers around just like they did before" so "what the hell are you fighting for, you have no flag," Carpenter insisted, "you do not have a Country."[42]

Unamused, the U.S. government charged Carpenter with treason. The community immediately turned to the NAACP for help and the Association's staff turned to Thurgood Marshall to defend the poor man whose "statement could certainly be shown to be 'warranted' by facts. No?"[43] To be sure, those facts, as an editorial in *PM* made clear, questioned how any African Americans could remain loyal to the United States after having the Red Cross "carefully segregate" their blood, after having a brother "in an Army hospital [with] a Southern constable's bullet in his lung," and after burying a "cousin in Missouri last month," or rather "what they could find after the lynchers touched off his gasoline-soaked body."[44] In February 1942, editorial cartoonist Oliver W. Harrington visually summarized the outrage. The first panel in his cartoon depicted a slain European crumpled beneath a hail of bullet holes and a flag bearing

39. Alfred E. Smith, "'Bad Negro with a Ph.D.'—And Logan's Proud of It," n.d., ca. 1943, newspaper clipping, found in Box 181-7, Folder 1, *Logan Papers-MSRC*.
40. "Birth of the 'Double V,'" n.d., Box 239, File "Double 'V' Campaign: *Pittsburgh Courier*, 1940–43," *Papers of the NAACP*.
41. "Negro Jailed as 'Traitor' Reported to Have Said: 'This Is a White Man's War,'" February 16, 1942, *PM* found in Box 195, File "Civilian Morale, 1942," ibid.
42. Theodore Spaulding to Almena Davis, March 4, 1942, ibid.
43. CC [Charlotte Crump] to TM [Thurgood Marshall], memo, n.d., ibid. The charge of treason against Carpenter was subsequently changed to sedition, and then the case was dismissed.
44. "The Crime is Ours," *PM*, n.d., found in ibid.

the swastika. In the very next panel was a dead black man, a rope around his neck, slumped against a sign reading "Sikeston, MO, U.S.A."[45]

The deadly parallels to Nazi Germany prompted NAACP Board member William H. Hastie to tell the secretary of war that, "As long as we tolerate such vicious nonsense, we can be respected neither by the forces of fascism which we condemn nor by the forces of democracy which we assume to lead."[46] America's "vicious nonsense" had, in fact, made it very easy for the Japanese to "depict the American people as having 'run amuck' in an orgy of Jim Crowism."[47] "Every lynching," Walter White warned, "every coldblooded shooting of a Negro soldier in Louisiana or Mississippi or Georgia, every refusal to abolish segregation in our armed forces, every filibuster against an anti-poll tax or anti-lynching bill, every snarling, sneering reference by a Mississippi Senator like [James O.] Eastland to 'burr headed niggers' in fulmination against an appropriation for the Fair Employment Practice Committee builds up a debit balance of hatred against America which may cost countless lives of Americans yet unborn."[48] To stop the orgies, the bloodbaths, and the hypocrisy, it was time, *Pittsburgh Courier* editor Percival Prattis noted, that America "got religion" on the issue of racial equality.[49]

The bible for that religious conversion, as far as the black leadership was concerned, was the Atlantic Charter. Issued in August 1941, British Prime Minister Winston Churchill and President Franklin Roosevelt tried to convince an isolationist Congress that England needed American assistance not, as many suspected, to fatten the British Empire, but to defeat the Nazis and ensure that the world could enjoy justice, equality, and democracy. The Atlantic Charter, therefore, eloquently supported the principle of self-determination, committed the Allied Powers to improving the quality of life for the world's inhabitants, and promised a peace that would secure for all peoples the Four Freedoms, especially freedom from fear and want. Congress was not particularly impressed nor was Republican foreign policy advisor John Foster Dulles, who described the Four

45. M. Thomas Inge, ed., *Dark Laughter: The Satiric Art of Oliver W. Harrington* (Jackson: University Press of Mississippi, 1993), xxiv.
46. Untitled fragment, n.d., Box 300, File "Hastie, William H.: Resignation as Civilian Aide to Secretary of War, 1943," *Papers of the NAACP.*
47. Philleo Nash to Jonathan Daniels, memo, August 15, 1944, Box 29, File "OWI-Files Alphabetical-Race Tension-Jonathan Daniels File-News Analysis," *Nash Papers.*
48. Address by Walter White .... at closing meeting of Wartime Conference, July 16 [1944], Reel 19, *Roosevelt.*
49. Speech made in Charleston, West Virginia, February 1944, Box 144-20, Folder 18 *Percival Prattis Papers*, Manuscript Division, Moorland-Spingarn Research Center, Howard University, Washington, D.C. (hereafter *Prattis Papers).*

Freedoms as "lofty generalities" that "pander" to Americans' sense of moral superiority.[50]

For African Americans, however, the Atlantic Charter was revolutionary. It was something, as NAACP Board member Channing Tobias declared, that black people would be willing to "live, work, fight and, if need be, die for."[51] It appeared that the world's largest capitalist nation had joined with the greatest colonial power and admitted that the world they created in 1919 with the Treaty of Versailles had only led to the rise of a racism so virulent that it even offended the Anglo-Saxons. Chastened by the mistakes of 1919, the Atlantic Charter appeared to be the United States' and Great Britain's pledge to correct the injustices of the past and create a much more humane world order. The embrace of self-determination, for example, implied that the federal government, or at least Roosevelt, would now fight to end the poll tax, white primary, and other voting restrictions that disfranchised millions of African Americans in the South. Similarly, the vow to create a world in which people could live without fear could only mean that the president, who had been reluctant even in the wake of the gruesome Claude Neal lynching, was finally willing to support a federal anti-lynching law.[52] In short, African Americans, as Walter White noted, took "literally the shibboleths of the Four Freedoms" and "[t]hey intend to secure and enjoy those freedoms and to put an end to the old order in which men, solely because they are colored, can be worked to exhaustion, exploited, despised, spat upon and derided by those whose chief right to sovereignty is whiteness of skin."[53]

The NAACP leadership realized, however, that if the promises of the Atlantic Charter were to become a reality, the Association itself would have to make some significant changes. Issues of institutional structure, priorities, partnerships, and vision began to seep into the NAACP's consciousness. A key element in this reappraisal was Ralph Bunche's analysis

50. "Radio Address by John Foster Dulles: Station WJW (Blue Network Local Broadcast) Cleveland, Ohio," January 16, 1945, Box 26, File "Re: Dumbarton Oaks Proposals, 1945," *Papers of John Foster Dulles*, Seeley Mudd Manuscript Library, Princeton University, Princeton, New Jersey (hereafter *JFD-Princeton*).

51. "Address [by Channing Tobias] at Tenth Anniversary Celebration of the Reichstag Trial: Carnegie Hall," December 22, 1943, Reel 18, *Roosevelt*.

52. Eleanor Roosevelt to Walter White, May 2, 1934, ibid.; White to Eleanor Roosevelt, November 8, 1934, ibid.; Eleanor Roosevelt to Walter White, November 23, 1934, ibid. For a description of the Claude Neal lynching, where he was castrated and forced to eat his genitalia, see Grace Elizabeth Hale, *Making Whiteness: The Culture of Segregation in the South, 1890–1940* (New York: Pantheon Books, 1998), 222–27.

53. "Address by Walter White . . . at closing meeting of Wartime Conference," July 16, 1944, Reel 19, *Roosevelt*.

of the NAACP for Gunnar Myrdal's *An American Dilemma*. In his review, Bunche, a black political scientist, acknowledged the Association's legal accomplishments but seriously questioned the NAACP's overemphasis on civil rights and virtual neglect of economic rights. Bunche warned that, without an economic program, all of the NAACP's courtroom battles, while impressive, would be nothing more than shadow victories. This was not earth-shattering news. In 1939, White was already trying to persuade the NAACP's Annual Convention to confront the economic issues in the black community. Later that year, he confided to Myrdal that it would be fatal for the NAACP to be preoccupied "with civil rights cases [while] ignoring" the "issues which affected the great masses of Negroes who were in dire poverty." A focus on civil rights alone, White observed, was much too narrow, and fighting discrimination in restaurants and theaters, while noteworthy, "failed to attack problems of employment and the like which affect the lives and destinies of persons who are not financially able to go" to those establishments.[54] White was not the only one in the NAACP concerned about the organization's limited trajectory. A staff report advocated a "reformulation of the Association's ultimate objectives" because, even during the depths of the Great Depression, the "work of the Association in the economic field has been conducted as an incidental phase of its civil liberty program." The report noted that the major problem with consistently relegating economics to the periphery was that, in the United States, ownership of property was "the substantial basis of... freedom." Yet, for the most part, African Americans were a "landless proletariat in the country and a propertyless wage-earner in the city" and thus, like slaves, would continue to be "exploited as cheap labor." In short, without economic power, African Americans could no more protect their hard-won constitutional rights than could the Freedmen after Reconstruction. Therefore, the NAACP would have to find some way to combine the fight for economic rights with its already well-developed strategy for civil rights.[55]

Roy Wilkins, the NAACP's assistant secretary, however, was not convinced. Wilkins declared that the NAACP was not equipped to handle an economic program, which, as he saw it, was the job of the Urban League. And while conceding that the NAACP had "given too little attention to the economic questions which are so important to the great masses of our people," Wilkins also believed that it would be "suicidal" for the NAACP

54. Walter White to Ralph Bunche, July 27, 1939, Box L22, File "Myrdal Study, 1939," *Papers of the NAACP-Addendum*; Ralph Bunche to Walter White, August 2, 1939, ibid.; Walter White to Gunnar Myrdal, December 20, 1939, ibid.

55. "Future Plan and Program of the NAACP," n.d., ca. December 1941, Box 439, File "NAACP Programs: General, 1941–42," *Papers of the NAACP*.

to champion a "political and economic revolutionary program."[56] Yet, even Wilkins could not ignore the unequivocal militancy in the black community, the "rising wind" of disgust with imperialism and colonialism, and the paradox of America's fight for global democracy with its concurrent support of domestic injustice. He finally had to concede that the Second World War "was no war," rather it was a "social revolution," a "people's revolution" that was obliterating the distinctions between race and class. He also believed that it was "crystal clear" and "marked down so plainly" that the NAACP had to be at the forefront of this revolution.[57]

That revolutionary fusion of race and class strongly suggested that the NAACP needed to work more closely with a broader range of organizations, especially those on the political Left. This was not to suggest, however, that the NAACP was willing to cede any of its autonomy, relinquish any of its dominance in the area of civil rights, or, in its search for partners, cross that threshold that distinguished the political Left from the Communists. In fact, the NAACP leadership despised the Communists.

In the 1930s, the battles between the Communist party (CP) and the NAACP over a series of racially and politically charged legal cases left deep, bitter scars. The two organizations waded into a pool of insults and accusations about the other. The party leadership derided the NAACP as being "comfortably situated under the influence of the big white bourgeoisie" and using that position to advance the Association's "own narrow class interests . . . at the expense of the mass of the Negro people."[58] The NAACP, however, could give as good as it got. When the Communists proposed the creation of a separate black nation in the Deep South, the NAACP immediately accused the "red brain trust" of conspiring with "the southern ruling class" to exile black Americans into an irreversible state of Jim Crow.[59]

56. Roy Wilkins to Walter White, memo, March 12, 1941, Box 166, File "Carnegie-Myrdal Study Negroes in America, 1941–42," ibid.

57. "Address of Roy Wilkins to the Thirty-third Annual Convention of the NAACP," July 14, 1942, Part 1, Reel 11, *NAACP*; Walter White's "Rising Wind," quoted in Brenda Gayle Plummer, *Rising Wind: Black Americans and U.S. Foreign Affairs, 1935–1960* (Chapel Hill: University of North Carolina Press, 1996), frontispiece.

58. William Z. Foster, *The Negro People in American History* (New York: International Publishers, 1954), 475.

59. See Dan T. Carter, *Scottsboro: A Tragedy of the American South* (Baton Rouge: Louisiana State University Press, 1969); Wilson Record, *Race and Radicalism: The NAACP and the Communist Party in Conflict* (Ithaca, New York: Cornell University Press, 1964); Kenneth Robert Janken, *Rayford W. Logan and the Dilemma of the African-American Intellectual* (Amherst: University of Massachusetts Press, 1993), 108–09; Robin D. G. Kelley, *Hammer and Hoe: Alabama Communists during the*

The NAACP's hatred did not abate even when party officials were clearly being persecuted by the U.S. government. In 1940, when the head of the Communist Party, USA, Earl Browder, was convicted on a relatively minor passport violation and sentenced to 20 years, Walter White was sure that "the motivation back of this conviction was in large measure due to [Browder's] Communist views and affiliation." Justice had not been served, of that White was certain. Nevertheless, he continued, Browder was "technically guilty," and there was no way that the NAACP would participate in any effort to free the CP leader.[60]

It comes as no surprise then that when the National Negro Congress (NNC), which had Communists interwoven throughout, was founded in 1936, the Association's leaders were immediately suspicious. Although the NNC counted among its ranks A. Philip Randolph as president, Ralph Bunche as a co-founder, and John P. Davis, who, as the head of the Joint Committee on National Recovery, received 75 percent of his salary from the NAACP, Walter White and Roy Wilkins remained leery and skeptical.[61] Randolph even admitted that "the National Negro Congress had Communists in it." And he anticipated that "they would naturally seek to shape and control [the NNC's] policy, but it was [his] feeling that that could be prevented."[62] The NAACP was not so sure. Allies on the Left were one thing, but this was clearly another. The NAACP leadership believed that the NNC was just the black manifestation of the Kremlin's directive for the Communist party to form a "united front" with other anti-fascist organizations. Convinced that the Congress would eventually be "sold down the river [by the] reds," White and Wilkins wanted no part of the NNC or its united front.[63] As a result, the NAACP, as Walter White

Great Depression, Fred W. Morrison Series in Southern Studies (Chapel Hill: University of North Carolina Press, 1990), 134, 181, 213; "*Crisis* Editorial Comment," *The Crisis* Magazine, October 1935, Box 68, File "Articles: Communism, on—1950–55," *Papers of the NAACP*.

60. Max Yergan to Walter White, September 30, 1941, Box B6, File "Browder Passport Case, 1941–42," *Papers of the NAACP-Legal*; Walter White to Max Yergan, October 4, 1941, ibid.; Walter White to Sidney R. Edmonds, May 13, 1942, ibid.; Walter White to Gloster Current, December 4, 1941, ibid.; Roy Wilkins to George Dozier, telegram, March 18, 1942, ibid.

61. Minutes of the Meeting of the Joint Committee on National Recovery, December 14, 1934, Part 1, Reel 3, *Papers of the National Negro Congress* (Washington, DC: University Publications of America, 1988). Microfilm (hereafter *NNC*).

62. A. Philip Randolph to Ernest Angell, November 1, 1950, Box 29, File "National Negro Congress, 1936–51," *Papers of Asa Philip Randolph*, Library of Congress, Washington, DC (hereafter *Randolph Papers*).

63. Quoted in, John Baxter Streater, Jr., "The National Congress, 1936–1947," Ph.D. diss. (University of Cincinnati, 1981), 241.

made clear, "did not affiliate nor did it participate in recent meetings and activities of the Congress."[64]

Yet, the NNC had a perspective on the condition of black inequality that, as White admitted in 1939, was desperately needed in the NAACP. In its founding manifesto, the NNC declared that, although the "fight for civil and political liberties . . . had been brilliantly waged by the NAACP," it was obvious that "the gravity and complexity" of achieving black equality required more than the Association was designed to do. African Americans were in a "hell hole of slavery . . . hunted down, harassed, and hounded." They "face a hard, deceptive, and brutal capitalist order." Thus, the NAACP's tradition-bound, legalistic strategy alone was unlikely to secure equality. Moreover, the Association's faith in either the Republican or Democratic party was also misplaced because "Negroes have watched themselves disfranchised and lynched under both regimes, Republican and Democratic." Rather than depending solely on the New Deal, the courts, or the electoral process, the solution to black equality lay in a strategy that would "place human rights above property rights." The NNC, therefore, urged a "united front" of labor, civil rights, and other progressive forces to confront the racial, political, and economic disarray in Depression-era America.[65]

By the end of the decade, however, the NNC itself was in disarray. Randolph was immersed in running the Brotherhood of Sleeping Car Porters and soon realized that he did not have the time "to break the grip of the communists on the Congress."[66] His influence was, therefore, being eclipsed by John P. Davis, the NNC's national secretary. The situation had disintegrated so badly that Davis, without fear of reprisal, refused to provide any current information on the NNC to Bunche, who was gathering research materials for the Myrdal study. Davis "bluntly suggested" that he was not going to "become a prostitute" for the Myrdal team and then declared that, although "free booty" was out of the question, he would sell Bunche the information.[67] To complicate matters, Davis' rise was accompanied by that of Max Yergan, a Communist fellow traveler

64. Walter White to Mrs. Kermit Ross and Miss Mamie Knight, May 18, 1940, Box 444, File "National Negro Congress: 1940–44," *Papers of the NAACP*.
65. "The Official Proceedings of the National Negro Congress," February 14, 1936, Box 29, File "National Negro Congress, 1936–51," *Randolph Papers*.
66. Eleanor Rye to Jack Beel, January 12, 1936, Part 1, Reel 3, *NNC*; A. Philip Randolph to Ernest Angell, November 1, 1950, Box 29, File "National Negro Congress, 1936–51," *Randolph Papers*.
67. William B. Bryant to Ralph Bunche, October 26, 1939, Reel 2, *Papers of Ralph Bunche* (Los Angeles: University of California, Los Angeles, 1980). Microfilm (hereafter *Bunche*); John P. Davis to Ralph Bunche, November 8, 1939, Reel 3, ibid.

and former YMCA missionary in South Africa, whom Bunche described as a self-promoting status seeker.[68]

This potent mix of rising red stars and declining black giants exploded at the Congress' 1940 convention. Following the signing of the Nazi-Soviet Non-Aggression Pact and the Soviet's participation in the dismemberment of Poland, the NNC dropped both its united front mask and its non-Communist leadership. The NNC ousted Randolph as president and immediately replaced him with Max Yergan. Then, in a carefully stage-managed process, resolutions streamed through denouncing the war in Europe as a battle between imperialist Britain and fascist Germany and not worth the bones of one Appalachian grenadier. Conversely, the NNC delegates praised the Soviet Union for its wisdom in staying above the fray in Europe, for its humanitarianism, and for its commitment to justice and equality. For Bunche, this was just too much. All of it – Randolph's ouster, Yergan's coronation, and the NNC's thick Russian accent – made him clearly "out of step" with the rest of the organization. He resigned.[69]

Randolph, however, did not go quietly into the night. Standing before 1,700 booing delegates, two-thirds of whom then initiated an "exodus" of biblical proportions, Randolph assailed the NNC's rush into the Soviet camp. He had grown weary of hearing delegate after delegate "hail" the Soviet Union "as a land without poverty or race prejudice." It was rather easy to make that assertion, Randolph noted, when "there are no Negroes in Soviet Russia" to discriminate against. He believed, however, that there were other indicators that strongly suggested that the Soviets' commitment to justice was highly suspect. First, he pointed to the series of purges that had wiped out millions of Russians. Then he zeroed in on an issue that resonated deep in the African American community – the Italians' desecration of Ethiopia in 1935. "It is significant to note," Randolph observed, "that Bolshevik Russia freely sold oil to Fascist Italy to assist in the murderous war of invasion of the peace loving and ancient kingdom of Ethiopia." Given that track record, Randolph warned, the "Negro would be foolish to tie up his own interests with the foreign policy of the Soviet Union or any other nation of the world." His warnings, however, just got trampled in the stampede toward a Communist utopia. I had to "quit the Congress," Randolph later said, "because it [was] not truly a

68. Fourth U.S. Civil Service Region Investigations Division: Report of Special Hearing, testimony, April 29, 1943, Reel 1, ibid.

69. "Notes on the Third National Negro Congress: From Ralph Bunche," April 28, 1940, Box 166, File "Carnegie-Myrdal Study Negroes in America, March 22–June 30, 1940, *Papers of the NAACP*; Ralph Bunche to Max Yergan, April 29, 1940, Reel 2, *Bunche*.

Negro Congress"; instead, the convention made it abundantly clear that "the Communists were firmly in the saddle."[70]

Randolph's ouster made the NAACP leadership even more determined that the Association would have absolutely nothing to do with the NNC. White and Wilkins consistently rebuffed Davis's offers to work together. And White, when asked by several NAACP branches for permission to cosponsor events with the NNC, made it perfectly clear that the Association and the NNC were "two distinct organizations" and "the National Negro Congress runs it affairs and we run ours."[71]

For a little more than a year after the convention, Max Yergan dutifully ran with the marching orders handed down during the convention. He described the war in Europe as nothing more than a "greedy struggle" between imperialists and fascists. He argued that, because the British and the Nazis were virtually indistinguishable, it was irrelevant who won.[72] Yergan therefore concluded that Americans had "no business allying themselves with either belligerent" and African Americans, in particular, had no stake in what was happening in Europe because the "battle for democracy lies at home."[73] Consequently, the NNC's program ignored the issue of the war, focused on the gaping wounds in American democracy, and urged African Americans to concentrate their efforts on domestic issues. Yet, the moment the Nazis attacked the Soviet Union, everything changed and the Congress was faced with an organization-killing dilemma.

With Hitler's armies rushing toward Moscow, CP doctrine slammed into reverse. No longer indifferent about the bloody spat between greedy imperialists and goose-stepping fascists, the party derided the "appeasers and... propagandists... who still prate about an 'imperialist war.'" The Communists, now fearing for the very survival of the Soviet Union, praised this "progressive war" and declared that anything that even

70. Ralph J. Bunche, "Notes on the Third National Negro Congress," April 28, 1940, Box 166, File "Carnegie-Myrdal Study Negroes in America, March 22–June 30, 1940," *Papers of the NAACP*; Ralph Bunche, "Critique of the National Negro Congress," 1940, Reel 1, *Bunche*; A. Philip Randolph, "Why I Would Not Stand for Reelection for President of the National Negro Congress," press release, May 4, 1940, Box 444, File "National Negro Congress: 1940–44," *Papers of the NAACP* (Emphasis added).

71. Walter White's marginalia on John P. Davis to Friend, February 23, 1940, ibid.; Roy Wilkins to John P. Davis, April 9, 1940, ibid.; Walter White to Mrs. Kermit Ross et al., May 18, 1940, ibid.; Walter White to Lucille Miller, April 7, 1941, ibid.

72. "Democracy and the Negro People: Address Given by Max Yergan... at the General Convention of the Episcopal Church at Kansas City, Missouri," October 16, 1940, Reel 3, *Bunche*.

73. Quoted in Cicero Alvin Hughes, "Toward a Black United Front: The National Negro Congress Movement," Ph.D. diss. (Ohio University, 1982), 191.

remotely looked like it would interfere with America's ability to supply Soviet forces with war materiel, had to be dealt with quickly and without remorse.[74]

Most telling was the CP's cold response to African Americans' continued fight for equality, especially in the defense industries. Party officials blasted the tendency "among certain Negro leaders" to "attempt to win gains" from "the Administration by threatening" to encircle the White House with a sea of black people. Instead of marching on Washington, the party thundered, African Americans needed to demonstrate "unity" with their white brethren, even if those brethren continued to discriminate and lynch. The party was equally disdainful of the black press, which spread its "appeasement poison" by demanding justice for black people after this war. As far as the Communists were concerned, that was a "distracting side issue" and irrelevant to the task at hand, namely, defeating the Nazis. In the 1930s, the CP had been one of the most vocal proponents of black equality. Yet now, with the Soviets imperiled, the party preached patience instead of revolution and urged tolerance instead of righteous indignation. The "Negro people" simply had to turn the other cheek, overlook Jim Crow, and "serve the nation." The Communist party tried to soften the harsh edges of its new message by offering assurances that, despite the relentless terrain of lynch victims dotting the American landscape, there would be no replay of the First World War's infamous Red Summer.[75] The point was to ensure that the Soviet Union survived so that Josef Stalin could "guarantee ... that the peace will not be Versailles."[76]

What the Communists failed to realize, of course, was that the issue for African Americans was not as simple as the party had cast it. Blacks knew how reprehensible the Nazis were. That was never in question. It was just that there was the American brand of Naziism that also had to be dealt with. "We Negroes," NAACP Board member Earl B. Dickerson explained, "are violently opposed to fascism because *we* know from our experience in the slave docks and on the plantations the meaning of fascism. We have endured a form of fascism since the first Negro was sold into bondage at Jamestown." Indeed, he continued, the "poll tax, the 'white primary,' the intimidation of masked men parading through the streets and warning our brothers of the South to stay away from the polls – *all* of these acts are cut from the same social pattern as Hitler's treatment

74. Report to the Young Communist League, n.d., Box 167-4, Folder 9, *Edward Strong Papers*, Manuscript Division, Moorland-Spingarn Research Center, Howard University, Washington, DC (hereafter *Strong Papers*); Edward P. Johanningsmeier, *Forging American Communism: The Life of William Z. Foster* (Princeton, New Jersey: Princeton University Press, 1994), 287–90.

75. Report to the Young Communist League, n.d., Box 167-4, Folder 9, *Strong Papers*.

76. Ibid.

of the Jews."[77] Even Harry Truman had to admit that "a lot of our Americans have a streak of Nazi in them."[78] Because of that, blacks were not backing down.

The NNC, which up to now, had willingly followed the CP line, was obviously in a tough spot. African Americans were demanding "Democracy in Our Time!" and the Communists were insisting that blacks wait because, as far as the CP was concerned, there was a much more important struggle being waged.[79] Many African Americans were enraged by the CP's attitude and became convinced that the Communists only supported the fight for black equality when it was expedient, brought in revenue, and advanced the needs of the party and the Soviet Union.[80] Yergan and Davis quickly grasped that if the NNC blindly followed this latest twist in CP doctrine, the Congress would lose all credibility in the black community and never become a mass organization.[81] The NNC, therefore, decided to ignore what was clearly a red quagmire, and opted, instead, to join in the *Pittsburgh Courier*'s "Double V" campaign. The "Double V" asserted that African Americans were determined to have victory over the Nazis, both in Germany and at home, and it served as the rallying cry for black equality during the Second World War. Indeed, the *Pittsburgh Courier* and the NAACP leadership were ready to "'go to town'" on pushing for the "Double V" because "victory abroad is futile unless there is victory at home also."[82]

Consequently, one of the first policies that emerged out of this realization was the need to influence the nature of the postwar world. On Churchill's assertion that the Atlantic Charter was for whites only, both the NAACP and the NNC called for a Pacific Charter to explicitly extend the Four Freedoms to people of color and create a "people's peace."[83] This

77. "Political Action for the Negro: Delivered by Earl B. Dickerson, at the Philadelphia 31st Annual Conference of the National Association for the Advancement of Colored People," June 19, 1940, Part 1, Reel 10, *NAACP* (Emphasis in original).
78. Harry Truman to Eleanor Roosevelt, December 21, 1945, Box 4560, File "Harry S Truman, 1945–1948," *Roosevelt Papers*.
79. Ottley, *New World-A-Coming*, 253.
80. Ibid., 242.
81. Hughes, "Toward a Black United Front," 191.
82. W. P. Bayless to Walter White, April 20, 1942, Box 239, File "Double 'V' Campaign: *Pittsburgh Courier*, 1940–43," *Papers of the NAACP*; Ira F. Lewis to Walter White, May 13, 1942, ibid.; Walter White to Ira F. Lewis, telegram, May 12, 1942, ibid.
83. Walter White to Franklin D. Roosevelt, May 4, 1942, Reel 19, *Roosevelt*; "Speech of Walter White ... to be delivered at the Madison Square Garden Mass Meeting of the March on Washington Movement," June 16, 1942, ibid.; Resolutions of the 33rd Annual Conference of the National Association for the Advancement of Colored People, July 19, 1942, Part 1, Reel 11, *NAACP*; "Address of Walter White," July 19, 1942, ibid.; "Announcing the Eastern Seaboard Conference [of the NNC] on the Problems of the War and the Negro People," April 11, 1943, Box 29, File "National Negro

peace, as William Hastie understood, went well beyond the Axis Powers' defeat. African Americans, he argued, "seek a peace that is more than just a breathing space between the death of an old tyranny and the birth of a new one.... Our choice is not between a Hitler slave-world and an out of date holiday of 'normalcy.'" There had to be a better alternative, Hastie explained, because those "who talk about going back to the good old days of Americanism mean the time when there was plenty for the few and scarcity for the many."

> We cannot offer the blueprints and the skills to rebuild the bombed-out cities of other lands and stymie the rebuilding of our own cities. Slums have no place in America. We cannot assist in binding the wound of a war-stricken world and fail to safeguard the health of our own people. We cannot hope to raise the literacy of other nations and fail to roll back the ignorance that clouds many communities in many sectors of our own nation...all people [must] have the opportunity for the fullest education.[84]

The options for a people's peace therefore incorporated not just an international commitment to civil liberties, but an equally strong commitment to basic quality of life standards that all – regardless of race, class, sex, creed, nationality, or religion – could enjoy. "Our choice is between democracy for everybody or for the few – between the spreading of social safeguards and economic opportunity to all the people – or the concentration of our abundant resources in the hands of selfishness and greed." To bring about the kind of nontraditional peace that Hastie had in mind, he was insistent that the "peace-makers must have more daring and vision than the war-makers."[85]

Even as Hastie spoke, however, tradition-bound organizations across America, such as the U.S. Chamber of Commerce, as well as bureaucrats buried deep in the State Department, were hard at work crafting the contours of the postwar world. Yet, as one woman explained to White, "on every hand there are discussions and plans by groups in and out of the gov[ernmen]t...but none seem to include us." Instead, African Americans were like a "dangling participle," in the context of things but "not really connected."[86] Another woman told Channing Tobias that she was tired of black people being "overlooked," and she wanted the

Congress, 1936–51," *Randolph Papers*; Edward Strong to Herman Osborn, March 24, 1943, Part 2, Reel 4, *NNC*.

84. No title, document begins "We have come far in twenty months of war." n.d., Box 299, File "William H. Hastie – General, July 1943–August 1944," *Papers of the NAACP*.
85. Ibid.
86. Bertha Lomax to Walter White, November 18, 1943, Box 439, File "NAACP Programs: Postwar, 1943–44," ibid.

NAACP to "exert sufficient pressure" on the State Department to make sure that there was an African American at the peace table. Tobias and Walter White could not have agreed more.[87] White confessed that he "shudder[ed] to think of what would happen" if the war ended immediately and there was "no concrete plan, proposed by a Negro" on what the postwar world should look like.[88] White was convinced that the Allies simply could not grasp that if they tried to trot out the same old discredited peace plan, especially a peace "based on the perpetuation of white overlordship, ... another war is inevitable." To save the Allies from committing "the folly of another Versailles Treaty," the NAACP, "on behalf of the Negroes not only of America, but of Africa, the West Indies and other parts of the world," was going to have to make its "voice heard."[89]

Once again, however, Roy Wilkins came at the question from a very different angle. Wilkins's revolutionary ardor of 1942 had withered in the fires of the 1943 riots. Although the uprisings were sparked by intolerable housing conditions in Detroit and police brutality in Harlem, white Southerners immediately denounced the riots as nothing but "'Negro agitation for instant social equality.'" When he heard Northerners join in the refrain, Wilkins' concern quickly transformed into panic. The words "social equality," as he knew all too well, often unleashed a reign of white terror on the black community. Wilkins therefore insisted that the NAACP focus on a postwar program "right here in America" that would prevent a repeat of the lynching spree that accompanied the end of the First World War. It was obvious to him that not much had changed since then. In a 1943 nationwide poll, for example, whites "overwhelmingly endorsed segregation," were "willing to grant Negroes [most] what ... Negroes want least," and showed "not much disposition to make any fundamental concessions" to rid the nation of lynching, Jim Crow schools, and restrictive covenants. The situation would become even more volatile, he feared, after the returning veterans ignited the inevitable competition for jobs. For Wilkins, this was not speculation, but experience. Nightmarish images of black corpses haunted him. In 1920, while on summer break from the University of Minnesota, he saw a frenzied mob in Duluth methodically terrorize and lynch three black men, one by one. The fact that this carnage could happen in Minnesota – not Mississippi – seared an image in

87. Elizabeth T. Meijer to Channing Tobias, n.d., ca. March 1943, Box 466 File "Peace Conference Committee, to Present Views of Negroes at Upcoming Peace Conference, 1943–1944," ibid.

88. Walter White to Paul Williams, May 23, 1942, Box 392, File "Leagues: Post-War Planning Organizations, 1942–43," ibid.

89. Address by Walter White ... at the closing meeting of Wartime Conference," July 16, 1944, Reel 19, *Roosevelt*.

his mind that he would never forget. Wilkins, who was "not a street kid of the ghettos or a child of the South," declared that on that night he lost his "innocence on race once and for all." That loss of innocence and a strong sense of foreboding made him assert that, although this talk about black people being at the peace table was interesting, "it was more important" that the Association "get down to earth on the problems which will arise between our people and white people in this country the instant the war is over."[90] Walter White, however, was not convinced that that was the best strategy, and his doubt was critical to the path that the NAACP would take.

Although he had once remarked that "the ways of white folks... are so often beyond understanding," perhaps no one in the NAACP understood the psyche of lynchers better than Walter White.[91] As a blond hair, blue-eyed black man from Georgia, he often passed for white to investigate some of the most gruesome lynchings in the United States. White would visit the town, pose as a newspaper man or just a traveler passing through, then sit down and talk, Southerner to Southerner, to the lynchers, who were often proud of their "accomplishment." White would listen to them proudly describe how and why they killed African Americans at will. There was the aerial bombing and massacre in the black section of Tulsa, Oklahoma, because African Americans had worked hard, saved their money, and kept up their property. They simply appeared to be doing financially better than whites and, therefore, had to die. In that one assault, at least 300 were killed, including two who were decapitated while they prayed for deliverance. There was also the lynching of an 18-year-old in her third trimester of pregnancy and the joy of listening to her "howl" when she was "strung up" because she had defied social custom and stood up to a white man although everyone, white and black alike, agreed he was a "brute."[92] After years of listening to Southerners explain

90. Radio Talk for Station KGFJ... by Roy Wilkins, July 16, 1942, Part 1, Reel 11, *NAACP*; Roy Wilkins to Walter White, memo, September 11, 1943, Box 439, File "NAACP Programs: Postwar, 1943–44," *Papers of the NAACP;* Roy Wilkins with Tom Mathews, *Standing Fast*, introduction by Julian Bond (New York: Viking, 1982; reprint, New York: Da Capo Press, 1994), 41–44 (page references are to reprint edition); Office of War Information (Surveys Division), "The Negroes' Role in the War: A Study of White and Colored Opinions, Memorandum No. 59," July 8, 1943, Box 29, File "OWI Files-Alphabetical File Race Tensions-Jonathan Daniels File-Research," *Nash Papers.*

91. Walter White to Walter King, December 1, 1941, Box 181, File "Churchill, Winston: Letter Regarding Negro Service in British Armed Forces, General, 1941–42," *Papers of the NAACP.*

92. Sondra Kathryn Wilson, ed., *In Search of Democracy: The NAACP Writings of James Weldon Johnson, Walter White, and Roy Wilkins (1920–1977)* (New York: Oxford University Press, 1999), 229–31.

why blacks had to die and how important those lynchings were to the white community, White fully grasped the dangers inherent in the words "social equality."[93] Yet, he also knew that there was more at work here.

White supremacy and its deadly implications for people of color, transcended national borders. What was killing black people, ultimately, was beyond the scope of Mississippi, or even the United States. His experience in 1921 with the Pan-African Congress "played a profound role in opening [his] eyes to the world implications of the race question." The symbiosis between white supremacy and global capitalism, which was "intimately involved with the causes of war and the very bases of civilization," convinced him that he was confronting an international problem that required an international solution.[94] This, by no means, implied that each nation could abdicate its responsibility to put its own house in order. Indeed, the NAACP would continue its relentless efforts to pressure local, state, and federal government to do just that. But White believed that the reach of the NAACP would have to extend further. He wanted the NAACP at the peace conference and he wanted to be sure that the Association was ready to shoulder that responsibility.

White, therefore, pushed his Board to sponsor and underwrite a series of conferences with officials from some of the most influential organizations in the United States to help the NAACP determine the specific elements of a just peace.[95] The participants included not only the traditional mainstream stalwarts such as Mary McLeod Bethune, president of the National Council of Negro Women and Walter Reuther, president of the United Auto Workers, but also NNC president, Max Yergan, whom

93. For the importance of lynching and spectacle lynching to Southern communities see, Hale, *Making Whiteness*, 199–239.

94. White, *A Man Called White*, 60.

95. John W. Fowler to Walter White, February 12, 1942, Box 507, File "A. Philip Randolph, 1942–55," *Papers of the NAACP*; Walter White to Board of Directors, memo, February 8, 1943, Box 466, "File "Peace Conference Committee to Present Views of Negroes at Upcoming Peace Conference, 1943–44," ibid.; "Minutes of the Meeting of the Committee on Personnel of the Committee to Place before the Peace Conference the Facts regarding the Negro and the Colored Peoples of the World," March 13, 1943, ibid.; List of Persons Asked to Serve on the Committee to present the Cause of the Negro at the Next Peace Conference, June 17, 1943, ibid.; William H. Hastie to Walter White, August 27, 1943, Box 299, File "William H. Hastie – General, July 1943–August 1944," ibid.; Walter White to William H. Hastie, November 12, 1943, Box 466, File "Peace Conference Committee to Present Views of Negroes at Upcoming Peace Conference, 1943–44," ibid.; Walter White to Harcourt A. Tynes, November 12, 1943, ibid.; Memorandum for the Secretary (For the Files), December 16, 1943, ibid.; Metz T. P. Lochard to William Hastie, August 10, 1943, Box 299, File "William H. Hastie – General, July 1943–August 1944," ibid.

Board member Hastie asked for specifically.[96] It was clear that Yergan, who had worked for 15 years in South Africa, had invaluable expertise in the area of globalized oppression. Yergan was also the executive director of the Council on African Affairs (CAA), an organization dedicated to disseminating accurate information about the conditions in Africa. Similarly, White included in his task force Paul Robeson, entertainer and chairman of the CAA and Rayford Logan, who had written the definitive work on the League of Nation's colonial mandate system. Colonialism, however, was but one part of the equation. Issues about the conditions under which people of color would be emancipated, as the history of African Americans since 1865 had starkly revealed, were also important. Political freedom without economic independence was just enslavement by another name. The Association, therefore, would expand its platform from civil rights to include the international human rights agenda, with its strong emphasis on economic rights and racial equality, that was emerging out of the horrors of Nazi atrocities.[97] Yet, while the conference participants praised the NAACP for its "foresight" and "sanity" in working to develop a plan before the war ended, White knew that the Association had to do more.[98]

His sense of urgency was heightened by the Allies' announcement that, at the end of the war, they would create a new international organization to replace the ineffective League of Nations. White sensed that this new organization, the UN, if properly developed, could be the vehicle to break the back of white supremacy, ensure a just peace, and implement the Four Freedoms. Yet, he was certain, given the Allies' questionable history, that the UN's development could not be left solely in their hands. Soviet purges, British colonialism, and American lynching did not inspire confidence in the Allies' commitment to human rights.

Nor was White at all comfortable about the deals President Roosevelt would cut with the Senate to ensure that the United States would be allowed to join this new international organization. The problem was the Southern Democrats. "Consider," Earl Dickerson exhorted, "'Cotton Ed' Smith [D-SC] with his ravings against the Negro and organized labor," who because of the widespread disfranchisement of black voters, was

96. William Hastie to Walter White, August 27, 1943, ibid.

97. For an excellent discussion on the emergence of human rights as an international principle, and particularly the importance of the Holocaust in that development, see Paul Gordon Lauren, *The Evolution of Human Rights: Visions Seen*, Pennsylvania Studies in Human Rights, ed. Bert Lockwood, Jr. (Philadelphia: University of Pennsylvania Press, 1998), 139–71.

98. Mary McLeod Bethune to Walter White, June 22, 1943, Box 466, File "Peace Conference Committee, to Present Views of Negroes at Upcoming Peace Conference, 1943–1944," *Papers of the NAACP*; Mercer Cook to Walter White, June 23, 1943, ibid.

"elected by less than 20 percent of the people of his home state." This, of course, was the senator who referred to the NAACP as the "'nigger advancement society,'" who defended "lynching as necessary 'to protect the fair womanhood of the South from beasts,'" and who walked out of the Democratic national convention because a "'Nigra'" was going to give the invocation, and he was not going to be prayed over by some "'slew-footed, blue-gummed, kinky-headed Senegambian!'"[99] Smith and his ilk, Walter White angrily explained, "head or dominate more than sixty percent of the Senate and House Committees which determine not only domestic legislation but foreign affairs and the shape of the post war world."[100] "The plain, bitter truth," White declared, "is that thinking and action on the problem of race in our own country are determined almost completely by the most fascist-minded element in the deepest and darkest South. This element – which practiced Naziism long before Hitler was born – almost completely dominates our federal government."[101] Frustrated and angry about the situation, White railed that no one in Washington had "the guts to stand up like men and fight the Tom Connally-Bilbo-'Cotton Ed' Smith filibustering gang which comes from the states where lynchings are most frequent and where the Federal Constitution is violated with impunity every day in the week."[102] In fact, on many occasions White watched President Roosevelt "appease Southern bigots" and just walk away from issues that were critical to the very survival of black people.[103]

The UN, White feared, could suffer the same fate because a Southern regime that "spit upon democracy whenever the Negro is involved" and which "utilize[d] hatred of the Negro precisely as Hitler used prejudice against Jews, Catholics and Christians" would, of course, be unwilling to ratify a UN treaty that guaranteed justice and racial equality.[104] The issue was further complicated because Texas Senator Tom Connally chaired the Senate Foreign Relations Committee, which had responsibility for

99. Quoted in, White, *A Man Called White*, 108, 168; quoted in Ashmore, *Civil Rights and Wrongs*, 8.
100. Address by Walter White, . . . at Closing Meeting of Wartime Conference, July 16, [1944], Reel 19, *Roosevelt*.
101. Address by Walter White . . . at the Closing Session of the Thirty-First Annual Conference of the National Association for the Advancement of Colored People," June 23, 1940, ibid.
102. Ibid.
103. Walter White to David Niles, July 26, 1944, Box 458, File "Niles, David K., 1944–47," *Papers of the NAACP*.
104. Speech of Walter White . . . to be delivered at the Madison Square Garden Mass Meeting of the March-on-Washington Movement," June 16, 1942, Reel 19, *Roosevelt*; Address by Walter White, . . . at closing meeting of Wartime Conference, July 16, [1944], ibid.

managing the process for the ratification of U.S. participation in the UN. White knew Connally's position on racial equality and justice all too well, because the Texas senator had led the "determined opposition" that "side-track[ed] the anti-lynching bill" in 1937, 1938, and 1940. In fact, the senator's filibusters were so "vindictive" that they compelled one man to sarcastically suggest that while Connally was at it, he might as well "sterilize all negro babies at birth" and "chloroform all old Negroes at 65 years of age." White therefore asserted that it was just too frightening to envision the "kind of world Connally would trowel out with his attitude of contempt for colored people."[105]

For White, Connally's influence in the shaping of the postwar world made it even more important that the NAACP be at the peace table, that it present a definitive set of demands, and that it have the wherewithal to follow through. Just as those ideas were beginning to crystallize, the preeminent authority on issues of colonialism, race, and economics was available for hire. This man's appointment could give the NAACP the intellectual resources, depth of vision, and personnel it needed to fight this all important battle for black equality. There was only one problem, the man was W. E. B. Du Bois. He despised Walter White . . . and the feeling was mutual.

Besides being a clash of Titanic-sized egos, their dispute was over control. Control of the Association's magazine, *Crisis*, and control over the bedrock ideology that would guide the Association into the future. Du Bois, one of the co-founders of the NAACP in 1909, had squired *Crisis* from the beginning. Brilliant, iconoclastic, insightful, and unrepentant, *Crisis* was a true reflection of its editor, Du Bois. For years, although it was the official organ of the NAACP, it had remained a separate, self-supporting, financial entity. But the Depression and years of resulting red ink forced *Crisis* in the mid-1930s to be subsumed under the NAACP. That, however, did not stop Du Bois from launching into a thought-provoking series on segregation that ran headlong into the NAACP's declared policy to destroy Jim Crow. Du Bois worried that the Association's tendency to immediately connote anything that was all-black as "inferior," in fact, undermined the very argument that the NAACP was making – namely, that African Americans were equal. Du Bois declared that it was not the racial composition of the schools, hospitals, or

105. Alben Barkley to Walter White, April 13, 1940, Box 62, File "Anti-Lynching: Barkley, Alben, 1940," *Papers of the NAACP*; Walter White to Franklin Roosevelt, April 2, 1940, ibid.; C. L. Brooks to Tom Connally, January 29, 1940, Box 64, File "Anti-Lynching: Tom Connally," ibid.; *The Congressional Record*, August 11, 1937, 7581, 7583–84, 7593–95; White, *A Man Called White*, 169–70, 173.

Photo 1.2. W. E. B. Du Bois, Director, Special Research, National Association for the Advancement of Colored People.
Special Collections and Archives, W. E. B. Du Bois Library, University of Massachusetts, Amherst.

even neighborhoods that created the appallingly inferior conditions that engulfed black life in America. Rather, it was the eagerness of whites to starve black institutions of resources that was at the root of the problem. The point, Du Bois continued, was not to fight for some glorious day when all-black institutions would disappear, the point was to strengthen and rely on those institutions for what they could bring to the African American community. Not surprisingly, when *Crisis* hit the stands, Walter White hit the roof. White wanted the next issue of *Crisis* to include a retraction and an unqualified statement that the NAACP was opposed to racial segregation, period. Du Bois refused, submitted his resignation, and went to teach at Atlanta University.

Despite this rancorous parting of the ways, by the Spring of 1944, Walter White wanted Du Bois back. Du Bois had been White's mentor at the Pan-African Congress in 1921 and White now had to admit that the NAACP's co-founder knew more "than any other living human being" about the global "problems faced by colored peoples."[106] Arthur B. Spingarn, President of the Board of Directors, while acknowledging Du Bois's enormous talents, warned White that working with the scholar may again prove difficult.[107] It appears, though, that White believed that the 76-year-old Du Bois, who had just been fired from Atlanta University without a pension, had been humbled by the experience and would be grateful for the NAACP's offer to help him out of his financial bind.

Three factors, however, would undermine White's thesis. First, the NAACP was not the only group vying for Du Bois' services. The moment word reached the black community that Atlanta University had fired him, ostensibly because he was past retirement age, but more likely because he had infuriated President Rufus Clement, offers from several universities poured in. Du Bois was carefully reviewing each one to determine which institution would give him the resources, flexibility, visibility, and autonomy he needed to continue his work on the issues of race, class, and colonialism.[108] Second, although there were many strong, able scholars like Rayford Logan, there was only one genius, W. E. B. Du Bois. He had the analytical rigor, theoretical deftness, and leaps of intuitive brilliance that elevated him above anyone else. Du Bois knew it and he knew that the NAACP knew it, too. Finally, because he was the only one who could really do the job, the NAACP desperately needed Du Bois' expertise more than he needed the Association.

Thus, although White personally invited Du Bois to return to the NAACP as the director for special research, Du Bois bypassed him and negotiated his return directly with three powerful members of the Board.[109] Du Bois' seemingly successful contract negotiations made him the second-highest paid employee of the NAACP and provided him with a hand-picked assistant, Dr. Irene Diggs, an expense account, office space, and clerical support to continue his work. Over time, the NAACP leadership would chafe under Du Bois' contract, and this would add fuel to the smoldering fire between Du Bois and White. For the moment, however, Du Bois eagerly set to work on his new assignment to champion the cause

106. Ibid., 60; White to William H. Hastie, April 21, 1944, Box 240, File "William E. B. Du Bois: General, 1943–44," *Papers of the NAACP.*

107. White to Arthur Spingarn, October 8, 1948, Box 94-8, Folder 181, *Spingarn Papers.*

108. Kendall Weisiger to Arthur B. Spingarn, May 5, 1944, Box 94-20, Folder 448, ibid.

109. Louis T. Wright to Kendall Weisiger, April 20, 1944, Box 240, File "William E. B. Du Bois: General, 1943–44," *Papers of the NAACP*; Eugene M. Martin to Walter White, April 24, 1944, ibid.; Eugene M. Martin to Walter White, April 24, 1944, ibid.; Minutes of the Meeting of the Committee on Administration, April 24, 1944, Box 127, File "Board of Directors: Committee on Administration, 1942–1944," ibid.; Du Bois to White, July 5, 1944, Reel 56, *W. E. B. Du Bois Papers* (Sanford, North Carolina: Microfilming Corporation of America, 1980). Microfilm (hereafter *Du Bois*).

of "the American Negro and the colored peoples of the world" at the San Francisco Conference, where 50 nations would meet to define the powers of the United Nations.[110]

Du Bois' first task, however, was to evaluate the proposals drawn up by the Allied powers at the Dumbarton Oaks Conference of October 1944, which outlined the UN's basic structure and formed the basis for discussion in San Francisco. The meeting at Dumbarton Oaks was divided into two phases. The first, in which all of the important decisions was made, involved the Americans, the British, and the Soviets. The second phase served two purposes. It was designed to acknowledge Roosevelt's concept of the "Four Policemen" – the U.S., Great Britain, the Soviet Union, and China – as the major peacekeepers in the postwar world. It was also designed to recognize the Soviet Union's refusal to accord China world power status and, thus, refusal to meet with Beijing's representatives. Winston Churchill shared the Soviets' view and dismissed China "contemptuously as not being a world power at all but only a 'faggot vote on the side of the United States.'"[111] Nevertheless, the British reluctantly agreed to meet with the Chinese and the Americans for the second phase of the Dumbarton Oaks Conference. China's participation in the conference, however, was but one of many disagreements between the Americans and the British.

The most salient and critical point of dispute was the issue of colonialism. The argument, however, was not over the merits of colonialism. Indeed, the Americans were not opposed to colonial rule at all, they just wanted to be more coy and subtle about their ambitions than the British, who flaunted Empire at every turn. Before the first phase of Dumbarton Oaks, the State Department had played with some language that would initially provide for minimal international oversight of colonial rule. The British immediately rejected the State Department's "naive" and "idealistic" proposal and found a willing accomplice in the U.S. military. For both the British and the military, "minimal" was still too much. Britain's very identity was enveloped in Empire, yet, the indigenous peoples in the British Empire were demanding independence. The British government recognized that it would be impossible to put the genie of freedom back in the bottle, while UN observers witnessed the quashing of one bloody insurrection after another. As for the U.S. military, there were several strategic islands that the armed forces had wrested from the Japanese, and the War Department had no intention of giving them back or

110. Walter White to W. E. B. Du Bois, 17 May 1944, ibid.; "Fragment of NAACP Minutes," May 1944, ibid.

111. Churchill quoted in Lauren, *Evolution of International Human Rights*, 170.

allowing some international organization to constantly look over the Navy's shoulder to make sure that the inhabitants were treated fairly. Caught between the British on one side and the War Department on the other, the State Department decided that this issue was not worth the fight and opted to omit any discussion of colonies or trusteeships from the Dumbarton Oaks agenda. The Soviets, while feigning disappointment and calling it a "pity" that colonialism would not be debated, agreed to the deletion, especially because it implied that there would be no discussion of Soviet territorial expansion.[112]

The question of human rights fared only slightly better at Dumbarton Oaks. Several weeks after the first phase of the conference began, Benjamin Cohen, President Roosevelt's personal liaison, registered great concern that the issue of human rights had not been included in the draft Charter for a United Nations. Given the congressional power of the Southern Democrats and the pervasiveness of Jim Crow throughout America, Cohen was well aware that the United States could not be overly strident about human rights. But he also recognized that without at least an acknowledgment of human rights, especially in light of the Holocaust, the proposed UN would appear to be nothing more than a facade for power politics as usual. The solution to this dilemma, the American delegation believed, was to accord human rights status as an "important international principle," while leaving its enforcement to individual states. Even this mild proposal was too strong for the British, who believed that it would render them vulnerable to interference in how they ruled the Empire. Although the Soviets initially described the issue of human rights as "not germane" and made it clear that "they weren't interested in bringing... economic and social matters" into the deliberations, the Allies concluded after much debate that they had to put human rights somewhere in the UN proposals. After all, they conceded, "it would be farcical to give the public [the] impression that the delegates could not agree on the need to safeguard human rights." The Allies finally concurred that the most innocuous place to insert language on the subject was in the section on the responsibilities of the Economic and Social Council. The Council would "promote respect for human rights and fundamental freedoms," but have no power to enforce them. The British were concerned that even this mild language would permit international meddling in the domestic affairs of member states. They therefore included an additional clause that prevented the UN from involving itself in the internal matters

112. Robert C. Hilderbrand, *Dumbarton Oaks: The Origins of the United Nations and the Search for Post War Security* (Chapel Hill and London: The University of North Carolina Press, 1990), 37, 173–76.

of states, unless the violations presented a direct threat to world peace.[113] The Soviet and American delegations agreed that this was a good, sound compromise and accepted it. The Allies' decision to severely limit the UN's power in human rights and colonial affairs dimmed the hopes raised by the Atlantic Charter's declaration of self-determination and equality. The Chinese phase of Dumbarton Oaks did nothing to improve the outlook.

Before the conference, the Chinese had proposed incorporating human rights, justice, and especially racial equality in the UN Charter. The Soviets immediately denounced the idea and refused to even consider it during the first phase of the conference. The British and Americans were also vehemently opposed to the idea, but realized that they had to be more circumspect in their denunciation. Sir Alexander Cadogan telegraphed the Foreign Office and explained the dilemma. Because Britain was a "liberal power" and the denial of racial equality "figure[d] so prominently in Nazi philosophy," it would be a public relations disaster for the British to openly oppose the inclusion of racial equality in what was essentially the Magna Carta of the United Nations. Undersecretary of State Edward R. Stettinius, Jr., echoed Cadogan's analysis and made it very clear that although the United States would concede that human rights deserved some recognition, under no circumstances would America support an explicit reference to racial equality.[114] As the Chinese delegation reviewed the work done during the first phase of the conference, they immediately recognized that with human rights mentioned only in the Economic and Social Council section and not in the Charter nor in the outline of the Security Council, the basic right to exist had been pushed to the very periphery of the organization and, thus, to the fringes of international importance. When the second phase began, China's delegation, fully understanding its precarious world power status and its sponsor's adamant opposition to racial equality, gingerly suggested several human rights and international law revisions to strengthen the draft UN Charter. Britain and the United States remained bitterly opposed to elevating human rights as a central theme of the UN, but decided that it was important to let the "Chinese save face" and agreed to incorporate into the draft UN Charter three "harmless" proposals on cultural cooperation and international law.[115] As John Foster Dulles would later explain, the Dumbarton Oaks proposals "had the defects which usually occur when a few big powers get together to decide how to run the world. They generally, and naturally,

113. Andrei Gromyko quoted in, Lauren, *The Evolution of International Human Rights*, 169; Durward V. Sandifer Oral History, Harry S Truman Presidential Library, Independence, Missouri (hereafter *Sandifer*); Hilderbrand, *Dumbarton Oaks*, 91–93.

114. Ibid., 231, 236–240; Lauren, *The Evolution of International Human Rights*, 166–70.

115. Hilderbrand, *Dumbarton Oaks*, 240.

conclude that the best of all possible worlds is a world which they will run."[116]

Du Bois immediately noticed the disrespectful way in which the Allies treated China and saw that treatment as indicative of Western contempt for nonwhites.[117] His meeting with State Department officials about the Dumbarton Oaks proposals, reaffirmed his position. Du Bois was "depressed" to realize how consistently the Allies had disfranchised the 750 million people who lived in the colonial world. He described the Dumbarton Oaks proposals as "intolerable, dangerous," and irreconcilable "with any philosophy of democracy."[118] According to the proposals, for example, only states could join the UN, bring a complaint before the Security Council, or appeal to the International Court of Justice. Colonies had no rights. Most importantly, the UN lacked the power to investigate human rights abuses; it could only consider complaints filed by member states. Provisions like these, according to Du Bois, made it clear to the millions shackled by colonial rule that "the only way to human equality is through the philanthropy of masters."[119] But what else could be expected, Du Bois wondered, when the Allies had chosen as their conference site the old Southern plantation of Dumbarton Oaks to decide the fate of 750 million people of color.[120] The Council on African Affairs leadership was equally disturbed by the proposals emanating from Dumbarton Oaks. In a letter to Walter White, Robeson and Yergan emphasized that colonial issues, especially in Africa, had not been effectively addressed. The Council therefore asked for White's cooperation in working out "constructive supplementary recommendations."[121]

Although they did not see it initially, there was a fundamental difference between the Council's and the NAACP's assessment of the flaws in the Dumbarton Oaks proposals. The most important element in the Council's vision was continued Allied unity. In this scenario, the Soviet Union – not the UN – would prevent the reimposition of the old imperial

116. "Address of John Foster Dulles at the Foreign Policy Association Luncheon," June 29, 1945, Box 26, File "Re: Dumbarton Oaks Proposals: 1945," *JFD-Princeton*.

117. W. E. B. Du Bois, *Color and Democracy: Colonies and Peace* (New York: Harcourt Brace, 1945), 7.

118. W. E. B. Du Bois, "The Negro and Imperialism," transcript of radio broadcast, November 15, 1944, Box 527, File "Speakers: W. E. B. Du Bois, 1944–48," *Papers of the NAACP*.

119. Du Bois to American Friends Service et al., October 21, 1944, Reel 55 *Du Bois*; Du Bois, *Color and Democracy*, 4; Du Bois, "The Negro and Imperialism," transcript of radio broadcast, November 15, 1944, Box 527, File "Speakers: W. E. B. Du Bois, 1944–48,"*Papers of the NAACP.*

120. Du Bois, *Color and Democracy*, 3–4.

121. Robeson and Yergan to White, November 29, 1944, Reel 55, *Du Bois*.

structure.[122] Robeson argued that, without the Soviets' constructive influence, the United States would "pursue a selfish path" toward "further imperialistic ambitions."[123] The Council therefore stressed that, "above everything else," the objective of the upcoming UN Conference was to establish a Charter that "will permanently hold together the great powers." Without that unity, the Council declared, no international problems, including that of the colonies, could be solved.[124] The Association insisted, however, that peace depended on a strong UN with the authority to rein in the Great Powers. "International collective security" was critical, the NAACP asserted, because the Great Powers depended on the continued existence of colonial empires to rebuild their war-devastated economies.

Despite these differences, the Council and the Association agreed that the colonial issue had received little or no attention in the Dumbarton Oaks proposals and that this oversight had to be corrected.[125] Du Bois strongly believed that the unsatisfactory proposals developed at Dumbarton Oaks were "substantially the American plan," but he was also convinced that the United States had to rise above the swamp of traditional diplomacy, indeed, the swamp of its own political tradition and history, and force the imperial powers to provide full citizenship and autonomy for the colonial people.[126] Unlike Robeson and Yergan, however, Du Bois and the NAACP were unwilling to rely primarily on the Soviet Union to champion the rights of colonial people, or anyone else, at the upcoming UN Conference on International Organization (UNCIO) at San Francisco.

As a result, Du Bois lobbied the State Department to be named as a consultant to the American delegation at the San Francisco Conference. He asked both Secretary of State Stettinius and his assistant, Leo Pasvolsky, who was the true power behind the throne, if the department had made

122. "The San Francisco Conference and the Colonial Issue: Statement of the Council on African Affairs," found in Reel 56, ibid.; "Editorial," *New Africa* 4, no. 3 (March 1945): 3; "Resolutions Adopted at the War-Time Conference," July 16, 1944, Part 1, Reel 11, *NAACP*.

123. "American Negroes in the War: Address delivered by Paul Robeson at the *New York Herald Tribune* Forum on Current Problems," November 16, 1943, Reel 1, *The Paul Robeson Collection* (Bethesda, Maryland: University Publications of America, 1991). Microfilm (hereafter *Robeson*).

124. "The San Francisco Conference and the Colonial Issue," found in Reel 56, *Du Bois*.

125. Max Yergan to Du Bois, telegram, December 11, 1944, Reel 55, ibid.; Du Bois to Yergan, December 12, 1944, ibid.; "Dumbarton Oaks and Africa," *New Africa* 3, no. 11 (December 1944): 1, 5–6.

126. Clark Eichelberger to Organization Representatives, February 13, 1945, Reel 56, *Du Bois*; Minutes of the Board of Directors' Meeting, December 1944, Part 1, Reel 3, *NAACP*; Du Bois to Clark Eichelberger, March 9, 1945, Reel 56, *Du Bois*.

any arrangements for African Americans to "advocate" for themselves and "for other peoples of African descent whom they, in a very real sense, represent?"[127] Du Bois was particularly insistent that the State Department allow the NAACP, an organization with more than 400,000 members and indirectly representing 13 million African Americans, to send two delegates to participate in the debates at San Francisco.[128]

As improbable as citizen participation in a peace conference may have sounded, State Department officials liked the concept. They immediately saw the need for a public relations campaign that would help the UN Charter avoid a fate similar to the one that befell the Treaty of Versailles in 1919. The State Department believed that a lack of widespread public support for the 1919 treaty, which included the Covenant of the League of Nations, had enabled the Senate to reject it and thus prohibit American participation in the League. This time the State Department was determined to build a broad base of support for the forthcoming UN treaty. With this goal in mind, it eventually asked 42 national organizations, ranging from the conservative National Association of Manufacturers to the liberal NAACP, to serve as official consultants to the U.S. delegation.[129]

To Walter White's chagrin, however, it soon became evident that the consultants were to be nothing more than "window dressing."[130] Stettinius wanted the consultants to act as cheerleaders, not coaches, for the new international organization.[131] The UNCIO, as far as the State

127. Du Bois to Stettinius, March 10, 1945, Reel 58, ibid.; Du Bois to Leo Pasvolsky, telegram, April 10, 1945, ibid.; Donald C. Blaisdell Oral History, Harry S Truman Presidential Library, Independence, Missouri (hereafter *Blaisdell*); *Sandifer*.

128. Du Bois to Leo Pasvolsky, telegram, April 10, 1945, Reel 58, *Du Bois*.

129. Dorothy B. Robins, *Experiment in Democracy: The Story of U.S. Citizen Organizations in Forging the Charter of the United Nations* (New York: The Parkside Press, 1971), 34–56 and 81–99.

130. White, *A Man Called White*, 295.

131. Stettinius to George E. C. Hayes, telegram, April 12, 1945, Reel 57, *Du Bois*; "Minutes of the Second Meeting (Executive Session) of the United States Delegation, Held at Washington, Friday, March 23, 1945, 10 A.M.," Department of State, *Foreign Relations of the United States*, Vol. 1, *General: The United Nations, 1945*: 148–49 (hereafter *FRUS*); "Memorandum by Mr. Charles E. Bohlen, Assistant to the Secretary of State for White House Liaison, of a Meeting at the White House, Thursday, March 29, 1945, 11:45 A.M.," ibid., 167; "Minutes of the Third Meeting of the United States Delegation, Held at Washington, Friday, March 30, 1945, 11 A.M.," ibid., 171; "Minutes of the Fourth Meeting of the United States Delegation, Held at Washington, Tuesday, April 3, 1945, 10 A.M.," ibid., 187–88; Stettinius diary, Meeting with Consultants, 10 A.M., April 26, 1945, Box 30, File "Stettinius Diary—San Francisco Conference, Vol. I: April 23, Midnight–May 31, 1945 (1 of 5)," *Files of Harley A. Notter: RG 59, General Records of the Department of State*, National Archives II, College Park, Maryland (hereafter *Notter*).

Department was concerned, was "exclusively a conference of governmental delegations" with simply no place in its deliberations for private citizens.[132] In fact, while the State Department sought wide public discussion about the proposed UN Charter, it simultaneously made clear that "aside from wording and phraseology, actual changes [in the Charter] would be few."[133] Stettinius was adamant that his "job in San Francisco was to create a charter... not to take up subjects like... 'the negro question'" or to allow something as "ludicrous" as "a delegation of American Indians... to present a plea... for recognition for the independence of the Six Nations (The Iroquois)."[134]

Undaunted, Du Bois and the NAACP prepared to present a strong case in San Francisco for African Americans and colonial peoples.[135] Following Stettinius's announcement that the Association would be an official consultant at the UN conference, the NAACP surveyed 151 African American organizations for their opinions on the important issues to be addressed in San Francisco.[136] The groups, ranging from the National Urban League to the Negro Ministers of New Haven, Connecticut, urged the Association to push for an end to racial discrimination and the abolition of colonialism.[137]

Confident that through years of research, meetings, conferences, and surveys they had compiled the most crucial elements for a just peace, White and Du Bois left for San Francisco hoping that the NAACP could induce the UNCIO participants to "face what is one of the most serious problems of the twentieth century – the question of race and color."[138] White's hopes would be dashed, however.

The conference began on April 25 but as late as May 1, 1945 the U.S. delegation, which included Texas Senator Tom Connally as one of its most

132. Benjamin Gerig to Du Bois, April 12, 1945, Reel 58, *Du Bois.*

133. Irene Diggs to Walter White, memo, November 6, 1944, Box 634, File "United Nations: Bretton Woods Conference, 1944–46," *Papers of the NAACP.*

134. Stettinius, diary, Box 29, File "Stettinius Diary, Week of 8–14 April 1945," *Notter*; Stettinius, diary, Box 29, File "Stettinius Diary, Week of 15–23 April 1945 (Section Ten)," ibid.

135. The NAACP also sponsored a Colonial Conference in March and April of 1945. See, "Resolution of the Colonial Conference in New York," April 6, 1945, Box 197, File "Colonial Conference, 1945," *Papers of the NAACP*; Logan to Du Bois, telegram, February 22, 1945, Reel 57, *Du Bois*; "Resolution of Board of Directors," March 12, 1945, Box 197, File "Colonial Conference, 1945," *Papers of the NAACP.*

136. Du Bois to Walter White, memo, April 12, 1945, Reel 57, *Du Bois*; Du Bois and White to the National Urban League et al., telegram, April 13, 1945, ibid.

137. "Summary of Survey," ([April 1945]), Reel 58, ibid.; Du Bois to Walter White, April 17, 1945, ibid.

138. White to Du Bois and Mary McLeod Bethune, memo (n.d. [May 1945]), Reel 57, ibid.; "Report of the Secretary," May 1945, Part 1, Reel 7, *NAACP.*

Photo 1.3. The hope of the UN. Crowd gathering outside of the San Francisco Opera House trying to catch a glimpse of American and foreign delegates as they leave the first session of the UNCIO Conference in April 1945.
Corbis.

dominant and "articulate" members, had yet to adopt a public position on the colonial empires and had decided not to press for a strong human rights plank or a UN agency to monitor human rights violations.[139] In a "brutally frank" exchange with Stettinius, Du Bois, White, and the other consultants argued that millions had died in vain if the war had not been fought for human rights and self-determination. After years of Nazi brutality and aggression, they said, it should be painfully clear that any international conference for world peace must take up such issues as human rights and colonialism. Neither the NAACP nor any of the other 41 organizations designated as "official consultants" would support a UN

139. *Sandifer*; "The Acting Secretary of State to the Ambassador in France (Caffery)," *FRUS* (1945), 1:67–68; "Minutes of the Fifth Meeting of the United States Delegation Held at Washington, Monday April 9, 1945, 3:15 P.M.," ibid., 221; "Minutes of the Twenty-Eighth Meeting of the United States Delegation, Held at San Francisco, Thursday, May 3, 1945, 6:20 P.M.," ibid., 581.

that did nothing to address these underlying causes of war.[140] That "acrimonious" barrage caught Stettinius and the U.S. delegation offguard, and they quickly promised to submit proposals on these two issues. Indeed, the State Department assured the consultants that this "pounding" and "pressure had not been without effect."[141]

The consultants were not placated by the State Department's assurances. The consultants therefore decided on May 2, 1945 to present their own human rights proposal to the American delegation. At the ensuing meeting, White turned to Stettinius and made clear that the clause pledging equality and justice was particularly applicable to colonial and other dependent people. The secretary of state responded with a "somewhat embarrassed, cryptic smile" and followed with a bewildering request to know which planks in the proposed amendment could be jettisoned if other delegations complained. The consultants were dumbstruck. The proposal, they said, was their "minimum demand." Instead of gutting it, and thus discrediting the moral leadership of the United States, they urged Stettinius to take the lead in the global fight for human rights. The secretary of state promised to do what he could and then left the room.[142]

What Stettinius could or would do was quite limited. With the Grand Alliance crumbling, the United States sought to isolate the Soviet Union and develop even stronger ties to Europe's imperial powers. American policy makers, particularly in the Pentagon, were therefore prepared to woo their allies by limiting the authority of the UN in colonial affairs. They made sure that the conference would only establish the procedure for placing colonies under the trusteeship system and emphasized that no specific territories would be discussed. The mounting tensions between the Soviet Union and the United States also meant that the U.S. military was more determined than ever to hold onto those key strategic islands in the Pacific. The goal, as one State Department official noted, was to make sure that Americans had a "free hand" to"use those islands as we saw fit."[143] Therefore, the United States moved authority for the islands from the Trusteeship Council to the veto-protected Security Council, dared

140. White to Du Bois and Mary McLeod Bethune, memo (n.d. [May 1945]), Reel 57, *Du Bois*; "Report of the Secretary," May 1945, Part 1, Reel 7, *NAACP*.
141. "Minutes of the Twenty-First Meeting (Executive Session) of the United States Delegation, Held at San Francisco, Friday, April 27, 1945, 8:55 P.M.," *FRUS* (1945), 1:484; "Minutes of the Twenty-Sixth Meeting of the United States Delegation, Held at San Francisco, Wednesday, May 2, 1945, 5:30 P.M.," ibid., 532–41; "Handwritten Notes from Consultants Meeting in Room 312" (n.d.), Reel 56, *Du Bois*.
142. White to Du Bois and Bethune, memo, (n.d. [May 1945]), Reel 57, ibid..
143. *Blaisdell*.

any nation to challenge that decision, and thereby satisfied the military's hunger for Pacific bases.[144]

Domestic pressures were also instrumental in derailing any "moral leadership" the United States might have taken. The Southern Democrats ruled the Senate. That was the bottom line. Circumventing the Constitution already required their eternal vigilance, the last thing they wanted was a UN Charter that provided yet another legal instrument that the NAACP and African Americans could use to break Jim Crow. State Department officials were well aware of this and even admitted that, "when you had men like ... Connally [on the delegation] ... you didn't go sailing off into the blue. You had to keep your eye all the time on not putting too much limitation on American sovereignty."[145] Or, to put it more specifically, on limiting states' rights. Those who did not understand this basic concept

144. U.S. Min. 6 Summary Record Meeting of the United States Delegation, April 26, 1945, Box 84, Folder 17, *Papers of Hamilton Fish Armstrong*, Seeley Mudd Manuscript Library, Princeton University, Princeton, New Jersey (hereafter *Armstrong Papers*). For the U.S. position on trusteeship, see Stettinius, diary, Box 29, File "Stettinius Diary Week of 15–23 April 6, 1945 (Section Ten)," 50–52, 92 *Notter*; Stettinius, diary, Box 29, File "Stettinius Diary Week of 8–14 April 1945," 14, 40–43 ibid.; "The Acting Secretary of State to the Ambassador in France (Caffery)," *FRUS* (1945), 1:80; "Minutes of the First Meeting of the United States Delegation, Held at Washington, Tuesday, March 13, 1945, 11 A.M.," ibid., 117; "Memorandum by the Interdepartmental Committee on Dependent Areas," ibid., 135; "The Secretary of State to Mr. Leo Pasvolsky, Special Assistant to the Secretary of State," ibid., 194–95; "Minutes of the Twelfth Meeting of the United States Delegation, Held at Washington, Wednesday, April 18, 1945, 9:10 A.M.," ibid., 349; "Minutes of the Nineteenth Meeting of the United States Delegation (A), Held at San Francisco, Thursday, April 26, 1945, 8:40 P.M.," ibid., 445–52; "Draft United States proposals for Trusteeship [San Francisco], April 26, 1945," ibid., 459–60; "Minutes for the Twenty-Fourth Meeting of the United States Delegation, Held at San Francisco, Monday April 30, 1945, 6:20 P.M.," ibid., 504; "Minutes of the Fiftieth Meeting of the United States Delegation (A), Held at San Francisco, Tuesday, May 22, 1945, 9:05 A.M.," ibid., 845; "Minutes of the Sixtieth Meeting of the United States Delegation, Held at San Francisco, Friday, June 1, 1945, 9 A.M.," ibid., 1390; "Press Release: Statement by the Honorable Edward R. Stettinius, Jr., Chairman of the American Delegation," May 5, 1945, Reel 58, *Du Bois*. For the U.S. military's stance on strategic areas within the trusteeship plan, see "Memorandum by the Chairman of the State-War-Navy Coordinating Committee (Dunn) to the Secretary of State [Washington], February 26, 1945," *FRUS* (1945), 1:93–95; "Memorandum of Conversation, by the Adviser on Caribbean Affairs (Taussig) [Washington], March 15, 1945," ibid., 122; "Extracts from the Diary of Edward R. Stettinius, Jr., Secretary of State, December 1, 1944–July 3, 1945, March 18–April 7, 1945 (Section Eight)," ibid., 140–41; "The Secretary of the Interior (Ickes) to the Secretary of State, Washington, April 5, 1945," ibid., 198–99; "The Secretary of State to President Roosevelt," April 9, 1945, ibid., 211–13; "Memorandum by the Secretaries of State, War, and Navy to President Truman, Washington, April 18, 1945," ibid., 350–51; "The Chairman of the United States Delegation (Stettinius) to the Acting Secretary of State, San Francisco, May 6, 1945," ibid., 614.

145. *Sandifer*.

were omitted from the core delegation or eased out of power in the State Department. The end result of this unnatural selection process was that America's human rights policy could barely evolve beyond the Mason-Dixon line.[146]

Moreover, because Tom Connally would be the one to "steer... the Charter through both the Committee hearings and the Senate debate," his opposition to human rights carried an inordinate amount of weight. For example, although several delegations wanted to include educational cooperation as one of the UN's functions, Connally was vehemently "opposed to any plan to provide educ[ation] irrespective of race." The delegation was therefore totally unresponsive, if not openly hostile, to the consultants' demand for "explicit use of 'educational'" in the UN's text. One delegate voiced fears that the "word 'educational' would provoke widespread controversy" and "repercussions in Congress." Another "emphasized the extent to which Congress [was] opposed to international educational programs." He then described the way Congress had even denied funds to rebuild bombed-out schools. Connally's opposition and clout easily led the delegation to reach the "consensus opinion that the inclusion of the word 'education'" was too risky because it "might provoke opposition in Congress to the whole document." The consultants would therefore just have to accept defeat because, as far as the delegation was concerned, the issue of education was "settled."[147]

Yet, for a nation desperate to portray itself as the embodiment of democracy and for a delegation fighting to have the word "justice" embedded in the UN treaty, the whole discussion of human rights was far from settled.

146. "Minutes of the Seventh Meeting of the United States Delegation, Held at Washington, Wednesday, April 11, 1945, 9 A.M.," *FRUS* (1945), 1:252–53; "Minutes of the Tenth Meeting of the United States Delegation, Held at Washington, Monday, April 16, 1945, 9 A.M.," ibid., 308; "Minutes of the Twelfth Meeting of the United States Delegation, Held at Washington, Wednesday, April 18, 1945, 9:10 A.M.," ibid., 338–42; "Minutes of the Twenty-Fifth Meeting of the United States Delegation, Held at San Francisco, Wednesday, May 2, 1945, 9 A.M.," ibid., 527; "Minutes of the Thirty-Seventh Meeting of the United States Delegation, Held at San Francisco, Wednesday, May 16, 1945, 6 P.M.," ibid., 765; "Minutes of the Seventy-First Meeting of the United States Delegation, Held at San Francisco, Thursday, June 14, 1945," ibid., 1301–02; Lauren, *The Evolution of International Human Rights*, 159–65.

147. Hamilton Fish Armstrong to Tom Connally, July 30, 1945, Box 16, File "Connally, Tom, 1943, 1945, 1949," *Armstrong Papers*; Walter White's handwritten notes of meeting with Corps Com., 9:30 A.M. 68 Post St., ca. May 1, 1945, Box 639, File "United Nations: United Nations Conference on International Organization—General, 1945–July 1946," *Papers of the NAACP*; Meeting of the American Delegation, April 27, 1945, Box 84, Folder 17, *Armstrong Papers*; Meeting of the United States Delegation: Summary Record, April 27, 1945, Box 84, Folder 18, ibid.; Hamilton Fish Armstrong's handwritten minutes of U.S. Delegates Meeting 5:30, May 2, 1945, Box 84, Folder 23, ibid.

If anything, it was clearly unsettling. Dulles knew, for instance, that the Soviets no more wanted the word "justice" than the United States wanted "education." He found distasteful, however, the Soviets' willingness to throw "education" on the scrap heap if the United States would treat "justice" as contemptuously. This was particularly disconcerting because the United States believed that the American judicial system was one of the hallmarks of democracy and a way to clearly distinguish the United States from the Soviet Union and its horrific "show trials." The problem was deeper than this, though. The Soviets may have had show trials, but the United States had Southern Justice. America also had Jim Crow, internment of the Japanese, genocide of the Native Americans, debt slavery, racist immigration laws, and a host of other human rights violations. Obviously, an open and frank debate about human rights could quickly unmask the reality of American democracy. Moreover, because San Francisco was not Dumbarton Oaks, this unmasking was a real possibility.[148] With 47 other nations and a contingent of headstrong consultants, the United States could not keep the debates over human rights from billowing out of the tight parameters established at Dumbarton Oaks. State Department officials knew, for example, that the United States was "'backward'" when it came to issues of "the right to work" and, in fact, was so far "behind other governments" in recognizing social rights that it became awkward and embarrassing. It was especially obvious when questions over "some of the economic and social provisions like full employment" sparked "animated debates" with "delegates like... Connally" on one side and the Australians, who "sought a guarantee of full employment," on the other.[149] It was just tremendously difficult to limit human rights to the comfortable areas of civil and political rights and then to craft an international enforcement mechanism as weak as the one that protected those rights in the United States.

The consultants exposed this problem when they demanded, of all things, establishment of a human rights commission. The American delegation may have been appalled at the suggestion, but the horrors of the Holocaust and, frankly, the horrors of America compelled the Jewish and African American consultants to view an international commission as absolutely essential. State Department official Leo Pasvolsky, clearly bristled

148. Arthur Vandenberg to John Foster Dulles, March 9, 1944, Box 25, File "Vandenberg '44," *JFD-Princeton*; Warren R. Austin to John Foster Dulles, March 22, 1945, Box 26, File "Austin, Warren R.," ibid.; Vandenberg's comments on Dumbarton Oaks discussions, April 1945, Box 26, File "Re: Dumbarton Oaks Proposals, 1945," ibid.

149. *Sandifer;* J. P. Humphrey and J. P. Hendrick, memo of conversation on Human Rights, September 18, 1946, Box 8, File "Human Rights: March 1945–December 31, 1947," Lot File 55D429, *RG 59*.

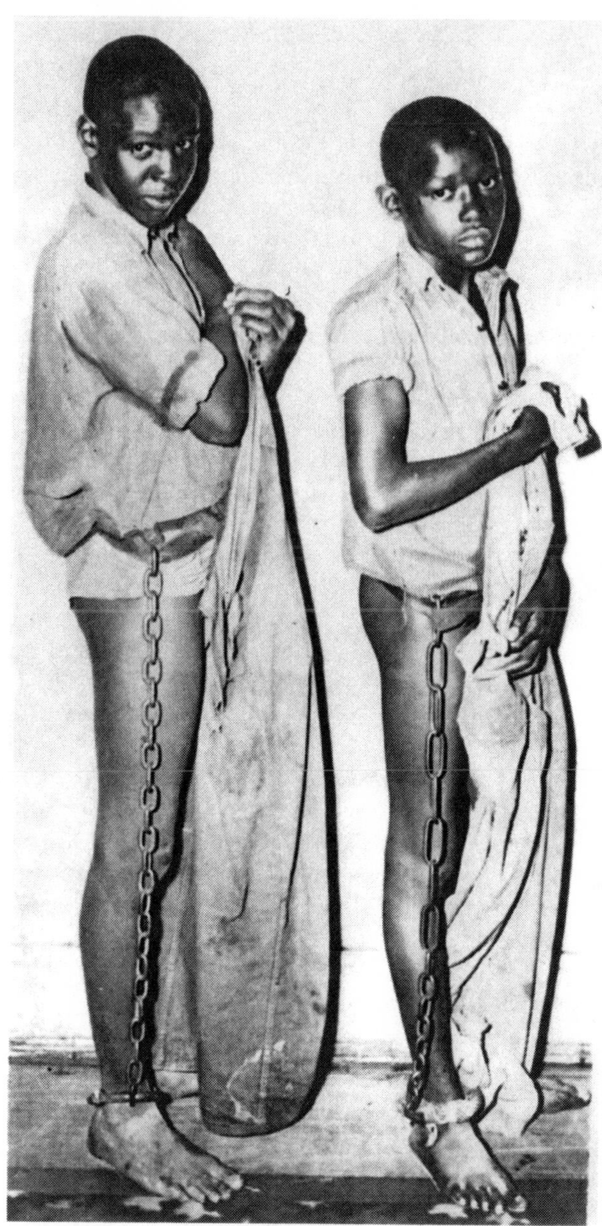

Photo 1.4. "Atrocities Strike Close to Home," June 1945. Two 15-year-old African American boys, shackled and stripped for trying to escape from the Colored Industrial Farm in Atlanta, Georgia. Photo taken at about the same time that the United States inserted the domestic jurisdiction clause in the UN Charter to keep the United Nations from investigating human rights abuses, especially in the South.

Corbis.

at the suggestion. "Pasvolsky was the key man" for the U.S. delegation in San Francisco.[150] In fact, "Leo Pasvolsky was pretty much writing his own ticket" at the UNCIO, and he had privately assured the Senate leadership that he would handle things in San Francisco to their liking.[151] He therefore pounced on the consultants' request for a human rights commission and sought to discredit the idea. If the United States caved into the consultants' unreasonable demands, Pasvolsky asserted, the UN would become a Hydra sprouting specialized commissions all over the place, first one for human rights, then an "Opium Commission," and heaven could only imagine what else.[152] Much to his surprise, though, Pasvolsky, who was a usually "genius at manipulating people," could not get Stettinius to accept that argument.[153] Although the secretary of state "was not an intellectual giant," he knew that the delegation had to do something "along [the] lines" that the consultants suggested. The whole point of having the consultants there in the first place was to get them to buy into the concept of the UN and generate enthusiastic, widespread support for the upcoming treaty. If they were denied everything they asked for, the State Department's public relations ploy could backfire and create a determined, well-financed, influential, and vocal opposition.[154]

Understanding the problem, John Foster Dulles was confident that he could devise a human rights plan that would pacify the consultants and satisfy the Southern Democrats. His solution was simple. Amid an unequivocal statement "guaranteeing freedom from discrimination on account of race, language, religion, or sex," Dulles inserted an amendment that "nothing in the Charter shall authorize ... intervention in matters which are essentially within the domestic jurisdiction of the State concerned." The American and Soviet delegations immediately embraced Dulles' stroke of genius.[155]

150. *Sandifer*.
151. *Blaisdell*; Arthur Vandenberg to John Foster Dulles, March 21, 1945, Box 27, File "Vandenberg, Arthur H., 1945," *JFD-Princeton*.
152. Hamilton Fish Armstrong's handwritten minutes of U.S. Delegates Meeting 5:30, May 2, 1945, Box 84, Folder 23, *Armstrong Papers*.
153. *Sandifer*; Hamilton Fish Armstrong's handwritten minutes of U.S. Delegates Meeting 5:30, May 2, 1945, Box 84, Folder 23, *Armstrong Papers*.
154. *Sandifer*; Hamilton Fish Armstrong's handwritten minutes of U.S. Delegates Meeting 5:30, May 2, 1945, Box 84, Folder 23, *Armstrong Papers*.
155. "Proposed Article to be inserted as a new chapter in the Charter," May 3, 1945, Box 216, File "UNCIO-Domestic Jurisdiction (General)," *Notter*; Meeting of the Big Four, 12 noon, May 4, 1945, Box 84, Folder 25, *Armstrong Papers*; Meeting of the United States Delegation, 6:20 P.M., May 3, 1945, Box 84, Folder 24, ibid.; United Nations, "Amendments Proposed by the Governments of the United States, the United Kingdom, the Soviet Union, and China," May 5, 1945, *United Nations Conference on*

The other nations and the consultants, however, sent up a wail of protest. Du Bois and White declared that, under those restrictions, the UN would be unable to prevent another Holocaust. Still worse, the amendment applied only to member states, not colonies where people of color were routinely the victims of discrimination and abuse. Certainly, they argued, the clause prevented the UN from doing anything to stop the human rights abuses that blacks suffered in the United States. That, of course, was the point. Stettinius did not want the United States to "be put in a position of having matters of domestic concern interfered with by the Security Council," and Dulles wanted to make sure that the UN could not "requir[e]" a state to "change [its]...immigration policy or legislation."[156]

Panama and Chile therefore argued, with good reason, that Dulles' clause "would leave the door too wide open for nations to escape the jurisdiction of the Organization." The Belgian delegation pleaded that "domestic jurisdiction" was so broadly defined that it created a "formidable," if not impenetrable, barrier. Why not use the phrase "solely within the domestic jurisdiction," the Belgians asked. As it stood, the UN had zero authority to censure human rights violations that were "essentially" within the domestic sphere.[157] It was obvious to the Australian delegation that the domestic jurisdiction clause circumvented the real problem. If the point of inserting human rights into the UN Charter was "to protect minorities," the Australians declared, then the "proper course is either to . . . recognize the protection of minorities as a matter of legitimate 'international,' and not merely of 'domestic' concern, or to make a formal international convention providing for the proper treatment of minorities."[158] After listening to delegation after delegation criticize the domestic jurisdiction clause, Dulles went on the offensive. He complained that the other delegations had gone hog-wild inserting one economic and social rights provision after the other. The United States had to protect itself. Dulles then made it

International Organization San Francisco, 1945: Documents, Volume 3, *Dumbarton Oaks Proposals Comments and Proposed Amendments* (London and New York: United Nations Information Organizations), 622–23.

156. "Report of the Secretary," May 1945, Part 1, Reel 7, *NAACP*; Walter White et al. to Stettinius, telegram, May 7, 1945, Reel 58, *Du Bois*; Informal Consultation on Domestic Jurisdiction of the United States, the United Kingdom, and Australia, June 1, 1945, Box 216, File "UNCIO-Domestic Jurisdiction (General)," *Notter*.

157. *Summary of Debate on Domestic Jurisdiction: Joint Four-Power Amendment*, June 1, 1945, ibid.

158. Informal Consultation on Domestic Jurisdiction of the United States, the United Kingdom, and Australia, June 1, 1945, ibid.; *Domestic Jurisdiction*: New Paragraph in Chapter II (Principles), Proposed by the Sponsoring Governments, n.d. (ca. June 1, 1945), ibid.

abundantly clear that the domestic jurisdiction clause was America's price for allowing human rights to seep into the UN Charter. This "is as far as we can go." "If [the domestic jurisdiction clause] is rejected," Dulles warned, "we shall be forced to reexamine our attitude toward increases in the economic and social activities of this Organization." After Dulles clarified the American position, the debate stopped and the other nations agreed to accept the domestic jurisdiction clause. The United States had just won an important battle in keeping human rights from darkening America's doorstep.[159]

Just as the plan for human rights had been severely weakened, Stettinius' plan for colonial trusteeships was just as troubling. The American proposal side-stepped the issue of independence as the ultimate goal of the plan and paternalistically described colonialism as a caretaking arrangement for those unable to handle the "strenuous conditions of the modern world."[160] Du Bois was incensed. Instead of recognizing that the plight of colonial peoples was "due to oppression and exploitation" and capitalist demands for "cheap... labor and forced servitude," the U.S. amendment "intimated" an inherent inferiority of colonial peoples. Du Bois lashed out that this was nothing but "a covert defense of the exploiters... against the exploited."[161] Worse yet, the American proposal would bring only three percent of the colonial world under the authority of the UN's Trusteeship Council. The U.S. plan allowed international oversight only for current mandates, colonies controlled by the Axis nations, and any dependency "voluntarily placed under the system by states responsible for their administration."[162] The latter was highly unlikely but Pasvolsky quickly dismissed a more comprehensive plan as a "wild

159. *Summary of Debate on Domestic Jurisdiction: Joint Four-Power Amendment*, June 1, 1945, ibid.

160. "Minutes of the Fifth Meeting of the United States Delegation, Held at Washington, Monday, April 9, 1945, 3:15 P.M.," *FRUS* (1945), 1:221; "Minutes of the Forty-Fourth Meeting of the United States Delegation, Held at San Francisco, Thursday, May 17, 1945, 6 P.M.," ibid., 789–90; "Minutes of the Sixtieth Meeting of the United States Delegation, Held at San Francisco, Friday, June 1, 1945, 9 A.M.," ibid., 1055; "Minutes of the Sixty-Fourth Meeting of the United States Delegation, Held at San Francisco, Tuesday, June 5, 1945, 9:01 A.M.," ibid., 1167–70; "Minutes of the Seventieth Meeting of the United States Delegation, Held at San Francisco, June 13, 1945, 9 A.M.," ibid., 1279–80; United Nations Conference on International Organization, "Working Paper for Chapter on Dependent Territories and Arrangements for International Trusteeship," May 15, 1945.

161. Du Bois to the Delegates of the USA UNCIO, draft (n.d. [May 1945]), Reel 58, *Du Bois*.

162. "Arrangements for International Trusteeship: Additional Chapter Proposed by the United States" (n.d. [May 1945]), ibid.

idea."[163] Du Bois, on the other hand, thought it equally ridiculous for the United States to rush blindly into the arms of the colonial powers simply because it had allowed itself to be "estranged from Russia by the plight of a dozen reactionary, ... Jew-baiting Polish landlords."[164] He confided to Metz Lochard, editor of the *Chicago Defender*, that "We have conquered Germany but not [its] ideas. We still believe in white supremacy, keeping negroes in their places and lying about democracy, when [what] we mean [is] imperial control of 750 million human beings in colonies."[165]

The CAA concurred in Du Bois' assessment. The Council denounced the American trusteeship plan as "unctuous rhetoric" designed to "avoid a clear guarantee ... of independence for colonial peoples."[166] Before the San Francisco Conference, the Council was confident of the Soviet Union's ability to prevent the reimposition of colonial rule. That, however, was confidence misplaced. It was evident that the Soviets and Americans, despite their major public disagreements over Poland, worked in harmony to thwart a strong UN commitment to human rights and decolonization. Indeed, the Soviets' anti-colonial stance grew more pronounced only as its alliance with the United States disintegrated, and Moscow needed some means to project itself on the world stage as the only true proponent of democracy. Unfortunately, the CAA leadership was oblivious to Soviet motives and only understood that visible tensions between the United States and the Soviet Union threatened the Council's concept of peace. The CAA's frustration was compounded by the NAACP's refusal to support the Soviet position on key issues and more aggressively attack the Western powers. Indeed, Max Yergan had urged White to join him in an anti-U.S. press conference that would praise the vision of Soviet Foreign Minister V. I. Molotov. White refused. In a fit of fury and in front of a room full of people, Yergan grabbed the NAACP's executive secretary by the lapels, berated him for being "obstructionist" and a "betrayer" of his people, and demanded that White adopt a more pro-Soviet position. Although Yergan soon regained his composure, the damage was done. White made sure that he avoided the Council's president for the rest of the conference, and the NAACP – which believed that, as Yergan went, so

163. "Minutes of the Seventy-Seventh Meeting of the United States Delegation, Held at San Francisco, Wednesday, June 20, 1945," *FRUS* (1945) 1:1390–91.
164. Du Bois to American Delegation—UNCIO, May 16, 1945, Box 639, File, "United Nations—UNCIO—General, 1945—May 11–June," *Papers of the NAACP*.
165. Du Bois to Metz L. P. Lochard, telegram, May 4, 1945, Reel 56, *Du Bois*.
166. Council on African Affairs, "Text and Analysis of the Colonial Provision of the United Nations Charter" (n.d.), Box 639, File "United Nations—UNCIO—General, 1945—May 11–June," *Papers of the NAACP*.

went the NNC – again began to distance itself from the National Negro Congress.[167]

Yergan had also continued to alienate Ralph Bunche, who was now both the highest ranking African American in the State Department and the U.S. delegation's expert on trusteeships. Not only was the fallout from the NNC convention and Bunche's resignation still smoldering, but in San Francisco Bunche saw an FBI report in which Yergan had implicated him in a plot to assure a pro-Soviet outcome of the UNCIO.[168] Bunche was furious. He railed that Yergan was nothing but a "phoney" and a "slicker who was milking nice old Quaker ladies for money" and who had "abandoned his fine Negro wife and children" for an Afrikaner.[169] Bunche quickly set up a *cordon sanitaire* between himself and Yergan. He declined repeated invitations to meet and refused to get Yergan the security passes the Council president needed to participate fully in the conference.

Without question, the tenuous unity that characterized African Americans' postwar plans was rapidly fracturing along the U.S.–Soviet fault line. Nevertheless, Walter White shared Yergan's disillusionment with the meager results of the conference. The executive secretary was well aware of the "difficulty of reconciling security needs with humanitarian considerations," but believed that a savvy, skillful delegation could find that balance. Instead, White contended, the American delegation was "patently weak," with Stettinius "completely out of his depth."[170] Although White was pleased that the consultants had forced the U.S. delegation to agree to a human rights commission, he was dismayed that fundamental flaws still remained in the Charter. He recognized that the NAACP stood little chance of getting the "domestic jurisdiction" clause overturned. He also held little hope for the colonial trusteeship plans,

167. White to Wilkins, memo, May 14, 1945, Reel 57, *Du Bois*; White to Bunche, February 3, 1954, Reel 3, *Bunche*; Yergan to White, (n.d.), Box 639, File "United Nations: United Nations Conference on International Organization—General, 1945–July, 1946," *Papers of the NAACP*; "Informal Gathering at San Francisco Office, Council on African Affairs," May 4, 1945, Box 639, File "United Nations: United Nations Conference on International Organization—General, March–May 10, 1945," ibid.; Edward Dudley to Roy Wilkins, memo, August 25, 1945, Box 393, File "Leagues: Post War Planning Organizations, 1945," ibid. Also see, Robert L. Harris, Jr., "Racial Equality and the United Nations Charter," in *New Directions in Civil Rights Studies*, eds., Armstead L. Robinson and Patricia Sullivan, Carter G. Woodson Institute Series in Black Studies (Charlottesville: University Press of Virginia, 1991), 126–45.

168. Ralph Bunche, "Summary of Reply: Allegation 14" (n.d. [1954]), Reel 2, *Bunche*.

169. Ralph Bunche, "Max Yergan, Notes for Interventions" (n.d. [1954]), Reel 3, ibid.

170. "Draft Minutes of Committee on Administration Meeting," May 28, 1945, Box 127, File "Board of Directors: Committee on Administration, 1945," *Papers of the NAACP*.

"all of which," in his estimation, "were ineffective." White castigated the U.S. delegation for being "timorous" and for losing "the bold moral leadership which it should have taken." He bemoaned that Russia and China had taken the high ground on colonialism, whereas "the smart boys like [British Foreign Secretary Anthony] Eden" had "outsmarted our delegation" and positioned the United States as a staunch supporter of imperialism. Or, as Du Bois noted, at San Francisco, it was painfully obvious that "not a whisper against colonialism could be heard except from Molotov."[171]

Bunche, who served as the staff expert for U.S. delegate Harold Stassen, agreed. "Stettinius," Bunche confided, "is a complete dud . . . in a job for which he has utterly no qualifications and about which he knows nothing."[172] Bunche was already upset that decolonization had been derailed at Dumbarton Oaks. Now, he feared that, under Stettinius' inept leadership, the United States would end up firmly in imperialism's corner. He therefore helped orchestrate a campaign to pressure the U.S. delegation to embrace a trusteeship plan that included independence as the ultimate goal of the system. Stassen had already made "one bad blunder" by opposing independence when the governor could have easily let the British, who were strenuously arguing against it anyway, do so. To overcome this debacle, Bunche slipped his own unauthorized American trusteeship proposal to the Australian delegation, which had taken a much more liberal stance on colonialism than Britain. This sleight of hand allowed the Australian delegation to become the champion of the American version of a trusteeship plan in the deliberations.[173]

Fearful that this strategy alone may not be enough, Bunche was also instrumental in helping to implement a newly hatched NAACP plan. As Walter White prepared to leave San Francisco, he turned to his trusted aide, Roy Wilkins, who was coming to replace him at the UNCIO. White asked for Wilkins' advice on the best way to force the U.S. delegation to strengthen the trusteeship plan. Wilkins responded that Governor Stassen was "politically ambitious" and susceptible to public pressure. Wilkins counseled White to have the NAACP branches barrage Stassen with telegrams indicating their ire that the U.S. delegation had "dealt a body blow

171. White to Roy Wilkins, memo, May 14, 1945, Reel 57, *Du Bois*; Du Bois to Arthur Spingarn, May 30, 1945, Box 94-20, Folder 448, *Spingarn Papers*. The U.S. delegation also feared that it had aligned itself too closely to the colonial powers. See "The Acting Secretary of State to the Chairman of the United States Delegation (Stettinius)," May 8, 1945, *FRUS* (1945), 1:652.

172. Brian Urquhart, *Ralph Bunche: An American Life* (New York: W. W. Norton, 1993), 118.

173. Ibid., 119–20.

to colonial people." Wilkins then suggested that this effort be followed up with a massive press campaign directed out of the NAACP's New York office.[174] White loved the idea and immediately set the plan in motion and followed it up by meeting with the new president of the United States, Harry S Truman, to discuss "certain matters which worr[ied] him about the San Francisco Conference...such as human rights," "equal rights, etc."[175]

As pressure from the NAACP and the press began to mount, Wilkins' strategy, for the moment, appeared to work. Bunche assured Wilkins that Stassen felt the pressure and became "much firmer" in his deliberations with Britain and France.[176] Satisfied with this assessment and pressed to deal with the other political and legal issues on the Association's agenda, Wilkins quickly joined White and Du Bois back in New York. Bunche warned the executive secretary, however, that the Association's absence from the conference had made it clear that there was no one "on the job watching" the American delegation, and there was a "distinct likelihood of compromises" now that the pressure from the NAACP was off.[177]

Disturbed by this turn of events, White telegrammed Stettinius. He urged the U.S. delegation to "take the highest moral and practical ground" and insist on independence as the goal for all colonial peoples.[178] The secretary of state maintained that the United States supported independence, but only for "peoples of trusteeship areas who...are capable of it."[179] The NAACP's position, however had been that independence must be for *all* colonial peoples, not just the 3 percent who came under the trusteeship

174. Wilkins to White, telegram, May 18, 1945, Box 639, File "United Nations—UNCIO—General, 1945—May 11–June," *Papers of the NAACP*; White to Wilkins, May 21, 1945, Box 639, File "United Nations—UNCIO—General, 1945—May 11–June," *Papers of the NAACP*; White to Conseulo Young, letter, May 18, 1945, ibid.

175. R. B. to Matt Connelly, memo, May 23, 1945, Box 1235, File "413 (1945–49)," *Papers of Harry S Truman: Official File*, Harry S Truman Presidential Library, Independence, Missouri (hereafter *Truman:OF*); Memorandum for the Files, May 23, 1945, Box 525, File "85-B, United Nations Conference," ibid.

176. Wilkins to White, May 24, 1945, Box 639, File "United Nations—UNCIO—General, 1945—May 11–June," *Papers of the NAACP*.

177. White to Wilkins, memo, June 4, 1945, ibid.; "Memorandum for the Files from the Secretary—RE: Long Distance Telephone Conversation with Ralph J. Bunche in San Francisco, California, June 3, 1945," June 4, 1945, ibid.

178. White to Stettinius et al., telegram, June 12, 1945, ibid.; White et al. to Stettinius, May 7, 1945, Box 639, File "United Nations: United Nations Conference on International Organization—General, March–May 10, 1945," ibid.; White to Stettinius, telegram, June 20, 1945, Box 639, File "United Nations—UNCIO—General, 1945—May 11–June," ibid.

179. White to Stettinius, telegram, May 18, 1945, ibid.; White to Stettinius, telegram, June 20, 1945, ibid.

Photo 1.5. President Truman signs the UN Charter as Secretary of State James F. Byrnes looks on, 1945.
AP/Wide World Photos.

plan. Moreover, because the proposed Trusteeship Council would have "no Native representation," only the imperial powers had the authority to determine if a colony was "capable" of independence. This proviso was unacceptable. White again urged Stettinius to rectify the flaws in the proposed UN Charter, but his pleading went unheard and there emerged, instead, a "denatured 'shell' of a Trusteeship system," limited to a handful of territories.[180] Du Bois accurately described San Francisco as "a beginning, not an accomplishment." The United States simply "would not take a stand for race equality or for colonies" and instead "back[ed] a contradictory statement on human rights." Rayford Logan was less diplomatic and angrily denounced the UN Charter as a "tragic joke."[181]

180. White to Stettinius, telegram, June 20, 1945, ibid.; White et al., to Stettinius, May 7, 1945, Box 639, File "United Nations: United Nations Conference on International Organization—General, March–May 10, 1945," ibid.; Du Bois to Lawrence Spivak, May 22, 1945, Reel 56, *Du Bois*; Urquhart, *Bunche*, 121.

181. Rayford W. Logan, diary, June 20, 1945, *Papers of Rayford W. Logan*, Library of Congress, Washington, DC (hereafter *Logan Papers*); Du Bois to Arthur Spingarn, May 30, 1945, Box 94-20, Folder 448, *Spingarn Papers*.

After the disappointment at San Francisco, African Americans needed to regroup. "There is not a day to be lost," Max Yergan declared as he invited the top African American leaders to a meeting to stress the "importance of unity in action."[182] Yergan's emphasis on "unity" was deliberate. After his assault on Walter White in San Francisco, there was a real possibility that the NAACP would not participate.[183] Anticipating trouble, Yergan convinced NAACP board vice-president Mary McLeod Bethune to serve as the official convener of the Conference of Negro Leaders.

White, nevertheless, still searched for some excuse to avoid the conference all together. Wilkins, who had even less patience than White, understood the executive secretary's frustration but thought that, politically, the Association could not "afford to turn down [the] invitation." White mulled it over and cautioned Wilkins to get a copy of the agenda before the NAACP committed itself. Given "Max Yergan's performance in San Francisco," White said, Bethune might be "unwittingly playing into the hands of the CP" and trying to align the NAACP with the Communist party. White conceded that the Association would have to "handle this situation with maximum tact and intelligence – neither [of] which, under the circumstances, [he] possess[ed] at the moment." Wilkins finally convinced White that the Association could not risk boycotting the Conference of Negro Leaders; the NAACP had to be represented.[184]

At the June 23, 1945 meeting of 34 black organizations, which included the NAACP, the conference participants noted that "recent international developments . . . demanded continued and strengthened unity of purpose." Rayford Logan chaired the committee on colonialism, which included Max Yergan and Walter White, and drafted a report that found that the San Francisco Charter provided "scant hope for liberation" for the

182. Max Yergan to Mary McLeod Bethune, May 28, 1945, Part 2, Reel 26, *NNC*; Thelma Dale to Max Yergan, May 3, 1945, ibid.; Yergan et al. to Brown, May 3, 1945, ibid.; Yergan to Dale, telegram, May 10, 1945, ibid.; Yergan to Dale, telegram, May 22, 1945, ibid.; Bethune to White, telegram, May 22, 1945, Box 639, File "United Nations: The United Nations Conference on International Organizations—Mary McLeod Bethune, 1945," *Papers of the NAACP*; Bethune to Wilkins, June 5, 1945, ibid.

183. Max Yergan to Mary McLeod Bethune, May 28, 1945, Part 2, Reel 26, *NNC*; Thelma Dale to Ben Davis, May 28, 1945, ibid.

184. White to Wilkins, telegram, May 24, 1945, Box 639, File "United Nations: The United Nations Conference on International Organizations—Mary McLeod Bethune, 1945," *Papers of the NAACP*; Wilkins to White, telegram, May 24, 1945, ibid.; Wilkins to White, telegram, May 28, 1945, ibid.; White to Wilkins, May 31, 1945, ibid.; White to Bethune, telegram, June 7, 1945, ibid.; White to Wilkins, June 15, 1945, ibid.

750 million people in non–self-governing areas.[185] Bethune spoke forcefully on how the UN Conference had drawn into "bold relief" that "common bond" between African Americans and the colonial peoples. If anything, Bethune remarked, the UNCIO had made it very clear that the "Negro in America" held "little more than colonial status in a democracy."[186]

The similarities were clear. The fight for colonial self-determination paralleled the battle to overturn the South's racist voting restrictions. The efforts to revise the UN's "domestic jurisdiction" clause matched the assault on the states' rights philosophy of the South. And the dissatisfaction with a trusteeship plan that denied colonies the right to lay their grievances before an international tribunal mirrored the opposition to America's separate and unequal system of justice. The Conference of Negro Leaders, with organizations representing more than eight million African Americans, vowed to move on all fronts to secure civil and human rights.

In the days ahead, however, this resolve would be greatly challenged. As Senator Arthur Vandenberg warned, "Peace without some semblance of general justice is a fake which not even the UN . . . could indefinitely sustain."[187]

185. Rayford W. Logan, diary, June 24, 1945, *Logan Papers*; "Conference of Negro Leaders," June 23, 1945, Part 2, Reel 26, *NNC*.

186. "Statement of Mrs. Mary McLeod Bethune," June 23, 1945, Box 3, Folder 17, *Mary McLeod Bethune Papers*, Amistad Research Center, New Orleans; "Negro Leaders Issue New Program," *Congress View* 3, no. 4 (July 1945): 8.

187. Arthur Vandenberg to Hamilton Fish Armstrong, December 24, 1945, Box 63, File "Vandenberg, Arthur H., 1945–1951," *Armstrong Papers*; Vandenberg's comments on Dumbarton Oaks discussions, April 1945, Box 26, File "Re: Dumbarton Oaks Proposals, 1945," *JFD-Princeton*.

2

The Struggle for Human Rights

African Americans Petition the United Nations

The American black man is the world's most shameful case of minority oppression.... How is a black man going to get "civil rights" before he first wins his human rights? If the American black man will start thinking about his human rights, and then start thinking of himself as part of one of the world's greatest people, he will see he has a case for the United Nations.

Malcolm X[1]

Roy Wilkins, the prophet. The rumblings of white terror that he sensed in 1943 exploded all over the black community in 1946. In Alabama, when an African American veteran removed the Jim Crow sign on a trolley, an angry street car conductor took aim and unloaded his pistol into the ex-Marine. As the wounded veteran staggered off the tram and crawled away, the chief of police hunted him down and finished the job with a single bullet, execution style, to the head.[2] In South Carolina, another veteran, who complained about the inanity of Jim Crow transportation, had his eyes gouged out with the butt of the sheriff's billy club.[3] In Louisiana, a black veteran who defiantly refused to give a white man a war memento, was partially dismembered, castrated, and blow-torched until his "eyes 'popped' out of his head and his light complexion was seared dark."[4] In Columbia, Tennessee, when African Americans refused to "take lying down" the planned lynching of a black veteran who had defended his mother from a beating, the sheriff's storm troopers, in an "attack ... on a

1. Malcolm X and Alex Haley, *The Autobiography of Malcolm X* (New York: Ballantine Books, 1964), 207. (Emphasis in original.)
2. "Ex-Marine Slain for Moving Jim Crow Sign," *Chicago Defender*, February 23, 1946, found in Box 54, File "WH Files-Minorities-Negro-General-Individuals-Newsclipping: 1945–1946," *Nash Papers*.
3. "Cops gouge out Negro vet's eyes," n.d. (ca. July 1946), found in Box 543, File "OF 93 May–December 1946 [1 of 2]," *Truman:OF*.
4. Lynching Record for 1946: Chronological Listing, n.d. (ca. 1946), Box 408, File "Lynching: Lynching Record, 1946–52," *Papers of the NAACP*.

scale reminiscent of military operations in the last war," "'drew up their machine guns and tommy guns,... fired a barrage of shots directly into the black area of town, and then moved in.'"[5]

As horrific as this violence was, however, the threshold for savagery was clearly breached in Monroe, Georgia. It was an ambush. Witnesses described screams. Piercing, agonizing screams ripping through a blanket of gunfire. Bound and surrounded, two sisters and their husbands were defenseless against the trunk load of firepower brought to the killing fields at Moore's Ford. All they could do was scream. At first, the lynchers planned to only murder the two black men, but then, when one of the women recognized a member of the lynch party, no one was spared. One of the women, seven months pregnant and at the center of a brawl between her husband and a white man rumored to have raped her, was "dragged out of the car" and then shredded by a firestorm of sixty bullets. The same gruesome fate befell her husband, who knew after he defended his wife and stabbed that white man in Georgia that "'I ain't gonna get out of this, they're gonna kill me.'" The pregnant woman's sister endured the agony of having both hands crushed before her spine was pulverized by the firing squad. The final victim, a veteran and the brother-in-law, was pistol whipped before the mob splattered his body into the red Georgia dirt.[6]

This alchemy of slaughtered veterans and mutilated women was the last straw. One black veteran asserted that, "This time it has gone too far, they are killing our women."[7] In a gasp of anguish, African American veterans pleaded with Truman. "Our lives are in jeopardy."[8] The National Council of Negro Women was "stunned beyond all expression" and called on Truman, in the "name of human justice," to stop the "brutal massacre

5. "The NAACP in 1946–47: Address of Dr. Louis T. Wright... at 38th Annual Conference," June 24, 1947, Box 130-6, Folder 15, *Papers of Louis T. Wright*, Moorland Spingarn Research Center, Howard University, Washington, DC (hereafter *Wright Papers*); "Report of Grand Jury in the Matter of the Racial Disturbance at Columbia, Tennessee," attachment to Tom Clark to Eleanor Roosevelt, October 8, 1946, Box 3338, File "NAACP, 1945–47," *Roosevelt Papers*; Jason Parkhurst Guzman, ed., *Negro Year Book: A Review of Events Affecting Negro Life, 1941–1946* (Tuskegee, Alabama: Department of Records and Research Tuskegee Institute, 1947), 246–53.
6. Lynching Record for 1946: Chronological Listing, n.d. (ca. 1946), Box 408, File "Lynching: Lynching Record, 1946–52," *Papers of the NAACP*; Hyde Post, Andy Miller and Peter Scott, "Murder at Moore's Ford," *Atlanta Journal–Constitution*, May 31, 1992, A/01.
7. Sammye T. Lewis to Truman, telegram, July 27, 1946, Box 548, File "OF 93a Lynching of (4) Negroes at Monroe, GA July 25, 1946," *Truman:OF*.
8. Kenneth C. Kennedy (United Negro and Allied Veterans of America) to Truman, telegram, July 30, 1946, ibid.

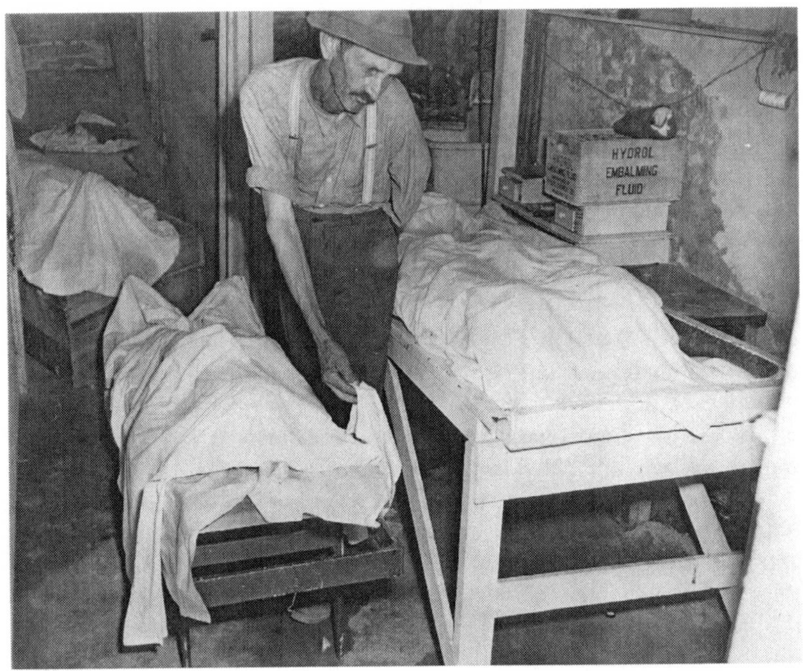

Photo 2.1. An ignoble end. Coroner W. T. Brown(?) places yet another sheet over the body of one of the four Monroe, Georgia, lynch victims, July 1946. *AP/Wide World Photos.*

of our people."[9] The killings were so repulsive that they even compelled the NAACP to set aside its serious reservations about working with suspected Communist organizations, including the newly organized Civil Rights Congress (CRC), which the NAACP had described as a "distinct threat to the Association." On August 6, 1946, Walter White met with the leadership from the Civil Rights Congress and the NNC, as well as representatives from other organizations, to "express our determination to combine together for the purpose of bringing before the bar of justice for conviction the perpetrators of these lynchings and to check the rising tide of mob violence."[10] For its part, the NAACP had uncovered eyewitnesses

9. Mary McLeod Bethune to Truman, telegram, July 27, 1946, ibid.
10. Roy Wilkins to Walter White, memo, May 1, 1946, Box 369, File "Leagues: Civil Rights Congress; 1946–47," *Papers of the NAACP*; Roy Wilkins to D. E. Byrd, May 25, 1946, ibid.; Marian Wynn Perry to Walter White, memo, May 7, 1946, ibid.; Walter White et al., to Truman, telegram, August 6, 1946, Box 548, File "OF 93a Lynching of (4) Negroes at Monroe, Georgia July 25, 1946," *Truman:OF*.

to the crime and immediately forwarded their names and affidavits to the Department of Justice. The Association also verified that law enforcement officers, acting "under the color of law," were involved in the killings and, therefore, that a federal crime had been committed.[11] That should have been enough. But it was not. Nor was presidential concern.

Truman, who was also a veteran, was distressed that men who had served their country were clearly being targeted for elimination. He "expressed his horror" at the crimes and told his staff that he was "very much alarmed at the increased racial feeling all over the country." The president urged his staff, and especially U.S. Attorney General Tom Clark to "push with everything you have" to determine if there has been a "violation of any Federal statutes."[12] It just seemed to Truman that "when the mob gangs can take four people out and shoot them in the back, and everybody in the country is acquainted with who did the shooting and nothing is done about it, that country is in a pretty bad fix from a law enforcement standpoint."[13]

To explain away its continuing inability to prosecute killers, the Department of Justice pointed to a lack of evidence, a lack of statutory authority, and a tight-lipped, closed Southern society that protected lynchers.[14] Unpersuaded, Walter White observed that, instead of using the authority it did possess, the "federal machinery for justice" demonstrated an uncanny ability to "collapse" consistently in the face of Southern opposition.[15] For many African Americans, the reason for that collapse led straight to Attorney General Clark, a man from Tom Connally's Texas, and a man, in the eyes of the black community, who never seemed able to find any law that any lyncher had ever broken. One woman even suggested that,

11. See, *Screws v. United States*, 325 U.S. 91 (S. Ct. 1945); Walter White to Tom Clark, telegram, July 29, 1946, Box 412, File "Lynching—Walton County, Georgia, Correspondence: 1946–1948," *Papers of the NAACP*; Walter White to Tom Clark, August 1, 1946, ibid.; Theron Caudle to Walter White, August 6, 1946, ibid.; Walter White to Tom Clark, August 12, 1946, ibid.

12. Truman to Tom Clark, September 20, 1946, Box 26, File "Civil Rights/Negro Affairs, 1945–June 1947," *Papers of David K. Niles*, Harry S Truman Presidential Library, Independence, Missouri (hereafter *Niles Papers*); David K. Niles to Mrs. Calvin Ricks, August 6, 1946, Box 38, File "WH Files Correspondence—Sample Letters, 1946–1952," *Nash Papers*; Truman to David K. Niles, memo, September 20, 1946, Box 26, File "Civil Rights/Negro Affairs, 1945–June 1947," *Niles Papers*.

13. Post, "Murder at Moore's Ford," A/01.

14. R. R. Wright to Truman, July 18, 1946, Box 543, File "OF 93 May–December 1946 [1 of 2]," *Truman:OF*; David K. Niles to R. R. Wright, July 25, 1946, ibid.; David K. Niles to Omar N. Bradley, July 25, 1946, ibid.

15. Walter White to Mrs. (Marian Wynn) Perry, memo, 4 October 1946, Box B112, File "Perry, Marian, Wynn, 1945–49," *NAACP–Legal*; Walter White to Truman, telegram, June 15, 1946, Box 543, File "OF 93 May–December 1946 [1 of 2]," *Truman:OF*.

as long as "Texas Tom Clark represents the federal government," Georgia has "nothing to fear so far as murdering Negroes is concerned."[16] Echoing that sentiment, a group of black Texans argued that with Clark at the helm of the Justice Department, whites obviously "feel free to kill Negroes at will."[17]

Nothing the Justice Department did in Monroe, Georgia, altered that assessment. One attorney in the Civil Rights section explained that "caution and restraint" were their guiding principles, even if that did irritate "some of the civil rights people."[18] That, however, was not the source of the NAACP's critique. Rather, it was how "caution and restraint" consistently translated into lynchers getting away with murder. And it looked like nothing was going to be done again. Clark explained that, "We have found in some communities that they just won't talk, like in Georgia. We had a Grand Jury down there in addition to quite a number of FBI men who had been on the job for several months, but we just couldn't get any citizens there to give us information, although we know they have it."[19]

In a letter to J. Edgar Hoover, one disgusted man wrote, "Am I to believe" that the FBI, which has captured "spies, gangsters, [and] men of the most practiced villainy" has been outsmarted and "defeated by country bumpkins... hillbillies... [and] Georgia crackers?"[20] Thurgood Marshall was equally incensed as he ripped into Clark. It was incomprehensible that the Association's own "inexperienced investigators" were able to identify members of the lynch mob while the professionals in the FBI could not. That just did not seem plausible. The Bureau, Marshall noted, had established an "uncomparable record for ferreting out" every other criminal under the sun, so why was it so difficult for the FBI to "produce the name of a single individual responsible for the acts of violence [against]... Negroes"?[21]

The Justice Department's seemingly *laissez-faire* attitude, juxtaposed to the U.S. government's vigorous prosecution of Nazi war criminals, added

16. Eunice Wright to Truman, telegram, July 29, 1946, Box 548, File "OF 93a Lynching of (4) Negroes at Monroe, Georgia, July 25, 1946," ibid.
17. Negro Retail Beer Dealers and Merchants of Texas to Truman, telegram, July 29, 1946, ibid.
18. *Eleanor Bontecou Oral History*, Harry S Truman Presidential Library, Independence, Missouri (hereafter *Bontecou*).
19. "Tom Clark's Testimony to the President's Committee on Civil Rights," Record Group 220, Box 14, *Papers of the President's Committee on Civil Rights*, Harry S Truman Presidential Library, Independence, Missouri.
20. Broadus Mitchell to J. Edgar Hoover, October 16, 1946, Box 412, File "Lynching—Walton County, Georgia: Correspondence, 1946–48," *Papers of the NAACP*.
21. Thurgood Marshall to Tom C. Clark, December 27, 1946, File "NAACP, General Correspondence, 1945–52," *Roosevelt Papers*.

fuel to the resentment and frustration burning in the black community. For many, it was sheer "lipocrisy" for the United States to flex its moral muscle at Nuremberg while claiming impotence in Monroe, Georgia.[22] Another fired off that the whites who had "declared war upon the Negroes" were "no less criminals than those in Nuernberg."[23] Similarly, White complained to Eleanor Roosevelt that, "Negro veterans . . . have been done to death or mutilated with savagery equalled only at Buchenwald." What added to the horror, he explained, was the very real possibility that, with "no visible action in the form of arrests and convictions," lynch mobs would see this as a "green light . . . to substitute the law of the jungle for the democratic process."[24]

White clearly had in mind Georgia's Governor-elect Eugene Talmadge, whom many had identified as the chief instigator of the violence at Moore's Ford. In what historian Kari Frederickson described as "the year's most racist political campaign," Talmadge "campaigned largely on the issue of 'keep the niggers where they belong!'" He asserted that, "'if the good white people will explain it to the negroes around the state just right I don't think they will want to vote.'"[25] He repeatedly warned African Americans to ignore the U.S. Supreme Court's ruling that the white primary was unconstitutional. If blacks approached the voting booth, Talmadge suggested, they were fair game for whatever punishment white Georgians chose to dole out. Indeed, one white man, disgusted by African Americans' determination to vote, stated matter-of-factly that, "'[Lynching has] got be done to keep Mister Nigger in his place . . . . Gene told us

22. "America's Unfinished Business Becomes an International Disgrace," *Resumé*, August 31, 1946, found in Part 2, Reel 31, *NNC*; Jason J. Palmer to Truman, telegram, July 26, 1946, Box 548, File "OF 93a Lynching of (4) Negroes at Monroe, Georgia July 25, 1946," *Truman:OF*; Adrian Johnson and George Weston to Truman, telegram, July 27, 1946, ibid.; Barbara Boucree to Truman, telegram, July 27, 1946, ibid.; Leo Jandreau to Truman, July 29, 1946, ibid.; James C. Arnold to Truman, telegram, July 29, 1946, ibid.; Tom Clark to Eleanor Roosevelt, October 8, 1946, Box 3338, File "NAACP, 1945–47," *Roosevelt Papers*; David Niles to Mrs. Frances L. Legge, May 6, 1946, Box 543, File "OF 93 May–December 1946 [2 of 2]," *Truman:OF*; Theron F. Caudle to Harry F. Ward, June 5, 1946, Part 2, Reel 1, *Papers of the Civil Rights Congress* (Washington, DC: University Publications of America, 1989) microfilm (hereafter *CRC*).

23. Adrian Johnson and George A. Weston to Truman, telegram, July 27, 1946, Box 548, File "OF 93a Lynching of (4) Negroes at Monroe, Georgia July 25, 1946," *Truman:OF*.

24. Walter White to Eleanor Roosevelt, telegram, September 18, 1946, Box 3338, File "NAACP, 1945–47," *Roosevelt Papers*.

25. Kari Frederickson, *The Dixiecrat Revolt & the End of the Solid South: 1923–1968* (Chapel Hill and London: University of North Carolina Press, 2001), 54; "Persecution of Negroes Still Strong in America," *Fiji Times and Herald*, December 23, 1946, enclosure with Despatch 96, Winfield H. Scott to Secretary of State, December 27, 1946, memo, Box 4684, Decimal File 811.4016/12-2746, *RG 59*.

what was happening, and what he was going to do about it. I'm sure proud he was elected.'"[26] Not surprisingly then, Macio Snipes, a black veteran who tried to vote, was soon gunned down in cold blood. His murder and the quadruple lynching at Moore's Ford, one labor group was certain, were a direct result of the "violence preached by Governor-elect Talmadge."[27] Over half of Southern newspapers and nearly 71 percent of those in the North agreed and identified Talmadge's clarion call as the primary catalyst for the murders.[28] Walter White, in fact, had reports that Talmadge was at the meeting when the "vengeance on [the pregnant woman's husband] was planned or discussed."[29] The governor-elect had purposely sent a strong signal that the state's lawmakers not only condoned, but also encouraged anti-black violence, particularly if African Americans believed that they had any rights that any white man was bound to respect. In fact, one of the suspected lynchers defiantly asserted that when he thought about why four black people had to die at Moore's Ford, it was obvious. "'It was civil rights that got them killed.'"[30]

Talmadge, however, was not alone in pushing his constituency to do whatever it took to keep blacks "in their place." Senator Theodore Bilbo (D-MS) championed the deportation of millions of African Americans to Liberia. He blasted the children of mixed marriages as the "'motley melee of miscegenated mongrels.'" His harangue for white racial purity led him to predict that, if African Americans achieved any form of equality, the United States would become a racial cesspool in which there was nothing but "'mestizos, mulattoes, zambos, terceroons, quadroons, cholos, musties, fusties, and dusties.'"[31] Bilbo vowed to do everything in his power to see to it that this never happened. Thus, while on the campaign trail in 1946, in a state where nearly half the population was African American, he fired up his "red-blooded Anglo-Saxon" constituency with a rejoinder that "'the best way to keep the nigger from voting... [was to] do it the night before election.'" He then instructed his followers that, "'If any nigger tries to organize to vote, use the tar and feathers and don't forget the matches.'" After a round of cheers and laughter, Mississippi's

26. Frederickson, *The Dixiecrat Revolt*, 54.
27. "Resolution on Terrorism in the South: Adopted by Pacific States Council of Furniture Workers," August 10–11, 1946, Box 548, File "OF 93a," *Truman:OF.*
28. Guzman, *The Negro Year Book*, 303.
29. Walter White to Tom Clark, telegram, July 29, 1946, Box 412, File "Lynching—Walton County, Georgia: Correspondence, 1946–1948," *Papers of the NAACP.*
30. Post, "Murder at Moore's Ford," A/01.
31. A. Wigfall Green, *The Man Bilbo* (Baton Rouge: Louisiana State University Press, 1963), 100, 104.

"reign of terror" began, and a black veteran was immediately "flogged" within an inch of his life for trying to register to vote.[32]

The black leadership erupted. It demanded, at bare minimum, that the election be ruled invalid and Bilbo barred from taking his seat in the Senate.[33] Others, however, called for much more drastic measures. One woman declared that Bilbo "should be shot" just like the "Nazi war lords."[34] A man from Ohio took it a step further and urged Truman to spare the Bikini atoll and just drop the next atom bomb on Bilbo and Mississippi.[35] Most, however, demanded that federal troops, led by General Douglas MacArthur, take over the South and teach those "white ignorant hoodlums" a thing or two about democracy. Although this may have sounded like a return to Reconstruction, its roots were in a much more recent war. MacArthur, as many African Americans knew, had chief responsibility for democratizing Japan. Certainly, one couple observed, blacks should at least be able to "enjoy as much democracy here as MacArthur guarantees the Japanese."[36]

That, however, was not the case. In fact, the economic maelstrom swirling around African Americans was even more insidious and deadly than all of the "mad rantings of Senator Bilbo."[37] The National Urban League warned the president that in postwar America, "full and unrestricted employment" would be "the Number One domestic problem . . . of the Negro minority." To be sure, employment in the defense

32. Guzman, *Negro Yearbook*, 2; quoted in, Jerry A. Hendrix, "Theodore G. Bilbo: Evangelist of Racial Purity," in *The Oratory of Southern Demagogues*, eds. Cal M. Logue and Howard Dorgan (Baton Rouge and London: Louisiana State University Press, 1981), 167; quoted in, Martha Coble, "Bilbo Demands: 'Keep Negro from Polls,'" *Akron Beacon Journal*, n.d. (ca. June 26, 1946), found in Box 543, File "OF 93 May–December 1946 [1 of 2]," *Truman:OF*; quoted in, "Death of a Demagogue," *American Heritage*, July/August 1997, 99–100; Sidney Hillman to Truman, telegram, June 24, 1946, Box 543, File "OF 93 May–December 1946 [1 of 2]," *Truman:OF*; Frederickson, *The Dixiecrat Revolt*, 48.
33. "Petition: Vote Bilbo Out of Senate . . . Send Troops to Georgia and Mississippi," August 14, 1946, Box 548, File "OF 93a," *Truman:OF*; Sidney Hillman to Truman, telegram, June 24, 1946, Box 543, File "OF 93 May–December 1946 [1 of 2]," ibid.
34. Lillian Stemerman to Truman, telegram, June 23, 1946, ibid.
35. Charles L. Snowden, Sr. to Truman, June 26, 1946, ibid.
36. Jason J. Palmer to Truman, telegram, July 26, 1946, Box 548, File "OF 93a Lynching of (4) Negroes at Monroe, GA July 25, 1946," ibid.; Adrian Johnson and George A. Weston to Truman, telegram, July 27, 1946, ibid.; Mr. and Mrs. George W. Harrison to Truman, telegram, June 23, 1946, Box 543, File "OF 93 May–December 1946 [1 of 2]," ibid.; E. H. Heslip et al. to Truman, telegram, June 23, 1946, ibid.; Edgar G. Brown to Truman, telegram, May 26, 1946, ibid.
37. Sidney Hillman to Truman, telegram, June 24, 1946, ibid.

industries had finally added one million blacks to the ranks of the gainfully employed. Yet, this was deceptive and concealed deeper, systemic problems. The Urban League directed the president's attention to rampant discrimination by employers and labor unions, competition from returning white veterans, a potentially flaccid industrial market weakened by defense reconversion, an insecure future for the Fair Employment Practices Committee (FEPC), and an educational system that continued to groom African Americans for obsolescence. African Americans, the Urban League pointed out, were overwhelmingly employed in those sectors of the industrial economy that were most likely to suffer massive layoffs and were hired so late in the war that seniority rules would wipe them out first. The Urban League predicted that "some 400,000 Negro war workers would lose jobs between V-E Day and V-J Day." Moreover, the occupations in which nearly 60 percent of all African Americans worked, as farm laborers and domestic help, were outside the parameters of the Social Security system. As a result, the overwhelming majority of black workers had no safety net.[38]

This specter of widespread unemployment and poverty hovered over the black community and exacerbated the housing and health care issues laying siege to African Americans. This was not just a Southern phenomenon, it was a national phenomenon. In Detroit, African Americans faced "formidable," indeed, "almost insurmountable," barriers to living in decent housing. As historian Thomas Sugrue noted:

> Because blacks were confined to the poorest-paying, most insecure jobs, they had less disposable income than their white counterparts, and could not afford the city's better housing.... Overpriced rental[s]... added to blacks' economic woes, forcing them to spend a higher percentage of their income on housing than whites,.... Homeownership was also an unrealistic expectation for a majority of black Detroiters in the 1940s.... White real estate brokers shunned black clients and encouraged restrictive covenants and other discriminatory practices.... Bankers seldom lent to black home buyers, abetted by federal housing appraisal practices that ruled black neighborhoods to be dangerous risks for mortgage subsidies and home loans. The result was that blacks were trapped in the city's worst housing, in the strictly segregated sections of the city.[39]

38. "Racial Aspects of Reconversion: A Memorandum Prepared for the President of the United States by the National Urban League," August 27, 1945, attachment to Lester B. Granger to Truman, August 27, 1945, Box 542, File "OF 93: September 1945," *Truman:OF*; Guzman, *The Negro Year Book*, 14, 139.
39. Thomas J. Sugrue, *The Origins of the Urban Crisis: Race and Inequality in Postwar Detroit*, Princeton Studies in American Politics: Historical, International, and Comparative

Detroit was no aberration.[40] In Baltimore, although "Negroes comprise[d] 20 percent of the population," they were "crammed into 2 percent of the residential area." As African Americans remained trapped in teeming, overcrowded ghettoes, rats and infectious diseases raced through the black community at an alarming rate. In the black ghetto of Detroit, for example, the rodent population was so out of control, and the rat bites inflicted on African Americans so numerous, that the area became known as the "rat belt."[41]

The diseases brought on by unsanitary overcrowded living conditions were aggravated by a segregated, grossly underfunded health care system. Black doctors and nurses were scarce, quality medical facilities were nonexistent, and the need for both was overwhelming. The chairman of the NAACP's Board of Directors, Dr. Louis Wright, asserted that "thousands of Negroes have died for lack of medical care. The American Medical Association is chiefly responsible for this cruel and inhuman attitude.... They give lip service to the health of the Negro in almost the same way that a Talmadge or a Bilbo would have done." This systematic denial of basic health care meant that eight to ten times as many African Americans died in the United States from tuberculosis and malaria as whites. In Harlem, "a record of nearly ten deaths from tuberculosis [occurred] each week." Indeed, although tuberculosis barely cracked the top ten leading causes of death for whites, it was the third leading cause of death for African Americans. In fact, on every key health care benchmark – infant mortality rates, life expectancy, etc. – it was clear that African Americans were dying young, dying fast, and dying unnecessarily.[42]

Again, Truman was more than aware of the housing, health care, and employment issues ripping apart the black community. He was also aware that racism was at the epicenter of this disaster. The president admitted

Perspectives, eds. Ira Katznelson, Martin Shefter, and Theda Skocpol (Princeton, New Jersey: Princeton University Press, 1996), 34.

40. See, Douglas S. Massey and Nancy A. Denton, *American Apartheid: Segregation and the Making of the Underclass* (Cambridge and London: Harvard University Press, 1993), 26–55.

41. Sugrue, *Origins of the Urban Crisis*, 37.

42. "The NAACP in 1946–47: Address of Dr. Louis T. Wright... at 38th Annual Conference," June 27, 1947, Box 130-6, Folder 15, *Wright Papers*; "Tuberculosis Survey in Harlem: Three Groups Join in Two-Month X-Ray Campaign Among New York Negroes," *National Negro Health News*, 14:1 (January–March 1946), 23; Guzman, *Negro Yearbook*, 320–38; *To Secure These Rights: The Report of the President's Committee on Civil Rights*, with an introduction by Charles E. Wilson (New York: Simon and Schuster, 1947).72.

that he was deeply troubled that, "in this country," there was "disturbing evidence of intolerance and prejudice, similar in kind, though perhaps not in degree" to the Nazis.[43] He lamented that the "better world we fought for" was just not here yet. It "will come to pass," the president asserted, "only as we are able ... to increase the practice of political democracy, economic democracy, and racial democracy." The president then became more explicit. "We must house the veteran – and I mean every veteran. We must get the veteran work at fair wages without discrimination by employers or unions." That same vision of what must be done echoed through in Truman's assertion that "[t]he ballot is both a right and a privilege ... [which] must be protected." He also recognized that this very foundation of democracy was being threatened by "organized terrorism" and "mob violence."[44]

After stating such a strong agenda for American democracy, Truman then waffled and concluded that "[n]o government can do these things alone."[45] Thus, as certain as Truman was about the defects in American democracy, he was equally certain that the U.S. government could not protect its own soldiers from domestic violence. Nor could it guarantee the right to vote, even in elections for federal office. Nor, it seemed, did it have any control over the segregationist mortgage loan policies of the Federal Housing Administration.

Even the much-heralded President's Committee on Civil Rights (PCCR), which Truman appointed in response to Monroe, Georgia, and the eye gouging in South Carolina, was steeped in the politics of "can't."[46] In one case, with the word "kill" scrawled repeatedly across the top, a graphic was deleted from the PCCR's final report that asked why the federal government could "attack crimes, such as kidnaping, auto thefts, white slavery, etc.," but not "safeguard the civil rights of *all* Americans?"[47] On another occasion, after listening to a litany of civil rights violations, one committee member suggested that the PCCR initiate an ad campaign to alert the American public to the corrosive effects of racism. That simple suggestion "provoked a good deal of dissension," met with stiff

43. Truman to Charles G. Bolte, August 28, 1946, Box 543, File "OF 93 May–December 1946 [2 of 2]," *Truman:OF*.

44. Truman to Walter White, June 6, 1946, Box 10, File "'N' (folder 1)," *Papers of Harry S Truman, Files of Philleo Nash: Official Files* (hereafter *Truman:Nash Official Files*).

45. Ibid.

46. Truman to Tom C. Clark, September 20, 1946, Box 26, File "Civil Rights/Negro Affairs, 1945–June 1947," *Niles Papers*.

47. Marginalia on "Methods Used to Deny Negroes the Right to Vote," n.d., Box 36, File "WH Files—Civil Rights—President's Committee on Oct. 1947 and Dec. 1946 (folder 1)," *Nash Papers*.

Photo 2.2. The NAACP's Leslie Perry (far left), Walter White (to the very right of Truman), and Channing Tobias (far right) – as members of the National Emergency Against Mob Violence Committee – call on the president to put an end to the wave of postwar lynching in the United States, September 1946. *Visual Materials from the NAACP Records, Library of Congress.*

opposition, and was dismissed with a terse White House reply that that activity exceeded the PCCR's authority. The committee was to write a report for the president and nothing more.[48]

Similarly, on the international front, as historian Thomas Borstelemann observed, "Truman demonstrated just how little the opinions of African Americans counted in American public life in 1945, and how much influence white Southerners had, by making James Byrnes his first appointed secretary of state."[49] For African Americans, Byrnes was the apocalypse. A "calamity." An appointment that could only be viewed with "great trepidation." White pointed out that Byrnes was a "notorious South Carolina Negro-hater" whose "hostility" to African Americans was "unbroken."

48. Robert K. Carr to David K. Niles, memo, May 2, 1947, Box 26, File "Civil Rights/Negro Affairs 1945–June 1947," *Niles Papers*; Philleo Nash to David K. Niles, memo, May 19, 1947, ibid.; Roger Baldwin to Steering Committee on Civil Rights Program of PCCR, May 3, 1948, Box 1100, Folder 8, Papers of The American Civil Liberties Union, Seeley Mudd Manuscript Library, Princeton University, Princeton, New Jersey (hereafter *ACLU Papers*).

49. Borstlemann, *The Cold War*, 51.

In 1919, as a U.S. congressman, Byrnes asked the attorney general to "prosecute editors of [the] *Crisis* and *Messenger* because they demanded equal rights for Negroes." After all, Byrnes insisted, "this is a white man's country, and will always remain a white man's country."[50] Byrnes therefore "fought virtually every piece of legislation designed to better the lot of Negroes" from federal support to Howard University to the distribution of New Deal funds to starving black sharecroppers in the South.[51] As a member of the Senate, Byrnes joined with Tom Connally in derailing proposed anti-lynching bills. He even went so far as to mock a triple lynching in South Carolina where one of the victims, a pregnant African American woman who had been dubiously convicted of murder, was "dragged fighting and screaming down the jail stairs to a car which took her to a woods, where a laughing mob of 1,000 kicked her and shot her and set her clothes on fire." Her brother "was finished off in the same woods after the mob had dragged him behind a murder car for a mile and a half." A 15-year-old cousin suffered an equally gruesome death.[52] In the face of such brutality, Byrnes, blamed the lynching on the NAACP. "'The facts are,'" he said, "'that the two Lowman boys would have quickly burned in the electric chair – they had been sentenced – and Bertha Lowman would have begun serving a life sentence, had the NAACP not taken the case to the Supreme Court of the State.'"[53] Byrnes explained to his Senate colleagues that the lynching occurred because "the National Association for the Advancement of Colored People intervened and employed counsel who were not residents of the county." That Northern interference, Byrnes insisted, simply enraged the locals and, thus, "[t]he responsibility for it [the triple lynching] can be placed at the door of these nonresidents, these people in New York who intervened." In further arguing against the bill, Byrnes also offered that the number of lynchings had actually decreased over the years, because "there has been fewer assaults by Negroes on white women." Byrnes was certain that the growing hesitancy of black men to defile white women could be traced, in part, to the very existence of lynching and "the certainty

50. Walter White to Editors, memo, June 4, 1945, Box 163, File "Byrnes, James F., General, 1941–46," *Papers of the NAACP*; Walter White to Truman, telegram, June 29, 1945, Box 164, File "OF-20A 'A–C,'" *Truman:OF*; "Record of James F. Byrnes on Civil Rights Issues," Box 163, File "Byrnes, James F., General, 1950–55," *Papers of the NAACP*.

51. White to Truman, telegram, June 29, 1945, Box 164, File "OF 20 A 'A–C,'" *Truman:OF*; Carl Murphy to Truman, telegram, June 30, 1945, ibid.; "James F. Byrnes," fact sheet, n.d. (1945?), Part 2, Reel 7, *CRC*.

52. "James F. Byrnes, [a compilation of press releases, articles, and speeches]" n.d., ibid.

53. Walter J. Brown, *James F. Byrnes of South Carolina: A Remembrance* (Walter J. Brown, 1992), 73; "James F. Byrnes," fact sheet, n.d. (1945?), Part 2, Reel 7, *CRC*.

of punishment," which has brought "fear to the hearts of the criminal Negro."[54]

As comfortable as Byrnes was in justifying lynching and Southern Justice, he was even more at ease in advocating massive disfranchisement. While governor of South Carolina, a state where almost 43 percent of the population was African American, Byrnes, a former U.S. Supreme Court Justice, worked assiduously to devise a method to circumvent the Supreme Court's 1944 ruling that outlawed the white primary. Byrnes' efforts were so successful that for years South Carolina's "lily white Democratic primary" was a "model for other Southern States seeking to keep their party affairs free from Negro participation."[55]

As the Cold War emerged and the United States sought to draw into stark terms the differences between American democracy and Soviet terror, African Americans were mystified how the same Byrnes who disfranchised millions of blacks in South Carolina could turn around and insist on free and unfettered elections in Eastern Europe.[56] One journalist wryly asked if Byrnes included "the people of South Carolina" in his demands that "subjugated minorities" "have a voice in their Government."[57] Du Bois told a captivated audience that the secretary of state was going straight to hell for his overwrought concern about "oppressed minorities" in Eastern Europe, while he systematically oppressed African Americans in the United States.[58] The greatest fear, of course, was that Byrnes had the power to do on the world stage what he had done in South Carolina. Robeson and White shared a "grave fear" that, "if as secretary of state, [Byrnes] follows the same philosophy toward . . . peoples of trusteeship and colonial areas as he has toward American Negroes," then "there is little hope," – the residents of the colonies were doomed. Walter White further agonized over the fact that Byrnes, as secretary of state,

54. Congress, Senate. Senator Byrnes of South Carolina speaking on the Prevention of and Punishment for Lynching, H.R. 1507, 75th Cong., 3rd sess., *Congressional Record* (January 11, 1938), Vol. 83, Pt. 1, 303–10.

55. Del Booth, "Suit Claims Loophole in South Carolina's 'Lily White' Primary," *Washington Post*, March 16, 1947, found in Box 485, File "Negroes (Politics)—Voting South Carolina," *RNC*.

56. Carl R. Johnson to Truman, telegram, June 30, 1945, Box 164, File "OF 20A 'A–C,'" *Truman:OF*; James F. Byrnes, *Speaking Frankly* (New York and London: Harper & Brothers Publishers, 1947), 98, 105; Krenn, *Black Diplomacy*, 14.

57. Thomas L. Stokes, "Do They Mean It?", news clipping, September 4, 1945, found in Box 49, File "WH Files-Minorities General-Newsclipping: 1945–1954 (folder 2)," *Nash Papers*.

58. George Streator, "Negro Youth Told Future is in South: Dr. Du Bois says the Region Should be Freedom 'Firing Line'—Byrnes Assailed," *New York Times*, October 21, 1946; "UN and the Negro," *People's Voice*, June 8, 1946.

"would have much to say regarding implementation of the San Francisco Charter, particularly ... its provision for granting human rights."[59]

Unfortunately, the department that Byrnes oversaw shared many of the secretary's values. The State Department had a "'notorious reputation'" for overt and covert discrimination against African Americans. In 1947, "less than 200 of the 7,000 departmental employees were black, and 'most of these were classified as custodial or minor clerical.'" Just as important, the department was intent on keeping it that way. African Americans who applied for upper-level positions and breezed through the rigorous written exams were deemed "unqualified" the moment they arrived for the face-to-face interviews. And the handful of black diplomats who did manage to squeeze through the barricades were trapped for decades in the State Department's chitlins' circuit of Liberia, Madagascar, and the Azores. This organization clearly did not have the capacity to address its own internal Jim Crowed universe. It, therefore, as historian Michael Krenn noted, could "barely comprehend" that "America's treatment of its minority citizens was a foreign policy liability of the first degree."[60] The best that the department was able to discern was that the "Negro problem" made the job of selling America to the rest of the world just a little more difficult. Thus, when newspapers in Mexico provided extensive coverage on the lynching at Moore's Ford, the embassy staff complained that the murders were given "prominence ... out of proportion to [their] importance." As far as the embassy was concerned, it was typical of the foreign press to exaggerate "matters regarding racial discrimination in the United States."[61] Other articles on lynching or Jim Crow were also summarily dismissed as "Soviet propaganda" or, worse yet, "pro-Negro," as if that automatically meant anti-American.[62]

Not surprisingly, then, when the State Department sat down to craft a human rights strategy that would effectively position America as "the tower of strength and the innovator and the pioneer in the field of human rights," it simply could not do it.[63] Assistant Secretary of State Robert

59. Paul Robeson to Truman, July 2, 1945, Box 164, File "OF 20A 'A–C,'" *Truman:OF*; Walter White to Truman, telegram, June 29, 1945, ibid.; "James F. Byrnes," fact sheet, n.d. (1945?), Part 2, Reel 7, *CRC*.

60. Krenn, *Black Diplomacy*, 6–7, 15, 21–27.

61. S. Walter Washington to Secretary of State, July 29, 1946, Box 4684, Decimal File 811.4016/7-2946, *RG 59*.

62. Howard Donovan to Secretary of State, memo, June 20, 1946, Box 4684, Decimal File 811.4016/6-2046, ibid.; L. Randolph Higgs to Secretary of State, memo, June 12, 1947, Box 4685, Decimal File 811.4016/6-1247, ibid.; Smith to Secretary of State, memo, November 20, 1946, Box 4684, Decimal File 811.4016/11-2046, ibid.

63. *Blaisdell*.

Lovett "said that to promise everyone the right to health, for example, was to promise the impossible."[64] The State Department and its legal experts also had "real difficulty ... in formulating the 'social' rights, such as those dealing with standards of living, conditions of work and social security."[65] In particular, the Department had "'serious difficulties' with the right to work" because it was "incompatible ... with the principles of a private enterprise economy."[66] The State Department's Harley Notter, therefore, advised that, in the field of human rights, it was time to be realistic. "We need to help the doers of good will stay down to earth in this field," he counseled. The truth of the matter, Notter admitted, was that no nation had an exemplary human rights record – not even the United States. "[T]he United States with all its power," Notter explained to his supervisors, "has not yet been able even to get up on the first rung of the ladder, namely elections which are free enough to provide the prerequisite basis for the honoring of even the most tangible of human rights, which are the legal ones." If the United States could not do it, Notter noted, then there was no sense in raising anyone else's hope that the UN would be able to guarantee and protect human rights anywhere in the world.[67]

Although agreeing with Notter's premise, the State Department still wanted to find some way to "assert ... [America's] moral leadership in [the] field" of human rights.[68] The goal, as novelist Ralph Ellison so eloquently stated, was to find a way to "reconcile democratic ideas with an anti-democratic reality."[69] The Department therefore tried to stabilize America's human rights house of cards with the cornerstone of democracy, the First Amendment. The Department's logic was simple. Without free speech, the oppressed would never be able to bring their grievances before the public, and there would be no hope of ever improving the situation. Thus, it was free speech that separated tyrannies like the Soviet Union from democracies like America. And it would be free speech in which the United States would stake its claim as the global leader in the struggle for human rights. The Americans therefore immediately pushed for and won, under the aegis of the Commission on Human Rights (CHR), a

64. Memorandum of Conference, November 20, 1947, Box 2, File "Human Rights Memorandum," *Papers of James Hendrick*, Harry S Truman Presidential Library, Independence, Missouri (hereafter *Hendrick Papers*).
65. Memorandum of Conversation regarding Commission on Human Rights, April 10, 1946, Box 4589, File "Mrs. Franklin D. Roosevelt," *Roosevelt Papers*.
66. James Hendrick to Eleanor Roosevelt, handwritten notes, n.d., Box 4594, File "UN Human Rights Commission, 1946–June 1947," ibid.
67. Harley Notter to Dean Rusk and Mr. Thompson, memo, March 14, 1947, Box 2187, Decimal File 501.BD/3-1847 (1945–49), *RG 59*.
68. Ibid.
69. Ralph Ellison, *Shadow and Act* (New York: Random House, 1964), 28.

Subcommission on Freedom of Information and of the Press. The United States also managed to secure agreement that a conference would be held in 1947 to survey the status of these freedoms throughout the world.[70]

The USSR, which could never be mistaken for a free speech stronghold, quickly sensed a set-up and refused to let the United States win round one so easily. The Soviets thus argued persuasively for two additional subcommissions – one dealing with the protection of minorities and the other for the prevention of discrimination. Of course, the Holocaust and the ongoing trial at Nuremberg only served to reinforce the Soviets' position.[71] Nevertheless, State Department officials were "doubtful of the necessity for a Subcommission on Minorities" and believed that there was "no urgency" in seeing the Soviets' proposed subcommissions become a reality.[72] Durward Sandifer, who was the State Department's UN specialist, admitted that his "reluctance to recommend immediate establishment [of the sub-commissions] springs from the fact that the problem is fraught with the most serious difficulties."[73] Put simply, the Kremlin's proposals would create a much too tempting international forum for the airing of America's "Negro problem." And that is exactly what the Soviets had in mind.

Recognizing the trap, Auschwitz on one hand and Mississippi on the other, the State Department decided to support simultaneously the Kremlin's proposals while also neutralizing the threat they posed to America's human rights image. A State Department report on the "Problems of Discrimination and Minority Status in the United States" finally acknowledged that America's "Negro problem" had now become America's foreign policy problem. "No other American group is so definitely subordinate in status or so frequently the victim of discriminatory

70. "Commission on Human Rights of the Economic and Social Council: Summary Record of Meetings—13 May 1946," May 17, 1946, E/ER/23, Box 4589, File "Mrs. Franklin D. Roosevelt," *Roosevelt Papers*; Durward Sandifer to Mr. Green, Mr. Hiss et al., memo, May 21, 1946, Box 8, File "Human Rights: March 1945–December 31, 1947," Lot File 55D429, *RG 59*; Durward V. Sandifer to Eleanor Roosevelt, April 22, 1946, Box 4593, File "Mrs. Roosevelt," *Roosevelt Papers*; State Department Instructions for "Commission on Human Rights: First Session of Commission, January 1947," n.d., SD/C.S.4/4a, Box 4594, File "UN Human Rights Commission, 1946–June 1947," ibid.

71. Drafting Committee on Reports in the Social Field (Commission on Human Rights): Summary Record of Fifth Meeting, June 14, 1946, Box 4594 (no file), ibid.

72. Durward V. Sandifer to Eleanor Roosevelt, April 22, 1946, Box 4593, File "Mrs. Roosevelt," ibid.; Commission on Human Rights: First Session of Commission, January 1947, SD/C.S.4/4a, Box 4594, File "UN Human Rights Commission, 1946–June 1947," ibid.

73. Walter Kotschnig and Durward V. Sandifer to Alger Hiss, memo, April 22, 1946, Box 16, File "Discrimination and Protection of Minorities, Subcommittee on Prevention," Lot File 55D429, *RG 59*.

practices" as the Negro. The report then detailed what those discriminatory practices were.

> Among the more important of these practices are: segregation legislation in southern and border states; restrictive covenants which limit the residential mobility of Negroes in many of the municipalities of the United States; economic restrictions and vocational discrimination – about 80 percent of the complaints before the Fair Employment Practice Committee from July 1943 to December 1944 were from Negroes; lynching; restriction of the Negro's access to the courts and various limitations on his participation in political activities, particularly in reference to the use of the franchise and office-holding; unequal access to schools, public facilities and social services generally; and the social restrictions placed on the Negro by custom and convention. These practices, many of which are nationwide, are obviously in conflict with the American creed of democracy and equality of opportunity for all.[74]

These conditions, the State Department understood, made the United States a prime candidate for a UN hearing. "There is an alert and intelligent public, composed of Negroes and whites, keenly aware of the disabilities suffered by the Negro. Elements within this public," the report warned, "may be inclined to press for consideration of the Negro's case before the Human Rights Commission." The State Department further realized that the goodwill intentions of American democracy were simply not enough to forestall a determined international inquest. Although in "theory discrimination is not allowable under the American constitution and law," in truth, the State Department had to admit, "facilities are on an unequal basis; and this and other discriminatory practices may give us some trouble before an international body concerned with preventing discrimination."[75]

The State Department therefore sought refuge in semantic legerdemain. The Department agreed to the formation of the Subcommission on the Protection of Minorities, but then filleted the definition of "minority" so finely that it automatically excluded African Americans from the subcommission's purview. African Americans, the Department reasoned, were not a "national minority." They did not seek to secede from the United States, they had no distinct culture or language, and all they wanted was to be an integral part of the United States. Using equally deft reasoning for Mexican Americans, Asian Americans, and Native Americans, the State Department concluded that "there probably are no national minorities in the United States." Once that fact was established, the report went on

74. "Problems of Discrimination and Minority Status in the United States," January 22, 1947, Box 43, File "SD/E/CN.4/1-43," Lot File 82D211, ibid.

75. Ibid.

to argue that it was evident that only true "national minorities" became the source of international conflicts, and therefore, those were the only ones whose issues could validly be presented before the subcommission on minorities.[76]

As inventive as that strategy was, however, it did not address the problem of discrimination. The State Department was concerned that some nation, with credibility, would present the issue of Jim Crow before the UN. Of course, the Soviets would try, but the United States could easily dismiss that as a "stunt" or as "propaganda." The Europeans, however, who had a tendency to be very critical of the treatment of African Americans, could not be dispatched as easily. The *London Sunday Express*, for example, ran a cartoon depicting two Southern planters strolling blithely past the corpse of a lynched black man while discussing how absolutely "Shameful" it was "the way these British are handling this Palestine business!" The Department, which had had enough of this kind of disapproving condescension, advocated combining the minority and discrimination subcommissions into one. That way, the United States could checkmate any European discussion about discrimination in the United States with an ominous hint that Europe's extensive "national minorities" problems could just as easily be opened up for international scrutiny. The staff who devised this ploy believed it would force the Europeans, who often blasted the United States for lynching, Jim Crow, and disfranchisement, to "view problems of discrimination, real or imaginary, in their true perspective."[77]

Jonathan Daniels, a Southern liberal, whom the State Department had tapped as the U.S. representative on the now combined Subcommission on the Prevention of Discrimination and Protection of Minorities (MINDIS), was still concerned. He wondered how the United States was supposed to sell its brand of democracy when a Mississippi Congressman could get elected with only 5,000 votes in a district that had over a quarter million people? How credible could the United States seem, he asked, when it would wring its hands about starving children in Albania and simultaneously ignore the emaciated babies in Alabama? And how, he wondered, could the United States serve as a beacon of hope for millions

76. "Discussion on Principles and Problems Relating to Minorities with a View to Prepare Instructions to the United States Delegate," SD/E/HR/MINDIS/D-3, August 27, 1946, Box 47, File "SD/E/HR/MINDIS/1-4," Lot File 82D211, ibid.

77. "Commission on Human Rights and Subcommissions: Suggested Terms of Reference," SD/CS.4/4, January 17, 1947, Box 4594, File "UN Human Rights Commission, 1946–June 1947," *Roosevelt Papers*; Borstlemann, *The Cold War*, 78; Department of State, "A Survey of National Minorities in Foreign Countries," January 2, 1947, Box 4594, File "UN: Human Rights Commission Documents 1946–June 1947," *Roosevelt Papers*; Edward M. Groth to Secretary of State, memo, June 10, 1947, Box 4685, Decimal File 811.4016/6-1047, *RG 59*.

of immigrants when the torch in the Statue of Liberty's hand was actually a warning flare to "discourage late comers."[78]

The answer, quite simply, was to contain the terms of the debates and modify the UN's organs to fit the needs of the United States. Thus, while perfecting its plans to corral the Europeans and MINDIS, the State Department began to grapple with ways to box in the CHR, as well. The impact, however, of the Nuremberg and the Tokyo War Crime trials on the international conscience kept getting in the way of the State Department's plans. Sickened by the revelations coming out of those deliberations, prominent European members of the CHR were arguing early on, that the Commission had to have the authority via a "control agency" to identify and punish human rights violators. Members of the CHR toyed with the idea of moving the enforcement of human rights out of the Economic and Social Council and into the Security Council, where the domestic jurisdiction clause would automatically become null and void. They played with the notion of creating a new international court that could overrule the opinions of, say, a U.S. Supreme Court in cases of human rights violations. The French representative on the CHR, Rene Cassin, argued strenuously that there were cases that "transcend national concern" and that in those instances, "the violation of human rights principles may be so serious that the right of the United Nations to discuss them must be stressed." The Belgian representative went even further and "vigorously advocated establishment of [a] supervisory organ for implementation." Thus, on June 21, 1946, the Economic and Social Council, acting on the recommendations of the CHR, decided that "the Charter of the United Nations . . . can only be fulfilled if provisions are made for the implementation of human rights and of an international bill of human rights."[79]

78. Jonathan Daniels, "Why am I a Liberal?," enclosure to Carl Brandt to Jonathan Daniels, August 26, 1947, Folder 584, *Papers of Jonathan Daniels*, Southern Historical Collection, Wilson Library, University of North Carolina at Chapel Hill (hereafter *Daniels Papers*); Jonathan Daniels to Charles S. Johnson, August 29, 1947, Folder 585, ibid.

79. "Commission on Human Rights of the Economic and Social Council: Summary Report of Meetings," May 6, 1946 at 3:00 P.M., Box 4587, File "Human Rights Commission, 1946," *Roosevelt Papers*; "Commission on Human Rights of the Economic and Social Council: Summary Record of Meetings, Twelfth meeting held on Monday, May 13, 1946 at 2:00 p.m.," May 13, 1946, Box 4589, File "Mrs. Franklin D. Roosevelt," ibid; "Commission on Human Rights: Working Paper on an International Bill of Rights," E/CN.4/W.4, January 13, 1947, Box 4593, File "Secretariat Documents: Working Papers," ibid.; Secretariat Memorandum D: Commission on Human Rights, Points for Discussion on Item 8 of Agenda Concerning Examination of Documents, May 7, 1946, Box 4587, File "Human Rights Commission, 1946," ibid.; "Commission on Human Rights: Memorandum on Implementation Prepared by the Secretariat at the Request of the Committee," June 19, 1947, E/CN.4/AC.1/12, *Papers of the United Nations*, Cleveland Public Library, Cleveland, Ohio (hereafter *UN*); Draft Resolution

That decision, especially for a nation that had not even reached "the first rung" of the human rights ladder, was like throwing down the gauntlet. The last thing the United States wanted was a CHR with power. If the Unites States had its way, Sandifer admitted, the Commission would be "of little use," regardless of the extent of the human rights violation. Sandifer observed that even the "ghastly" treatment of the "natives of the Belgian Congo or the persecution of the Christian Armenians by the Turkish Empire" would not have been enough to warrant international intervention. He was sure, therefore, that before there could be any further discussion about implementation or intervention, the CHR had to have a much more refined definition of what constituted a legitimate, peace-threatening human rights violation. That debate, of course, could take years. Meanwhile, the discussion about a "control agency" would have to be postponed indefinitely.[80]

To thwart further the implementation madness gripping the CHR, the State Department wanted to be sure that the Commission had a chairman who would be understanding about the quirks and pitfalls in American democracy, such as the distribution of power between the federal and state governments, the existence of Jim Crow, and the unyielding power of the Southern Democrats. Thus, Sandifer was elated that Eleanor Roosevelt, who had the charisma, credibility, and trust of the delegates, appeared to be the consensus candidate for chair. For the State Department, this was an incredible boon. Sandifer informed his colleagues that "there is no doubt that" the chair "can by guiding the discussion, and by recognizing or not recognizing particular speakers at critical moments exercise considerable influence on the Commission."[81] Not only was it fortuitous that Roosevelt would be that person, but it helped immensely that the relationship between Sandifer and her was like "love at first sight," and she immediately "adopted [him] as her confidential and personal adviser."[82]

The next important battle the State Department waged was to ensure that the CHR and its subcommissions had no authority to review the thousands of petitions from "individuals and groups throughout the world protesting against wrongs which might be righted by the Commission on Human Rights."[83] The State Department firmly believed that the UN

Concerning the Report of the Commission on Human Rights, E/56/Rev.1, June 19, 1946, Box 4594 (no file), *Roosevelt Papers*; Commission on Human Rights: Resolution Adopted June 21, 1946, E/56/Rev.2, 1 July 1946, ibid.

80. Durward V. Sandifer to Mr. Green, Mr. Hiss et al., memo, May 21, 1946, Box 8, File "Human Rights: March 1945–December 31, 1947," Lot File 55D429, *RG 59*.

81. "Human Rights Working Group—Minutes of First Meeting, September 30, 1946," October 1, 1946, Box 45, File "SD/E/CN.4/Min 1," Lot File 82D211, ibid.

82. *Sandifer*.

83. "Human Rights Working Group—Minutes of First Meeting, September 30, 1946," October 1, 1946, Box 45, File "SD/E/CN.4/Min 1," Lot File 82D211, *RG 59*;

should not "dignify [the petitions] beyond their importance," and that organizations and people who tried to bring a human rights matter before the UN, "without official sponsorship by a Member State" should be "put . . . on notice as to the treatment they may expect to have accorded their communications."[84] There was a concern that "crack-pot complaints" would inundate the UN and cause its machinery to collapse under the strain. The State Department was also clear that, "even if some system existed for automatically excluding communication from crackpots, difficulties would still be encountered in screening the petitions, for oppressed people are often ignorant, unable to express themselves clearly, and as their oppression grows their sense of balance and accordingly their accuracy of expression deteriorates." As the "moral leader" in the crusade for human rights, the State Department couched its disdain in the velvet fist of an organization simply wanting to spare people who were in bleak circumstances, including those below the "Mason-Dixon line," from having "false hopes." Yet, its real concern, naturally, was to shield America from international scorn. "The peculiar disadvantage of the United States," one official wrote to the assistant secretary of state, "would be that with the seat of the United Nations in this country and with a freer flow of information here than elsewhere the United Nations could be flooded with petitions relating to United States abuses . . . thus giving the impression that the United States was the chief offender against rather than defender of civil liberties."[85]

Those were the debates that were raging both in the State Department and in the United Nations when the National Negro Congress decided to petition the UN. Asserting that the conditions in postwar America were

"Commission on Human Rights: Working Paper on Consideration of Communications Received," E/CN.4/W.3, January 13, 1947, Box 4593, File "Secretariat Documents: Working Papers," *Roosevelt Papers*; "Commission on Human Rights: Summary Record of the Third Meeting," E/CN.4/SR.3, 28 January 1947, *UN*; "Commission on Human Rights: Summary Record of the Fourth Meeting," E/CN.4/SR.4, January 29, 1947, ibid.; "Commission on Human Rights: Summary Record of the Sixteenth Meeting," E/CN.4/SR.16, February 6, 1947, ibid.; "Commission on Human Rights: Summary Record of the Twentieth Meeting," E/CN.4/SR.20, February 7, 1947, ibid.

84. "Rules of Procedure on Handling of Private Communications for the Attention of the General Assembly," SD/A/C.6/4, August 26, 1946, Box 32, File "SD/A/C.6/1-52," Lot File 82D211, *RG 59*.

85. "Commission on Human Rights, First Session of Full Commission, January 1947: Consideration of Communications Received," SD/CS.4/5, January 16, 1947, Box 4594, File "UN Human Rights Commission, 1946–June 1947," *Roosevelt Papers*; Robert McClintock to Robert A. Lovett, November 25, 1947, memo, Box 4595, File "Book I: Position Book for Second Session of Commission on Human Rights, Geneva, Switzerland, December 1–19, 1947," ibid.; Marginalia on Harley Notter to Dean Rusk and Mr. Thompson, memo, March 14, 1947, Box 2187, Decimal File 501.BD/3-1847 (1945–49), *RG 59*.

"intolerable" and that the federal government had refused to ameliorate those conditions, the Congress' leadership decided to take African Americans' plea for justice and equality to the UN.[86] At the NNC's request, historian Herbert Aptheker drafted an eight-page report to the UN that outlined African Americans' economic, political, and social oppression. Aptheker began by stating that 10 million of 12.5 million African Americans lived in the South and were subjected to a range of inhumane conditions, of which lynching was only the most obvious. Economically, African Americans were trapped in backbreaking, poorly paid manual labor occupations. As a result, more than 40 percent of African Americans had an annual household income of less than $200, more than 70 percent lived in housing with no electricity or indoor plumbing, and the infant mortality rate among African Americans was almost double that of white Southerners.[87]

This "wholesale oppression," despite the "prattle about 'separate but equal' facilities," carried over into education. South Carolina, which had almost the same number of African American as white children, spent a total of $1.2 million to bus white students to school and less than $7,000 on its black students. The same pattern of abuse and neglect obtained throughout the South and led to more than 40 percent of African Americans completing less than four years of formal education.[88]

Southern politicians, Aptheker noted, were also intent on restricting the right to vote and perpetuating an unconstitutional oligarchy. As a result, only 27.9 percent of the potential electorate in the South actually voted in the 1944 Presidential election, compared with almost 62 percent of the electorate in the rest of the nation. The figures were even worse for poll-tax states like Mississippi, Georgia, and South Carolina, where only 19 percent of the potential voters turned out on election day. Southern racism, Aptheker concluded, "has spread its poison throughout the life of America . . . throttling and killing . . . the entire nation."[89]

The NNC prefaced Aptheker's searing report with a brief rationale that laid out the UN's authority to "end the oppression of the American

86. Max Yergan and Revels Cayton to Truman, June 1, 1946, Box 58, File "WH Files-Minorities-Negro-Organizations-National Negro Congress," *Nash Papers*; National Executive Board, "Recommendations of the UN Committee," May 30, 1946, Part 2, Reel 26, *NNC*; R. A. Guerin to J. Edgar Hoover, May 31, 1946, Reel 2, *FBI File on National Negro Congress* (Wilmington, Delaware: Scholarly Resources, 1987), microfilm.

87. Herbert Aptheker, "The Oppression of the American Negro: The Facts," Part 2, Reel 26, *NNC*.

88. Ibid.

89. Ibid.

Negro."[90] NNC Executive Director Revels Cayton presented this document to 1,000 delegates at the Congress' national convention on June 1, 1946. As he read it, the delegates gave Cayton a "universal storm of applause" and authorization to forward the petition to the UN.[91] On June 6, 1946, the National Negro Congress presented its concise petition on the plight of black Americans to the UN secretary general's office. The NNC's leaders expressed their "profound regret" that they had to bring the oppression of 13 million African Americans to the UN's attention. But, after exhausting all constitutional avenues in the United States, they were "forced" to appeal their case to "the highest court of mankind – the United Nations." This court, unlike any in the United States, would understand that blacks had been "bound to the soil in semi-feudal serfdom," "lynched," "terrorized," and "segregated like pariahs."[92]

The NNC's entreaty to the United Nations was exactly what the State Department was afraid would happen. The FBI tried to play down the petition by remarking that "it is well to keep in mind that the National Negro Congress is a Communist Front Organization" that has been identified as repeatedly engaging in "un-American activities."[93] Yet, no amount of red baiting could dispel the fact that the "news story regarding the appeal to UNO by 13,000,000 American negroes was disseminated throughout the Middle East by Reuter (sic)." Nor could it wash away that lingering doubt about America's true commitment to human rights. An editorial in an Iraqi paper, for example, applauded the NNC's petition and noted that the United States was obviously treating African Americans "cruelly and robbing them of all the rights enjoyed by American citizens. Yet," the editorial continued, "the Statue of Liberty still stands . . . and the Americans do not feel ashamed!"[94] As could be expected, the Soviets joined the chorus. They launched their editorial with a description of the "bestial" murders at Monroe, Georgia, and the killing in Louisiana in which a "crowd of white men tortured a negro war veteran, John Jones, tore his arms out and set fire to his body." Noting that the "murderers, even

90. Ibid.; National Negro Congress, "The Jurisdiction of the Economic and Social Council of the United Nations," ibid.

91. "National Negro Congress Petitions UNO to End Nat'l Bias," *New York Age*, June 8, 1946.

92. National Negro Congress, *A Petition to the United Nations on Behalf of 13 Million Oppressed Negro Citizens of the United States of America* (New York: National Negro Congress, 1946), 2–3.

93. "Negro: New York, New York," July 16, 1946, Reel 3, *FBI File on Eleanor Roosevelt*, Franklin Delano Roosevelt Presidential Library, Hyde Park, microfilm (hereafter *FBI File on ER*).

94. James S. Moose, Jr. to Secretary of State, June 10, 1946, Box 4684, Decimal File 811.4016/6-1046 CS/RH, *RG 59*.

though they are identified, remain unpunished," the Soviets concluded that "the progressive negro association, 'The National Negro Congress'" had no other option than to petition the UN "inasmuch as 'the negro people, not having received aid through constitutional recourse in liberation from oppression, is compelled to direct the attention of the international organ towards this vitally important question."[95] In addition, groups in Bolivia and the West Indies, as well as almost 20 organizations in the United States, including the NAACP and several locals of the Congress of Industrial Organizations (CIO), wrote to the UN in support of the NNC's petition.[96]

Yet, despite "bestial" lynchings, widespread disfranchisement, and life-threatening poverty, the secretariat's office determined that, before the petition could be reviewed, the NNC had to prove that the rights of African Americans were, indeed, being violated. UN officials also made it quite clear that, according to the Charter, the United Nations had little, if any, authority to receive petitions from nongovernmental organizations and no power to "intervene in domestic affairs" and investigate human rights abuses. After that sobering message, Petrus Schmidt, secretary of the UN Commission on Human Rights, remarked that if the NNC still felt compelled to provide any additional evidence to buttress its complaint against the United States, it was free to do so.[97]

How free the NNC actually was to respond, however, was debatable. Organizational changes during the end of the Second World War, as well as the emerging Cold War and the rise in anti-Communist hysteria had made it difficult for the NNC to answer the UN's challenge. During the Second World War, the draft had sent most of the Congress's national leadership into the military, and the eventual lure of high-paying defense industry jobs had enticed many local NNC organizers to abandon their work with the Congress. The final blow came when Max Yergan, motivated by personal ambition and ideological zeal, facilitated the resignation of John P. Davis, the power behind the throne and engineer of Randolph's ouster. Held together by bale and hitching wire and the sheer will and determination of acting Executive Secretary Thelma Dale, the NNC had begun to show

95. Charge d'Affaires ad interim Moscow to Secretary of State, memo, August 26, 1946, Box 4684, Decimal File 811.4016/8-2642 CS/A, ibid.

96. "List of Communications Submitted to the Commission on Human Rights," n.d. (ca. 1946), Box 4592, File "Commission on Human Rights, Second Session–UN Documents," *Roosevelt Papers*.

97. National Negro Congress to Council & Affiliates, memo ([1946]), Part 2, Reel 12, *NNC*; Russell Barnes, "UN Action Doubtful on Negroes' Petition: Appeal for Relief from Discrimination Could Prove Embarrassing to the U.S.," *Detroit News*, June 3, 1946; Summary Record of the Presentation of a Petition by Dr. Max Yergan, President, National Negro Congress," June 6, 1946, Part 2, Reel 28, *NNC*.

new life only toward the end of the war. But just as the Congress was reinvigorating its local branches, the NNC leadership fell under the sway of the Communist party line again and decided to centralize authority and let the locals atrophy. This proved to be a disastrous move.[98]

The UN secretariat's request for proof of human rights abuses in the United States essentially required the NNC to have local organizations in place to document the allegations in the Congress' petition. But thanks to CP policy, the National Negro Congress did not. Nevertheless, the NNC gamely tried to deliver. The Congress would forward articles about lynching to the UN secretariat as proof of the extensive human rights violations in the United States.[99] Most importantly, however, the NNC set up "People's Tribunals" in Los Angeles, Chicago, Detroit, Cleveland, Birmingham, New Orleans, New York, and Washington, D.C., to get direct testimony about "Negro oppression."[100] The Tribunals initially met with a degree of success. The NNC collected several thousand signatures in support of its UN petition, but then, after the initial excitement, the drive began to stall. An NNC informant to the FBI complained that he "had no faith" that the UN petition campaign would succeed because the Congress simply did not have the organizational structure to maintain the momentum.[101] For example, when the national office pressed one local organizer to turn in his signed petition, he confessed that his children had "ransacked" his papers, his wife could not find the petition, and, besides, he did not have any signatures on it anyway.[102] This fairly typical response led one NNC official to bemoan how difficult it was to have a successful signature drive "without [the] dramatics" of an overall UN campaign. Indeed, the Congress leadership feared that generating any additional support would be "comparable to reviving a corpse."[103]

Hoping for a resurrection miracle, the NNC turned first to the black churches, which were noticeably absent in voicing their support for the

98. Streater, "The National Negro Congress, 1936–1947," 241, 299–342; Hughes, "Toward a Black United Front," 189–229.

99. "List of Communications Submitted to the Commission on Human Rights," n.d. (ca. 1946), Box 4592, File "Commission on Human Rights, Second Session–UN Documents," *Roosevelt Papers*.

100. "The American People's Tribunal," n.d., Part 2, Reel 29, *NNC*; Untitled, n.d., Part 2, Reel 26, ibid.; "UN Commission Seeks More Data on Negroes," *People's Voice*, July 6, 1946.

101. Dorothy K. Funn: Report–Activities, April–October, 1946, October 27, 1946, Box 167-6, Folder 18, *Strong Papers*; Guy Hottel to J. Edgar Hoover, memo, October 3, 1946, Reel 2, *FBI File on NNC*.

102. Celia Forman to Horace Perryman, October 15, 1946, Part 2, Reel 28, *NNC*; Perryman to Forman, (n.d.), ibid.

103. "Summarization—UN Signature Campaign," (n.d.), ibid.

Congress's petition. The NNC stressed that there was an "urgent need" for the churches to "give leadership" to the cause and erase the "dry rot of racial injustice" in America. The NNC leadership complained that the CHR, which had taken "no action" on the petition, would continue to ignore the plight of America's black population until the churches, with their unimpeachable moral authority, forced the UN to investigate. The NNC's exhortations, however, were in vain, and the black church refused to answer Yergan's prayers.[104]

The NNC president was equally unsuccessful when he reached out to Mary McLeod Bethune, whom he had earlier cajoled after the UNCIO into hosting the Conference of Negro Leaders. Bethune blasted Yergan with a stinging rejoinder that the plight of blacks was a "national" problem that the NNC had inappropriately dropped on the UN's doorstep. That terse rebuke, according to the NNC leadership, was a direct result of Bethune's too close association with the Truman administration. Star struck by her proximity to power, the NNC grumbled, Bethune was now blinded to the simple fact that "all problems of oppression are international."[105]

The Congress next tried to arrange a meeting in which Metz Lochard, editor of the influential *Chicago Defender*, would present UN officials with additional evidence about the "degradation" of African Americans. Like Bethune, however, Lochard balked at the Congress' plans. He ostensibly found other pressing engagements that would keep him out of New York and made clear that he was unavailable. In reality, though, Lochard was in New York but he had plans of his own, which did not include openly aligning himself with the red-tainted NNC. Thus, while he was rejecting Yergan's pleas to go to the UN, Lochard was simultaneously trying to arrange a meeting with Eleanor Roosevelt to "present additional evidence on the oppression of the Negro American" that a *Chicago Defender* reporter had pulled together. Mrs. Roosevelt, who was more than "familiar with the [NNC's petition's] contents," brushed Lochard off with a brief note that she was "now serving as a U.S. delegate" and that it would be inappropriate for her to receive any kind of petition. Lochard, she advised, should therefore put his comments "in writing" and "present [his] report to the Ec[onomic] & Social Council for

104. Revels Cayton and Dorothy Funn to Rev. R. B. Hurt, September 16, 1946, ibid.; Cayton and Celia Forman to Rev. F. W. Jacobs, September 16, 1946, ibid.; Cayton and Forman to Rev. George C. Wainright, September 16, 1946, ibid.; Moselle Edwards to Dorothy Funn, (n.d. [September 1946]), ibid.; Edward Strong to Rev. P. A. Bishop, October 26, 1946, ibid.; Celia Forman to Moselle Edwards, September 17, 1946, ibid.

105. Max Yergan to Mary McLeod Bethune, November 15, 1946, ibid.; Mary McLeod Bethune to Max Yergan, November 20, 1946, ibid.; Ruth Jett to Max Yergan, November 21, 1946, ibid.

reference to [the] proper body."[106] Cold shoulders, stonewalls, and end-runs, however, were not the worst of the NNC's problems at this time. The FBI, through its dark warren of informants, was certain that the Communist party and its "front groups" intended to "exploit all possibilities" to embarrass the United States on "the Negro question." The FBI was therefore convinced that the NNC's attempts to bring the "plight of 13 million underprivileged Negroes" before the UN was nothing but a "move to detract attention from the Soviet setback in Greece," where British and Royalist forces were battling a Communist insurgency.[107] In short, affiliation with the NNC was beginning to carry a hint of treason. This led its major financial supporter, organized labor, to join the race with Bethune, Lochard, and the black churches in distancing themselves from the NNC.

The CIO tried to steer clear of "the Communist taint" by ordering 267 affiliated unions to "drop all association with the National Negro Congress."[108] Although several unions vigorously protested the order, Philip Murray, president of the CIO, and a member of the NAACP Board of Directors, had "no damn use for American Communists meddling in [union] affairs" and fully supported the directive.[109] The result was financial disaster.

The NNC, which had hoped to use the UN petition as a marketing tool to increase membership and augment its donations from the CIO, was now so short of cash that its fledgling local councils had to "shoulder the responsibility" for developing all "promotional material."[110] The central office did not even have the resources to create posters, and certainly lacked the funding and personnel to develop the "dramatics" of an overarching UN campaign.[111]

106. Adelaide Bean to Thelma Dale, memo, (n.d. [November 1946]), ibid.; "Statement on the Presentation to the Human Rights Commission of the United Nations of a Document, 'Jim Crow America,' in Evidence of the Oppression of Negro Americans," (n.d. [November 1946]), ibid.; Metz T. P. Lochard to Eleanor Roosevelt, telegram, October 25, 1946, Box 4587, File "Human Rights Commission, 1947," *Roosevelt Papers*; Cover memo to "Summary Record of the Presentation of a Petition by Dr. Max Yergan, President, National Negro Congress," June 6, 1946, ibid.

107. Scheidt to Director, teletype, September 11, 1946, Reel 2, *FBI File on NNC*.

108. FBI Report NY 100-3633, (n.d.), ibid.; Mary Sperling McAuliffe, *Crisis on the Left: Cold War Politics and American Liberals, 1947–1954* (Amherst: The University of Massachusetts Press, 1978), 14.

109. Anne Benda to John Brophy, January 15, 1947, Part 2, Reel 34, *NNC*; Fred Williams to John Brophy, December 18, 1946, ibid.; Hodges E. Mason to George L. C. Weaver, December 16, 1946, ibid.; Joseph and Stewart Alsop, "Chicago Parley of Progressives Turned Liberals Against Reds," *Chicago Herald Tribune*, October 7, 1946.

110. "Publicity Cost for Exploitation of United Nations Petition," (n.d.), Part 2, Reel 26, *NNC*; Edward E. Strong to Rowena Sudduth, September 19, 1946, ibid.

111. Ibid.

The "dramatics" came, instead, from an unexpected source. On June 22, 1946, India, incensed by discriminatory treatment of Indian laborers in the Union of South Africa, lodged a complaint before the UN. The South Africans, the Indians charged, had violated a series of treaties whereby India would provide South Africa with laborers and the South African government would, in turn, ensure that the Indian workers enjoyed all "the rights and privileges of citizenship."[112] Instead of honoring this agreement, however, the Indians contended that South Africa had passed a series of discriminatory laws that violated the treaties. The South African government countered that there was no treaty and that this was strictly a domestic matter outside the jurisdiction of the UN. To stem the Indians' "growing commercial success" in South Africa, the government passed the Asiatic Land Tenure and Indian Representation Act of 1946, which prohibited Indians from buying land in "whites only" areas. The South Africans vigorously contended that this was obviously a domestic matter. The South African government also concluded that it could not have violated anyone's human rights because no "internationally recognized... rights [existed], and the [UN] Charter... did not define them."[113]

While making its plea, the South African delegation turned to the United States for support.[114] The South Africans declared that they were tired of getting "crucif[ied]" for codifying their racial beliefs and "being the guinea pig" for UN challenges to racial discrimination. The South Africans also made it very clear that they were not "fighting the domestic jurisdictional battle... only for themselves" because, as they were quick to point out, other nations, especially the United States, had "racial and minority problems."[115]

The U.S. delegates understood the full import of the South Africans' message and, frankly, they were angry with the Indians for raising and pushing the issue. One State Department analysis equated the Indians' battle to protect their people from the brutality of South African racism to Adolf Hitler's "protection" of the Germans in Czechoslovakia and Poland and, thus, depicted the Indians – not the South Africans – as

112. United States Delegation to the United Nations, July 10, 1946, US/A/2, Box 48, File "US/A/1-75," *RG 84*.

113. United Nations, *Yearbook of the United Nations: 1946–1947* (Lake Success, New York: United Nations, 1947), 144–148.

114. For a full discussion of the "alliance" between South Africa and the United States see, Thomas Borstlemann, *Apartheid's Reluctant Uncle: The United States and Southern Africa in the Early Cold War* (New York: Oxford University Press, 1993).

115. Memorandum of Conversation, October 29, 1946, US/A/70, Box 48, File "US/A/1-75," *RG* 84; Memorandum of Conversation, November 6, 1947, US/A/C.1/546, Box 38, File "US/A/C.1/451-550," ibid.

unreasonable, self-serving, and willing to destroy world order because of an obsession with race. Therefore, over the course of several meetings, the U.S. delegation wrestled with how to fend off the Indians' assault. UN Ambassador Warren Austin noted that the Indian complaint took on enormous "importance" if the delegation "simply imagined" what would happen if the UN's investigatory powers "were applied against the United States." This was particularly troubling to Senator Vandenberg, who confessed that he had great difficulty discerning the difference between "Indians in South Africa and negroes in Alabama." And because the differences were "not very great," Eleanor Roosevelt worried that an "oppressed" minority "could get its case before the United Nations in spite of its own government."[116]

The delegation, therefore, struggled to understand what level of protection the "domestic jurisdiction" clause provided. Tom Connally was convinced that it overrode everything else in the UN's charter and would shield the United States from unwanted intrusions. John Foster Dulles admitted that he had designed it to function just that way because he feared that the UN would otherwise engage in "promiscuous international action." Dulles further asserted that it was "debatable" whether the UN meddling in domestic affairs would be any more productive than the federal government interfering in Mississippi, and decided that the United States must sidetrack the Indians' complaint. Vandenberg then suggested throwing the issue into several committees, blurring lines of jurisdiction, and bogging the complaint down in the UN bureaucracy. Although Roosevelt voiced some discomfort that this strategy might undermine the UN's credibility, she agreed that the Indians' complaint could not come before the General Assembly and decided to go along with whatever her colleagues decided. Dulles, therefore, proposed that the United States keep the General Assembly focused on the question of the treaties between India and South Africa, not on the human rights issue. That way, he concluded, the Americans could limit the discussion, keep the UN from expanding its query beyond the original issue, and, most importantly, escape international scrutiny of the "negro problem." Connally, however, worried that "the debate could not be limited" and that there would be

116. "Commission on Human Rights: First Session of Full Commission, January 1947: Consideration of Communications Received," SD/CS.4/5, January 16, 1947, Box 4594, File "UN Human Rights Commission, 1947–June 1947," *Roosevelt Papers*; Minutes of the Tenth Meeting of the General Assembly Delegation, US/A/M (CHR)/10, October 28, 1946, Box 60, File "US/A/M/(CHR)/1-32," *RG* 84; Minutes of the Eleventh Meeting of the United States General Assembly Delegation, US/A/M/(CHR)/11, October 28, 1946, ibid.; Minutes of the Fifteenth Meeting of the General Assembly Delegation, US/A/M/(CHR)/15, November 12, 1946, ibid.

"no stopping" the UN once it "was turned loose."[117] Frightened by the prospect of a precedent-setting vote that would allow the UN to investigate racially discriminatory practices, the United States tried to move the Indians' complaint out of the UN's jurisdiction altogether and into the International Court of Justice, where the court could focus only on the nature of the treaties and completely ignore the issues of human rights and domestic jurisdiction.[118]

To the consternation of the U.S. delegation, the emerging Third World and the Soviet bloc banded together. Johannesburg's openly racist policies, the delegations concluded, threatened to make a "complete mockery" of the UN Charter and, therefore "an example [had to] be made of South Africa." The General Assembly therefore discounted the "domestic jurisdiction" argument and declared that every nation that signed the UN Charter had "made a certain renunciation of their sovereignty." The Assembly further asserted that the "Charter imposed upon each member an obligation to refrain from policies based upon race discrimination." The General Assembly's January 1947 resolution condemned South Africa's racist policies as a violation of human rights and "contrary to the Charter," and strongly advised South Africa to bring its policies into "conformity with the principles and purposes of the Charter."[119]

A jubilant Yergan believed this was just the opening the NNC needed to garner not only national backing, but also international support.[120] He contended that the problem stalling UN action on the Congress' petition was "the barrier of national sovereignty," which, as he saw it, was "the equivalent of the 'states rights' obstacle to federal action in the United

117. Minutes of the Tenth Meeting of the General Assembly Delegation, US/A/M/(CHR)/10, October 28, 1946, ibid.; Minutes of the Eleventh Meeting of the United States General Assembly Delegation, US/A/M/(CHR)/11, October 28, 1946, ibid.; Minutes of the Fifteenth Meeting of the General Assembly Delegation, US/A/M/(CHR)/15, November 12, 1946, ibid.; Minutes of the Tenth Meeting of the United States Delegation to the Third Regular Session of the General Assembly, US(P) A/M/(CHR)/10, October 5, 1948, Box 60, File "US(P)/A/M/(CHR)/1-34," ibid.

118. Memorandum of Conversation, US/A/C.1/160-US/A/C.4/38, September 23, 1947, Box 37, File "US/A/C.1/101-200," ibid.; Minutes of the Tenth Meeting of the General Assembly Delegation, US/A/M/(CHR)/10, October 28, 1946, Box 60, File "US/A/M/(CHR)/1–32," ibid.; Minutes of the Eleventh Meeting of the United States General Assembly Delegation, US/A/M/(CHR)/11, October 28, 1946, ibid.; Minutes of the Fifteenth Meeting of the General Assembly Delegation, US/A/M/(CHR)/15, November 12, 1946, ibid.; Minutes of the Tenth Meeting of the United States Delegation to the Third Regular Session of the General Assembly, US(P) A/M/(CHR)/10, October 5, 1948, ibid.

119. Memorandum of Conversation, US/A/C.1/501, November 3, 1947, Box 38, File "US/A/C.1/451-550," ibid.; *Yearbook of the United Nations: 1946–1947*, 144–148.

120. United Nations Conference Summary Proceedings, February 8, 1947, Part 2, Reel 28, *NNC*.

States."[121] Yet, the recent UN action seemingly set an outstanding precedent. If the emerging system of *apartheid* was a violation of human rights, then certainly Jim Crow had to be as well. If the Asiatic Land Tenure and Indian Representation Act was contrary to the principles of the UN Charter, then America's well-worn restrictive covenants had to be equally unacceptable. The *New York Amsterdam News* declared that "American arrogance, English chicanery, and [America's] bootlicking stooges" had just lost an important battle in the United Nations, and this could only give "new impetus" to the Congress' petition.[122]

Yergan agreed. "The time is ripe," he euphorically declared, to get the United Nations to act. The NNC therefore made one last gesture to broaden the financial and organizational support for its UN petition. Yergan quickly invited representatives from 200 organizations to meet together to "map...out joint plans" that would force the UN to investigate the "conditions of oppression...experienced by the Negro in the United States."[123] This required, as the NNC well knew, a carefully crafted protest that could demonstrate how American racism projected itself into the international arena. At the February 8, 1947 strategic planning meeting, 75 representatives from a range of labor, fraternal, and civil rights organizations decided to draft a supplement to the original NNC petition that would expand the original focus from African Americans alone to all peoples of color under U.S. jurisdiction. The proposed supplement would first outline the legal basis of oppression in Puerto Rico, the Virgin Islands, the Panama Canal Zone, and the prized Pacific Islands that the military had wrested from Japan. Second, the supplement would describe how America's Jim Crow laws discriminated against Third World UN delegates. That way, "the problem is not only domestic in character, but is of direct concern to the governments from which these nationals come." Third, the supplement would emphasize the patently racist nature of America's immigration laws, which were heavily biased against Indonesians, Japanese, and other people of color. Finally, the supplement would conclude that these patterns of abuse were symptomatic of and emanated directly from the "basic pattern of Negro discrimination in the United States." As a result, America's "Negro question" was "far more than an internal problem." It had critical "international implications" that had to be addressed by the world community.[124]

121. Max Yergan to Dwight Bradley, January 29, 1947, ibid.
122. "Editorial," *New York Amsterdam News*, December 14, 1946.
123. Max Yergan to Dwight Bradley, January 29, 1947, Part 2, Reel 28, *NNC*.
124. "Proposals for Extending UN Petition Campaign as Adopted by the Conference on United Nations and Minorities," February 8, 1947, ibid.; "United Nations Conference: Summary Proceedings," February 8, 1947, ibid.; "Suggested Contents of Supplementary Petition to the United Nations," February 8, 1947, ibid.

The next stage in this plan was to produce the kind of international and national support that would place the issue of African Americans squarely on the UN's agenda. A small subcommittee suggested visiting Latin America and Europe "to organize such support." That required money, however, and the Congress had none. The NNC leadership therefore asked each organization at the conference to: (1) become an official sponsor of the UN campaign; (2) name a permanent representative to work with the NNC on the petition; (3) use its own national and local organizational structures to distribute information about the campaign and garner support; (4) provide financial backing to assist in the campaign; and (5) organize "People's Tribunals" throughout the United States.[125] In short, the NNC asked the other organizations to carry out the tasks that its own financially and structurally weak organization could not.

For all intents and purposes, that February UN strategy session was the NNC's last big hurrah. The Congress was rapidly disintegrating, and the leadership had to focus all of its efforts on trying to save the organization. The major problems were money and membership. Not only had labor withdrawn its financial support, but also the national office had difficulty collecting the pledges made both at the Tenth National Convention and in the UN signature campaign. The Chicago Council of the NNC had managed to deliver only $669 of its $2,500 pledge. The Washington, D.C. Council, which, along with Detroit and Chicago, was supposed to be one of the strongest locals, had stopped reporting altogether about its UN membership drive. Perhaps that silence was to be expected. The Washington and Chicago Councils, in fact, were on the verge of having their telephones disconnected and being evicted from their offices. Other financial worries also plagued the Congress. Bertha Tipton, executive secretary of the Chicago Council, had allegedly embezzled NNC funds and then disappeared. The National Office could not meet its payroll. Edward Strong, a senior staff member, was reduced to scrawling "WHERE IS MY MONEY?" at the bottom of a report. Fiscal insolvency also put an abrupt halt to plans to move the NNC's headquarters from New York to the United Auto Workers' Detroit stronghold.[126] In short, the lack of adequate financial resources made it impossible for the NNC

125. "Proposals for Extending UN Petition Campaign as Adopted by the Conference on United Nations and Minorities," February 8, 1947, ibid.

126. Alfred McPherson et al. to Revels Cayton, July 6, 1946, Part 2, Reel 29, ibid.; Edward Strong to Marie Harris, October 22, 1946, ibid.; Bertha Tipton to Revels Cayton, July 8, 1946, ibid.; Edward Strong to Dorothy Funn, (n.d), ibid. (emphasis in original); FBI Report, January 8, 1947, Reel 2, *FBI File on NNC*; FBI Report, February 17, 1947, ibid.; FBI Report, October 22, 1946, ibid.

to carry out the broad agenda it had set for itself. At the same time, the rising tide of anti-Communist hysteria kept potential supporters away. Membership drives were abysmal "failures," and there was a "severe lack of participation" in NNC activities even by its own card-carrying members. To give one example, although the Washington, DC Council boasted more than 3,000 members, only "a dozen or so ever appeared" at meetings.[127]

The Communist party had seen enough. The CP had hoped that the Congress would be the party's entree into the African American community. But a series of doctrinal blunders made this impossible. After the party denounced the "Double V" campaign during World War II, the CP, quite simply, lost its credibility in the larger black community.[128] Of course, the party leadership did not believe that its problems in the African American community were a direct result of the "Double V" debacle. Instead, the CP openly derided the rudderless direction of the National Negro Congress and concluded that the NNC desperately needed "political leadership by the Communist Party." Angered at being "stalemated by the National Office," the party leadership cavalierly discussed letting the NNC "die" and allowing the more suitable Civil Rights Congress to "carry on [the NNC's] work in the Negro field."[129]

Sparked by the CP's open disapproval, financial insolvency, dwindling membership, and plummeting staff morale, the National Board of the NNC met on June 22, 1947 to decide the organization's fate.[130] After heated debate, the Board opted for a "holding operation" that maintained the Congress as a national organization with a centralized office. This decision resolved nothing. The NNC had so many intricately woven problems that the National Board was finally compelled to appoint a subcommittee to do an "exhaustive" study of the organization and report back to the full Board.[131] The subcommittee examined issues surrounding personnel, finances, program, strength of local councils, and the

127. Ibid.; Special Agent in Charge, Washington to Director, FBI, memo, January 10, 1948, ibid.

128. George M. Frederickson, *Black Liberation: A Comparative History of Black Ideologies in the United States and South Africa* (New York: Oxford University Press, 1995), 181–82; Record, *Race and Radicalism*, 114–16.

129. Edward C. Pintzuk, *Reds, Racial Justice, and Civil Liberties: Michigan Communists during the Cold War* (Minneapolis, Minnesota: MEP Publications, 1997), 75–76; FBI Report, February 17, 1947, Reel 2, *FBI File on NNC*; Special Agent in Charge, Detroit to Director, FBI, memo, May 15, 1947, ibid.

130. National Executive Board Meeting: Summary Minutes, June 22, 1947, Part 2, Reel 34, *NNC*.

131. Ibid.; "Untitled," June 22, 1947, ibid.

UN supplementary petition.[132] Its recommendations, submitted to the National Board on July 7, 1947, ensured that the organization's drift and decline would continue. The subcommittee "reaffirmed" the National Board's June 22 resolution, recommended keeping the NNC headquartered in New York City, and suggested reducing the executive staff to two. The last recommendation was borne of sheer necessity. Sensing the inevitable end of the NNC, Revels Cayton and Edward Strong had already submitted their resignations. The subcommittee was at a loss about how to fix the Congress's financial woes. The financial statement showed only $104 in the bank, but over $3,200 in bills. The Communist party finally decided that its grand experiment had failed and agreed to "gradually dissolve" the Congress.[133] Declaring that the CP had "sabotaged" the National Negro Congress, Yergan began an agonizing reappraisal of his and his organizations' alignment with the Communist party and, as a result, abandoned the NNC in its death throes.[134]

With the resignations of Cayton, Yergan, and Strong, Thelma Dale was left "with pretty much everything on her hands." She began to negotiate the transfer of remaining assets from the NNC to the Civil Rights Congress.[135] According to the November 23, 1947 Agreement, the National Negro Congress merged into the CRC. The prized New York office now became the Harlem local of the Civil Rights Congress and the NNC's paid members automatically became CRC members. Because there was already a rich cross-fertilization between the CRC and NNC National Boards, those who had not already done so were formally invited to sit on the Executive Board of the CRC.[136] Thus, 11 short years after its inception, the National Negro Congress ceased to exist. The NNC's blind loyalty to the Communist party, its weak organizational structure, and financial problems meant that its most innovative program, the petition to the UN, was destined to fail.

Roy Wilkins was not surprised. The moment the NNC's petition hit the UN, Wilkins advised White to "find out absolutely that this cannot be done," then "damn the action" by acknowledging that it was an "excellent

132. National Executive Board Meeting: Summary Minutes, June 22, 1947, ibid.; "Untitled," June 22, 1947, ibid.

133. Special Committee Meeting: Minutes, July 7, 1947, ibid.; National Negro Congress Financial Statement, July 23, 1947, ibid.; Pintzuk, *Reds*, 75–76; Unsigned to P. Kenneth O'Donnell, February 3, 1961, Reel 2, *FBI File on NNC*.

134. "Max Yergan Obituary," *New York Times*, April 13, 1975.

135. Special Agent in Charge, Detroit to Director, FBI, memo, August 15, 1947, Reel 2, *FBI File on NNC*.

136. "Statement on Merger of the National Negro Congress with the Civil Rights Congress," December 4, 1947, ibid.; Press Release from Civil Rights Congress and National Negro Congress, December 6, 1947, ibid.

publicity stunt" that would prove to be "a dud."[137] White and Du Bois, however, were not as pessimistic or cynical as Wilkins, and believed that the Congress had, in fact, stumbled on a great idea. After conferring with Bunche, White became convinced that the petition was, indeed, more than a leftist "publicity stunt," and came to recognize that the NNC had "captured the imagination" of African Americans by "lifting the struggle of the Negro" out of the "local and national setting and placing it in the realm of the international."[138] Indeed, according to NAACP Board member, Theodore Berry, Bunche "encouraged" White to pursue the issue and have the NAACP craft its own petition to the UN.[139] White was tempted. In his assessment, it was not the message but the NNC's Communist leanings that sealed the petition's fate. He contended that the Association, which had worked diligently to prevent Communist infiltration, would be able to appeal the case of African Americans before the UN while dodging the Red bullet that had killed the NNC's chances. Du Bois was eager to take up the challenge.[140]

After White's and Du Bois' disappointing experience in San Francisco, it may seem odd that these two men were now eager to work through the UN organization founded in that city. Important changes had occurred since May 1945, however, and these changes seemed to cast the UN in a new light. In addition to being the chair of the CHR, Eleanor Roosevelt had also joined the NAACP's Board of Directors.[141] For Walter White, this meant that a powerful, apparently sympathetic, ally would be available to champion the cause of African Americans before the international body. Du Bois, on the other hand, had come to the conclusion that the United States, because of the emerging Cold War, was vulnerable to a skillfully publicized expose on American racism.[142] This publicity would force the

137. Roy Wilkins to White, memo, June 6, 1946, Box 444, File "National Negro Congress: 1945–47," *Papers of the NAACP*.

138. Gloster Current to Walter White, June 4, 1946, ibid.; White to Bunche, June 7, 1946, ibid.

139. Theodore Berry, Sr. of Cincinnati, telephone interview by author, August 20, 1994, Columbus, Ohio, handwritten notes in author's possession.

140. Du Bois to B. R. Ambedkar, July 31, 1946, Reel 58, *Du Bois*; White to Du Bois, memo, August 1, 1946, Box 634, File "United Nations—General, 1945–46," *Papers of the NAACP*; Du Bois to White, memo, August 1, 1946, Reel 59, *Du Bois*; Du Bois to White, memo, January 29, 1947, Box 241, File "William E. B. Du Bois—General, 1947," *Papers of the NAACP*.

141. Minutes of the Board of Directors Meeting, May 8, 1945, Reel 3, *NAACP Board of Directors Meeting, 1944–1953* (Washington, DC: Library of Congress), microfilm (hereafter *NAACP/LC*); Minutes of the Board of Directors Meeting, June 11, 1945, Reel 3, *NAACP*.

142. "Report of the Department of Special Research, NAACP: June 4 to September 7, 1946," Reel 59, *Du Bois*.

nation to address the needs of its 13 million African Americans, regardless of what the UN could or would do.

On August 1, 1946, Du Bois requested several copies of the NNC petition, which he believed was "too short" and "not sufficiently documented" to spur the UN or the United States to action.[143] He sought to craft a scholarly 150–200 page treatise that documented both the effects of human rights abuses on America's black population and the UN's obligation to intervene. Du Bois believed that he and a team of scholars and attorneys, including Rayford Logan and Earl Dickerson, could pull together a petition in time for the UN General Assembly's September 1946 meeting. White forwarded the plan to the Board of Director's powerful Committee on Administration for its advice.[144]

The committee members agreed with the overall thrust of the plan, but suggested some major revisions, including expansion of the editorial board beyond "the New York family" to include, perhaps Roscoe Dunjee, editor of Oklahoma's *Black Dispatch*.[145] Thurgood Marshall thought the September deadline completely impractical; it was already Labor Day weekend. He also questioned whether the attorneys, who had thriving law practices, would have the time to devote to the petition. Instead, Marshall recommended Milton Konvitz, a Cornell University professor, as one who had done "the best job" on the legal rights of African Americans. The main issue for Marshall was whether the Association wanted to "do a real job or not" in presenting an airtight case before the UN. If it did, he advised, then it needed to slow down, determine who was going to do the work, and decide what, exactly, the Association wanted to accomplish.[146]

Du Bois took the suggestions under advisement and replaced one of the attorneys with Konvitz. Du Bois thought Dickerson was indispensable and pressed to keep him on the team. Dickerson's expertise was valued because, as a key member of the National Lawyer's Guild, he may have helped draft the NNC's petition on the duties of the UN to protect human rights. Not only did Du Bois seek to maintain Dickerson, he also believed that Marshall was too pessimistic about the timeline. The General Assembly would begin its session on September 23, and Du Bois

143. Du Bois to NNC, August 1, 1946, ibid.

144. Du Bois to White, memo, August 26, 1946, Box 637, File "United Nations Petition, 1946," *Papers of the NAACP*; White to Committee on Administration, memo, August 28, 1946, ibid.

145. Roy Wilkins to White, memo, September 3, 1946, Reel 59, *Du Bois*; Channing Tobias to White, August 30, 1946, ibid.; Ruby Hurley to White, memo, August 29, 1946, ibid.; Charles Toney to White, September 4, 1946, Box 637, File "United Nations Petition, 1946," *Papers of the NAACP*.

146. Thurgood Marshall to White, August 31, 1946, Reel 59, *Du Bois*.

believed that it would not get down to business until late October. Du Bois therefore contended that there was "no reason why" the petition could not be ready for the General Assembly by November.[147] But then reality set in. One of the co-authors, Robert Ming, Jr., former associate general counsel for the Office of Price Administration and a professor of law at the University of Chicago, failed to send in his chapter by the original October 26 deadline, missed an extended November 15 deadline, and ignored Du Bois's repeated telegrams.[148] Finally, on January 2, 1947, Ming's chapter arrived in "good" shape, but "45 days late."[149]

Du Bois troubles were far from over. At every turn, friends and foes warned him about the impotence of the UN. As Rayford Logan researched materials for his section, he began to seriously question whether the UN had any authority at all to safeguard human rights. The dreaded "domestic jurisdiction" clause, which the NAACP had fought so hard and futilely to overturn in San Francisco, seemed to block effectively all action by the UN. When international intervention did occur, such as in the case of the Nuremberg and Tokyo War Crime Trials, it was the result of "treaties imposed upon weak nations," which certainly did not describe the United States.[150]

Leslie S. Perry, director of the Association's Washington, D.C. Bureau, warned Du Bois that the NAACP was asking the UN to go to the very "brink of its authority." And after reading Ming's and the others' chapters, Perry determined that the draft petition would hardly compel the international organization to exceed its powers and challenge the United States. If the UN could be budged to move, Perry decided, it would need more than the legal treatise that Du Bois's team had drafted. Perry was "disturbed" by the authors' inability to convey fully "the low state of Negro welfare" in the United States or "the disabilities under which the Negro works and lives." He called for "sociological data" on employment stratification and resulting wage differentials, on illiteracy and per capita expenditures on African American and white students, on the high-rent urban ghettos and rural plantation shacks that blacks were forced to live in, and on the high infant mortality rate, low life expectancy, and dangerously inadequate health care facilities for 10 percent of the American population.[151] Perry's stinging critique struck a chord, and Du Bois challenged the former social worker to write that chapter. Perry assented.

147. Du Bois to White, memo, September 5, 1946, ibid.
148. Du Bois to Charles Houston, telegram, November 20, 1946, Reel 58, ibid.
149. Du Bois to White, memo, January 2, 1947, Reel 60, ibid.
150. Logan to Du Bois, October 12, 1946, Reel 58, ibid.; Logan to Du Bois, October 12, 1946, ibid.; Logan to Du Bois, October 27, 1946, ibid.
151. Leslie S. Perry to Du Bois, January 7, 1947, Reel 60, ibid.

Robert Carter, an attorney in the NAACP's legal office, shared Logan's and Perry's concerns about the UN's authority to intervene. The draft petition simply did not set up the "prerequisite" conditions that would explain why the UN had to have jurisdiction in this case. "Nowhere," Carter contended, "do I find a clear-cut, strong statement to the effect that the states will not protect the Negroes." Nor did Carter find any direct statement that the federal government was "powerless" to stop human rights violations. It is "impossible for Negroes to attain justice within the United States," and this compelling fact, Carter concluded, meant that "the only recourse left" was "direct action [by] the United Nations." This was the ground work that Du Bois had to lay if he wanted the UN to take some action.[152]

Getting the UN to act, however, was going to be very difficult. The CHR could not agree if it even had the authority to acknowledge, much less do anything about, the thousands of petitions it had already received. Untangling that basic level of authority sparked a series of heated debates among the Commission members. The Philippine representative, General Carlos Romulo, argued that the UN should assume the "role of a Supreme Court of Appeal." The sheer number of petitions indicated, at least to him, that something was terribly wrong with the state of human rights in the world. He then proposed that a subcommittee review all of the petitions, determine their merit, and present the valid ones before the Commission for discussion. Mrs. Roosevelt, as chair, quickly observed that "the Commission had no power to conduct an enquiry, or to put its decisions into force." Charles Dukes, the British representative, concurred and said that he "saw a certain danger in making these communications . . . available to members of this Commission." The Commission's primary function, Dukes asserted, was to draft an International Declaration on Human Rights and no more. William Hodgson, the Australian delegate, added that to even consider accepting petitions or doing anything with them at this point was "hasty." The "Commission," as far as he was concerned, "was on dangerous ground . . . . [T]he Commission's first duty," he asserted, "was to draft the International Declaration on Human Rights . . . . The examination of complaints did not enter the Commission's functions or powers." The Belgian, Roland LeBeau, reaffirmed his colleagues' stance when he insisted that "the principal task of this Commission was not to examine these communications or to give the impression that it could redress grievances." General Romulo then sought to clarify his reference to a Court of Appeal. He conceded that the Commission did

152. Robert L. Carter to Du Bois, memo, January 22, 1947, Box 637, File "United Nations Petition (NAACP): 1947, Jan.–Sept.," *Papers of the NAACP*.

not have that function, but, he added, "that was how the public regarded it." He believed, however, that even though the CHR was not really a court of last resort, it could "be said to represent the world conscience" and his proposal was only to have a subcommittee determine how to handle the thousands of communications the CHR received. The Soviet representative, V. F. Tepliakov, had heard enough. "The Human Rights Commission was not a court of justice. It had a definite task, namely, to draw up a Declaration of Human Rights." Hodgson then jumped in again. "He agreed with the USSR representative.... The public must not be allowed to think that the Commission was a tribunal." Mrs. Roosevelt believed, however, that Romulo was not seeking to set up a tribunal, but rather some mechanism so that "the authors of communications [would not] feel that they were... writing for nothing." With Mrs. Roosevelt's support, the Philippine motion carried.[153]

By early February 1947, however, the tide had turned. Before the next round of meetings, Durward Sandifer sent Mrs. Roosevelt explicit instructions that "[t]he establishment of a special organ to supervise and enforce human rights would seem to be an extreme measure." He then attempted to explain why any activity that suggested enforcement of basic human rights was a radical, dangerous concept. The Charter only "employs such phrases as 'promoting and encouraging respect for'" human rights. "It does not speak of the 'supervision and enforcement of' human rights and fundamental freedoms." "Furthermore," he asserted, "Article 2 (7) specifically denies authority to the United Nations to intervene in matters which are essentially within the domestic jurisdiction." It is, therefore "the view of the United States that the establishment of machinery for international supervision of human rights... cannot be an immediate objective of the Commission on Human Rights."[154]

Thus, as the subcommittee to review petitions set about its job to determine the procedure and the machinery for receiving and handling petitions, the chair of the CHR was under explicit orders to rein in this and all other activities hinting at implementation and enforcement. The Subcommittee on the Handling of Communications had met on February 1, with Dukes elected chair. The first item, the three-man panel, decided was that, "it was not its task to examine the communications received." With that piece of business out of the way, the second major decision the panel reaffirmed was that "the Commission has no power to take any action in regard to any complaints regarding human rights." It then

153. "Commission on Human Rights: Summary Record of the Fourth Meeting," E/CN.4/SR.4, January 29, 1947, *UN*.

154. Durward Sandifer to Eleanor Roosevelt, February 5, 1947, Box 4594, (no file), *Roosevelt Papers*.

recommended that the secretariat compile a confidential list of communications, circulate the list to members of the Commission, and "inform the writers of all communications concerning human rights ... that their communications will be brought to the attention of the Commission on Human Rights."[155]

That last suggestion set off a firestorm of protests. P. C. Chang of China admonished that it was "premature to say that the Commission was qualified to receive communications officially" and this body had to "refrain from raising false hopes." Roland LeBeau could not have agreed more. By even suggesting that the communications would be brought to the attention of the CHR, he said, it would "give rise to the mistaken impression that the Commission was a tribunal whose function was to redress wrongs." Rene Cassin was beside himself. The defeatist, futile attitude permeating the discussions led him to suggest that the Economic and Social Council (ECOSOC) needed to know "the serious gap resulting from the Commission's absence of power to deal with communications." Although Mrs. Roosevelt convinced Cassin that it was not necessary to spell out this "gap" in any official documentation to ECOSOC, Tepliakov wanted it to be understood by everyone that the Commission "was not empowered" to handle petitions. Dukes rightly observed that the Soviets' position would mean that "the communications would be simply filed." That just did not sit well with Charles Malik of Lebanon. He exhorted that, "it was the Commission's duty to receive all communications dealing with human rights, otherwise it might appear that it was not doing its job." Roosevelt had to agree. She also added, however, that limiting the distribution of the petitions to members of the Commission and ensuring that the list was confidential would "reduce" the "risk of indiscretions." Thus, after a few more exchanges about confidentiality and keeping the press at bay, the subcommittee's recommendations were adopted without amendment. That is to say, although the Commission had "no power to enforce human rights," and all petitions would be kept confidential and out of the press, the simple act of receiving a petition would still allow the Commission to look like it was doing its job.[156] Thus, the stage was set for the barriers that the NAACP would face.

As daunting as the UN's obstacle course may have been, the Association would also have to contend with a Cold War that was getting hotter and

155. "Commission on Human Rights: Report of the Sub-Committee on the Handling of Communications," E/CN.4/14/Rev.2, February 6, 1947, Box 4593, File "Secretariat Documents: Working Papers," ibid.

156. "Commission on Human Rights First Session: Summary Record of the Sixteenth Meeting," E/CN.4/SR.16, February 6, 1947, *UN*; "Commission on Human Rights: Summary Record of the Twentieth Meeting," E/CN.4/SR.20, February 7, 1947, ibid.

hotter by the moment. The latest and most decisive blast came from the impending crisis in the Near East, where the autocratic regime in Greece could no longer be propped up by an increasingly weakened Great Britain. The British were flat broke and did not have the resources to support both the Labour government's social welfare agenda, as well as Britain's traditional foreign policy objectives. In a winter with record-setting freezing temperatures, Britain's food and fuel shortages, juxtaposed with Greece's continuous drain on the British treasury, caused Chancellor of the Exchequer Hugh Dalton to complain that "[w]e are, I am afraid, drifting in a state of semi-animation towards the rapids" and must stop the "endless dribble of British taxpayers' money to the Greeks."[157] After months of debate, Dalton finally convinced Prime Minister Clement Attlee to hand the Greek quagmire over to the Americans.

State Department officials, already convinced that the Greek Communists and their war machine were fully supported and directed by Moscow, were eager to crush the insurgency and hand the Soviets a major defeat. When State Department officials imagined a Communist victory in Greece, they saw the apocalypse. They envisioned a "world cut in half," with communism spilling out of the Near East into Iran, Africa, Italy, and France. The problem was that Congress and the American public saw neither the apocalypse nor any direct correlation between the outcome of the Greek civil war and U.S. interests. If the United States was going to take up the mantle of the British Empire, the White House and State Department knew that they would have to describe the conflict as if the fate of western civilization hung in the balance. And what better place to fight for western civilization than in the cradle of democracy – Greece.[158]

On March 12, 1947, in what would become known as the Truman Doctrine, the president laid before Congress his version of the apocalypse. Greece, the president declared, was threatened by Communist terrorists, who were supported by the Soviet satellite states of Bulgaria, Albania, and Yugoslavia. Besieged by the constant incursions on its northern border and the terrorists' disruption of its economy, the Greek government's "small and poorly equipped" army was simply "unable to cope." America, the president asserted, was the only nation "willing and able" to support the "democratic Greek government."[159] Truman, of course, knew that

157. Quoted in, Daniel Yergin, *Shattered Peace: The Origins of the Cold War and the National Security State* (Boston: Houghton Mifflin Company), 280.

158. Ibid., 281–82; Lawrence S. Wittner, *American Intervention in Greece, 1943–1949* (New York: Columbia University Press, 1982), xi, 73–74, 77–78.

159. Harry S Truman, "The Truman Doctrine," in *The Annals of America*, Vol. 16, *1940–1949: The Second World War and After* (Chicago: Encyclopedia Britannica, Inc., 1968), 435; Wittner, *American Intervention in Greece*, 79–80.

the Greek government was anything but democratic. U.S. officials had consistently characterized the ruling clique as "corrupt, incompetent, and repressive" and Truman, himself, was compelled to acknowledge that the "government of Greece [was] not perfect," that it had been "operating in an atmosphere of chaos and extremism." Nonetheless, the president continued to hammer home the point that only American support could protect Greece and allow it to become "a self-supporting and self-respecting democracy" – a democracy just like the United States, where there were "free institutions, [a] representative government, free elections, guarantees of individual liberty ... and freedom from political oppression."[160]

The democracy that Truman described, unfortunately, bore no resemblance to the one that African Americans experienced. And blacks in America knew it. Less than a month before Truman's speech, an epileptic Willie Earle had been dragged out of a South Carolina jail, mutilated, and virtually decapitated by a series of shotgun blasts and then, despite detailed confessions, his murderers were found "not guilty" by a jury of their peers. One journalist wrote that the verdict was what "one might have expected from twelve idiots in a madhouse." Walter Reuther, president of the United Auto Workers, explained to Truman that the jury's decision was a "farce" that could only create "skepticism on our claim that we are the most democratic nation in the world." "From all corners of the Earth" Reuther continued, "the eyes of the people of many races and colors are turned upon America today to see if we can practice the principles we preach in the councils of the United Nations." But the United States simply would not and could not do it. Tom Clark had made a pretty "good speech" on the case, but, as one Southerner noted, "Eloquence doesn't stop lynching." And he was appalled that Clark refused to take the necessary steps that would put an end to this horrible feature of American society. "Successful prosecution of lynchers and conniving sheriffs" who "surrender ... a prisoner to a lynching mob" was the only thing that "will stop them." It was the least the United States could do, he noted because "[w]hile proposing to make the world 'Democratic' by ... the arming of fascist governments like Turkey and Greece at a cost of millions (soon to become billions), it might be helpful to attempt even handed justice in the United States."[161] The administration, however, ignored the renewed

160. Yergin, *Shattered Peace*, 288, 292; Truman, "The Truman Doctrine,"*The Annals of America*, 435–36.

161. "South Carolina Negro First Lynch Victim of 1947," *P.M.* February 18, 1947, found in Box 55, File "WH Files-Minorities-Negro-General-Lynching-Newsclipping—Willie Earle South Carolina, Feb–Mar 1947," *Nash Papers*; Ted LeBerthon, "White Man's Views: Wrong for Acquitted Lynchers to Believe They Are Christians," *Pittsburgh Courier*, June 21, 1947, found in ibid.; Walter Reuther et al. to Truman, telegram,

pleas for an anti-lynching law and greater enforcement of existing federal civil rights statutes, and, instead, breathed a sigh of relief because the PCCR, which immediately issued statements about the case, had taken Truman "'off the hot seat.'"[162]

Robert Carter was right. As dismal as the UN may have looked, the American scene was even more bleak. Du Bois would have to make it clear that the UN was the only place that African Americans could secure justice. After Du Bois significantly revised the NAACP's petition to incorporate the changes suggested by the reviewers, he immediately began to lay the groundwork for a full UN hearing.[163] The venerable scholar operated under no illusions. He and Ollie Harrington, the Association's public relations director, knew the NAACP's petition was a "mass of homicide" that would obliterate whatever illusions anyone might have about American democracy. As a result, the two men understood that it would be extremely difficult to get the UN to accept the petition, much less "allow it to remain in the open."[164] Nevertheless, Du Bois contacted all of the UN delegations, as well as Secretary General Trygve Lie, asking for their support in bringing the NAACP's petition before the General Assembly.[165] One of Du Bois' colleagues, Harry E. Davis, a state legislator from Ohio, warned him that the "Anglo-American representatives" would make every effort to "sidetrack" the petition by throwing up the "internal domestic affairs" excuse.[166] The British, of course, met all of Davis' low expectations and refused to be of "any assistance."[167] Trygve Lie also replied that he was "not in a position" to receive the petition and suggested that Du Bois contact John Humphrey in the Human Rights Division.[168] Du Bois and Harrington had anticipated this chilly reception,

May 27, 1947, Box 548, File "OF 93a," *Truman:OF*; Albert E. Barnett to Tom Clark, May 24, 1947, Box 1099, Folder 7, *ACLU Papers*.

162. David K. Niles to Matt Connelly, memo, February 19, 1947, Box 26, File "Civil Rights/Negro Affairs 1945–June 1947," *Niles Papers*; David K. Niles to Mr. Connelly, February 19, 1947, Box 543, File "OF 93 1947 [3 of 3]," *Truman:OF*.
163. Du Bois to White, memo, August 28, 1947, Reel 60, *Du Bois*.
164. Oliver Harrington to Al Smith, October 2, 1947, Box 637, File "United Nations Petition (NAACP): 1947, Oct," *Papers of the NAACP*; Du Bois to William H. Stoneman, October 16, 1947, Box 637, File "United Nations Petition (NAACP): 1947, Jan–Sept," ibid.
165. Du Bois to Trygve Lie, September 11, 1948 (sic), ibid.; Du Bois to William H. Melish, September 18, 1947, Reel 60, *Du Bois*; Hugh H. Smythe to Afghanistan UN delegation et al., September 29, 1947, ibid.
166. Harry E. Davis to Du Bois, September 19, 1947, Reel 59, ibid.
167. Assistant Private Secretary (United Kingdom Delegation) to Hugh H. Smythe, October 2, 1947, Reel 60, ibid.
168. William H. Stoneman to Du Bois, September 29, 1947, Box 637, File "United Nations Petition (NAACP): 1947, Jan.–Sept.," *Papers of the NAACP*.

but felt that they could count on support from at least the Indian, Soviet, and "one or two South American" delegations to pressure the UN to receive the petition and openly and fully debate its merits.[169]

Because Walter White erroneously thought that Mrs. Roosevelt would be a strong ally in the NAACP's quest for UN intervention, he prodded Du Bois to consult her.[170] Well before White's urging, however, Du Bois had already found the former first lady to be less than supportive. Roosevelt was often unresponsive to his requests or only gave Du Bois "vague and meager advice." Nevertheless, he still tried. "I am writing again to beg that you use your good offices to give us the simple and reasonable right to present this petition . . . and to have the press and Visitors present. I think you will agree with me that American Negroes have grievances and that they have a right to make those grievances known." Yet, as Roosevelt demonstrated in her discussion about the Indians in South Africa, as well as her maneuvering to keep all petitions a closely guarded secret, no, she did not agree with Du Bois.[171] John Humphrey therefore told Du Bois that only member states could place a petition before the UN and the State Department had already decided that "no good would come" from putting a petition "of this character" on the General Assembly's agenda.[172]

At the same time, Marian Wynn Perry of the NAACP's Legal Defense Fund warned Du Bois of a law that placed "strict limitations and criminal penalties" on anyone who contacted a foreign government on a subject currently being negotiated. She urged Du Bois to get State Department approval before submitting the petition to the UN. Du Bois, alluding to the growing debate over Palestine, politely dismissed her concerns by joking that "the whole Jewish population of the United States" would

169. Vijaya Pandit to Du Bois, September 25, 1947, Reel 60, *Du Bois*; William Melish to Du Bois, September 30, 1947, ibid.; Harrington to Al Smith, October 2, 1947, Box 637, File "United Nations Petition (NAACP): 1947, Oct," *Papers of the NAACP*; Du Bois to William Melish, October 6, 1947, Reel 60, *Du Bois*; T. Tokina to Smythe, October 10, 1947, ibid.

170. White to Du Bois, memo, January 29, 1947, ibid.; Du Bois to White, January 31, 1947, ibid.

171. Du Bois to Eleanor Roosevelt, July 17, 1946, Reel 59, ibid.; Eleanor Roosevelt to Du Bois, July 22, 1946, ibid.; White and Du Bois to Eleanor Roosevelt, September 22, 1947, Box 637, File "United Nations Petition (NAACP): 1947, Jan.–Sept.," *Papers of the NAACP*; Du Bois to Eleanor Roosevelt, October 14, 1947, Reel 60, *Du Bois*; Du Bois to Walter White, memo, November 24, 1947, ibid.

172. Warren R. Austin to Hugh H. Smythe, October 9, 1947, ibid.; John P. Humphrey to Du Bois, October 9, 1947, ibid.; Du Bois to Warren R. Austin, October 14, 1947, ibid.; Du Bois to Trygve Lie, October 14, 1947, ibid.; Warren R. Austin to Du Bois, October 21, 1947, Box 637, File "United Nations Petition (NAACP): 1947, Jan.–Sept.," *Papers of the NAACP*.

be imprisoned if it were illegal to contact the UN. And, then, in a more somber tone, he declared that he would be "very happy to go to jail in defense of the right to petition the United Nations."[173]

That steely determination led Du Bois to force the issue. The relationship between White and Du Bois was already tense, and the scholar began to suspect that, with the impending release of the PCCR's report, the executive secretary was beginning to hedge his bets and pull back on the Association's UN efforts. Du Bois therefore decided to circumvent Walter White and independently put public pressure on the UN to act. Ollie Harrington had already intimated to members of the African American press corps that the Association had prepared a document that would humiliate the American government. It was, therefore, a relatively simple task for Du Bois to convince the public relations director to leak the petition, without White's consent, to the *New York Times* and several other influential newspapers.[174] Although White was furious with Du Bois, the plan worked. Sunday's *New York Times* carried Du Bois' charges that the American South, because of its racism and systematic corruption of the democratic process, posed a greater threat to the United States than the Soviets ever could. The *Times* could only conclude that it "is not the Soviet Union that threatens the United States so much as Mississippi: 'Not Stalin and Molotov but Bilbo and Rankin.'"[175] Humphrey capitulated and agreed to receive the NAACP's petition on October 23, 1947.[176]

Du Bois had won that round but the next battle, which was imperative for his plan, required a full press corps and numerous observers to witness the presentation and thus provide extensive coverage about the conditions in black America. As could be expected, the State Department and the UN balked at the NAACP's plans to turn the presentation into a media event. Sandifer therefore applauded the way Humphrey refused to let the Association "make a rather spectacular ceremony of the presentation

173. Marian Wynn Perry to Du Bois, memo, October 9, 1947, Reel 60, *Du Bois*; Du Bois to Marian Wynn Perry, October 14, 1947, ibid.

174. White to Du Bois, memo, October 11, 1947, Box 637, File "United Nations Petition (NAACP): 1947, Oct," *Papers of the NAACP*; Oliver Harrington to Agnes Meyer, October 11, 1947, ibid.; Rayford W. Logan, diary, November 16, 1947, *Logan Papers*.

175. George Streator, "Negroes to Bring Cause Before UN: Statement Charges that South Offers Greater U.S. Threat than Soviet Activities," *New York Times*, October 12, 1947, 52.

176. Du Bois to Walter White, memo, October 17, 1947, Reel 60, *Du Bois*; NAACP, *An Appeal to the World: A Statement on the Denial of Human Rights to Minorities in the Case of Citizens of Negro Descent in the United States of America and an Appeal to the United Nations for Redress* (New York: National Association for the Advancement of Colored People, 1947).

with several hundred people present." Indeed, the State Department was overjoyed that Humphrey insisted on "limiting those coming...to 12 or 15 of the leaders of the Association."[177]

The next order of business was to ensure that Eleanor Roosevelt, a press magnet, would steer clear of the presentation. After Sandifer advised "Mrs. R" that she "should not attend," she diplomatically turned down Walter White's invitation and conveyed that, "as an individual I should like to be present, but as a member of the delegation... I should not seem to be lining myself up in any particular way on any subject.... It is just a matter of proper procedure." White, who truly valued and wanted to continue to nurture his relationship with the highly respected Mrs. Roosevelt, graciously accepted her rationale and made clear that he did not want to do anything that would compromise her position or integrity. He therefore asked whether "there would be any value in the NAACP sending a representative" to the CHR meeting in Switzerland where the petition might come up for debate. "As to sending a representative to Geneva," Mrs. Roosevelt quickly replied, "I really do not think it necessary or of value." So who, exactly, the NAACP's standard bearer in Geneva would be was unclear. White appeared to believe that, in the end, Mrs. Roosevelt would come through. Du Bois, however, shared neither White's high opinion nor faith in the former first lady. That seismic difference in opinion would eventually rend two of the NAACP's greatest leaders apart. Until that time, however, the two men would present a united front before the UN.[178]

Walter White began the Association's significantly scaled-back presentation by noting that "freedom is indivisible," yet there had been repeated attempts to deny people of color their freedom by "exploiting" them solely on the basis of "color, race, or creed." White declared that the "injustice against black men in America" had "repercussions" for the "brown men of India, yellow men of China, and black men of Africa." As long as discrimination existed in the most powerful nation in the world, White surmised, the rest of the world would be caught in its wake and plagued with continued war and unrest. Du Bois then noted, in a veiled reference to the United States' declaration to save democracy in Greece, that there were twice as many African Americans as Greeks. If democracy was to be saved, its salvation had to begin at home. He then stated that African Americans were "as loyal" as any other citizens and demanded a world

177. Durward Sandifer to Warren Austin, memo, October 21, 1947, Box 20, File "General Assembly-Second Session-National Association for the Advancement of Colored People," *Records of the Bureau of International Organization Affairs, United Nations Delegations Position Papers and Background Books, 1945–1964, RG 59* (hereafter *Bureau of Int'l Organization: RG 59*).

178. Du Bois to Walter White, memo, November 24, 1947, Reel 60, *Du Bois*.

hearing to "persuade" the United States to "be just to its own people." This could not be achieved, he continued, if the UN insisted on burying the NAACP's petition in the "archives."[179]

Humphrey patiently listened to Du Bois' and White's pleas, then carefully articulated UN policy. "I must make clear to you," Humphrey declared, that the petition would be treated as "confidential." Even at that, he continued, "the Commission ... still has no power to take any action ... concerning human rights." Recognizing the inanity of his own statement and attempting to smooth what was becoming a tense session, Humphrey assured the NAACP officials that their effort would not be in vain. In fact, Humphrey offered, the Commission would review the petition as background material for "formulating an International Bill of Human Rights" and helping the Commission define the "'human rights and fundamental freedoms'" alluded to in the UN Charter.[180]

For Du Bois, that was so unsatisfactory. "What is wrong about human rights," Du Bois explained to White, was "not the lack of pious statements, but the question as to what application is made of them and what is to be done when human rights are denied in the face of law and declarations. For this reason," Du Bois concluded, "I have worked for a year on a specific case of denial of rights."[181] And that year of long, hard work meant that Du Bois would continue to push for a full-scale publicity campaign about the plight of African Americans in the United States. He urged UN Ambassador Austin to place the petition on the General Assembly's agenda because it would "be an excellent thing" if Americans could let the world know that they were "perfectly willing" to perfect democracy in the United States before they tried to export it abroad.[182]

State Department officials, of course, had no intention of putting the NAACP's petition on the UN docket, and thus, officially confirming what, to date, had been dismissed as exaggerations, rumors, and Soviet propaganda. Nonetheless, they were well aware of the international problems

179. "Introductory Statement by Walter White, Executive Secretary of the NAACP, October 23, 1947. On occasion of presentation of Petition to the United Nations," Box 68, File "Articles: W. E. B. Du Bois Preface to Statement on Denial of Human Rights to Negroes, 1947," *Papers of the NAACP*; "Statement of Dr. W. E. B. Du Bois to The Representatives of the Human Rights Commission and its Parent Bodies—The Economic and Social Council and the General Assembly," October 23, 1947, ibid.

180. "Statement by Professor John P. Humphrey, Director, Division of Human Rights, Social Affairs Department," October 23, 1947, Box 637, File "United Nations Petition (NAACP): 1947, Oct.," ibid.

181. W. E. B. Du Bois to Walter White, memo, November 24, 1947, Reel 60, *Du Bois*.

182. Du Bois to Warren R. Austin, October 28, 1947, Box 637, File "United Nations Petition (NAACP): 1947, Jan.–Sept.," *Papers of the NAACP*; Hugh H. Smythe to Estelle Robbins, November 26, 1947, Reel 60, *Du Bois*.

that America's Jim Crow system had caused. For example, in the summer of 1946, as the UN began its first session, Trygve Lie's office had secured lodging for all of the delegations at both the Waldorf-Astoria and in apartments owned by the Metropolitan Life Insurance Company. These establishments, however, had very strict Jim Crow housing policies and brusquely informed the diplomats from Ethiopia, Liberia, and Haiti that there was no room at the inn. Lie was stunned, and he became increasingly frustrated as he met with "great difficulty in placing these three delegations" in anything but "unacceptable" "second and third rate hotels." The exasperated secretary general knew that the problem was Jim Crow, and he insisted that the U.S. delegation "solv[e] this." He had done all that he could. Lie had personally intervened with the chairman of the board of the Waldorf-Astoria, who finally agreed to accept the Ethiopian and Liberian delegations, but not the Haitians. Met Life refused to budge at all. The company representative "bluntly" stated that "no persons of other than the white race, and few, if any, Jews would be admitted." The Philippine and Argentine delegations, which got an ugly glimpse of Jim Crow in operation, immediately registered "intense concern" about this "bad situation" and wanted to know what the U.S. delegation planned to do about it. The State Department scurried to clean up the mess and found a hotel in New York City that would provide shelter for the Haitians. But the Department's most valiant, sustained efforts were targeted at keeping the impending scandal out of the press.[183] The Department also had to scramble to explain away racist treatment of Indian businessmen in Washington, DC, manhandling of a West African dignitary and Haitian diplomats by police and custom officials in Miami and New Orleans, and the latest lynching in the Deep South.[184] In short, America's position as the Jim Crow leader of the "free world" posed a constant, nagging stumbling block to the full implementation of U.S. foreign policy.

Instead of "correct[ing] this sordid situation themselves," however, the United States looked for ways to deflect the NAACP's charges. The Department "anticipated that a number of [MINDIS] Subcommission Members may ... attack the United States for its shortcomings in the

183. Thomas. F. Power, Jr. to Samuel DePalma, memo, June 20, 1947, Box 78, File "Discrimination: Race—U.S., 1947," *RG 84*; Thomas F. Power, Jr. to Warren Austin, memo, August 26, 1947, Box 78, File "Discrimination, 1947," ibid.

184. Gallman to Marshall, telegram, January 10, 1947, Decimal File 811.4016/1-1047, *RG 59*; Memorandum of Conversation, January 15, 1947, Decimal File 811.4016/1-1547, ibid.; Dean Acheson to Morris Rosenthal, March 3, 1947, Decimal File 811.4016/2-1147, ibid.; Rosenthal to Acheson, February 11, 1947, Decimal File 811.4016/2-1147, ibid.; Barber to Briggs, memo, May 8, 1947, Decimal File 811.4016/5-847, ibid.; John J. Macdonald to Marshall, November 5, 1947, Decimal File 811.4016/11-547, ibid.; Walter White to Truman, telegram, October 22, 1947, Box 543, File "OF 93 1947 [2 of 3]," *Truman:OF*.

treatment of Negroes." To blunt this assault, the Department surveyed its missions "throughout the UN Membership asking for information on discrimination occurring in those countries." The object, of course, was to give Jonathan Daniels the ammunition he needed "so that if the U.S. is specifically attacked, he could reply with a specific statement showing that the U.S. is not the only country" that discriminated against sizeable portions of its population. The Department was especially interested in having the final report on the "Study of the USSR Minorities Problems" ready for Daniels to use in Geneva. The State Department also determined that, on a more positive note, it would be "extremely useful" for Daniels to have a "'self-serving' statement that would indicate the very real forward strides" that the United States had made in attaining civil rights for all of its citizens.[185]

The timing for a "self-serving" statement, however, could not have been worse. Not only had the NAACP developed a beautifully written, well-documented petition, but the PCCR had also just issued its official report, *To Secure These Rights*. Jonathan Daniels confided to Mrs. Roosevelt's aide that "whatever may be the difficulties between the historic European idea of a minority and our own, this report frankly, even vigorously, presents the fact that minorities do need protection in the United States." Worse yet, Daniels noted, the report not only revealed the United States as a nation inflicted with "all the evils with which the sub-commission was set up to deal, but" it also illustrated how deeply the United States was "unable or unwilling to . . . do anything effective about it." "In other words," Daniels continued, "between this report and the United States Senate, it seems . . . that [the U.S.] is caught . . . in a strategic position in terms of world opinion which is almost desperate." From that melancholy but accurate assessment, Daniels suggested that the United States should just walk into the UN meeting and "throw . . . [*To Secure These Rights*] on the table . . . before anybody else brings up this document or the discriminations with which it deals."[186] That strategy would eventually come into play, but for now, the U.S. delegation members hoped to defuse the situation by either inviting the NAACP leadership to meet with them directly or having the revered Eleanor Roosevelt handle the matter through a "personal appeal" to Walter White.[187]

To thwart the State Department's efforts, Du Bois barraged the popular and scholarly press with the NAACP's petition and the press

185. Hugh H. Smythe to Estelle Robbins, November 26, 1947, Reel 60, *Du Bois*; Memorandum of Conversation, July 24, 1947, Folder 580, *Daniels Papers*.
186. Jonathan Daniels to James P. Hendrick, October 29, 1947, Folder 597, ibid.; Jonathan Daniels to John W. Halderman, October 30, 1947, Folder 598, ibid.
187. P. M. Burnett to Durwald V. Sandifer, n.d., (October 1947), Box 78, File "Discrimination, Race: U.S., 1947," *RG 84*.

responded.[188] The *Chicago Defender* called the petition, *An Appeal to the World*, a "searing indictment" of America's "failure to practice what it preaches."[189] The National Urban League's editor hailed the petition as "the most strategic move" in race relations for a long time and hoped that it would "make democracy a living force in America and throughout the world."[190] *P.M.* described the NAACP's "memorandum" as "an unpleasant jolt" and a reminder of "the considerable gap between American preaching and practice." For journalist Saul Padover, the Truman Doctrine and the constant American harping about human rights abuses in Eastern Europe now had an "unconvincing sound." He saw that, "if there is not much democracy in Hungary and Bulgaria, there is possibly even less of it . . . in South Carolina and Mississippi."[191] In the same issue, *P.M.* carried Attorney General Tom Clark's speech to the National Association of Attorneys General. Clark said that he was "humiliated" that African Americans had to seek redress of their grievances from the UN and vowed to use the full power of the Justice Department, "as is permitted under the law," to "protect the life and liberties" of African Americans. All of the press, however, was not positive. The *San Francisco Chronicle* concluded that the NAACP leadership must obviously like "rejection," because there was no way that the Association would be able "to get around" the UN's "domestic jurisdiction" clause. For the *Morgantown Post* in West Virginia, the NAACP's action was nothing but a "publicity" stunt that would "embarrass" the United States and "furnish . . . Soviet Russia with new ammunition."[192]

At the meeting in Geneva, just as the *Morgantown Post* predicted, the Kremlin, with *An Appeal to the World* strapped in its holster, went gunning for the United States. This, of course, was the same Soviet delegation that, just a few months earlier, argued strenuously that the CHR "was not empowered" to even acknowledge petitions. But now, the Soviets were not about to miss an opportunity to take a direct shot at the nation which, under the guise of strengthening democracy in Greece and Europe, had launched the multibillion dollar Truman Doctrine and the Marshall Plan. Daniels' nightmare was coming true. The United States was getting ready

188. Du Bois' Department of Special Research mailed copies of the NAACP's petition to a variety of newspapers. See, "Review Copies of NAACP UN Petition Sent to:," January 15, 1948, Reel 62, *Du Bois*.
189. Robert S. Abbott, "An Important Appeal," *Chicago Defender*, November 1, 1947.
190. Dutton Ferguson to Hugh H. Smythe, October 20, 1947, Reel 60, *Du Bois*.
191. Saul K. Padover, "How About Democracy for Negroes Too?" *P.M.*, October 14, 1947.
192. A digest of press responses is included in, Hugh H. Smythe to Cedric Dover, November 3, 1947, Reel 60, *Du Bois*. Also see, Hugh H. Smythe to *Common Sense*, "American Negroes Petition the United Nations for Help in Removing Discrimination," October 29, 1947, Reel 60, *Du Bois*.

Photo 2.3. In a clearly staged photograph that bore no resemblance to the coming blow-up over *An Appeal to the World,* Mrs. Roosevelt and Board member Dr. James McClendon chart the NAACP's 1947 course of action with Walter White (rear left), Roy Wilkins (rear right), and Thurgood Marshall. *Visual Materials from the NAACP Records, Library of Congress.*

to be attacked "at its most vulnerable points" and exposed as a "nation of hypocrites."[193]

The combatants in MINDIS unsheathed their weapons early. At the very first session, Daniels launched his preemptive strike and announced that the "recent report of President's Committee on Civil Rights" reflected the concerns and seriousness with which the U.S. government viewed racial discrimination, and it also embodied the president's commitment to develop "measures to improve [the] situation."[194] The Soviet delegate, Alexander P. Borisov, in turn, exploited every opportunity to launch into a "severe attack on U.S. discrimination practices." He "dwelt on lynchings and . . . [on] the UN petition of the NAACP." He "cited [the] writings of Ex-senator Bilbo," and he reminded his subcommission colleagues that discrimination in the United States could also be very "subtle" as in the

193. Jonathan Daniels to James Hendrick, October 29, 1947, Folder 597, *Daniels Papers.*
194. Troutman to Secretary of State, telegram, November 26, 1947, Folder 603, ibid.

case of "New York hotels [that] . . . refus[e] to accept colored guests" by saying there is a "lack of accommodations."[195] This was clearly turning into the "pretty hot job" that Daniels predicted, and there was no relief in sight.[196] When Daniels proposed that MINDIS review all petitions except those in which a nation invoked the domestic jurisdiction clause, Borisov said that the Americans' proposal did "not have the purpose of dealing with minorities problems," at all " but rather of avoiding them . . . . Such proposals," he added, "were natural coming from [a] country which wished to avoid dealing with discrimination." At that point, Daniels had clearly had enough and fired back that "such remarks came with poor grace from [a] country which achieved equality by uniformly suppressing human rights, which refused to allow wives of alien husbands to leave [the] country, which used minorities as puppets, and which concealed information about internal conditions."[197] Those impassioned and embittered exchanges were just the opening volley as MINDIS turned its attention to *An Appeal to the World.*

Borisov argued vigorously for the inclusion of the NAACP's – and the National Negro Congress's – petition on the UN's agenda. Daniels countered by rhetorically throwing *To Secure These Rights* on the table again and acknowledging that "he was aware of the problem of the Negroes in the United States . . . , and that the President himself [had already] authorized a comprehensive investigation of this problem." In other words, it was being handled, at the highest levels, and thus, there was no reason for UN interference. Daniels knew, of course, that "this report of the President's Committee ha[d] no force and effect beyond its publicity value," but that did not need to be discussed at Geneva. What was important was that the United States *appeared* to be solving its human rights problems with vigor, honesty, and forthrightness. Could other nations, namely the Soviet Union, say the same? Daniels then made clear that it would be "invidious" to elevate one group's petition over the others, and he taunted Borisov with the unconfirmed rumors that the Soviets were running a gulag system that would make Alabama's chain gangs look like a stroll through Central Park. Daniels even hinted that there were petitions floating somewhere in the UN bureaucracy that could attest to the horrors of Siberia. Afraid that this was yet another "trick" by the Americans, Borisov parried every attempt to include all petitions on the subcommission's agenda and continued to press for the NAACP's and

195. Halderman to Secretary of State, telegram, November 29, 1947, ibid.; Troutman to Secretary of State, telegram, December 1, 1947, ibid.; Troutman to Secretary of State, telegram, December 4, 1947, ibid.
196. Jonathan Daniels to Charles S. Johnson, August 29, 1947, Folder 585, ibid.
197. Troutman to Secretary of State, telegram, December 3, 1947, Folder 603, ibid.

the NNC's. Daniels countered, in a line of reasoning similar to that of South Africa's a year earlier, that because the UN had no International Bill of Human Rights, it would be impossible to determine if blacks had a legitimate complaint. Finally, Daniels asserted, the UN simply did not have in place the machinery to receive and investigate petitions alleging human rights abuses. After days of wrangling and numerous points of order, Borisov's attempts to place the NAACP's petition before the UN went down to resounding defeat.[198]

Back home in North Carolina, Daniels walked away from his sojourn in international diplomacy absolutely furious with Walter White. The Southern liberal railed that "our colored friends led by Walter White are now damning me up and down the street in connection with the meeting" simply "to cover . . . [their] embarrassment . . . that their petition was used as a political weapon by our Russian friends." Daniels then began to gloat, "I suspect that right now he is threshing around in pretty difficult waters." "The espousal of the N.A.A.C.P. petition by the Russian member of our Subcommission at Geneva . . . must be creating a rather disturbing situation for . . . White." And that situation was going to get even worse, Daniels was sure, because the NAACP had made a big "mistake in defending [the] Russian position."[199]

198. "Sub-Commission on Prevention of Discrimination and Protection of Minorities, Draft Resolution proposed by Mr. A. P. Borisov," E/CN.4/SUB.2/24, December 1, 1947, *UN*; Jonathan Daniels to James Hendrick, October 29, 1947, Folder 597, *Daniels Papers*; Troutman to Secretary of State, airgram, November 26, 1947, Folder 603, ibid.; "Proposal of Mr. M. R. Masani (India) with Regard to the Implementation of Human Rights," December 1, 1947, *UN*; "Amendment to Mr. Borisov's Resolution (E/CN.4/Sub.2/24) Proposed by Mr. M. A. Masani (India)," December 2, 1947, ibid.; "Sub-Commission on the Prevention of Discrimination and the Protection of Minorities: First Session, Summary Record of the Thirteenth Meeting," E/CN.4/Sub.2/SR/13, December 2, 1947, ibid.; "First Session: Summary Record of the Fourteenth Meeting," E/CN.4/Sub.2/SR.14, December 3, 1947, ibid.; "First Session: Report Submitted to the Commission on Human Rights by the Sub-Commission on the Prevention of Discrimination and the Protection of Minorities," December 5, 1947, ibid.; "First Session: Summary Record of the Eighteenth Meeting," December 7, 1947, ibid.; Marian Wynn Perry, "Untitled," (n.d. [1948]), Box 635, File "United Nations General Assembly, November 1948–49," *Papers of the NAACP*; "UN Turns Down Petition," *Philadelphia Tribune*, December 13, 1947. The editorial announced that "The United States will be spared, for a while at least, the washing of its dirty 'racial' linen in full view of the entire world . . ."; "UN Group Kills Probe of Bias on U.S. Negro," *Daily News*, December 4, 1947, in Box 637, File "United Nations Petition (NAACP): 1947, Nov.–Dec.," *Papers of the NAACP*.

199. Jonathan Daniels to Mrs. Robert Alexander, December 20, 1947, Folder 602, *Daniels Papers*; Jonathan Daniels to Peter Bagley, December 23, 1947, ibid.; Jonathan Daniels to Philleo Nash, December 29, 1947, Folder 603, ibid.; Jonathan Daniels to A. G. Mezerik, December 29, 1947, ibid.; Jonathan Daniels to Mark McCloskey, December 31, 1947, Folder 604, ibid.

Eleanor Roosevelt could not have agreed more. Although Du Bois and, possibly White, believed that she was just following State Department orders in Geneva, her advisors and colleagues knew better. Mrs. Roosevelt was actually "following her own inclinations in this matter."[200] Thus, in an article and a series of letters that read like "The Education of Walter White," she emphasized that she was in total accord with the vote and with Daniels's position at Geneva. She was particularly impressed with the way the Southern liberal "made a good fight for the U.S. in the subcommission meetings." She stressed that the NAACP's petition should not have been "singled out in preferance (sic) to others." She intimated that the NAACP had erred in going to the UN because the only petitions the Soviets ever supported were those authored by known "communist dominated" groups. And, even more important, White needed to understand, in no uncertain terms, that the U.S. delegation "could not let the Soviet (sic) get away with attacking the United States" and dodge having their own "shortcomings" exposed.[201] Then, in the ultimate lesson, shortly after the Geneva meeting, Roosevelt submitted her resignation from the NAACP Board of Directors. Although she did not mention the debacle in Geneva, the timing of her resignation seemed to carry with it a very distinct, ominous message. White, of course, pleaded with her to reconsider. The Association "would suffer irreparable loss if you were to resign." She held firm. He begged her again. "[U]nder no circumstances would we want you to resign from the Board. Your name means a great deal to us." His pleas, astutely, never mentioned the UN but only how much needed to be done domestically and how only she had the clout to make that happen. Roosevelt eventually agreed to stay. And White began to rethink seriously the NAACP's investment in the struggle for human rights.[202]

200. Du Bois to Walter White, memo, November 24, 1947, Reel 60, *Du Bois*; John Halderman to Jonathan Daniels, December 30, 1947, Folder 603, *Daniels Papers*.

201. Eleanor Roosevelt to White, December 8, 1947, Box 635, File "United Nations General Assembly, 1946–August 1948,"*Papers of the NAACP*; Eleanor Roosevelt, "My Day: The Delegate from Lebanon was Missing," December 5, 1947, found in Folder 603, *Daniels Papers*; Eleanor Roosevelt to Walter White, January 20, 1948, Box 3389, File "White, Walter, 1947–50," *Roosevelt Papers*.

202. Walter White to Eleanor Roosevelt, December 31, 1947, ibid.; Walter White to Eleanor Roosevelt, January 10, 1948, ibid.; Eleanor Roosevelt to Walter White, January 20, 1948, ibid.

3

Things Fall Apart

I as a man of color... recognize that I have... [o]ne duty alone: that of not renouncing my freedom through my choices.

Frantz Fanon[1]

Nineteen forty-eight was a year of peril. The combination of a presidential election, an intensified Cold War, a hotly debated "International Bill of Human Rights" and a polarized black leadership meant that neither the NAACP nor the Council on African Affairs would emerge unscathed. It did not start out that way, however. It looked like this would be an incredible opportunity to capitalize on shifting political fortunes, the first enunciation of an international human rights standard, and the president's need for the black vote.

From his vantage point, presidential aide Clark Clifford was certainly aware that the Democrats, and especially Truman, could not continue doing business as usual. A full year before the election, Clifford saw threats to Truman's presidency everywhere. New York Governor Thomas Dewey, undoubtedly the Republican party's presidential nominee, was surrounded by a group of shrewd political strategists who had the wherewithal to make him virtually invincible. Clifford warned Truman that the New York governor would "be a highly dangerous candidate," who would be "even more difficult to defeat than in 1944." Yet, while the GOP seemed unified and ready to seize the White House, the Democratic party was "an unhappy alliance" of "three misfit groups" who, Clifford worried, may or may not show up at "the polls on the first Tuesday after the first Monday of November 1948."[2]

1. Frantz Fanon, *Black Skins White Mask* (New York: Grove Press, Inc., 1967), 228–29.
2. Clark Clifford to Truman, November 19, 1947, Box 23, File "Confidential Memo to the President [Clifford-Rowe Memorandum of November 19, 1947] (1 of 2)," *Papers of Clark Clifford*, Harry S Truman Presidential Library, Independence, Missouri (hereafter

The fractures in the party were even more apparent as Roosevelt's former vice president, Henry Wallace, prepared to wrench the left wing of the Democratic party away and run as a third-party candidate.[3] Wallace had also served as Truman's secretary of commerce but was fired for openly denouncing the strategy of containment. Wallace's anti-Cold War stance immediately attracted a range of supporters, including the Communist Party, USA. Clifford, however, cautioned the president that it would be foolish to believe that the Communists were Wallace's only base of support. As Clifford well knew, despite his plan to "identify" Wallace with the Communists and thereby "isolate him in the public mind," the former vice president's idealism and outspoken aversion to war with the Soviet Union had also attracted a very active, articulate core of young progressives as well. Moreover, Wallace's brand of racial liberalism, his seemingly genuine desire to address the major civil rights issues in America, could prove overwhelmingly appealing to African American voters who were disgusted with the Southern Democrats' intransigence. Finally, Clifford continued, Wallace was even more dangerous than the political analysts believed because "there is something almost Messianic in his belief today that he is the Indispensable Man."[4]

Eleanor Roosevelt joined Clifford's chorus of impending doom and counseled that if Truman continued on the same do-nothing course, he would lose the election. The president had "produced very little in the past few years," Roosevelt warned. As a result, "Mr. Wallace will cut in on us because he can say we have given lip service" and not much else to desperately needed social reforms. She, therefore, predicted that Truman would pay the ultimate price for his administration's stalled progressive agenda and "domination" by the "Military and Wall Street." Cozying up to the GOP's power base, Roosevelt implied, was just plain stupid. "Believe me" she warned, "it is going to be impossible to elect a Democrat...by appealing to conservatives." Truman simply could not beat the GOP at its own game. It was time, instead, for Truman to play to the Democrats' strength, which meant that he was "going to need Jewish and Negro votes and" just as important, he would have to do something "about it from that point of view." Truman knew that she was right. He admitted that the neverending attempts by the Southern Democrats to

Clifford Papers); Clark Clifford with Richard Holbrooke, *Counsel to the President: A Memoir* (New York: Random House, 1991), 192.

3. Zachary Karabell, *The Last Campaign: How Harry Truman Won the 1948 Election* (New York: Alfred A. Knopf, 2000), 31–33.
4. Clark Clifford to Truman, November 19, 1947, Box 23, File "Confidential Memo to the President [Clifford-Rowe Memorandum of November 19, 1947] (1 of 2)," *Clifford Papers*.

"turn the clock back" rather than deal with the pressing housing, labor, and civil rights issues on the nation's agenda had put his election prospects in serious jeopardy.[5]

Truman's electoral journey was made even more tortuous by Roosevelt's son, Jimmy, and other New Dealers, who believed that the paucity of social reforms reflected Truman's betrayal of FDR's legacy. In a desperate search for an alternative to the seemingly unelectable Missouri plow horse, the New Dealers openly courted World War II hero, General Dwight D. Eisenhower. Eisenhower, however, had never publicly stated his ideological stance on any of the important social issues, nor had he declared that he was, in fact, a registered Democrat. It seemed as if the Roosevelt faction believed that a total political unknown was still infinitely better than Truman. Given those horrible odds – a Republican juggernaut on one side, the Messianic, Indispensable Man on the other, and treacherous allies at his back – Truman appeared destined to lose. But Clifford had a plan.[6]

Clifford's strategy rested on two key premises. First, Truman had to find some way to attract the all-important, yet "up for grabs," black vote.[7] This would not be easy. The stunning 1946 midterm election, which resulted in the Republicans seizing both houses of Congress, was "due in large part to the black vote," because although African Americans had abandoned the Party of Lincoln in 1936; "they had slowly begun to return to the Republican Party, which seemed to be more amenable and sensitive to their demands."[8] Obviously, as Clifford explained to the president, blacks were becoming "increasingly restive under President Truman, mostly because of the reactionary domination exercised over the Democratic Party by the Congressional Southerners." To turn this around, Clifford advised, Truman would have to make some "new and real efforts (as distinguished from mere political gestures which are today thoroughly understood and strongly resented by sophisticated Negro leaders)." "Under the tutelage of Walter White," Clifford continued, "the Negro

5. Eleanor Roosevelt to Truman, January 16, 1948, Box 4560, File "Harry S Truman 1947 and 1948," *Roosevelt Papers*; Eleanor Roosevelt to Truman, February 20, 1948, ibid.; Roosevelt to Truman, n.d., ibid.; Truman to Eleanor Roosevelt, January 19, 1948, ibid.

6. For the full story on the Memorandum, its initial authorship by James Rowe, who was too closely allied with an avowed enemy of Truman, Thomas Corcoran, for the president to accept any of the recommendations, and its subsequent redrafting by Clifford see, Clifford, *Counsel to the President*, 189–94, and David McCullough, *Truman* (New York: Simon and Schuster, 1992), 590–92.

7. Clark Clifford to Truman, November 19, 1947, Box 23, File "Confidential Memo to the President [Clifford-Rowe Memorandum of November 19, 1947] (1 of 2)," *Clifford Papers*.

8. Frederickson, *The Dixiecrat Revolt*, 52.

voter has become a cynical, hard-boiled trader," who now held "the balance of power in Presidential elections for the simple arithmetical reason that the Negroes not only vote in a bloc but are geographically concentrated in the pivotal, large and closely contested electoral states such as New York, Illinois, Pennsylvania, Ohio, and Michigan." The South, Clifford acknowledged, would undoubtedly get very indignant about anything that even hinted at "measures to protect the rights of minority groups," but, given the very real possibility of Truman's defeat, the South's displeasure was "the lesser of two evils." Clifford's second premise therefore flowed naturally from his first. Regardless of how liberal Truman's policies evolved in the upcoming year, Clifford was convinced that the South, which despised the Party of Lincoln, could never revolt. It simply had nowhere else to go.[9]

African American leaders had also done their own analysis of the 1948 election. Clifford was right, no "Tammany turkey" or "mere political gesture" was going to be enough. The black leadership wanted something big. A determined Walter White told Truman that it was time for the federal government to "put its own house in order," and he urged the president to issue an executive order that would eliminate discrimination in hiring and promotion in federal agencies.[10] Similarly, A. Philip Randolph, as chair of the Committee to End Jim Crow in the Military, was equally determined that Truman prove his civil rights mettle. In January 1948, Randolph demanded an audience with the president to discuss desegregating the armed forces. When he was rebuffed, Randolph fired back that it was just impossible to conceive of anything that Truman could possibly be working on that took precedence over the "long-accumulated grievances" of 15 million black Americans. Taken aback, Truman's staff belatedly recognized that "Phil Randolph . . . is an important Negro" and arranged for a meeting the first week of February – *after* Truman's landmark message to Congress.[11]

On February 2, 1948, in a move that was clearly an integral component of Clifford's electoral strategy, Truman struck at the core of the Old South's antebellum value system.[12] Before a hostile, Southern-dominated Congress, Truman presented an omnibus civil rights package that included

9. Clark Clifford to Truman, November 19, 1947, Box 23, File "Confidential Memo to the President [Clifford-Rowe Memorandum of November 19, 1947] (1 of 2)," *Clifford Papers*.
10. White to Truman, January 28, 1948, Box 633, File "Harry S Truman, 1946–49," *Papers of the NAACP*.
11. A. Philip Randolph to Truman, January 12, 1948, Box 548, File "OF 93B 1945–June 1948, [2 of 2]," *Truman:OF*; David K. Niles to Matt Connelly, January 20, 1948, memo, Box 548, File "OF 93B 1948–June 1948, [2 of 2]," ibid.
12. Frederickson, *The Dixiecrat Revolt*, 69.

anti-lynching and anti-poll tax measures, as well as a Fair Employment Practices Commission. Moreover, the president announced that, in the near future, he would issue executive orders to end segregation in the armed forces and discrimination in the federal government.[13]

Elated, Walter White immediately congratulated Truman for his "courage." Then, in his syndicated columns, the executive secretary blasted the "Southern Bourbons," "conservative Republicans," and "supporters of Henry Wallace" for accusing Truman of "'playing politics'" with the black vote. To refute that charge, White recited Truman's "quiet, ... consistent" support of anti-lynching legislation during the president's years in the Senate. White pointed to the PCCR and *To Secure These Rights* as proof that the president's commitment remained strong even after he entered the White House. As further evidence of the president's sincerity, the executive secretary reminded his readers of Truman's rousing address at the NAACP's 1947 National Convention. White then summarized what he believed to be an extraordinary record of civil rights achievement and declared that this clearly was not the career of a political opportunist. It was simply Truman being Truman. The president did not "play politics" by "evading or postponing action on this most explosive of American issues." Rather, "in his quiet Missouri fashion Truman has demonstrated that he is earnest when he says that 'we must correct the remaining imperfections in our practice of Democracy.'"[14]

Editorials in the *Chicago Defender* and other major newspapers were equally effusive as they called the speech "'Lincolnesque.'" In doing so, they paid Truman the highest compliment imaginable from the black community. Those glowing reviews, the White House beamed, were rippling through the hands of millions who read the black press. Of course,

13. Text of President's Statement to Congress February 2, 1948 Regarding Civil Rights, SD/A/C.3/53, Box 175, File "Background Book: Committee III (Social Humanitarian, and Cultural), Volume IV," *RG 84*; "Dixie Democrats to Present Protest to McGrath Monday Opening Intra-Party Battle," February 21, 1948, *Providence Journal* found in Box 59, File "Civil Rights and Southern Splits: Desk Corresp. Clippings–Senatorial," *Papers of Senator John J. McGrath*, Harry S Truman Presidential Library, Independence, Missouri (hereafter *Sen. McGrath Papers*); Nadine Cohodas, *Strom Thurmond and the Politics of Southern Change* (New York: Simon & Schuster, 1993), 127–42; "Transcript of Conference of Southern Governors with Senator J. Howard McGrath, Chairman of the Democratic National Committee," February 23, 1948, Box 26, File "Governors, Southern Conference of 1948, Proposed Legislation–Senatorial," *Sen. McGrath Papers;* McCullough, *Truman*, 593; Clifford, *Counsel to the President*, 203–08.

14. White to Truman, February 2, 1948, telegram, Box 633, File "Harry S. Truman, 1946–49," *Papers of the NAACP*; Walter White, ["The President Means It"], February 12, 1948, Box 81, File "Articles: Walter White Syndicated Column, 1949," *Papers of the NAACP;* Walter White, Untitled Article, February 27, 1948, Box 74, File "Articles: Walter White *Chicago Defender* Columns, 1948," ibid.; Walter White, untitled *Chicago Defender* article, April 5, 1948, ibid.

Photo 3.1. The alliance that infuriated Du Bois. Walter White with President Truman and Mrs. Roosevelt at the Lincoln Memorial shortly before Truman addressed the NAACP Convention, June 29, 1947.
National Park Service Photograph – Abbie Rowe. Courtesy of Harry S Truman Library.

it was going to take more than a mere speech to sway the African American leadership fully; but, make no mistake, the seduction had definitely begun.

It is also true, as well, though, that the South's vehement response – an angry meeting with the head of the Democratic National Committee (DNC) demanding a retraction of Truman's "un-American" message of racial equality, followed by a very public and embarrassing boycott of *the* major Democratic function in Washington, and punctuated by a delegation of Southern "liberals" who told Truman exactly where he and his civil rights message could go – shook the White House's confidence about Clifford's prediction. To give the South some time to calm down, Truman refused to issue either of the executive orders, and his courting of the black vote quickly began to look more like harmless, misguided flirtation that neither he nor the South were going to let get out of hand.[15] Years later, Truman recalled that his February speech had

15. White to David Niles, February 16, 1948, Box 27, File "Civil Rights/Negro Affairs, July 1947–48," *Niles Papers*; David K. Niles to Truman, memo, February 16, 1948,

"stirred up a hornets' nest" of trouble. Southerners were furious because it looked like "the nigras" had successfully seduced him into destroying Jim Crow. And then "the niggers were upset" because he appeared to be reneging on his civil rights promises and knuckling under to the South's threats.[16] All Truman wanted in 1948 was just some time for things to cool down.

Walter White disagreed. All a cooling off period would do was freeze the status quo. Thus, in early April, he alerted the president that, although the speech was wonderful, it was not enough. The African American community, White declared, was "eagerly awaiting the issuance of your promised executive order against discrimination in the Federal service." In New Orleans, for example, White noted, "eighty percent of the persons rejected for appointment by one Federal agency were colored." After detailing other instances of blatant discrimination in hiring by the federal government, White then reaffirmed the importance of the executive order and remarked, in a veiled, threatening way, that in this critical election year, the implementation of the civil rights program would be "*the* measuring rod by which candidates . . . will be judged."[17]

Late the next month, with still no signs of an executive order on the horizon, White grew more and more concerned that Truman's inaction would allow Henry Wallace to gain a strong foothold in the black community. Wallace, in White's opinion, was devious, unelectable, a Communist dupe, and, above all else, a sure way to put the "coolly efficient" and "opportunistic" Dewey in the White House. Thus, to fill what he considered to be a dangerous void created by Truman's silence, White planned to issue a statement that would keep the president's promises squarely before African American voters.[18]

Box 27, File "Civil Rights/Negro Affairs 1949–52," ibid.; "Dixie Democrats to Present Protest to McGrath Monday Opening Intra-Party Battle," February 21, 1948, *Providence Journal* found in Box 59, File "Civil Rights and Southern Splits: Desk Corresp. Clippings–Senatorial," *Sen. McGrath Papers*; Cohodas, *Strom Thurmond*, 127–42; "Transcript of Conference of Southern Governors with Senator J. Howard McGrath, Chairman of the Democratic National Committee," February 23, 1948, Box 26, File "Governors, Southern Conference of 1948, Proposed Legislation–Senatorial," *Sen. McGrath Papers;* McCullough, *Truman*, 593; Clifford, *Counsel to the President*, 203–08; Frederickson, *The Dixiecrat Revolt*, 76–81, 98–100.

16. Harry S Truman, *Decision: The Conflicts of Harry S Truman*, Episode 16 "Give'em Hell Harry," produced by Independence Productions, Inc., Screen Gems, Inc., 1964, Harry S Truman Presidential Library, Independence, Missouri.
17. White to Truman, April 7, 1948, Box 1235, File "413 (1945–49)," *Truman:OF*. (Emphasis added.)
18. Report of NAACP Labor Department at the 38th Annual Conference in Washington, DC, June 26, 1947, found in Box 3338, File "NAACP, 1945–47," *Roosevelt Papers*; White, "The Candidates' Record: II–Thomas E. Dewey," September 16, 1948, Box 81, File "Articles: Walter White Syndicated Column, 1948," *Papers of the NAACP*.

Clarence Mitchell, NAACP labor secretary, vehemently disagreed with this approach and advised White to hold off on anything that even remotely looked like praise for Truman. Too much time had passed, and there was nothing, at least as far as he could tell, to show for all of the president's February bravado. Mitchell, therefore, insisted that Truman produce something "specific," before the NAACP went publicly out on a limb praising a man whose greatest accomplishment was a speech.[19]

This was excellent advice because White was dancing on the precipice. As early as December 1947, the Association leadership, in direct violation of the NAACP's nonpartisan rule, decided to support Truman, who "though far from perfect," was its best hope for securing the civil rights legislation the Association wanted. There was also a growing consensus within the upper echelons of the NAACP that Wallace, with his demonstrated commitment to civil rights, posed the greatest threat to Truman's election and, therefore, had to be discredited.[20]

As a result, White marshaled substantial NAACP resources as well as those of other organizations to find the most damning evidence. White especially targeted Wallace's record as secretary of agriculture under Roosevelt and the hiring practices in Wallace's Commerce Department.[21] The yield for all of this investigative work, however, was decidedly mixed. It was clear that Wallace's Department of Agriculture during the 1930s was a bastion of racism and bigotry. From employment to programs, African Americans were consistently the least, last, and worst served. Yet, it was also clear that, in the late 1940s, Wallace and his hand-picked assistants took on the entrenched racism at the Department of Commerce

19. Clarence Mitchell to White, May 20, 1948, Box 633, File "Harry S Truman, 1946–49," ibid.

20. Alfred Baker Lewis to White, December 19, 1947, Box 665, File "Wallace, Henry A.—General, 1945–48," ibid.; Claude Barnett to Channing Tobias, April 10, 1948, Box 14, File "'T' (folder 1)," *HST:Nash Files*; Channing Tobias to Philleo Nash, March 29, 1948, ibid.; William H. Hastie, interview, *William H. Hastie Oral History*, Harry S Truman Presidential Library, Independence, Missouri (hereafter *Hastie*).

21. White to P. L. Prattis et al., telegram, December 30, 1947, Box 665, File "Wallace, Henry A.—General, 1945–48," *Papers of the NAACP*; Clarence Mitchell to White, telegram, December 31, 1947, ibid.; Leslie Perry to White, memo, March 2, 1948, ibid.; Clarence Mitchell to White, memo, March 2, 1948, ibid.; White, untitled *Chicago Defender* article, January 6, 1948, Box 82, File "Articles: Walter White Syndicated Column Drafts, 1948," ibid.; White, untitled *Chicago Defender* article, "Henry Wallace's Supporters," June 10, 1948, Box 81, File "Articles: Walter White Syndicated Column, 1948," ibid.; White, untitled *Chicago Defender* article, January 9, 1948, Box 74, File "Articles: Walter White *Chicago Defender* columns, 1948," ibid.; White to Wilkins and Moon, memo, July 6, 1948, ibid.; George Streator, "Wallace Attacked by Negro Leader: Accused of 'Muddling' Political Waters by Walter White Before NAACP Meeting," *New York Times*, June 23, 1948, 16.

and forced some of the most reactionary divisions, like the Bureau of the Census, to provide equal employment and promotion opportunities for African Americans. Moreover, at the Patent Office, which had one of the worst reputations in the federal government, one report noted that job opportunities for "Negroes are not quite the blind alleys they [once] were." The report concluded "unmistakably that, with respect to fair employment practices, the Wallace who headed the Department of Commerce was a different man from the Wallace who headed the Department of Agriculture."[22] The NAACP's own Leslie Perry had also alerted White that the only "concrete information" he had been able to uncover revealed that, under Wallace, "an entirely different feeling and spirit pervaded the Department" of Commerce. "It was... understood at all levels that [Wallace] wanted Negroes integrated."[23] That was not what White wanted to hear.

In a January 8, 1948 syndicated column, White had already dismissed Wallace's candidacy as nothing more than a three-ring circus. White predicted that, "once the excitement over a possible third party is tempered by [the] realization that such a move would only mean the election of a reactionary Republican, very few Negroes will throw away their votes." Then, turning his razor-sharp pen on the "reactionary" GOP, White denounced the Republicans' quadrennial concerns over lynching, the poll tax, and segregation as "sheer political opportunism." Like "trained seals," White scoffed, the GOP would agonize about the deplorable state of civil rights and then, after the polls closed, collude with the "Southern wing" of the Democratic party to keep blacks chained in second-class citizenship. White made sure, of course, that he clearly distinguished the "Southern wing" of the Democratic party from Truman's, which, he noted, produced the "courageous report of the President's Committee on Civil Rights... that had given hope... especially [to] the Negro."[24]

That hope, however, was quickly withering away. Since Truman's bold civil rights message in February, the president had done nothing.

22. White to Joseph Lohman, June 2, 1948, Box 665, File "Wallace, Henry A.—General, 1948–49," *Papers of the NAACP*; White to John Fischer, June 2, 1948, ibid.; Will Alexander to White, May 27, 1948, ibid.; White to Will Alexander, June 2, 1948, ibid.; John Fischer to White, July 1, 1948, ibid.; Joseph Lohman to White, June 18, 1948, ibid.

23. Leslie Perry to White, memo, March 2, 1948, Box 665, File "Wallace, Henry A.—General, 1945–48," ibid.

24. Walter White, "Will Henry Wallace Get the Negro Vote," January 8, 1948, Box 27, File "Civil Rights/Negro Affairs, July 1947–48," *Niles Papers*; Walter White, "A New Negro Emerges," July 1, 1948, Box 81, File "Articles: Walter White Syndicated Column, 1949," *Papers of the NAACP*; White to David K. Niles, January 14, 1948, Box 27, File "Civil Rights/Negro Affairs, July 1947–48," *Niles Papers.*

Absolutely nothing. Even the president's Universal Military Training bill, which was winding its way through Congress, still maintained Jim Crow in the armed forces.[25] White concluded that the president needed to understand that he (Truman) had a lot more to worry about than just the Southern Democrats. If Truman really wanted the presidency, White reminded him, he was going to have to wade through the deep waters of civil rights to get there. Therefore, in June, just as Truman prepared to take a "non-political" campaign tour through Chicago and several Western states, White sent him Henry L. Moon's *Balance of Power: The Negro Vote.* Moon's opening statement was unequivocal. Neither "party will be able to get away with the vague and inconclusive . . . party platforms of 1944." "Action is what is demanded, and action *now.*" Moon, like Clifford, had also worked the electoral math, and although they agreed about the importance of the black vote, they disagreed on one key important point – the South. "The Democratic party can afford to sacrifice the entire 127 electoral college votes of the Solid South and win," Moon proclaimed. "It cannot, however, hope for success in a presidential election without the Negro and organized labor."[26] The DNC agreed. The DNC's Kenneth Birkhead advised that, during this unofficial campaign trip, Truman should "appeal to the Negro voter" by emphasizing how the landmark report, *To Secure These Rights*, "offers them great new hope." Birkhead also outlined a series of strategies to woo the black leadership and dispel the pervasive rumor that "the President's Report on Civil Rights" was "nothing more than a 'flash' to corral Negro votes."[27] But, instead, to keep the South mollified, the president decided to say nothing – nothing whatsoever through 9,505 miles, 18 states, and 73 speeches – about civil rights.[28]

By early July, just as the nominating conventions were beginning, Walter White knew that he had done about all that he could to push Truman firmly into a civil rights corner. In March, he had maneuvered the 21 organizations, who drafted the 1948 Declaration of Negro Voters, into adopting the same tenor and tone that he had used in his January 8 article.[29] At the NAACP Annual Convention in June, White summarized

25. Grant Reynolds and A. Philip Randolph to Truman, June 29, 1948, Box 548, File "OF 93B 1945–June 1948," [2 of 2], *Truman:OF.*
26. White to Truman, May 20, 1948, [cross-reference sheet], Box 543, File "OF 93 1948 [3 of 3]," ibid.; William L. Batt, Jr., to Philleo Nash, June 8, 1948, Box 59, File "WH Files-Minorities-Negro Publications-Balance of Power of the Negro Vote by H. L. Moon-Review, June 1948," *Nash Papers* (emphasis in original).
27. Kenneth Birkhead to Bill Batt, memo, May 21, 1948, Box 27, File "Civil Rights/Negro Affairs 1949–52," *Niles Papers.*
28. McCullough, *Truman*, 593, 629.
29. White, untitled *Chicago Defender* article for "Straws in the Wind Department," n.d., Box 74, File "Articles, Walter White *Chicago Defender* Columns, 1948," *Papers of the NAACP*; "Statement by Continuations Committee of Twenty-One Negro

the insurgent, restless mood that pervaded the conference. He declared that the "Republican Tweedledum and Democratic Tweedledee . . . are indistinguishable to the NAACP delegates." African Americans were no longer hypnotized by the GOP's "rattling of Lincoln's bones" or awed by the specter of FDR's ghost. Rather, White declared, "a New Negro," "politically independent and potent" had emerged. This "New Negro," who controlled the electoral balance of power, demanded nothing less than full equality and a president who would deliver. Now, with the nominating conventions fast approaching, it was up to Truman, who was foolishly trying to straddle both the Confederacy and the Freedmen, to rise up and meet White's challenge.[30]

Yet, as the Democratic National Convention loomed, Truman's continued tenure as president was in jeopardy; there was even major doubt about whether he would get the nomination of his party. The factional strife had created seismic fissures in the left and right wings of the Democratic party, and the center was highly unstable and unpredictable. The Jewish community, angry about Truman's vacillation over the creation of a Jewish homeland in Palestine, had apparently repudiated the president's congressional candidate in New York City's midterm election and was ready to reject the president, too. Moreover, after Truman vowed to break a nationwide railroad strike by drafting the workers into the armed forces, only his veto of the anti-union Taft-Hartley Act had eased organized labor's antagonism toward him. The national press, sensing the collapse of the New Deal coalition, began to write Truman's political obituary. Even the site for the upcoming convention, with its wrinkled, used flags and banners left over from the GOP's convention, just added to the suffocating despair. By the time of the Democratic convention in mid-July, the Philadelphia cab drivers joked that, instead of taxis, the Democrats should have ordered hearses.[31]

At the convention, tempers flared in the 93-degree un-air-conditioned center as the Democratic bosses deadlocked over a platform that could satisfy all of the party's "misfit" constituencies. Not surprisingly, a major

Organizations in Presentation of 'Declaration of Negro Voters' to the Democratic National Platform Committee," July 8, 1948, ibid.

30. George Streator, "Wallace Attacked by Negro Leader," June 23, 1948, *New York Times*, found in Box 664, File "Wallace, Henry A.—Clippings and Printed Matter, 1941–48," ibid.; Walter White, "A New Negro Emerges," July 1, 1948, Box 81, File "Articles: Walter White Syndicated Column, 1949," ibid. The "rattling of Lincoln's bones" quote is from a later *Crisis* article, see Stephen J. Spingarn to Mr. Murphy, memo, December 19, 1949, Box 42, File "Internal Security File Civil Rights-Negro File," *SJ Spingarn Papers*.

31. Robert A. Divine, *Foreign Policy and U.S. Presidential Elections: 1940, 1948* (New York: New Viewpoints, 1974), 175–78, 184–88, and 194–200; McCullough, *Truman*, 632–37.

source of friction was the civil rights plank. Instead of incorporating the recommendations from the PCCR, earlier Truman had cut a deal with Mississippi Senator John Rankin to use the same plank from 1944, which "meant that the platform would not go beyond pledging Congress to 'exert its full constitutional powers' to protect the rights of blacks – leaving open the question of what those powers and rights really were."[32] When Walter White saw the do-nothing civil rights splinter in the Democrats' platform, he erupted. "Appeasement will gain [you] nothing," he warned the president, "but [it] will alienate many." And that "many" appeared to be the only people truly supporting Truman. The president even noticed that the only convention speakers who appeared to be "wholeheartedly" for him were two African Americans demanding that the Democrats address the issue of civil rights. The most forceful demand, however, came from Minneapolis Mayor Hubert Humphrey, a member of a vocal insurgency within the Democratic party, who refused to accede to the reactionary demands of the Southerners. As he stood at the podium before a wearied, listless crowd, Humphrey demolished the argument that it was too soon to press for civil rights. America, he declared, was already 172 years too late. "The time has arrived," Humphrey asserted, "for the Democratic Party to get out of the shadow of states' rights and walk . . . into the bright sunshine of human rights."[33]

The crowd went wild – all except the Southern delegates, who seethed in absolute fury. But, inspired by Humphrey's rousing address, the Democrats then fashioned a decidedly stronger civil rights plank that incorporated a commitment to anti-lynching, anti-poll tax, and FEPC legislation. Rep. Estes Kefauver (D-TN) was beside himself with anguish. In his opinion, this was the nation, once again, just like during Reconstruction, pandering to the black vote by trying to "make . . . a whipping boy of the South." The South, frankly, was not going to sit idly by and watch its cherished way of life, its time-honored traditions trounced by vote-grubbing politicians. The Southern Democrats therefore stalked out of the convention, formed their own political party, the Dixiecrats, and nominated South Carolina Governor Strom Thurmond for president. Thurmond noted that the break was absolutely necessary because, unlike FDR, "Truman really means it."[34]

32. Ashmore, *Civil Rights and Wrongs*, 71.

33. White to Truman, telegram, July 13, 1948, Box 1511, File "N," *Truman:OF*; McCullough, *Truman*, 632–40.

34. Quoted in, ibid., 645; Cohodas, *Strom Thurmond*, 126–27, 148, and 154–69; Congressional Record-House, July 29, 1948, found in Box 10, File "Civil Rights Official Memoranda 1956–1955," Records of E. Frederic Morrow, Dwight D. Eisenhower Presidential Library, Abilene, Kansas (hereafter *Morrow Records*).

"Let'em Walk!" a euphoric White declared.[35] "WHOOPEE!" exclaimed an editorial cartoon in the *Chicago Defender* that showed a bloodied, prostrate Southern boxer knocked out cold by Truman's *To Secure These Rights* and counted out by a "New Democratic Party."[36] A new Democratic party, indeed! The South's exodus had just destroyed Clifford's electoral formula for victory. Clifford had initially assumed that, as long as Truman carried the South, the president "could lose New York, Pennsylvania, Illinois, New Jersey, Ohio, Massachusetts – all the 'big' states – and still win."[37] Now, without the South, Truman could not afford to dismiss any vote, anywhere, especially in those "big states" with their substantial black populations. The NAACP had already made it very clear that the price for that vote was something real and significant on the civil rights front. Now, unshackled from the South's antebellum leg irons, Truman and the Democratic party finally took their first, real step out of the shadow of states' rights. On July 27, 1948, just a few days after the convention and the South's angry exit, Truman issued two executive orders, one desegregating the armed forces and the other forbidding discrimination in the federal government.[38]

The NAACP swooned. Words like "historic," "courageous," and "sincere" dripped from White's pen. The executive secretary admired the way Truman just "called the bluff" of the "race baiting" Southerners, ignored the bad recommendations of his "unwisely chosen advisors," and launched an all-out "assault on the citadels of prejudice." Yet, White did not stop there. He instructed the NAACP's public relations director, Henry Lee Moon, to provide a digest of clippings from the black press for the White House staff to analyze.[39] NAACP Board member William H. Hastie, governor of the Virgin Islands, was also mesmerized by

35. White to David Niles, July 21, 1948, Box 27, File "Civil Rights/Negro Affairs, 1949–52," *Niles Papers*.
36. "The Winner," July 24, 1948, *Chicago Defender* found in Box 62, File "WH Files-Political-1948-Campaign Democratic Convention, News Clippings," *Nash Papers*.
37. Clark Clifford to Truman, memo, November 19, 1947, Box 23, File "Confidential Memo to the President [Clifford-Rowe Memorandum of November 19, 1947] {1 of 2}," *Clifford Papers*.
38. Ibid.; Clifford, *Counsel to the President*, 208–11. For a full discussion on the desegregation of the military see, Richard M. Dalfiume, *Desegregation in the United States Armed Forces: Fighting on Two Fronts, 1939–1953* (Columbia: University of Missouri Press, 1969). For the battles for an FEPC, see Louis Ruchames, *Race, Jobs, & Politics: The Story of FEPC* (Westport, Connecticut: Negro Universities Press, 1971 [reprinted]).
39. Walter White, "President Truman and Civil Rights," July 29, 1948, Box 81, File "Articles: Walter White Syndicated Column, 1949," *Papers of the NAACP*; Walter White, "The Candidates' Record III: Harry S Truman," September 23, 1948, ibid.; White to David Niles, July 21, 1948, Box 27, File "Civil Rights/Negro Affairs 1949–52," *Niles Papers*.

Truman and convinced that the Association had to do whatever it could to keep Truman in the White House. Much to Hastie's chagrin, however, the Democratic National Committee acted as if it had already conceded defeat and was just "going through the motions of organizing a campaign" for Truman's election. Unwilling to let the DNC's defeatist attitude sabotage a man whom Hastie believed had a "deep, personal commitment" to civil rights, he insisted that the party leaders organize a 19-city, cross-country speaking tour for him so that he could spread the word about the president. Another NAACP Board member, Channing Tobias, who swore that in Truman's darkest hour he would not desert the president, vowed to "interpret [Truman's] motives in their true light," and then wrote a series of laudatory articles for the black press, which he religiously forwarded to Truman's staff.[40]

Of course, all of this violated, if not the letter, then certainly the spirit of the nonpartisan rule, which prohibited executive officers from endorsing any candidate for political office, speaking at political rallies or conventions, and maintaining or implying that the NAACP endorsed any political candidate. But the Association was convinced that Truman's election would finally result in the long-awaited and desperately needed anti-lynching, anti-poll tax, and FEPC legislation for which the NAACP had lobbied for years to secure. With so much at stake, the Association became hopelessly and all too easily embroiled in the campaign's "factional strife" and appeared, in the words of one editor, poised to "disintegrate . . . on the rock of partisan politics."[41]

Thus, in a move that would have devastating repercussions on the Association for years, the NAACP leaders had decided early in 1948 to quell any dissension in the ranks about the Association's barely veiled support of Truman's candidacy and therefore reaffirmed the Board of Directors' 1944 nonpartisan policy.[42] Obviously, this rule did not apply to those who supported Truman. Rather it was targeted directly at W. E. B. Du Bois,

40. "Statement of the Hon. William H. Hastie, Governor of the Virgin Islands," press release, October 13, 1948, Box 62, File "WH File—Political-1948 Campaign Hastie Governor-Political Tour Press Releases," *Nash Papers*; "Itinerary of Governor William H. Hastie: Campaign Tour for the Re-Election of President Truman," October 13, 1948, ibid.; *Hastie*; Channing Tobias to Philleo Nash, March 29, 1948, Box 14, File "'T' (folder 1)," *HST:Nash Files*; Channing Tobias to Truman, telegram, July 27, 1948, Box 1512, File "T," *Truman:OF*; Channing Tobias to David Niles, October 4, 1948, Box 27, File "Civil Rights/Negro Affairs, 1949–52," *Niles Papers*.

41. "Dissension in the NAACP," April 16, 1948, *St. Paul Recorder*, found in Box 665, File "Wallace, Henry A.—General, 1948–49," *Papers of the NAACP*.

42. White to Branch Officer, May 6, 1948, Box 143, File "Board of Directors Political Action, 1944, 1950–53," ibid.; "Report of the Committee on Re-Statement of the Association's Principles Re-Participation in Politics," March 13, 1944, ibid.; White to Staff, memo, February 25, 1948, Reel 62, *Du Bois*.

Photo 3.2. The alliance that enraged Walter White and the NAACP leadership. Du Bois with Progressive party presidential candidate Henry Wallace, 1948. © *Julius Lazarus/Special Collections, Rutgers University Libraries.*

who, along with Robeson, had been one of the few prominent African-American leaders working to elect Wallace to the presidency. Indeed, in January 1948, Du Bois noted that, without Wallace in the presidential hunt, African Americans would "be put in the embarrassing position of having to choose between fools and demagogues" and, a vote for either, Du Bois asserted, would cause blacks to lose all their "self respect." Not surprisingly, the NAACP leadership wanted Du Bois silenced.[43]

As fate would have it, Du Bois was on a cross-country speaking tour when the Board reaffirmed its nonpartisan stance. Panicked and "apprehensive" that the scholar might publicly endorse Wallace during the tour, White immediately air mailed Du Bois a copy of the notice.[44] The scholar

43. "Robeson, Fifty Other Negro Leaders Endorse Henry Wallace for President in 1948," press release, December 31, 1947, Reel 2, *Papers of W. Alphaeus Hunton,* Schomburg Center for the Study of Black Culture, New York, New York (hereafter *Hunton Papers*); White to Arthur Spingarn, March 12, 1948, Box 241, File "W. E. B. Du Bois—General (Jan.–Sept. 1948)," *Papers of the NAACP;* W. E. B. Du Bois, "The Winds of Time," January 3, 1948, *Chicago Defender* found in Box 241, File "William E. B. Du Bois—General, 1947," ibid.

44. Hugh H. Smythe to Du Bois, February 25, 1948, Reel 62, *Du Bois.*

was furious. He bypassed the executive secretary and went directly to Arthur Spingarn for clarification. Du Bois acknowledged that the present election had aroused "bitter feelings," but how, he asked Spingarn, could the Association "interfere with the political freedom" for which it had fought for nearly 40 years. Du Bois sympathized with the difficulty of maintaining unity in an organization of more than 500,000 members, but he could not believe that the Association would try to restrict private citizens from expressing their political beliefs just because they happened to be employees of the NAACP. He then laid out his own conditions. He would continue to endorse Wallace but would make it clear that he was speaking as a private individual, "not . . . for the NAACP."[45] Spingarn was noncommittal, but offered to submit Du Bois' statement to the full Board for consideration.[46] The Board decided, again, that there would be "no exceptions" to the nonpartisan policy.[47]

Du Bois' response was swift. The NAACP's "gag-law" threatened to "close his mouth and stop his pen," which was about "the sharpest threat a man can face at the end of his life," he railed.[48] Articles written for the *Chicago Defender* would now have to be reviewed and censored for political content; speaking engagements declined. The order was too broad, he informed Spingarn. Exactly what, in these intensely troubled times, was not political? Was he prohibited from discussing civil rights, the poll tax, segregation? What about China? Greece? Was he to avoid a meeting simply because one of the speakers, an NAACP branch officer, was a Progressive party candidate for Congress? Was he to risk "bread and butter" if he somehow crossed the NAACP's political demilitarized zone? Frustrated, Du Bois declared that if he had known about the "non-partisan" policy, he never would have returned to the Association.[49]

Nevertheless, despite the Board's warning shot, Du Bois continued to test the limits of the NAACP's political tripwire. On occasion after occasion, Du Bois gave pro-Wallace speeches and campaigned for the Progressive party candidate while consistently being identified by the media as "research director, National Association for the Advancement of Colored

45. Du Bois to Board of Directors, draft memo, n.d. (February 27, 1948), ibid.; Du Bois to Arthur Spingarn, February 27, 1948, ibid.; Du Bois to Board of Directors of the National Association for the Advancement of Colored People, memo, March 8, 1948, Box 241, File "W. E. B. Du Bois—General (Jan.–Sept. 1948)," *Papers of the NAACP*.
46. Arthur Spingarn to Du Bois, March 2, 1948, Reel 62, *Du Bois*.
47. White to Du Bois, March 11, 1948, ibid.; White to Spingarn, March 12, 1948, Box 241, File "W. E. B. Du Bois—General (Jan.–Sept. 1948)," *Papers of the NAACP*.
48. Du Bois to Hugh Smythe, March 16, 1948, Reel 62, *Du Bois*; Du Bois to Arthur Spingarn, April 2, 1948, ibid.
49. Ibid.

People."[50] Although this enraged Walter White, the NAACP's policy, in Du Bois' estimation, did not forbid employees from having political views and expressing them – as White was "doing daily" in his pro-Truman syndicated columns. Of course, White did not see it that way. As far as he was concerned, his articles could never be construed as "'openly campaigning for Truman.'" Rather, he was merely conveying to the American public the president's "contributions to a better America" and, conversely, the shortfalls of the other candidates. For White, though, Du Bois' actions were a direct affront to the Board's mandate, and he was determined to bring the Association's co-founder in line with the NAACP's partisan policy.[51]

The sparring between Du Bois and White soon erupted into a mudslinging, name-calling brawl as White would denounce Du Bois as "utterly vicious and dishonest," and Du Bois did everything in his power to make it clear that he "didn't like" or respect the "phenomenally selfish" White. In fact, since Du Bois' return to the NAACP in 1944, the two had suspiciously eyed each other, questioned the other's motives and tactics, and barely strained to find some *modus vivendi.* They perpetually dueled over office space, secretarial support, the San Francisco conference, the presidential campaign, and the scope of the NAACP's commitment to Africa and anti-colonialism. Unable to see past their personal grievances, the leadership that the African American community desperately needed – the visionary and the politically astute – tried to destroy each other. Oddly enough, their final battle ground would be on the treacherous terrain of human rights.[52]

50. W. E. B. Du Bois, interview, *W. E. B. Du Bois: A Recorded Autobiography*, interviewed by Moses Asch, 1961 (hereafter *Recorded Autobiography*); White to Du Bois, March 29, 1948, Reel 62, *Du Bois*; Du Bois to White, March 31, 1948, ibid.; White to Du Bois, memo, July 9, 1948, ibid.

51. Du Bois to White, memo, July 9, 1948, ibid.; "Excerpts from Speech Delivered by Dr. W. E. B. Du Bois," June 16, 1948, ibid.; White to Fred Taylor, September 2, 1948, Box 633, File "Harry S. Truman, 1946–49," *Papers of the NAACP*; Walter White, untitled article, November 23, 1948, Box 74, File "Articles: Walter White *Chicago Defender* Columns, 1948," ibid. For a sampling of the columns that infuriated Du Bois, see, Walter White, "The South vs. President Truman," February 26, 1948, Box 81, File "Articles: Walter White Syndicated Column, 1948," ibid.; White, "Governor Dewey's *Record* on the Negro Question," March 4, 1948, ibid. (emphasis in original); White, "The President Means It," February 12, 1948, ibid.

52. Du Bois, interview, *Recorded Autobiography*; White to Arthur Spingarn, October 8, 1948, Box 94-8, Folder 181, *Spingarn Papers*; White to Du Bois, September 22, 1944, Box 240, File "William E. B. Du Bois: General, 1943–44," *Papers of the NAACP*; Du Bois to White, memo, April 10, 1945, Reel 57, *Du Bois*; Du Bois to Vada Somerville, April 13, 1945, ibid.; "Statement of Expenses for Secretarial Expenses at UNCIO, San Francisco, California," May 18, 1945, Box 240, File "William E. B. Du Bois: General, 1943–44," *Papers of the NAACP*; Roy Wilkins to White, May 27, 1945, Box 639, File "United Nations—UNCIO—General, 1945—May 11–June," ibid.; Roy Wilkins to

After Eleanor Roosevelt's iceberg response to the NAACP's petition, White, while still committed to the development of a strong human rights platform, had begun to question the wisdom of pushing Roosevelt to the point where a valued ally could easily transform into a powerful enemy. Instead of putting the NAACP Board member once again in the untenable position of defending America's civil rights record, White wanted to downplay *An Appeal to the World* and turn the NAACP's efforts more fully to the crafting of the Declaration and Covenant on Human Rights, which were the major UN projects of the former first lady. Du Bois, however, cared little about protecting Roosevelt's human rights image, nor was he troubled by the inevitable shedding of her liberal skin to reveal a hard-bitten Cold Warrior. As far as Du Bois was concerned, the Association had not pushed Roosevelt hard enough to place *An Appeal to the World* on the UN's agenda, and because the systematic violations of African Americans' human rights continued apace, Du Bois believed that it was unconscionable for the NAACP to abandon *An Appeal to the World* simply because Mrs. Roosevelt did not like it. Du Bois' disdain for and suspicion of Roosevelt easily contaminated his opinion of the draft Declaration and Covenant on Human Rights, and he viewed the efforts to craft an International Bill of Human Rights, as the Declaration was becoming known, with utter contempt. The warped development of America's human rights policy did nothing to dispel Du Bois' suspicions.

Obviously, the United States clearly prided itself on its Constitution, its love of liberty, and its commitment to basic individual rights.[53] Indeed, John Foster Dulles conflated the terms civil rights and human rights and suggested that the United States should use human rights as its "'theme song'" at the upcoming UN meeting. Yet, that song, in reality, could only be sung with the background noise of lynching, disfranchisement and Southern justice repeating like a bitter refrain.[54] Moreover, because the

White, memo, June 7, 1945, Reel 57, *Du Bois*; Du Bois to Logan, June 21, 1945, ibid.; Du Bois to White, memo, June 26, 1945, Box 240, File "William E. B. Du Bois: General 1945," *Papers of the NAACP*; White to Du Bois, memo, June 27, 1945, ibid.; Du Bois to White, memo, July 2, 1945, Part 1, Reel 3, *NAACP*; Cathryn Dixon to Roy Wilkins, July 10, 1945, Reel 57, *Du Bois*; White to Du Bois, memo, July 12, 1945, ibid.; White to Du Bois, memo, July 12, 1945, ibid.; Wilkins to Du Bois, memo, July 17, 1945, ibid.; White to Du Bois, memo, July 18, 1945, ibid.; White to Du Bois, December 21, 1945, ibid.; and Rayford Logan, diary, September 18, 1945, *Logan Papers*.

53. Michael H. Hunt, *Ideology and U.S. Foreign Policy*, (New Haven, Connecticut: Yale University Press, 1987), 19–45.

54. Suggested Line for US Approach, n.d., Box 4588, File "Human Rights Commission, 1948," *Roosevelt Papers*; George Marshall to Eleanor Roosevelt, May 19, 1948, ibid.; Mr. Sanders to Acting Secretary, memo, October 13, 1948, Box 8, File "Human Rights: General, 1948," Lot File 55D429, *RG 59*; K. L. Rankin to the Secretary of State, memo, July 22, 1948, Box 4685, Decimal File 811.4016/7-2248, ibid.

ranking senators from Mississippi, Texas, Alabama, South Carolina, and Georgia wrote the lyrics, America's human rights policy could only be sung in the key of white supremacy and Jim Crow. For example, when Moscow refused to let Soviet wives of American and British nationals leave the USSR, the United States thought that it had a great issue to highlight the vindictive nature of the Soviet regime. Yet, as the United States sought to craft language to condemn "all legislative measures which forbid mixed marriages," its efforts ran headlong into the anti-miscegenation laws of the South. Similarly, other attempts to express in clear, unequivocal language basic human and civil rights, such as the right to vote, were consistently bent by the prism of Jim Crow and American racism as the efforts to craft a Declaration and then Covenant on Human Rights demonstrated.[55]

In December 1947, in Geneva, Switzerland, a subcommittee of the Commission on Human Rights, led by Eleanor Roosevelt, completed the initial draft of a Declaration of Human Rights, which was the first international enumeration of ideal standards. As John Foster Dulles later explained to a very wary and hostile American Bar Association (ABA), the Declaration of Human Rights, for all that it was, was not a legal document. Rather, it was more like America's "Sermon on the Mount," in "this great ideological struggle" between the United States and the Soviet Union.[56] Alexander E. Bogomolov, the Soviet ambassador in Paris, was not impressed. He argued that a gaping defect in the Declaration was its silence on exactly *who* was protected by these noble, elegant rights. The Declaration, Bogomolov noted, did not outlaw racial discrimination, nor did it prohibit racially inflammatory language. As a result, he said, singing his own version of America's theme song, the "lynching of negroes would continue."[57]

For Eleanor Roosevelt, however, although lynching was tragic, the omission of a clause on racial discrimination was a political necessity. The Southern senators, Roosevelt declared, would never agree to any document that outlawed racial discrimination. Therefore, not only did she argue forcefully against an article to eliminate discrimination committed by individuals, but she also challenged the clause prohibiting

55. Memorandum of Conversation with Mrs. Franklin D. Roosevelt, Mr. D. V. Sandifer et al., 24 August 1948, Box 8, File "Human Rights: General, 1948," Lot File 55D429, ibid.; James Simsarian to Eleanor Roosevelt, December 21, 1949, Box 4588, File "Human Rights Commission, 1949," *Roosevelt Papers*.

56. John Foster Dulles to W. Jefferson Davis, February 2, 1949, Box 8, File "Human Rights: General, 1949," Lot File 55D429, *RG 59*.

57. Commission on Human Rights, Second Session: Summary Record of Thirty-Fourth Meeting, December 12, 1947, E/CN.4/SR.34, Box 4589, File "E/CN.4/AC Documents," *Roosevelt Papers*.

government-sanctioned racial discrimination.[58] While she sought to craft a human rights document that would not offend or threaten the Southern way of life, others in the U.S. government simply voiced doubts about the merits of the Declaration altogether. George Kennan, the architect of containment, strongly questioned the wisdom of creating a Declaration of Human Rights at all. "I wish to say," Kennan explained, "that the Staff has great misgivings as to the wisdom of the Executive branch negotiating declarations of this nature setting forth ideals and principles which we are not today able to observe in our own country, which we cannot be sure of being able to observe in the future, and which are in any case of dubious universal validity. It seems to us that this invites charges of hypocrisy against us." Kennan therefore recommended that "before we embark on any further international discussions of broad general principles purporting to have universal validity, we give most careful examination to their consistency with our own practices and with world realities."[59]

The Declaration, a simple listing of basic human rights, was obviously difficult enough for the American government to embrace, but the Covenant, which, as a treaty, would have the force of law, engendered Truman's and the State Department's intense antipathy. In fact, after conferring with the president, Under Secretary of State Robert Lovett called Geneva at three in the morning and ordered the U.S. delegation "'to kill the Covenant.'" Roosevelt's ever-efficient State Department advisor, James Hendrick, however, had already distributed the drafts to the other delegations. Not surprisingly, Hendrick's supervisor "'bawled the hell out of'" him because the United States could not exactly deny a document that was firmly clutched in everyone's hands.[60] That gaffe ultimately cost

58. Commission on Human Rights: Drafting Committee, Second Session, Draft International Covenant on Human Rights (Document E/600) with United States Recommendations), May 3, 1948, E/CN.4/AC.1/19, Box 4595, (No File), ibid.; "Committee Discusses Covenant Article on Discrimination," Press Release, May 11, 1948, SOC/521, Box 634, File "United Nations: General, 1948–49," *Papers of the NAACP*; "Article 22 Adopted Against Opposition," Press Release, May 11, 1948, SOC/523, ibid.; Minutes of the Meeting of the Board of Directors of the American Association for the United Nations, January 14, 1949, Box 3249, File "American Association for the UN, 1948–49," *Roosevelt Papers*; Minutes of the Fifteenth Meeting of the United States Delegation to the Third Regular Session of the General Assembly, October 14, 1948, US(P)/A/M(Chr)/15, Box 60, File "US(P)/A/M(CHR)/1-34," *RG* 84. (Emphasis in original.)

59. John Foster Dulles to Eleanor Roosevelt, June 15, 1948, Box 4588, File "Human Rights Commission, 1948," *Roosevelt Papers*; George F. Kennan to Mr. Humelsine, July 8, 1948, Box 8, File "Human Rights: General, 1948," Lot File 55D429, *RG* 59.

60. Quoted in, Joseph P. Lash, *Eleanor: The Years Alone*, foreword by Franklin D. Roosevelt, Jr. (New York: W. W. Norton & Company, 1972), 70.

Hendrick his job, and it forced the United States to play the role of human rights champion and saboteur at the same time.[61]

Yet, Roosevelt, who, as one State Department official commented, "gracefully blended" "cunning and naivete," was perfectly suited for this job. Roosevelt had the will, the clout, and the skill to extract from the Commission on Human Rights virtually whatever she and the United States wanted. As her State Department advisors noted with pride, Roosevelt "drove that... Commission." "She wouldn't let them press her, she pressed them." She "pulled no punches." Roosevelt saw to it that the human rights documents emerging from her committee would position the United States as the moral leader of the free world, while the United States continued its amoral treatment of African Americans. She made sure that the proposed Declaration and, especially the Covenant, contained no viable implementation mechanisms. In addition, Roosevelt worked to ensure that neither individuals nor nongovernmental organizations would have any authority to petition the UN for redress of human rights violations. One of her State Department advisors would later lament that those restrictions were "exceedingly restrictive," but President Truman and Robert Lovett were greatly concerned that African Americans, as the NNC and NAACP had already done, would continue to petition the UN to resolve what America had neither the will nor the desire to fix. The State Department therefore worked diligently to "preserve the integrity of domestic jurisdiction," and discourage African Americans from appealing to the UN "until all available local remedies have been exhausted." In reality, that meant never. One State Department analysis fully acknowledged that, for African Americans, the "trinity of constitutional guarantees, judicial decisions and administrative support" was "impotent" in breaking the shackles of second-class citizenship. Yet, despite the lack of viable domestic remedies, the analyst concluded, it would be wrong to "lure" African Americans into believing that they could find redress for their "domestic maladjustments" at the UN.[62]

61. Dean Rusk to James Hendrick, July 7, 1948, Box 2, File "Human Rights: J. P. Hendrick Personal," *Hendrick Papers*; James Hendrick to Eleanor Roosevelt, July 22, 1948, Box 3301, File "Hendrick, James, P., 1947–1952," *Roosevelt Papers*; Jonathan Daniels to James P. Hendrick, August 20, 1948, Box 2, File "Human Rights: J.P. Hendrick Personal," *Hendrick Papers*.

62. Quoted in, Lash, *Eleanor*, 69; Isador Lubin, interview, *Isador Lubin Oral History*, Harry S Truman Presidential Library, Independence, Missouri (hereafter *Lubin*); *Sandifer; Blaisdell*; James Green is quoted in Robert E. Asher et al., eds., *The United Nations and Promotion of the General Welfare* (Washington, D.C.: Brookings Institution, 1957), 762; Charles S. Murphy to D. V. Sandifer, memo April 14, 1948, Box 533, File "85-Q Human Rights Commission Folder," *Truman:OF*; Durward V. Sandifer to Eleanor Roosevelt, April 16, 1948, Box 4595, (No File), *Roosevelt Papers*; Draft Memo

Thus, as supplicants appealed to the Commission on Human Rights for justice, Eleanor Roosevelt bluntly stated that the Commission was not "a tribunal before which individual cases are heard. It was not established for that purpose and has no machinery to carry on such work." People, Roosevelt chastised, simply needed to "take the trouble to ascertain the facts about HR Commission" because "it is a great pity to raise people's hopes only to have them unfulfilled."[63] Of course, the Commission on Human Rights had established in its very first session that it had "no power to take any action in . . . any complaints concerning human rights."[64] This "declaration of impotence," John Humphrey would later concede, made the Commission "the most elaborate wastepaper basket ever invented."[65]

America's emasculation of human rights did not stop there, however. Hendrick, in his "farewell memo," stressed to his replacement, James Simsarian, that Simsarian not only had "to watch like a hawk" any effort to "put measures of implementation in the Declaration," but also to realize that sometimes it was necessary to fight against phrases with which the United States was in complete agreement simply because they might open up a Pandora's box of social and economic rights.[66]

The Soviets, however, believed that *their* "theme song" was economic and social rights and complained that it was bad enough that the United States insisted on crafting a human rights document that would "not offer any hope" to "the Negroes in America or the Indians in South Africa," but the United States had also insisted on truncating the definition of

of Conversation with Roosevelt, Sandifer, Hendrick on March 4, 1948, April 20, 1948, Box 2, File "Human Rights Memorandum," *Hendrick Papers*; "Human Rights and International Organization," n.d., Box 4588, File "Human Rights Commission, undated," *Roosevelt Papers*; Statement of the Position of the United States on Petitions by Individuals in Relation to a Covenant on Human Rights, April 30, 1948, Box 4593, File "Mrs. Roosevelt," ibid.

63. Roosevelt to Xavier Leurquin, October 22, 1948, Box 4588, File "Human Rights Commission, 1948," ibid.; Roosevelt to Pauline W. Callaghan, April 9, 1951, Box 3274, File "Council A-Z," ibid.

64. UNESCO, "Human Rights Commission: Report of the Commission on Human Rights to the Economic and Social Council," February 11, 1947, found in Part 2, Reel 28, *NNC*; Commission on Human Rights-Second Session: Report of the Ad Hoc Committee on Communications, December 14, 1947, E/CN.4/64, *UN*; United Nations Commission on Human Rights Drafting Committee, Press Release SOC/504, May 4, 1948, found in Box 634, File "United Nations: General, 1948–49," *Papers of the NAACP*; United Nations Commission on Human Rights Drafting Committee, Press Release SOC/521, May 11, 1948, ibid.; United Nations Commission on Human Rights Drafting Committee, Press Release SOC/523, May 11, 1948, ibid.

65. Quoted in, Howard Tolley, Jr., *The UN Commission on Human Rights* (Boulder, Colorado and London: Westview Press, 1987): 16, 18.

66. James Hendrick to James Simsarian, July 27, 1948, Box 2, File "Human Rights Memorandum," *Hendrick Papers*.

human rights to include only legal and political rights, which had now rendered the entire document worthless. The Soviets contended that a real Covenant on Human Rights would "harmoniz[e] the economic and the political rights of man" and include such tenets as equal pay for equal work, the right to decent housing, health care, and education and more importantly, the statement that the government had a responsibility to ensure those rights. They lamented that the Commission was so blinded by the Western concepts of individual rights that it had completely disregarded the fact it was impossible to have true equality without having economic security. Instead, the Soviets argued, the draft Covenant did no more than give African Americans "the right... to be taken to a police station just like a white man." The U.S. delegation retorted that it was ridiculous to have a world "full of well-fed slaves" and dismissed the Soviets' arguments as the "inarticulate Slavic desire for the economic well-being of the masses."[67]

This desire for economic security, no matter how supposedly inarticulate, gave the Truman administration, the ABA, the Republicans, and the Southern Democrats fits. The Republicans, the Southern Democrats, and the ABA declared that social and economic rights reeked of "socialism" or even worse, communism. For Roosevelt and Truman, however, the issue was not so much "socialism," indeed, Truman's Fair Deal included many of the same components, but simply that *universal* social and economic rights were unattainable. Roosevelt candidly admitted that America already had "the jitters" because it did not even enforce its own Bill of Rights.[68] Truman had also been unequivocal. His "commitment was to desegregation" and even when addressing the 1947 NAACP Convention, "he was careful not to go beyond specified constitutional rights."[69] Obviously, then, the idea of a Covenant, which would commit the United States to provide economic and social rights for all of its citizens, was just too much to contemplate seriously. "Obstacles to the United States support for a Covenant," James Hendrick wrote, were the "nondiscrimination article" and "[i]ts import for other articles of substance" and the fact that "'we don't want others meddling in our affairs.'" He therefore

67. Commission on Human Rights: Second Session, Summary Record of Forty-Second Meeting, December 16, 1947, E/CN.4/SR/42, found in Box 4589, File "E/CN.4/AC Documents," *Roosevelt Papers*; Suggestions for the Press Conference, December 17, 1947, Box 4587, File "Human Rights Commission, 1946," ibid.; Committee Completes General Discussion on Human Rights, press release, May 4, 1948, SOC/504, found in Box 634, File "United Nations: General, 1948–49," *Papers of the NAACP*.

68. James P. Hendrick to Eleanor Roosevelt, July 23, 1948, Box 3301, File "Hendrick, James, P., 1947–1952," *Roosevelt Papers*; Minutes of the Meeting of the Board of Directors of the American Association for the United Nations, June 22, 1949, Box 3249, File "American Association for the UN, 1948–49," ibid.

69. Ashmore, *Civil Rights and Wrongs*, 66.

admonished that the United States had to have firm control of the human rights process to keep economic and social rights from creeping into the Covenant and to "show the Cov[enant] is essentially the same as U.S. Bill of Rights."[70] Secretary of State George Marshall also counseled Roosevelt to rein in these human rights discussions. Marshall was insistent that America's human rights efforts could be no more than a publicity ploy, and he wanted it understood that the Covenant, because it was a treaty, had to be much more "narrow in scope" than even the Declaration of Human Rights.[71] Roosevelt, although she believed that there at least had to be some faint recognition of economic and social rights, fell in line like a good soldier and argued that the Covenant could "not necessarily cover . . . all rights" and, as her efforts to squelch the anti-discrimination clauses attest, nor could the Covenant cover all people. As a result, for three years, the United States worked relentlessly to eliminate all mention of economic and social rights from the Covenant.[72]

Channing Tobias's son-in-law, William H. Dean, Jr., Chief of the UN's Africa Unit, alerted Walter White that the NAACP needed to secure immediately copies of the draft human rights documents and have the Association's legal team review them. Dean cautioned that "there were some things" in there that the Association "would not agree with."[73] He was right. The Association leadership recognized that as important as the NAACP's legal strategy was to overturn Jim Crow, the economic devastation in the black community could not be solely addressed by banning future discrimination. Centuries of repression, as the NAACP leadership also acknowledged, demanded ameliorative steps as well. Du Bois cogently noted that "it was not enough for us to ask simply for civil rights," there had to be massive "economic reconstruction," as well. Walter White clearly believed that the Declaration and especially the Covenant were crucial in moving beyond the limited parameters of civil rights. Nor was he the only one. State Department legal counsel, Herzel Plaine, even recognized it. As Plaine outlined those areas in which the Declaration surpassed current practice, he carefully explained to Eleanor

70. [James Hendrick] Covenant on Human Rights, draft letter, January 14, 1948, Box 2, File "Human Rights Memorandum," *Hendrick Papers*.

71. George Marshall to Eleanor Roosevelt, May 19, 1948, Box 4588, File "Human Rights Commission, 1948," *Roosevelt Papers*.

72. Eleanor Roosevelt to Gilbert W. Stewart, n.d. (December 29, 1949), Box 4588, File "Human Rights Commission, 1949," ibid.; James P. Hendrick to A. Glenn Mower, Jr., June 30, 1975, Box 2, File "Human Rights Correspondence," *Hendrick Papers*; "Committee Completes General Discussion on Human Rights," press release, May 4, 1948, SOC/504, found in Box 634, File "United Nations: General, 1948–49," *Papers of the NAACP*.

73. E(dna) M. W(asem) to White, memo, January 29, 1948, Box 635, File "United Nations General Assembly, 1946–August 1948," ibid.

Roosevelt that the social and economic articles in the draft Declaration, unlike anything else in existence, were for those who were "ill-fed, ill-housed, ill-clothed, without schools or proper education, and without the many benefits of a good life." Those articles offered a lifeline for African Americans who were mired in the economic chaos of Jim Crow America. In the Covenant, however, those rights could be more than a lifeline; they had the potential to reshape the racially degrading contours of American society.[74] Thus, the NAACP legal staff quickly discerned that the United States had consistently maneuvered to enervate or eliminate mechanisms to enforce human rights. "It seems essential," NAACP attorney Edward Dudley noted, that in addition to defining human rights, that there "must also . . . [be some] type of machinery to correct the abuses, once discovered." "The adoption of anything less," he continued, would give the UN, yet, another "Palestine" with "neither [the] moral nor physical forces," to carry out its mandate. Dudley concluded that, as currently written, the draft Declaration, as well as the Covenant on Human Rights, "added little" to the status of African Americans in the United States and "certainly added nothing" that would alleviate the plight of "minorities the world over." That was obvious after Marian Wynn Perry, another NAACP attorney, uncovered the federal–state clause embedded in the Covenant. That innocuous sounding addendum was, in fact, lethal. It asserted the primacy of states' rights even over the Constitutional principle that a treaty was the law of the land and would have allowed the South to ignore every provision in the Covenant guaranteeing the sanctity of human rights. Clearly, the State Department was trying to craft a Covenant that would not offend the most rabid Dixiecrat in the Senate. Although, political realities suggested this policy, there was something inherently desperate and disingenuous about trying to design a human rights document that would be acceptable to an audience that deified white supremacy, encouraged lynching, and condoned unconscionable medical experiments on African Americans.[75]

74. Herzel H. E. Plaine to Mrs. Eleanor Roosevelt, memo, June 16, 1948, Box 4588, File "Human Rights Commission, 1948," *Roosevelt Papers*; Du Bois to Lasker Smith, March 9, 1949, Reel 64, *Du Bois*.

75. Edward R. Dudley to White, memo, February 4, 1948, Box 635, File "United Nations General Assembly, 1946–August 1948," *Papers of the NAACP*; James H. Jones, *Bad Blood: The Tuskegee Syphilis Experiment* (New York: Free Press, 1981); Stefan Kèuhl, *The Nazi Connection: Eugenics, American Racism, and German National Socialism* (New York: Oxford University Press, 1994); Philip Reilly, *The Surgical Solution: A History of Involuntary Sterilization in the United States* (Baltimore: Johns Hopkins University Press, 1991); J. David Smith, *The Eugenic Assault on America: Scenes in Red, White, and Black* (Fairfax, Virginia: George Mason University Press, 1993); William H. Tucker, *The Science and Politics of Racial Research* (Urbana: University of Illinois Press, 1994), 5–7.

A State Department briefing in March 1948 did nothing to dispel that assessment. Rayford Logan, who attended the meeting with White, watched in horror and amazement as an article that was supposedly the bedrock of American democracy, the right to vote, was targeted for elimination because it violated Southern electoral policies. This shocking display, as nothing else could, made White realize that it was going to take a "very considerable amount of pressure ... to force the State Department and the American delegation" to toughen two horribly enervated texts on human rights.[76]

William Dean agreed, and he recognized that the Declaration and especially the Covenant were "of critical importance to Negroes," yet, he feared, things in those drafts were just "not right."[77] Dean told his father-in-law that the NAACP would have to use whatever resources it had available to pressure the American delegation. Tobias therefore insisted that someone from the Association keep a "very close watch" on the proceedings. This had to be a priority, Tobias declared, because "this will be a World Bill of Rights [and] we ought to scrutinize it carefully." He then noted that if the Board had considered sending White all the way to Geneva, Switzerland, to defend *An Appeal to the World*, it certainly could "send someone out to Lake Success," New York, where the Commission was currently meeting.[78]

White, however, believed that Lake Success was just a warm-up for the upcoming UN session in Paris where the real decisions would be made, and that is where he wanted the NAACP to be represented. The State Department's public relations strategy, which was to have major organizations involved as consultants to the U.S. delegation, dovetailed nicely with White's plans. After Chester Williams, the State Department's UN public relations officer, invited the NAACP, along with 44 other organizations, to attend the meeting in Paris, White advised the Committee on Administration that it was of the "highest importance" that the NAACP have a representative there. As White surveyed the names of the

76. White to Du Bois, March 12, 1948, Box 635, File "United Nations General Assembly, 1946–August 1948," *Papers of the NAACP*; Francis H. Russell to White, February 13, 1948, ibid.; Logan to White, memo, March 8, 1948, ibid.; James Simsarian to Eleanor Roosevelt, December 21, 1949, Box 4588, File "Human Rights Commission, 1949," *Roosevelt Papers*.

77. Marginalia from William Dean to Channing Tobias. Written on "Press Release SOC/504, Commission on Human Rights Drafting Committee," May 4, 1948, Box 634, File "United Nations: General, 1948–49," *Papers of the NAACP*; White to Wilkins, memo, May 10, 1948, ibid.

78. Wilkins to White and Thurgood Marshall, memo, May 17, 1948, ibid.; Channing Tobias to Roy Wilkins, memo, n.d. (May 1948), ibid.; White to Wilkins, memo, May 10, 1948, ibid.

other invited organizations, "not one," he noted "speaks directly for the Negro," and it was obvious that the State Department was trying to craft two landmark human rights documents that would leave black oppression untouched. Because of the complexities of the human rights issues and the importance they held for African Americans, White recommended that the NAACP send Du Bois as the Association's representative.[79] The Committee disregarded White's suggestion, however, and voted to have the executive secretary attend the Paris meeting, instead.[80]

According to White, the Committee members believed that they would be courting disaster to cast Du Bois in the role as a human rights lobbyist. The scholar's "refusal to descend from Mt. Sinai" and his well-advanced age had, in the Board's opinion, made Du Bois wholly inflexible.[81] No doubt there was another concern. The Communists' bloody overthrow of the moderate Czech government, the Soviets' ongoing blockade of Berlin, and the increasing success of Mao Zedong's Red Army in China had made the UN an increasingly tense and hostile arena. In this setting, Du Bois' avowed faith in socialism, his assertion that the difference between communism and capitalism was "the difference between heaven and hell," and his open hostility toward the Truman administration made him a major liability. The Board was clearly afraid that Du Bois, who "had a tendency to act on his own initiative," would be difficult, if not impossible, to restrain all the way on the other side of the Atlantic.[82] White, however, the ultimate consensus builder and politician, appeared tailor-made for the task. There was only one problem. Although he possessed the political acumen needed for the job and had an outstanding grasp of the broader foreign policy issues, White did not have the expertise to interpret and counter the sometimes arcane minutiae of the human rights debates. Recognizing this, he immediately requested meetings with Eleanor Roosevelt and Chester Williams, and he sought Du Bois' guidance.[83] All three of

79. Secretary (White) to Committee on Administration, memo, July 13, 1948, Box 635, File "United Nations General Assembly, 1946–August 1948," ibid.
80. White to Chester S. Williams, July 29, 1948, ibid.
81. Rayford Logan, diary, September 10, 1948, *Logan Papers*.
82. Du Bois to Anna Melissa Graves, July 9, 1946, Reel 58, *Du Bois*; "NAACP Conference Adopts Resolutions," June 28, 1947, Part 1, Reel 12, *NAACP*; "UN, Socialism Only Hope for World's Backward Races, Says Dr. Du Bois," *Pittsburgh Courier*, n.d. (June/July 1947), found in Reel 59, *Du Bois*; Chester S. Williams to Mrs. Roosevelt, memorandum of conversation, September 9, 1948, Box 78, File "Discrimination: Race, 1948–49," *RG 84*.
83. Walter White, untitled column, August 26, 1948, Box 74, File "Articles—Walter White, *Chicago Defender* Columns, 1948," *Papers of the NAACP*; White to Eleanor Roosevelt, August 18, 1948, Box 635, File "United Nations General Assembly, 1946–August 1948," ibid.; White to Du Bois, memo, August 20, 1948, Reel 62, *Du Bois*.

these would-be advisors, however, had their own agenda, none of which coincided with White's.

Du Bois, virtually ignoring the executive secretary's emphasis on the Declaration and Covenant on Human Rights, told White to "demand that the [NAACP's] Petition ... be placed on the agenda of the Assembly." Du Bois had watched suspiciously and with growing alarm the executive secretary's increasing support of Truman and Eleanor Roosevelt. Du Bois' distrust of Roosevelt had grown immeasurably after a very unpleasant meeting a few months earlier. The moment he raised the subject of the NAACP's petition, Roosevelt had insisted that *An Appeal to the World* remain entombed in the UN's bureaucracy. She asserted that the petition was "embarrassing; that it would be seized upon by the Soviet Government and others as an excuse for attacking the United States" and, as a result, she and her colleagues would be placed, once again, in the "unpleasant position of having to defend" the United States. Roosevelt then declared that if the NAACP placed her in that awkward position, "she would feel it necessary to resign from the United States Delegation to the United Nations." Du Bois, of course, was totally unaffected by that threat and bluntly told her that just because the petition made her and the United States uncomfortable, "that was no reason for suppressing the truth." He then intimated that there were other nations that were interested in championing the petition. Sensing Du Bois' threat, Roosevelt warned him that the NAACP did not want to "expos[e] the United States to distorted accusations by other countries." She then interjected that, "in my opinion, the ... colored people in the United States ... would be better served in the long run if the NAACP Appeal were not placed on the Agenda." Roosevelt then tried to compensate for her brusqueness by offering Du Bois the opportunity to make suggestions toward the development of the Declaration of Human Rights. Du Bois, however, no more trusted the Declaration than he trusted Mrs. Roosevelt. Therefore, in response to White's request for advice on the International Bill of Human Rights, Du Bois told the executive secretary that the world did not need further definition of human rights, it needed those rights enforced. Until Roosevelt and the U.S. delegation were willing to cross that threshold, further advice was just a waste of his time. Du Bois concluded his memo to White with the rejoinder that he had absolutely nothing to add about the Declaration that the executive secretary had not already heard.[84]

84. Du Bois to White, memo, August 23, 1948, Box 241, File "W. E. B. Du Bois—General (Jan.–Sept. 1948)," *Papers of the NAACP*; Du Bois to White, memo, July 1, 1948, ibid.; Comment Paper: Discrimination Against Negroes in the United States, August 30, 1948, SD/A/C.3/75, Box 175, File "Background Book: Committee III (Social, Humanitarian,

White, however, was greatly concerned about the serious imperfections in the Declaration, and he wanted more from the NAACP's foreign policy expert than just a terse, two-line response. He therefore thanked Du Bois for the synopsis, but asked to have the scholar prepare a more complete briefing paper and to then meet with him in preparation for the debates in Paris.[85]

Du Bois exploded. On September 7, 1948, in a well-crafted and widely distributed memo that blended Du Bois' boiling rage over the NAACP's blatant partisan politics and its Roosevelt-centered human rights strategy, he predicted that, until there was a change in leadership in Washington, D.C., Paris would be "just a waste of time." "It is certain," Du Bois asserted, "that no influence applied in Paris is going to have the slightest influence on our delegation. Their minds are made up and their policy set." As an example of the delegation's intransigence, Du Bois charged that one of the most implacable foes to African Americans' struggle for human rights was the NAACP's own Eleanor Roosevelt. So, just how, he demanded to know, could the NAACP truly fight for human rights when a powerful member of its own Board of Directors scuttled *An Appeal to the World* and had now threatened to resign if the NAACP fought for the advancement of colored people through the UN? The answer was simple. It could not. Du Bois, therefore, flatly refused to comply with White's request for a full briefing on human rights. Instead of wasting his time by fretting over where to put commas in the Declaration, Du Bois decided to deliver a jeremiad on what he considered to be the root cause of the NAACP's floundering human rights policy. The trail of incompetency and betrayal, Du Bois exclaimed, led directly to Walter White's political machinations. The executive secretary, Du Bois asserted, had "jump[ed] on the Truman bandwagon" and tied the NAACP to the "reactionary, war-mongering, colonial imperialism of the present administration." Clearly, Du Bois insisted, there was a double standard in operation. White was apparently rewarded with an all-expenses paid trip to Paris for his efforts to bring the black vote to Truman, while Du Bois had received "five threats and warnings from the officials of the NAACP" for informing African Americans about the only presidential candidate who was honestly committed to black equality. Moreover, White's foreign policy ascendancy, Du Bois contended, was due to the executive secretary's neverending efforts to erect a *cordon sanitaire* between the scholar and the Board of Directors, in effect, denying the NAACP the expertise it desperately needed in

and Cultural), Volume IV," *RG 84*; Du Bois to White, memo, November 24, 1947, Reel 61, *Du Bois*.

85. White to Du Bois, memo, August 24, 1948, Reel 62, ibid.

foreign policy issues. In Du Bois' opinion, the NAACP's incomprehensible support of the Marshall Plan was an indication of White's misguided leadership. As a consequence, Du Bois demanded greater involvement in the Board of Directors meetings and extensive discussion of the Association's direction on foreign policy matters.[86] As could be expected, this intemperate memo jeopardized his continued employment with the NAACP. The fact that the contents leaked to the *New York Times*, before the Board of Directors had a chance to review it, sealed Du Bois' fate.[87]

White could not believe it. He immediately demanded a full accounting of how much the Association had spent on Du Bois' salary, research assistants, and travel. The staggering four-year sum (in 1998 dollars) of almost a quarter of a million dollars, particularly for an organization that was bleeding red ink, was more than White could handle.[88] He expected a little loyalty, or a least gratitude, for financially rescuing Du Bois after the scholar's pensionless dismissal from Atlanta University. Instead, he felt like he had just been sucker-punched for stooping down to help an aging icon.[89] White had had enough. He wanted Du Bois gone.

In a draft memo that Roy Wilkins and Henry Moon futilely urged White to "ton[e] down," because "this thing will get publicity," the executive secretary lashed out in a blinding rage. White chided Du Bois for his "patent annoyance that someone else other than yourself was sent to . . . Paris." As far as White was concerned, the Board had "good and sufficient reasons" for choosing him over Du Bois, and it acted well within its prerogative in doing so. Moreover, for Du Bois to question the Board in this matter was the ultimate in hubris, when, frankly, it was the scholar's motives that needed to be examined. Du Bois did not scream about "being 'loaded on the Truman bandwagon'" when he went to the San Francisco Conference in 1945, so why raise the issue now? In White's opinion, it was an obvious attempt to discredit Truman and bolster Wallace's dimming political fortunes. No one, White asserted, was singled out by the Board for engaging in political activity. It was simply that Du Bois stubbornly refused to comprehend that "no exceptions" meant just that, no exceptions. White, of course, then pointed to his own resignation from the liberal, but decidedly

86. Du Bois to The Secretary (White) and Board of Directors of the NAACP, memo, September 7, 1948, Box 241, File "W. E. B. Du Bois—General (Jan.–Sept. 1948)," *Papers of the NAACP*.
87. White to Board of Directors, memo, September 13, 1948, ibid.
88. White to Lillian H. Waring, memo, September 8, 1948, ibid.; Lillian H. Waring to White, memo, September 9, 1948, ibid.; Bureau of Labor Statistics, Consumer Price Index-All Urban Consumers, http://www.stats.bls.gov/top20.html. The actual 1948 amount of $36,248.33 is $245,162 in June 1998 dollars.
89. White to Arthur Spingarn, October 8, 1948, Box 94-8, Folder 181, *Spingarn Papers*.

anti-Communist, Americans for Democratic Action, as proof that at least *he* took the nonpartisan rule seriously. He therefore charged that Du Bois was reprimanded because, unlike the other officers, the scholar chose to blatantly and publicly ignore the policy. White also dismissed Du Bois' "ridiculous" charge that the Association blindly supported the administration's foreign policy. The NAACP vigorously disagreed with the U.S. delegation in 1945, White intoned, and it would disagree with it in Paris, as well. As for being purposely isolated from the Board of Directors and kept uninformed about the agendas and meetings, Du Bois had no one to blame but himself. Although all division directors were "expected" to attend Board meetings, for the past year the scholar had willfully chosen to absent himself from those gatherings. Finally, White angrily concluded, it was "most unfortunate" that Du Bois, without giving White or the Board a chance to respond, released the memo to the press "apparently at the same time" that it was sent to the executive secretary's office. Given that White had only received the memo shortly before the end of the business day, he especially resented that George Streator of the *New York Times* "and other reporters telephoned [him] the next morning to ask for comment." White therefore insisted that the Board of Directors deal with this matter promptly, and he informed three key members of the Board that Du Bois had also given Shirley Graham, confidante, friend, and future wife, interoffice memoranda that she was now distributing to the press at the Progressive party convention in hopes that the media would "do a job on that s-o-b Walter White." Then, just before he left for Paris, White distributed copies of the September 9 *New York Times* article to all members of the Board and reemphasized how Du Bois' imperious actions had seriously undermined not only White's, but also the Association's ability to "secure action on such issues as human rights and trusteeship" in Paris.[90]

Thus, by the time of the September 13, 1948 Board meeting, the funeral pyre for Du Bois' NAACP career was fully ablaze. Yet, some members of the Board wanted more than just hearsay evidence, and they argued persuasively that they owed it to themselves and to Du Bois to hear from the scholar directly about what had transpired. When Du Bois stepped

90. White to Du Bois, draft memo, September 8, 1948, Box 241, File "W. E. B. Du Bois—General (Jan.–Sept. 1948)," *Papers of the NAACP*; Henry Moon to White, memo, September 8, 1948, ibid.; White to James Loeb, Jr., February 18, 1947, Box 17, File "Americans for Democratic Action, 1947, January–February," ibid.; James Loeb, Jr., to White, February 25, 1947, ibid.; White to Du Bois, memo, September 13, 1948, Box 241, File "W. E. B. Du Bois—General (Jan.–Sept. 1948)," ibid.; White to Louis Wright, Arthur Spingarn et al., memo, September 10, 1948, Box 240, William E. B. Du Bois: Dismissal—Individuals, 1948," ibid.

into the room, he immediately asserted that "he had no idea how it [the memo] got to the *New York Times*." Perhaps, Du Bois admitted innocently enough, he was ultimately responsible for the leak because he had distributed copies to his staff, as well as to all members of the Board. At that moment, the Board paused. That explanation was plausible. Maybe someone else on the staff, not Du Bois, released the memo. Just as the situation was being defused, however, the eloquent Du Bois uttered one phrase too many. "He added that if the newspapers had asked him about his memorandum, he would have given it to them because he did not consider the matter a secret." Stunned, one Board member asked him to repeat what he had just said. Du Bois blithely reasserted that "he would have given it" to the press.[91] With that incendiary admission, Du Bois left both the room and his tenure with the NAACP in ashes.

In a statement that was both elegiac and harsh in its assessment of the NAACP's co-founder, Arthur B. Spingarn acknowledged that, for many years, Du Bois' "voice was the voice of this organization," but now, Spingarn continued, the "board was convinced" that the NAACP could not function effectively when one of its officers, even if that officer was "one of the greatest leaders of his race," simply "refused to abide by [the Board's] directives."[92] As could be expected, Du Bois' termination, which would become effective at the end of his contract in December, provoked a massive outcry. Just how could Du Bois, "one of the greatest leaders of his race," and the NAACP, the greatest civil rights organization in the United States, be incompatible? Although the answers branched into three separate directions, they shared one unyielding hub – Walter White.

One theory, advanced by journalist Thomas L. Dabney described it as a personal problem – Walter's. White, Dabney asserted, was clearly "suffering from an inflated ego." The executive secretary was so "self-centered" that he actually had the audacity to try to "step in front" of Du Bois and usurp the scholar's hard-earned and well-deserved role in foreign affairs. "Walter White is a shoe shine boy in comparison to you," Dabney explained to Du Bois, "he has never been and never will be the scholar or statesman that you are."[93]

Some, however, argued that the NAACP's problems were not so much personal as political. White and the Board had become so ensnared in Truman's campaign, columnist Abner Berry asserted, that they were

91. Wilkins to White, September 14, 1948, Box 241, File "W. E. B. Du Bois—General (Jan.–Sept. 1948)," *Papers of the NAACP*.
92. Motion passed by NAACP Board of Directors, September 13, 1948, ibid.; "Statement by Arthur B. Spingarn, President of the NAACP," September 13, 1948, ibid.; Wilkins to White, September 14, 1948, ibid.
93. Thomas L. Dabney to Du Bois, September 24, 1948, Reel 61, *Du Bois*.

willing to give the "revered elder statesman of the Negro people, Dr. William Edward Burghardt Dubois (sic)... the boot." As proof, Berry noted that at that momentous Board meeting, where the fate of the NAACP's co-founder hung in the balance, "at least half" of the Board members in attendance were "active in pro-Truman politics or [held] political jobs."[94] The hypocrisy of the NAACP's top leadership being baptized in Democratic waters but firing Du Bois for his avowed faith in the Progressive party was too much for dues-paying NAACP members Stanley and Margaret Blumberg. "Please accept our resignation from the N.A.A.C.P. effective immediately," they wrote. "We cannot be part of any organization" that denies its members and officers the "basic American right to support political candidates." The most comprehensive repudiation of the Board's actions, however, came from the president of the Indiana State Conference of NAACP Branches, Willard B. Ransom. Describing Du Bois' firing as "arbitrary" and "incomprehensible," Ransom asserted that whether the Board wanted to admit it or not, White had, indeed, linked the NAACP to the Truman administration. Obviously, Ransom noted, "the endorsement of Mr. Truman is looked upon with favor [while] the endorsement of Mr. Wallace... creates consternation and fear." It was blatantly apparent that the "mumbo-jumbo" about Du Bois' insubordination was nothing but a smokescreen. It was much more likely, Ransom charged, that Du Bois was sacrificed "because of some strange desire to placate the Truman administration." White's appointment as a consultant to the U.S. delegation in Paris, Ransom asserted, was further evidence of the NAACP's capitulation. This was "clearly an implied, if not an open, endorsement of [the American] government's foreign policy," which meant that the Association had aligned itself behind the continued "enslavement and imperialistic exploitation of colonial peoples." Moreover, despite White's protests, there was simply no comparison between the UN Conference in 1945 and the one in 1948. Whereas in San Francisco, Du Bois had helped "aid... in the formation of the United Nations," an organization that held great promise for a new world order, the UN had now devolved into a Cold War sideshow, thereby making White just another carnival act for American foreign policy.[95] Put simply, the Council on African

94. Abner W. Berry, As We See It, "The NAACP Remains Silent on Some Important Questions," n.d. (September 1948), found in Reel 63, ibid.

95. Mr. and Mrs. Stanley Blumberg to NAACP, September 27, 1948, Box 241, File "William E. B. Du Bois—General, Oct–Dec 1948," *Papers of the NAACP*; Thomas L. Dabney to Du Bois, September 24, 1948, Reel 61, *Du Bois*; Willard B. Ransom to Roy Wilkins, September 30, 1948, Box 240, File "William E. B. Du Bois—Dismissal: Board of Directors—Branches 1948–49," *Papers of the NAACP*; Madison S. Jones, Jr., to

Affairs' Alphaeus Hunton explained, the NAACP could not "serve the interests of the Negro people if it tails along... [behind] the Truman administration."[96]

Dr. Henry Callis, a member of the CAA, could not have agreed more. Yes, White's ego was of mythic, legendary proportions, and the presidential campaign had exacerbated tensions within the NAACP, but the most important issue for Callis was the destructive influence that Walter White had had on the NAACP's – and consequently, African Americans' – foreign policy in the Cold War. The "NAACP cannot carry the State Department on one shoulder and the cause of oppressed peoples on the other," Callis charged. Indeed, the NAACP-endorsed Marshall Plan betrayed even the possibility of the advancement of colored people. "The very philosophy beneath the Marshall Plan," Callis wrote, "envisions the exploitation of Africa with the aid of American tax dollars."[97]

As a litmus test of the Association's independence and to gauge whether "the leaders of the NAACP" had "turn[ed] their backs on the fight" for true black equality, reporters demanded that Walter White explain his plans for placing *An Appeal to the World* on the UN's agenda. It was no secret, Abner Berry noted, that so far "the organization has not pushed its UN petition against colonial and national oppression."[98] Was that going to change? Or, would White meekly accept the fact that "Mrs. Roosevelt and Jonathan Daniels killed [the NAACP's petition] last December at the Human Rights Commission meeting in Geneva?" Indeed, Du Bois' airing of "Mrs. Roosevelt's role in this mess," had raised some serious questions about the NAACP and its most famous Board member. If Du Bois' allegations were true, journalist Horace Cayton wrote, then it was clear that even when a supposedly strong "friend of the Negro" emerged, "the Brother in black is always told to wait and defer his case in view of larger issues." "But," Cayton continued, "the Negro in America is the larger issue. He is the issue upon which two-thirds of the population of the

Willard B. Ransom, October 5, 1948, ibid.; "Letter to Board Members for October Board Meeting," (n.d.), Box 241, File "William E. B. Du Bois—General, Oct.–Dec. 1948," ibid.

96. George Canon, Ewart Guinier et al. to Louis T. Wright, October 6, 1948, Box 240, File "William E. B. Du Bois—Dismissal: Board of Directors—Branches, 1948–49," *Papers of the NAACP*; W. Alphaeus Hunton to Arthur B. Spingarn, September 14, 1948, Reel 62, *Du Bois*; W. Alphaeus Hunton (as Secretary, Council on African Affairs) to Arthur B. Spingarn, September 20, 1948, Reel 61, ibid.; Madison Jones to Wilkins, memo, June 29, 1949, Box 241, File "William E. B. Du Bois: General, 1949–55," *Papers of the NAACP*.
97. Henry Arthur Callis to Du Bois, October 8, 1948, Reel 61, *Du Bois*.
98. "Marshall Plan for NAACP," September 16, 1948, *Daily Worker*, found in Reel 1, *FBI File on ER*; Abner W. Berry, As We See It, "The NAACP Remains Silent on Some Important Questions," n.d. (September 1948), found in Reel 63, *Du Bois*.

world who are not white will make up their minds whether democracy will always mean white supremacy. I'm sorry Mrs. Roosevelt can't see this."[99] What the reporters did see, "to the eternal disgrace of Mr. White" and his supporters, was the existence of a "'gentlemen's agreement' among the U.S. delegation to 'hush-hush' the matter of Negro-American Civil Rights in the General Assembly of the UN."[100] Had White and the NAACP jumped so far onto the Truman bandwagon that they were now part of this "gentlemen's agreement" to squelch their own petition? "Walter White," Berry declared, "should assure those whom he will represent in Paris that he is pushing the same program that the NAACP was pushing on Oct. 23, 1947 [when it first presented *An Appeal to the World*]. This is no time to pull [America's] political chestnuts from the fire at the expense of an international movement for civil rights and peace."[101]

The State Department, which was closely following the White–Du Bois feud, certainly did not expect any help at all from White. In fact, the Department had braced itself for the NAACP's UN assault on American racism. State Department officials had culled together every scrap of evidence they could find to argue that there had been "steady improvement in [the] conditions of Negroes in the United States." Lynching, for example, had supposedly reached "a point where the occurrence of a single act of violence is a shocking event precisely because it is so out of keeping with our system of equal justice under the law." In addition, because *To Secure These Rights* had worked so well in Geneva, the Department was ready to throw it on the table again, as well as the president's recent executive orders, and several decisions by the "ever vigilant" Supreme Court to prove, beyond a shadow of a doubt, that American democracy worked and that the United States was fully committed to equality for all of its citizens. Of course, this position was impossible to reconcile with the other State Department report that admitted that the "trinity" of court decisions, the Bill of Rights, and executive orders, was "impotent" in stopping America's brutal treatment of African Americans. Nonetheless, the facade of democracy had to be maintained.[102]

99. Horace Cayton, "There's More to DuBois-White Feud Than Meets the Eye, Says Mr. Cayton," October 2, 1948, found in ibid.

100. George Canon, Ewart Guinier et al. to Louis T. Wright, October 6, 1948, Box 240, File "William E. B. Du Bois—Dismissal: Board of Directors—Branches, 1948–49," *Papers of the NAACP*.

101. Abner W. Berry, As We See It, "Walter White Forgets The Petition to UN," n.d. (September 1948), found in Reel 63, *Du Bois*.

102. Mr. Simsarian to Mr. Sandifer, memo, September 23, 1948, Box 4567 (no file), *Roosevelt Papers*; Discrimination Against Negroes in the United States, comment paper, SD/A/C.3/75, August 30, 1948, Box 27, File "SD/A/C.3/46-80," Lot 82D211, *RG 59*.

The Department was therefore especially concerned about which delegations the NAACP would approach to maneuver *An Appeal to the World* onto the UN's agenda. Mrs. Roosevelt had offered to find out whatever she could during her meeting with White and to pass along any information he divulged about "the question of racial discrimination being raised in the General Assembly." Given Borisov's strenuous defense of *An Appeal to the World*, and the fact that the Soviets always had a "field day" with Jim Crow, they, of course, looked like the most obvious choice. The Department complained that "It was typical of Soviet tactics to raise the question of discrimination against Negroes in the United States at every possible opportunity," to portray themselves as the saviors of the "poor and down-trodden," and to use the NAACP's petition to cast themselves as the heroes and the Americans as the villains in this Cold War melodrama. The British had warned the Department that the Kremlin would use the "'oppression' of minorities" in the United States to undermine America's position in the UN. A State Department survey of the other UN delegations revealed, however, that it was even worse than that. Confidence in the United States was already eroding. The delegations counseled that the United States had to "counteract widespread criticism on treatment of negroes and the . . . failure to act on the President's Civil Rights Program," and the only way to do that was to be at the forefront of securing passage of a strong Declaration of Human Rights. If the United States did anything to impede the development of the Declaration, especially against the backdrop of the "Negro problem," it was clear that doubt about America's real commitment to human rights would reverberate throughout world. The staff, therefore, agreed that the United States had no choice but to ensure that the Declaration of Human Rights was completed and approved at this meeting of the UN.[103]

103. Du Bois to Warren Austin, February 4, 1948, Reel 63, *Du Bois*; Warren Austin to Du Bois, February 26, 1948, Part 14, Reel 17, *NAACP Int'l*; Du Bois to Trygve Lie, September 11, 1948, Reel 63, *Du Bois*; White to Eleanor Roosevelt, August 18, 1948, Box 3338, File "NAACP, 1948," *Roosevelt Papers*; Eleanor Roosevelt to White, August 23, 1948, ibid.; Memorandum of Conversation with Mrs. Franklin D. Roosevelt, Mr. D. V. Sandifer et al., August 24, 1948, Box 8, File "Human Rights: General, 1948," Lot File 55D429, *RG 59*; Discrimination Against Negroes in the United States, position paper, August 30, 1948, SD/A/C.3/76, Box 173, File "Instructions to the United States Delegation to the Third Regular Session of the General Assembly: Committee 3 (Social, Humanitarian, and Cultural), *RG 84*; Minutes of the Tenth Meeting of the United States Delegation to the Third Regular Session of the General Assembly: October 1, 1948, October 5, 1948, US(P)A/M/(Chr)/10, Box 60, File "US(P)/A/M(CHR)/1-34," ibid.; Porter McKeever to Political Officers, memo, September 1, 1948, Box 179, File "Documentation for Rebuttal of Soviet Propaganda, Background Book," ibid.; Discrimination Against Negroes in the United States, comment paper, August 30, 1948,

What an opportunity. The State Department finally had to admit that the "Negro problem" was a foreign policy embarrassment of the first magnitude and that it had called into question the very essence of American democracy. And, with an *Appeal to the World* lurking in the shadows, the U.S. delegation would now have to go after a Declaration of Human Rights with a lot more vigor than it had initially planned. White, therefore, originally planned to use the mere existence of *An Appeal to the World* to move the United States toward a more comprehensive, enforceable Declaration and Covenant. He was particularly enthralled with the idea of an international court of human rights and believed that the U.S. delegation could be prodded to take much more "courageous action . . . on the basic issues." White, ever-mindful of Roosevelt's fury, had absolutely no intention of openly brandishing *An Appeal to the World* to effect his plan. But the State Department did not know that. In fact, the Department had no idea what the NAACP planned to do at this session, and Roosevelt's advisors feared the worst. That is, of course, until White's ego, anger at Du Bois, and need to ingratiate himself further with Mrs. Roosevelt superceded the fight for African American human rights.[104]

Only two days after receiving Du Bois' memo (and four days *before* the scholar was even fired), White informed Chester S. Williams, the State Department's public liaison officer, that the NAACP had absolutely "no intention" of pressing for a UN hearing for *An Appeal to the World*. The petition, which White had once called "magnificent," was now denigrated as Du Bois' "pet project." It was only because of Du Bois' age and "personal prestige," White said, that the NAACP had even lent its name and resources to the petition. Conveniently forgetting that he, too, was instrumental in its development, White insinuated that Du Bois, the "lone-wolf," had undertaken this massive effort without the consent or advice of the NAACP's Board of Directors. White then confided that, during this session of the UN, Du Bois probably would not approach any of the delegates in the Soviet bloc "to carry the ball," but would, instead, impose on the Liberians to sneak the petition onto the UN's agenda. White then pledged that, unlike Du Bois, the NAACP had committed itself wholly to the "positive work of the Human Rights Commission and the Declaration on the Human Rights."[105]

SD/A/C.3/75, Box 175, File "Background Book: Committee III (Social, Humanitarian, and Cultural), Volume IV," ibid.

104. Roy Wilkins to Harold Preece, August 4, 1948, Part 14, Reel 17, *NAACP Int'l*; Walter White, untitled column, August 26, 1948, Box 74, File "Articles Walter White, *Chicago Defender* Columns, 1948," *Papers of the NAACP*.

105. Walter White to the [NAACP] Board of Directors, October 22, 1947, Box 3338, File "NAACP, 1945–47," *Roosevelt Papers*; Chester S. Williams to Mrs. Roosevelt et al.,

What a major blunder from a man who was usually so astute and who had proudly boasted that "I am a politician, yes."[106] White quickly tried to cover his tracks, but at a certain level he knew the import of what he had just done. Instead of the bravado he evidenced in late August, White now proffered a series of excuses why African Americans' aspirations for human rights would go unfulfilled. He observed that "there is little to be expected from the UN General Assembly meeting" because the threat of war in Berlin and the political chaos in France had cast a pall over the entire session. Although White quickly asserted that he, of course, was no pessimist, he did remark that he was "realist enough to know that any advance towards the goal of human equality is unlikely to be made under existing circumstances." He failed to add, of course, that those circumstances included his complete abandonment of the NAACP's petition and sell-out to the State Department. He could only conclude that "[w]e have . . . only an outside chance of winning."[107]

The chances for African American equality, given the endemic racism in the United States, were never very great; but those chances dwindled significantly when the black leadership relentlessly attacked each other. What White and Du Bois failed to realize was that it was not of a question of either/or; it was a question of both. The struggle for African Americans' human rights required the NAACP's petition *and* a strong Declaration and Covenant on Human Rights. Du Bois was right on target. *An Appeal to the World* had struck a nerve because, unlike many of the smaller organizations, the NAACP had the clout, credibility, and prestige to be taken seriously. Thus, for the American delegation, especially as it tried to distinguish itself from the Kremlin with the "theme song" of human rights, the threat of *An Appeal to the World* was an omnipresent force that compelled the United States to maneuver and countermaneuver against consistent international "criticism about the treatment of the negroes." Legal historian Mary Dudziak, in fact, has documented how essential international pressure was in getting the Truman administration to support several desegregation lawsuits. Yet, those cases merely shaved the outer layers of a glacier that had frozen African Americans out of the political

memorandum of conversation, September 9, 1948, Box 78, File "1948–49, Discrimination: Race," *RG 84*.

106. *The University of Chicago Roundtable: Civil Rights and Loyalty, A Radio Discussion by Arthur Schlesinger, Jr., Walter White and Louis Wirth*, November 23, 1947, found in Box 36, File "WH Files-Civil Rights-Pamphlets (re: General Civil Rights Report, 1948–49 [folder 1]), *Nash Papers*.

107. Walter White, untitled column, September 14, 1948, Box 74, File "Articles—Walter White *Chicago Defender* Columns, 1948," *Papers of the NAACP*.

and economic mainstream of America for centuries. This is not to diminish the importance of those Supreme Court cases, but it is evident that legal strategies were only a partial answer to black inequality. Simply removing the legal barriers could not cause the whole edifice of oppression to crumble. But instead of recognizing this, Walter White had just ceded an important weapon in the fight for black equality.[108]

Du Bois was not blameless in this debacle either. He, too, had made an equally serious error in judgment. Although he viewed the Declaration and Covenant as trite and meaningless, they were not. This was the first attempt to define and codify standards of human rights that were the inherent rights of all people, regardless of race, color, sex, nationality, or citizenship. These were rights that transcended and permeated the boundaries of national sovereignty. This was not mere "pious" verbiage; this was an incredible opportunity. And because the "trinity" was truly "impotent," it was imperative to find an alternate power base to exact justice. That reality compelled William Dean and Walter White to recognize that because African Americans had the most to lose – as well as the most to gain – there had to be someone at or the near the Declaration's drafting table who spoke "for the Negro." Without that voice, the U.S. delegation, including Mrs. Roosevelt, felt very comfortable trying to insert the ultimate artifacts of American racism – states' rights and Jim Crow – into an international human rights document. Moreover, because there was a direct correlation between the breadth of the Declaration's enumerated rights and those that would eventually be placed in the Covenant, it was essential that the Declaration include those elements most important to African Americans. If key principles, such as equal pay for equal work, adequate housing, health care, education, and the right to social security, were absent from the Declaration, their exclusion from the Covenant was a virtual certainty. Yet, from his aerie on "Mt. Sinai," Du Bois remained entirely too dismissive of the moral and legal power that the Declaration and Covenant could hold. Indeed, by the time of Du Bois' withering attack on the Declaration, there had already been several precedent-setting cases, in which the courts used the human rights provisions in the UN Charter to overturn state-sanctioned racial discrimination. Thus, the Declaration's and Covenant's potential, especially harnessed to the incredible legal and political minds in the NAACP, could have helped transform the Civil Rights Movement into a human rights movement. Instead, the feud between Du Bois and White had left the NAACP's petition in the dustbin of history and African Americans' human rights hopes resting solely

108. Dudziak, "Desegregation as a Cold War Imperative," 61–120.

on Walter White's now compromised ability to influence the American delegation.[109]

White certainly was not prepared for the task before him. Although he had sought Rayford Logan's advice, the Howard University professor was inundated with work from the Haitian embassy and could only direct White to verify that issues concerning implementation, the right to petition, the right to vote, and the right to publicly supported education, which he had identified after the State Department's March briefing session, had now been addressed.[110] Thus, with no more information on the intricacies of the Declaration than he had before the Du Bois imbroglio, and with no partially concealed petition in his arsenal, White set sail for Paris.[111]

Nothing could conceal how far awry the NAACP's human rights plans had gone. During the debates on human rights, White soon came to realize how totally unprepared he was. He quickly became bored and irritated with the long, rambling arguments over "the nature of God" or the "quibbling" over the meaning of the word "birth." White further complained that the "work at Paris on the human rights . . . issues is painfully, annoyingly slow." He groaned that it would be a "miracle" if the General Assembly gave itself the authority to sanction human rights violators, and it was obvious that the most substantive debates would not begin until sometime in November, which, unfortunately, because of his pressing responsibilities stateside, he would have to miss.[112] White therefore was conveniently absent during the most intense debates on the draft Declaration, and he had returned to the United States by the time the General Assembly approved the International Declaration of Human Rights in December 1948.[113]

109. Memorandum of Conversation with Mrs. Franklin D. Roosevelt, Mr. D. V. Sandifer et al., August 24, 1948, Box 8, File "Human Rights: General, 1948," Lot File 55D429, *RG 59*; Bert B. Lockwood, Jr., "The United Nations Charter and United States Civil Rights Litigation: 1946–1955," *Iowa Law Review*, 69 (May 1984): 901–50; Jo L. Southard, "Human Rights Provision of the U.N. Charter: The History in U.S. Courts," *International Law Students Association Journal of International and Comparative Law*, 1 (Spring 1995): 41–65.

110. Rayford Logan, diary, September 10, 1948, *Logan Papers*; Rayford Logan to White, September 11, 1948, Box 635, File "United Nations General Assembly, October 1948," *Papers of the NAACP*.

111. Walter White, untitled *Chicago Defender* article, September 14, 1948, Box 74, File "Articles—Walter White *Chicago Defender* Columns, 1948," ibid.

112. White to Arthur Spingarn, October 8, 1948, Box 94-8, Folder 181, *Spingarn Papers*; Walter White, "World Insecurity Mirrored at UN Assembly," September 30, 1948, Box 81, File "Articles: Walter White Syndicated Column, 1949," *Papers of the NAACP*.

113. Wilkins to [Arthur] Spingarn, September 15, 1948, Box 635, File "United Nations—General Assembly, Sept. 1948," ibid.; White to the Office, September 17, 1948, ibid.;

White, however, remained in Europe just long enough to avoid the next round of the Du Bois wars. The Association's co-founder refused to go quietly into exile. Du Bois' cause was aided by the blistering deluge of protests from stalwart NAACP supporters and the rash of membership cancellations that the Association simply could not afford as its balance sheet poured red ink. The Board had therefore decided that, at its upcoming meeting in October, it would reevaluate the decision to fire Du Bois. In response, Shirley Graham immediately formed an Emergency Committee for Dr. Du Bois that would try to force the Board to rescind its termination order. Graham's strategy called for zero percent contrition and 100 percent confrontation. At Graham's insistence, the Emergency Committee flooded the NAACP branches with Du Bois' unrelenting, merciless attack on White's ties with the Truman administration.[114] In that missive, Du Bois charged that, instead of addressing the critical issues affecting African Americans, such as a plan for economic self-sufficiency, the 1947 NAACP Annual Convention was virtually a "Truman rally." He also charged that White had delayed printing the NAACP's petition, *An Appeal to the World*, just long enough to allow *To Secure These Rights* to steal its thunder. In Du Bois' eyes, White had sacrificed African Americans' best chance at human rights for a cheap political stunt to strengthen Truman's popularity in the black community and increase the president's election chances. Du Bois further charged that White had consistently thwarted his requests to the Board to fund research and publications on Africa and colonialism. The result, Du Bois insisted, was that the dictatorially run Association had no policy research wing and no ability to link its important legal work with the equally important, but neglected, economic and social agenda.[115]

Graham added her own inflammatory blast when, prior to the October Board meeting, she wrote Spingarn and launched into an harangue about

"Broadcast over UN Radio from Paris, by Walter White," October 1948, Box 635, File "United Nations General Assembly, October 1948," ibid.; "Report from Mr. White in Paris Received 10/11/48 (on UN General Assembly)," ibid.; "Report to the Office Not for Publication Until Later, Received from Walter White," October 19, 1948, ibid.; "Report on the Progress of the Efforts to Secure Action First on a Declaration on Human Rights by the General Assembly," October 19, 1948, ibid.; Jason Berger, *A New Deal for the World: Eleanor Roosevelt and American Foreign Policy,* Social Science Monographs (New York: Columbia University Press, 1981), 68.

114. Hugh Smythe to Du Bois, September 14, 1948, Reel 62, *Du Bois*; Lil (Murphy) to Hugh Smythe, September 29, 1948, ibid.; George B. Murphy, Jr., to Shirley Graham, memo, October 8, 1948, Reel 61, ibid.; White to Wilkins, memo, October 11, 1948, Box 635, File "United Nations General Assembly, October 1948," *Papers of the NAACP*.

115. W. E. B. Du Bois, "My Relations with the NAACP," Box 241, File "William E. B. Du Bois—General, Oct.–Dec. 1948," ibid.

the "vindictive" and "petty" behavior of Walter White and Roy Wilkins, who were "[l]esser men" who had seized "the controls of a bureaucratically run organization" and tried to "drive [Du Bois] away."[116] In the end, the only thing that Graham's confrontational strategy accomplished was to convince the Board that its initial decision was the right one. As Wilkins explained to one NAACP branch president, if Du Bois was not fired, "an intolerable situation would develop." Du Bois' tendency to "air issues... prior to taking them up through regular channels" was destructive and unacceptable. Moreover, as further proof of Du Bois' destructive impact on the NAACP, Wilkins shared his suspicions that the infamous September 7 memo was actually politically motivated. Wilkins laid out his thesis carefully:

> [A]lthough [Du Bois] had all the information as to the NAACP's plans on August 20, he did not raise any objection until September 7. If he felt that the NAACP was making a mistake he could have raised his objections promptly on August 20. He could have asked for a special meeting of the Board. He could have done a number of things. What caused him to wait from August 20 to September 7? Everyone knows that it does not take Dr. W. E. B. Du Bois two and one-half weeks to analyze a situation and make his views known. It seems fair to assume that the action of September 7 was a deliberate one, carefully timed for a purpose other than arriving at a solution of the situation as posed by Dr. Du Bois.[117]

Under those circumstances, there was no way that the Board was going to "budge an inch." Graham angrily declared that the Association had "fastened a cord about its own neck... that will eventually strangle it"; nevertheless, the September resolution stood.[118] Du Bois' contract would not be renewed. Instead, at the end of his contract in December, he would become, with the help of Henry Wallace and Paul Robeson, the vice chairman of the Council on African Affairs.[119]

With Du Bois out of the way, White was ready to enjoy Truman's election-day triumph. Both the NAACP's and the Administration's analysis showed that the black vote kept Truman in the White House, and

116. Shirley Graham to Arthur Spingarn, October 11, 1948, Box 240, File "William E. B. Du Bois: Dismissal—Individuals, 1948," ibid.; "Resolution Passed by the National Council, ASP, at the Academic Freedom Rally, in the Case of Dr. W. E. B. Du Bois," October 10, 1948, ibid.

117. Wilkins to Shirley Graham, October 13, 1948, ibid.

118. [Shirley Graham] to Clyde Miller, October 18, 1948, Reel 62, *Du Bois*.

119. Wilkins to A. R. Traylor, October 19, 1948, Box 240, File "William E. B. Du Bois—Dismissal: Board of Directors—Branches, 1948–49," *Papers of the NAACP*; Du Bois to Mrs. [Anita] Blaine, draft, n.d., Reel 61, *Du Bois*; Du Bois to Mrs. [Anita] Blaine, December 15, 1948, ibid.; Doxey Wilkerson to Du Bois, December 25, 1948, ibid.

the president appeared ready to deliver on his civil rights promises, even confiding to Eleanor Roosevelt that the Dixiecrats' exodus meant that the South was no longer "the tail wagging the Democratic dog."[120] The president was beholden, that was clear. In addition to the president's indebtedness to African American voters, the NAACP's leaders were even more confident that they could secure their civil rights goals because they had "access" to Truman and David Niles, the president's administrative assistant for minority affairs. In this regard, as with so much lately, the Association leadership was mistaken. Niles, according to White House aide Stephen J. Spingarn, was a "liability that HST inherited from FDR." Instead of taking his job seriously, "Dave made himself very scarce at the White House" and Niles "alone among the senior Presidential assistants never attended HST's daily morning staff meeting." When Niles was on the job, he viewed his role as a watchdog for the status quo not as a facilitator for minority rights. He told Stephen Spingarn that when it came to issues of civil rights and minority affairs "if you did nothing about a problem long enough it went away." Niles seemed to hope that not only the problem, but also the messengers for civil rights would evaporate. Thus, when Walter White sought an appointment with Truman, Niles "kissed him off" with some bogus excuse. And when an African American labor leader complained about racial discrimination, Niles suggested that the administration "give this gentleman the silent treatment." Or, "as an alternative," Niles offered derisively, "we could be so kind as to refer him to [the UN's MINDIS], of which our old friend Jonathan Daniels is the U.S. Representative."[121]

The problem of commitment, however, extended well beyond David Niles. It reached directly into the Oval Office. Even after the president recognized that this nation had to do better, had to be better, Truman still could not rid himself of Missouri's Confederate-leaning, slaveholding roots. Truman, for all of his strengths, was simply not philosophically or psychologically equipped to accept true black equality. His penchant for referring to African Americans as "niggers" was well known. His disdain for social equality was a matter of public record. And his contempt for nonviolent protests against Jim Crow was clearly documented. Paternalistically, he referred to Walter White, a man who led an

120. Truman to Eleanor Roosevelt, December 13, 1948, Box 4560, File "Harry S Truman 1947 and 1948," *Roosevelt Papers*.

121. *Hastie*; C[harles] G. R[oss] to Matthew J. Connelly, memo, August 23, 1945, Box 1235, File "413 (1945–49), *Truman:OF*; Stephen J. Spingarn to Donald R. McCoy, memo, April 4, 1969, Box 42, File "Civil Rights File-Civil Rights Correspondence Regarding—under Truman Administration," *SJ Spingarn Papers*; David K. Niles to Matthew J. Connelly, January 6, 1947 (sic), Box 543, File "OF 93 1948 [1 of 3]," *Truman:OF*.

organization with over a million dollar annual budget and 500,000 members, as a "kid" who needed to be "calm[ed] down" and he wanted the White House nursemaid, David Niles, to do it. None of this, of course, bode well for real access.[122] Instead, it looked like the Association had built its hopes for equality on a foundation of "wishy-washy liberalism" and old Southern paternalism.[123] And now a hurricane from below the Mason-Dixon Line threatened to blow the NAACP's house of cards away.

It quickly became clear that neither Truman nor his Congressional lieutenants, even in the face of the South's crushing electoral defeat, had the savvy or the commitment to secure the promised legislation. Indeed, words like "botched," "equivocated," "timid," and "fumbling" dominate the histories of Truman's postelection civil rights efforts. The level of incompetence was simply astounding. By the time Truman and his congressional aides had finished, not only was there no new civil rights legislation, but the filibuster rule, which allowed the Southern Democrats to talk proposed civil rights bills to death, had been strengthened immeasurably.[124] And after that stunning filibuster victory in March 1949, or as White labeled it "fiasco," the Southern Democrats' power was further enhanced by the appointment of Mississippi's James Eastland as chair of a subcommittee responsible for all civil rights bills in the Senate, except for the poll tax and FEPC, which came under the purview of the other senator from Mississippi, John Stennis. The NAACP braced as it could sense the South's resurgent, unrepentant power and how that power had chastened the once bellicose Truman. Throughout 1949, therefore, the plaintive wails from the African American community about Truman's "moral collapse," "betrayal," and "surrender to segregation" filled the air. And when DNC chairman John McGrath, for the sake of "'unity,'"

122. HST to Dave [Niles], November 24, 1945, Box 26, File "Civil Rights/Negro Affairs, 1945–June 1947," *Niles Papers*; Stephen J. Spingarn to Donald R. McCoy, memo, April 4, 1969, Box 42, File "Civil Rights File-Civil Rights Correspondence Regarding—under Truman Administration," *SJ Spingarn Papers*; McCullough, *Truman*, 247, 588, 971–72; "'President' Truman Said:" July 8, 1947, Box 544, File "OF 93 1949–1950 [1 of 2]," *Truman:OF*; Helen L. Kass to Truman, January 27, 1947, Box 548, File "OF 93B 1945–June 1948," ibid.; A. L. Reaves to Truman, January 23, 1947, ibid.; Harry Brand, Jr., to Truman, January 25, 1947, ibid.; Clarence T. R. Nelson to Truman, January 28, 1947, ibid.

123. Leonard Dinnerstein, comment paper on: Carol Anderson, "'With Friends Like These...': Eleanor Roosevelt, the NAACP, and the Limits of Liberalism," and Cheryl Greenberg, "Jews, Interracial Coalitions, and the Challenges to Liberalism," Organization of American Historians Conference, March 31, 2000.

124. Donald R. McCoy and Richard T. Ruetten, *Quest and Response: Minority Rights and the Truman Administration* (Lawrence: University Press of Kansas, 1973), 148–49, 171–200; William C. Berman, *The Politics of Civil Rights in the Truman Administration* (Columbus: Ohio State University Press, 1970), 137–81.

"welcomed" the Dixiecrats "back into the Democratic ranks" it was clear that the NAACP's Truman-or-nothing strategy had just backfired.[125]

By June 1949, White appeared beaten, crestfallen, and wearied. Citing health problems, he asked the Board to accept his resignation as executive secretary of the NAACP. After intense negotiations, the Board finally agreed to a one-year medical leave.[126] White, however, had exaggerated his health problems to conceal the fact that he was planning to violate one of the major taboos in Jim Crow America – black men and white women. His African American wife of 27 years, Gladys, had agreed to divorce him so that, within a week, he could wed the white, South African-born Poppy Cannon.[127] Wilkins, who was ambushed by reporters with the news during the Association's annual convention, later remarked that half of the NAACP's members with whom he spoke "wanted to lynch Walter for leaving Gladys, and the other half wanted to string him up for marrying a white woman."[128]

The marriage, some claimed, merely validated the Southern demagogues' contention that the NAACP was fighting to ensure that there would be a white woman in every black man's bed. Columnist J. Robert Smith therefore declared that White had just lost all of his credibility, and it would be difficult for him, as the head of the NAACP, to "fight the cause of the Negro" by day while "playing pappy with Poppy in the night.[129] White's choice for a new wife was further complicated by the fact that no

125. G. L. Bishop to Truman, July 8, 1949, Box 548, File "OF 93B July–December 1949," [2 of 2], *Truman:OF*; "The 40th Annual NAACP Conference," by Edward E. Strong and William Taylor, Box 167-1, Folder 18, *Strong Papers*; Roy Wilkins to Officers of Branches/State Conference/Youth Councils and College Chapters, memo, October 21, 1949, found in Box 167-6, Folder 5, ibid.; "The Dixiecrat Purge," November 15, 1949, *Providence Bulletin*, found in Box 59, File "Civil Rights and Southern Splits: Desk Corresp. Clippings-Senatorial," *Sen. McGrath Papers*.

126. White to Branch President, June 24, 1949, Box 610, File "Staff: Walter White, Leave of Absence, 1949," *Papers of the NAACP*; Louis T. Wright to Carl Murphy, draft, September 1, 1949, ibid.

127. "New Love for Walter?" *Pittsburgh Courier*, July 16, 1949; "Walter Whites Divorced," Baltimore *Afro-American*, July 16, 1949; "Wife Divorces Walter White: Mexican Decree Ends Marriage of 27 Years," *Chicago Defender*, July 16, 1949; "Walter White, Poppy Cannon Said Married," *Atlanta Daily World*, July 28, 1949; "Did Walter White Marry His White Sweetheart?" *New York Amsterdam News* (n.d.); "Hint Walter White Romance," *New York Amsterdam News*, July 9, 1949; Wilkins, *Standing Fast*, 203–04.

128. Ibid., 205.

129. McCoy and Ruetten, *Quest and Response*, 179; J. Robert Smith, "California Writer Raps Walter White for Taking White Bride," *St. Paul Recorder*, August 12, 1949; "C.C. Spaulding Chides Walter White for His Recent Marriage," *Chicago Defender*, September 3, 1949.

one had ever heard of Poppy Cannon, the fashion editor for *Mademoiselle* magazine, in civil rights circles. For many in the black community, she was this "bizarre creature" with three children by three different husbands, who, instead of working for the cause, had spent her energies relentlessly pursuing and seducing a very powerful African American man.[130] NAACP member Lucille Miller concluded that White's "philandering" behavior was grounds for instant dismissal.[131] Board member Carl Murphy agreed and declared that White had discredited the Association and should be permanently removed as executive secretary.[132]

William H. Hastie called for cooler heads to prevail. He countered that the NAACP could not fire White simply because the man married a white woman.[133] But not everyone saw it that way. Long-term Board member, Alfred Baker Lewis, was thoroughly disgusted with White's recent performance. Lewis had already voiced his disenchantment about White's "inept leadership" that had allowed the filibuster fiasco to happen in the first place. The executive secretary's case was further weakened by his article in *Look* magazine in which he advocated the use of skin bleaching creams to allow African Americans to "pass" as whites and thereby end America's racial problems. This "quackery," one editorial raged, "will accomplish" about as much to cure America's ills "as Mr. White's marriage to a white woman." "Walter White . . . is unfit to be a leader of 14,000,000 Negroes," another editorial exclaimed, and it was clear that White had taken "the coward's way out" by putting the onus of ending racial discrimination on African Americans instead of where it rightly belonged. Many then questioned if White's views were also the views of the NAACP.[134] White's antics had clearly made the NAACP a laughingstock and an object of derision. More importantly, Roy Wilkins

130. Wilkins, *Standing Fast*, 204–05; W. (from Washington, D.C.) to NAACP, postcard, August 23, 1949, Box 610, File "Staff: Walter White Marriage, 1949," *Papers of the NAACP*.

131. Lucille Miller to Louis Wright, August 2, 1949, ibid.; S. K. Bryson to NAACP, October 15, 1949, ibid.

132. Carl Murphy to Palmer Weber, August 31, 1949, ibid.; Carl Murphy to Palmer Weber, September 6, 1949, ibid.

133. William H. Hastie to Carl Murphy, October 3, 1949, ibid.; Palmer Weber to Carl Murphy, September 1, 1949, ibid.; Wilkins, *Standing Fast*, 205.

134. Walter White, "Has Science Conquered the COLOR LINE?" Box 79, File "Article: Walter White *Look* magazine, 1949," *Papers of the NAACP*; "Do You Want to be White?" August 26, 1949, *St. Louis Argus*, found in ibid.; "Leaders Ridicule White's Solution of Race Problem through Bleach," August 27, 1949, *Afro-American*, found in ibid.; "Critics Blast Walter White's Article on 'Turning White' in Look Magazine," August 27, 1949, found in ibid.; Walter White 'Conquers' Color Line, August 20, 1949, *Akron Informer*, found in ibid.

was certain that White's activities were partly responsible for the decline in membership that was plaguing some of the NAACP branches and thus the organization's coffers. Frankly, he resented having to clean up the mess that White had made. Alfred Baker Lewis decided, however, that instead of firing the executive secretary and generating more publicity, the Board should simply accept White's resignation when his leave of absence expired in June 1950. The Association had everything to gain and nothing to lose, Lewis noted, because Roy Wilkins' efficiency and talent made it clear that the NAACP would not miss a beat or Walter White.[135]

Wilkins' rising star would signal a definite shift in the direction of the NAACP. More domestically focused, dogmatic, and anti-Communist than White, Wilkins' strength lay in implementing someone else's vision. This was a critical asset for the number two man in an organization, but was a fatal flaw for the one entrusted with setting the NAACP's direction, tone, and pace. His lack of vision accelerated the NAACP's retreat from international issues, except in cases concerning South Africa and the Italian colonies in which the NAACP was more effective, strident, and resistant to Cold War dogma than even the black Left.[136] But other than that,

135. Roy Wilkins to Eugene E. Peterson, September 26, 1949, ibid.; Alfred Baker Lewis to Carl Murphy, August 30, 1949, Box 610, File "Staff: Walter White, Leave of Absence, 1949," ibid.

136. Walter White to the First Secretary of the Imperial Ethiopian Legation, September 9, 1948, Box 322, File "Italian Colonies Disposition of, Correspondence Regarding, 1948–49," ibid.; Marshall to Secretary of State, telegram, October 3, 1947, Box 140, File "921-980, 10/2/47-10/9/47," *RG 84*; E. Sylvia Pankhurst to Walter White, March 3, 1948, Box 404, File "Logan, Rayford, 1948–49," *Papers of the NAACP*; Logan, diary entry, September 5, 1948, Box 4, File "Diaries, Personal: 1948–49," *Logan Papers*; Logan, diary entry, October 1, 1948, ibid.; Logan, diary entry, May 28, 1949, Box 4, File "Diaries, Personal: 1948–49," ibid.; Madison S. Jones, Jr. to Michael Roche, September 19, 1949, Box 323, File "Italian Colonies, Disposition of, Correspondence Regarding, May 1949–50," *Papers of the NAACP*; Roy Wilkins to Trygve Lie, September 29, 1949, ibid.; "Action on Italian Colonies at Paris Conference is Test of Peace Aims," *New Africa*, Vol. 5, no. 7 (July–August, 1946); "Interpreting the Foreign Ministers' Discussion on Italian Colonies," *New Africa*, Vol. 4, no. 9 (October 1945); "A Six-Point Program for Africa and the Peace Settlement," *New Africa*, Vol. 4, no. 8 (August–September 1945); Du Bois to White, memo, August 23, 1948, Box 241, File "W. E. B. Du Bois—General (Jan.-Sept. 1948)," *Papers of the NAACP*; W. E. B. Du Bois, "Ethiopia and Eritrea," *New Africa*, Vol. 8, no. 3 (March 1949); Roy Wilkins to Editor *New York Times*, November 18, 1949, Box 323, File "Italian Colonies, Disposition of, Correspondence Regarding, May 1949–50," *Papers of the NAACP*; "Council Urges Just and Prompt Decision on Italian Colonies," press release, September 28, 1948, Reel 2, *Hunton*; Mr. Jones to Mr. Hickerson, memo with attachment "Anglo-American Co-Operation in Fourth Committee of the General Assembly," November 30, 1951, Box 2, File "6th General Assembly," Lot File 58D33, *RG 59*; Memorandum of Conversation, September 23, 1948, US(P)/A/32, Box 55, File "US(P)/A/1-70," *RG 84*;

Wilkins did not understand the international realm, its connections to the conditions ravaging black America, and was, therefore, not convinced that the Association's efforts in that arena justified the costs. He was also certain that internationalism was synonymous with communism.[137]

Wilkins's proclivities would seep out in the most destructive ways. For example, in 1947, Rosa Lee Ingram, a black sharecropper in Georgia, and her 14- and 16-year-old sons were convicted of murdering a white man who had "cursed her" and beat her "until the blood ran." Originally sentenced to death by hanging, the Ingrams' sentences were eventually reduced to life imprisonment. Yet, a life sentence for what was clearly self-defense prompted the National Committee to Free the Ingram Family to petition the UN in 1949 for help. The petition, written by Du Bois, carefully laid out the facts of the case and focused on the inequity of a criminal justice system that could let the quadruple lynching at Moore's Ford go unpunished, while simultaneously condemning two black boys and the mother of 12 to a grim existence in Georgia's prison system. Officials in the Department of Justice "warned" the State Department that, although they believed "the facts in the Ingram case are not as alleged in the petition," it would "prove difficult" to convince other nations that the Ingrams actually received a "fair trial." Because Ingram was a black-woman-sharecropper in Georgia, no less, the State Department believed that this was a tailor-made case for the Soviet propaganda mill and that there was a "likelihood that the USSR may raise the Ingram case in the General Assembly." Worse yet, the Department was afraid that "this may be the first in a series of petitions relating to such unfortunate incidents – petitions inspired by the Communist Party, U.S.A. acting on orders from the Cominform." When contacted by the State Department for advice, Roy Wilkins intimated that the State Department's analysis was right on target. Wilkins explained that, although the NAACP was handling the Ingrams' legal defense, the "Association had no connection with the National Committee" and then "implied" that the Committee was "communist-dominated." Wilkins's spin on the petition gave the Department all the ammunition it needed to undermine the credibility of the petition and the Ingram case, as well.[138]

Channing H. Tobias to Walter White, November 12, 1952, Part 14, Reel 4, *NAACP-Int'l*; Channing H. Tobias to John D. Hickerson, May 19, 1952, Box 2, File "6th General Assembly," Lot File 58D33, *RG 59*.

137. Wilkins to Logan, telegram, June 7, 1949, Box 404, File "Rayford Logan, 1948–49," *Papers of the NAACP*; Wilkins to Arthur Spingarn, September 15, 1948, Box 635, File "United Nations—General Assembly, Sept. 1948," ibid.

138. Maude White Katz to Du Bois, April 13, 1949, Reel 64, *Du Bois*; Du Bois to Maude White Katz, April 15, 1949, ibid.; Du Bois to Hugh Smythe, April 15, 1949, ibid.;

Wilkins's disdain for blending international issues with the struggle for black equality also came through in a venomous response to a speech by Paul Robeson in April 1949 to the World Peace Congress in Paris, where Robeson was deliberately misquoted as saying that African Americans would never fight against the Soviet Union.[139] In a blistering editorial in the *Crisis*, Wilkins went straight into attack mode. "While people in ... Texas and ... Alabama ... were battling ... and yelling for help," Wilkins wrote, "Robeson was writing and talking about Africa [and] singing Russian work songs." The pampered, rich, movie star barricaded himself from "ordinary American Negroes" and traded the leadership position he could have had in the United States for a "circle of international intellectuals ... and causes that [barely] touched the American Negro's plight."[140] Wilkins was joined in his attack by a group of African American leaders, including Brooklyn Dodger Jackie Robinson, who were paraded before Congress to denounce Robeson and prove that African Americans were loyal to the United States.[141]

For Robeson, the black leadership's attack on him was just the latest in a string of crises. In 1948, Robeson's Council on African Affairs, like the NAACP, went through its own bloodied episode of internecine warfare. Founded in 1936, the Council had a national membership of less than 100, a dedicated core of 25 Board members, and had evolved into Max Yergan's personal fiefdom. Ralph Bunche warned his colleagues to stay clear of the "opportunistic" and shallow Yergan. The "Kremlin apologist" openly played with the "CP boys," he said, and the Council itself was riddled

[Hugh Smythe] to Du Bois, memo, June 4, 1949, ibid.; Du Bois to Mrs. Katz, June 10, 1949, ibid.; "A Petition to the Human Rights Commission of the Social and Economic Council of the United Nations: And to the General Assembly of the United Nations; and to the Several Delegations of the Member States of the United Nations," August 22, 1949, Box 5048, Decimal File 811.4016/10-1041, *RG 59*; Durward V. Sandifer to George Washington, October 14, 1949, Box 5048, Decimal File 811.4016/10-1041, ibid.; Kotschnig to Sandifer, memo, October 10, 1949, Box 5048, Decimal File 811.4016/10-1049, ibid.; Memorandum of Conversation, August 29, 1949, Box 5048, Decimal File 811.4016/10-1041, ibid.; Sandifer to Mrs. Roosevelt, memo, October 12, 1949, Box 4685, Decimal File 811.4016/10-1041, ibid.

139. Martin Bauml Duberman, *Paul Robeson* (New York: Alfred A. Knopf, 1988), 341–42; Logan, diary, February 28, 1950, Box 5, File "Diaries, Personal: 1950–51," *Logan Papers*.

140. Hunton to Council Member, May 23, 1949, Reel 7, *Robeson*; [Roy Wilkins], "Robeson Speaks for Robeson," *Crisis*, Vol. 56, no. 5 (May 1949): 137.

141. Congress, House, Committee on Un-American Activities, *Hearings Regarding Communist Infiltration of Minority Groups*, 81st Cong., 1st sess., July 13, 1949, 454–55; P. L. Prattis, "What's All This Robeson Fuss?" August 17, 1949, *Pittsburgh Post-Gazette*, found in Box 144-17, Folder 11, *Prattis Papers*; Charley Cherokee, "Your Lips Tell Me No, No," July 23, 1949, *Chicago Defender* found in Reel 2, *Robeson*.

Photo 3.3. The alliance that outraged the U.S. government and Roy Wilkins. Paul Robeson with a petition sponsored by an American–Soviet friendship coalition in 1949 supporting peace.

© Julius Lazarus/Special Collections, Rutgers University Libraries.

with fellow travelers and had a well-known Communist sympathizer as its "financial angel," a charge that even Du Bois had to acknowledge was "probably true."[142]

142. FBI Report 100-949, October 28, 1946, Reel 2, *FBI File on NNC*; Ralph Bunche to Clark M. Eichelberger, April 11, 1944, Reel 2, *Bunche*; Du Bois to George Padmore, July 12, 1946, Reel 59, *Du Bois*; Hollis R. Lynch, *Black American Radicals and the Liberation of Africa: The Council on African Affairs, 1937–1955*, introduction by St. Clair Drake, Africana Studies and Research Center Monograph Series, no. 5 (Ithaca, New York: Cornell University Press, 1978).

Yergan's affinity for the Left was rapidly dissipating, however. He had just witnessed the Communist party's abandonment of the National Negro Congress and was determined to steer his last base of power, the Council, away from the Communist Party, USA. The CP was not his only concern, however as the U.S. government was quickly closing in on the CAA. In November 1947, Attorney General Tom Clark placed the Council's name on the list of subversive organizations that threatened to overthrow the U.S. government. Panicked at this development, Yergan confided to Rayford Logan that he was determined to sever the Council's relationship with the Communists and believed that this move would force a showdown with Robeson.[143]

The unavoidable and ugly confrontation occurred at a Council meeting on February 2, 1948. Robeson tried to pack that session with all of his "liberal-minded" supporters, especially Du Bois, who would not be cowered by the growing anti-Communist sentiment in America.[144] Yergan, on the other hand, argued that if the Council was to regain its influence and vigor, it had to distance itself from the Communists and become a "non-partisan [organization] loyal . . . to American democratic principles." He insisted that the Council make an official statement that it was "neither fascist, Communist, nor subversive."[145] Robeson, though, argued that Yergan's strategy would do nothing but capitulate to popular "red-baiting" and declared that the CAA would not be "diverted [by] the Justice Department's gratuitous labeling of the Council as 'subversive'." To make it clear to everyone where he stood on the issue, Robeson, the CAA's big-name draw, threatened to resign if the Council followed Yergan's lead.[146]

The intensity of the confrontation escalated when W. Alphaeus Hunton, education director and Robeson ally, accused Yergan of being incompetent and a thief. Hunton charged that the executive director had mismanaged the Council, missed numerous opportunities to publicize Africa's plight, stifled membership drives, failed to follow through on a mandate to develop branches nationwide, and embezzled funds intended for famine relief in Sub-Saharan Africa.[147] Although Yergan's supporters challenged

143. Logan, diary, November 16, 1947, *Logan Papers*.

144. Robeson to Council Member, January 27, 1948, Reel 61, *Du Bois*.

145. "Statement: Meeting of the Council on African Affairs," February 2, 1948, ibid.

146. "Commie Issue Splits African Affairs Group," *New York World-Telegram*, February 4, 1948, found in Box 4, File "Africa—General, 1947–49," *Papers of the NAACP*; "Tobias Firm in Stand Opposing Leftists," *New York Times*, February 4, 1948, found in Box 147, File "Board of Directors—Channing Tobias, General—1943–1949," ibid.

147. Report of the Educational Director, W. A. Hunton to the Meeting of the Council on African Affairs, February 2, 1948, Reel 1, *Hunton Papers*; Lack of Collective Planning and Functioning, n.d., ibid.; "Policy and Interim Committee and Definition of Its

Hunton's right to criticize the executive director's stewardship, Robeson's faction insisted that the charges be fully investigated.[148]

In an attempt to undercut Robeson's support, Yergan waged war through the media. He told the press that the Communists were trying to use the Council to secure the Negro vote for the Progressive party's presidential candidate, Henry Wallace. On the surface, it appeared that Yergan's charges were valid. Robeson served as vice-chair of the Progressive party and wholeheartedly agreed with Wallace on many fundamental issues. But, regardless of Robeson's close ties with Wallace, the campaign was not discussed at the February and March meetings of the Council. Yergan's publicity ploy revealed both his opportunism, his lack of ethics, and his desperation. Yergan was trying to divert attention from his mismanagement of the Council by "yelling about Communists," Robeson accurately told the press.[149]

Disgusted, three members of the Council, "whom" as Hunton noted, "no-one not even Dr. Yergan, has accused of being 'left-wing,'" formally charged Yergan with "mal-feasance, mis-feasance, and non-feasance." Yergan, they asserted, had hurled the "irresponsible charge of 'communism'" at the Council to "conceal his own political retreat" from progressivism. They further declared that he had "co-mingled" substantial amounts of Council funds with his own, including almost $2,000 intended for famine relief in Africa. In fact, they said, Yergan had sent less than "25 percent of the $8,918.56 collected" to Africa. His "one-man rule" and "crude, disruptive, high-handed [and] illegal" activities could no longer be tolerated. They demanded immediate action, and Robeson was more than willing to oblige.[150]

At a special Council meeting on May 26, 1948, Yergan was "immediately suspended" as executive director of the Council on African Affairs.[151] An expensive legal battle for the Council's property ensued. Only after Yergan was officially expelled from the membership in September 1948 did he formally resign and agree to drop all claims against the

Functions: Supplementary Statement to the Committee's Progress Report," n.d. (February 1948), Reel 61, *Du Bois*. (Emphasis in original.)

148. Lynch, *Black American Radicals*, 36.

149. Hunton to Du Bois, March 7, 1948, Reel 61, *Du Bois*; Du Bois to Smythe, March 7, 1948, ibid.; Du Bois to Robeson, March 8, 1948, ibid.

150. W. A. Hunton to the Editor *New York Times*, June 21, 1948, Reel 1, *Hunton Papers*; John Latouche, Mary Church Terrell, and Henry Arthur Callis to Robeson, May 15, 1948, Reel 61, *Du Bois*; Robeson to Members of the Executive Board, May 19, 1948, ibid.

151. Hunton to Council Member, May 26, 1948, ibid.; FBI Report NY 100-25857, n.d. (June 1948?), Reel 1, *FBI File on Paul Robeson* (Wilmington, Delaware: Scholarly Resources, 1987) microfilm. (Hereafter *FBI File on Robeson*.)

Council.[152] In fact, though, Yergan never really admitted defeat. There is strong evidence that as early as April and definitely by September 1948, he had decided to exact his revenge in another way. Yergan was now fully co-operating with and supplying the FBI with information that would fuel the Bureau's relentless persecution of both the CAA and the men he had once called his friends.[153]

Thus, as the United States was falling under the spell of anti-Communism and the resurgent power of the Southern Democrats, the African American leadership was in disarray and had begun to cannibalize itself, its strategies, and its vision. Unfortunately, the feeding frenzy, especially as the Cold War intensified, would only get worse.

152. Lynch, *Black American Radicals*, 37; Robeson and Hunton to Friend, October 7, 1948, Box 355, File "Leagues: Council on African Affairs, 1948–55," *Papers of the NAACP*.
153. SAC, New York to Director, FBI, February 7, 1948, *FBI Files on Max Yergan*, Federal Bureau of Investigation, Washington, D.C. [FOIA Request] (hereafter *FBI:Yergan*); SAC, New York to Director, FBI, April 27, 1948, ibid.; J. Edgar Hoover to SAC, New York, telegram, June 7, 1948, ibid.; SAC, New York to Director, FBI, September 20, 1948, ibid.; SAC, New York to Director, FBI, October 4, 1948, ibid.

4

Bleached Souls and Red Negroes

One ever feels his twoness—an American, a Negro; two souls, two thoughts, two unreconciled strivings; two warring ideals in one dark body.

W. E. B. Du Bois[1]

In a strange Dickensian way, these were the worst of times and the worst of times. The Cold War, McCarthyism, the Soviets' atomic explosion, and the Korean War unleashed a maelstrom of fear, xenophobia, and conformity that wreaked havoc across America's political and progressive landscape. Public Enemy No. 1, of course, was the Communist Party, U.S.A. and its supporters. Headline-grabbing politicians vied for the spotlight as they created a web of laws and internal security committees to trap all of the Communists – real and imagined – who had supposedly burrowed deep into the fabric of American society. One of the most potent weapons the sentries of American democracy uncovered was the Smith Act, a relic of the early 1940s that now allowed the Justice Department to virtually outlaw the CP.[2] The African American leadership surveyed this perilous landscape and chose sides. In the end, African Americans would pay dearly for those decisions.

The government's prosecution of twelve ranking members of the Communist party and the subsequent conviction and sentencing of eleven of the defendants not only caused the CP to almost collapse, but it also pulled the Civil Rights Congress slowly into the abyss. The CRC's future dimmed considerably after it staked its resources, its personnel, and its very survival on securing the freedom of the CP's imprisoned leadership.[3] The CRC bluntly asserted that the Communist party's legal

1. W. E. B. Du Bois, *The Souls of Black Folks*, with an introduction by Nathan Hare and Alvin Poussaint (New York: New American Library, 1969), 45.
2. Ellen Schrecker, *Many Are the Crimes: McCarthyism in America* (Boston, Massachusetts and New York: Little, Brown and Co., 1998), 162, 192.
3. Aubrey Grossman to Frederick V. Field, October 11, 1950, Part 2, Reel 2, *CRC*; "CRC Appeals for $60,000 to Fight McCarran, Smith Acts," news release, Part 2, Reel 8, ibid.;

battles were the "A1 civil rights problem in fact, as well as in word." As a result, the quest for black equality was quickly demoted to a secondary, supporting role.[4]

This moment in history would not be the NAACP's finest hour either. The internal witch hunt in the Association was "utterly ruthless." Roy Wilkins and eventually a resurrected Walter White vowed to "clean out" the NAACP and "make sure that the Communists were not running it."[5] They purged *suspected* Communists, rigged the elections in the San Francisco branch to oust its left-leaning president, and limited support for the victims of the government's loyalty program to those whose patriotism had been questioned solely because of race or membership in the NAACP.[6]

Ruthlessness had a price, however. Judge Jane Bolin, vice president of the NAACP, resigned in complete frustration because, as she said, the Association leadership had become more concerned with purging Communists than with fighting for civil rights.[7] Clarence Mitchell made a similar

National Office to All Chapters and Organizations, memo, December 19, 1950, ibid.; Patterson to the Australian Communist party, March 22, 1951, Part 2, Reel 2, ibid.

4. "Minutes: Resident Board Meeting, July 16, 17, & 18, 1949," July 18, 1949, Part 2, Reel 12, ibid.

5. "Press Releases," June 24, 1950, Part 1, Reel 12, *NAACP*; Wilkins to White, memo, July 21, 1950, Box 22, File "Communism, 1950," *Papers of Roy Wilkins*, Library of Congress, Washington, DC (hereafter *Wilkins Papers)*; White to NAACP Branches, memo, August 29, 1950, Box 369, File "Leagues: Civil Rights Congress, 1948–50," *Papers of the NAACP*.

6. Clarence Mitchell to Louis E. Hosch, March 1, 1950, Box H126, File "Loyalty Review Board Cases, 1947–1951," *Papers of the NAACP Washington Bureau*; Statement for the Press by Roy Wilkins, press release, June 23, 1950, Box 201, File "Communism: General, 1949–1950," *Papers of the NAACP*; Minutes of the Meeting of the Board of Directors, June 22, 1950, Part 1, Reel 3, *NAACP*; Resolutions Adopted by the 41st Annual Convention, June 23, 1950, Part 1, Reel 12, ibid.; NAACP Moves to Ban Communist Activity, press release, June 24, 1950, ibid.; Minutes of the Meeting of the Board of Directors, December 11, 1950, Reel 3, *NAACP/LC*; Clarence Mitchell to Arthur L. Johnson, April 18, 1951, Box H126, File "Loyalty Review Board Cases, 1947–1951," *Papers of the NAACP Washington Bureau*; Terressa E. Griffin to Roy Wilkins, January 12, 1949, Box C20, File "San Francisco, Calif, 1948–50," *Papers of the NAACP–Branch*; Jan R. Bosfield to Carlton B. Goodlet, March 22, 1949, ibid.; Noah Griffin to Roy Wilkins, November 21, 1949, ibid.; Noah [Griffin] to Roy Wilkins, November 23, 1949, ibid.; Noah W. Griffin to Gloster B. Current, November 25, 1949, ibid.; Current to Roy Wilkins, memo, November 28, 1949, ibid.; N. W. Griffin to Gloster B. Current, ibid.; Walter White to Franklin H. Williams and Cecil Poole, December 12, 1950, ibid.; Walter White to Thurgood Marshall and Robert Carter, memo, December 15, 1950, ibid.; Carlton Goodlett to Roy Wilkins, January 11, 1950, Box C416, File "San Francisco Branch-Election Controversy, 1949–50," ibid.

7. Quoted from, Cheryl Greenberg, "The Black/Jewish Dilemma in the Early Cold War," conference paper, August 8, 1998, American Historical Association–Pacific Coast Branch.

point. Already he had witnessed delegates at the annual convention attempting to eject Jack Greenburg of the Legal Defense Fund from an important meeting and quickly discovered that because Greenburg was white, the delegates automatically assumed that he was a Communist.[8] That sloppy, overzealous vigilance carried through to other areas of the NAACP's work.

In 1950, for example, the Association sponsored a Civil Rights Mobilization to put pressure on Congress and the Truman Administration to enact the civil rights legislation promised during the 1948 campaign. Roy Wilkins conceived of the mobilization as a method to bring together leaders from major civil rights and labor organizations to develop a common legislative strategy.[9] He was also determined that this would be an exclusive event for the NAACP's brand of liberals, who could squeeze through an elaborate credentialing scheme that required organizations to have his personal approval before they could participate.[10] Wilkins, however, trusted the CIO, which was going through its own purge, to determine which unions were acceptable. One excluded union balked and denounced the NAACP for "subjecting participants in the conference to the measuring rod of the House Un-American Activities Committee."[11] In many ways, that yardstick appealed to Wilkins, who was determined to weed out "irresponsible" organizations whose concern about civil rights was only a "sideline" to something more sinister.[12]

Although Wilkins applied that definition to the Civil Rights Congress, William Patterson, the CRC's national secretary, was not deterred and sought to involve the Congress in the Mobilization at all costs. He urged CRC branches to "bend over backwards" to work with the Association's local affiliates, not because he wanted to "build... the NAACP," but because it would enhance the CRC's visibility in the African American community, force the Association to confront the depth of economic and

8. Clarence Mitchell to White, June 28, 1950, Box H124, File "Legislation, Communism, Loyalty, Un-American Activities," *Papers of the NAACP Washington Bureau*.
9. Statement of Policy Objectives: NAACP Civil Rights Committee, October 15, 1949, Box 193, File "Civil Rights Mobilization 1950: Planning Meeting, 1949," *Papers of the NAACP*.
10. All Sponsoring Organizations in Civil Rights Mobilization, January 1950, ibid.
11. Bernard J. Mooney to Madison S. Jones, Jr., January 12, 1950, Box 193, File "Civil Rights Mobilization 1950, Organizations Not Accepted—General, 1949–1950," ibid.
12. All Sponsoring Organizations in Civil Rights Mobilization, n.d., Box 193, File "Civil Rights Mobilization 1950: Planning Meeting, 1949," ibid.; Wilkins and Arnold Aronson to All Sponsoring Organizations, December 21, 1949, ibid.

political disfranchisement in black America, and prevent the Mobilization from devolving into a Truman rally.[13]

Wilkins, however, had no intention of incorporating anything that the CRC advocated nor the CRC itself. The Mobilization will have nothing to do with "apologists for Soviet foreign policy," he declared.[14] This Mobilization was for America and "no other state," and he was adamant that he would not let the Communists "crash the gate."[15]

The battle between the NAACP and the Civil Rights Congress now began in earnest. The Association used its exclusion of the CRC and other left-wing organizations as an example of its patriotism, just as the CRC wore the NAACP's ostracism like a badge of honor.[16] In retaliation for being blacklisted from the Civil Rights Mobilization, Patterson launched a deftly crafted and widely distributed letter to publicize the NAACP's red-baiting tactics. He pleaded with the NAACP to get off the McCarthyist bandwagon and join with the CRC in the fight for civil rights. We must have unity, he declared.[17]

Wilkins coldly responded with his own well-publicized letter. As far as he was concerned, this was no genuine offer of unity and conciliation, but pure Communist drivel on what the CRC "chooses to classify as civil rights" and what it chooses to define as unity. He then went on to recite a laundry list of past grievances. There was no unity at Scottsboro, he said, nor after the Nazi invasion of the Soviet Union. There was no unity in the case of the Martinsville Seven, where the CRC allegedly tried to put the Association "out of business." Wilkins asserted that the Civil Rights Mobilization was designed to integrate African Americans more fully into the "American concept of democracy," which was something that Patterson and the Communists could not possibly understand. The CRC could complain all that it wanted, Wilkins said, but the answer was

13. Patterson to All Regional Directors, All Chapter and Branch Leaders, memo, November 7, 1949, Box 167-6, Folder 5, *Strong Papers*; Patterson to Mrs. Bobby Graff, December 14, 1949, Part 2, Reel 24, *CRC*.
14. Article by Roy Wilkins, Chairman, National Emergency Civil Rights Mobilization and Acting Secretary of the National Association for the Advancement of Colored People, for publication in *The New Leader*, January 1950, Box 186, File "Civil Rights Mobilization, 1950 Article," *Papers of the NAACP*.
15. Henry Lee Moon, "Mobilizing for Civil Rights," January 20, 1950, ibid.
16. Wilkins to Hugh Baillie, December 1, 1949, Box 186, File "Civil Rights Mobilization 1950: Communist Influence, 1949–50," ibid.; Patterson to Wilkins, November 29, 1949, Box 193, File "Civil Rights Mobilization 1950: Organization Not Accepted—Civil Rights Congress, 1949–50," ibid.
17. Patterson to Wilkins, November 14, 1949, ibid.

"no" and "no" it remained throughout the subsequent Mobilizations.[18] Wilkins's position pleased the House Un-American Activities Committee, which sent him its own report on the CRC to use as he saw fit, but it did not do him much good as Walter White's ambitious shadow dogged the acting secretary at every turn.[19]

Although White was officially on leave while the uproar over his surprise marriage to Poppy Cannon died down, he missed being the NAACP's official spokesman, resented the Board members who were seeking to make his one-year leave permanent, and apparently played on his close relationship with Eleanor Roosevelt to discredit Roy Wilkins and reinsert himself back into power. Shortly after meeting with White in November 1949, Roosevelt, the most influential and powerful person on the organization's Board of Directors, threatened to resign because Wilkins had allegedly denounced White's marriage in some of the most intemperate, inappropriate tones imaginable. Wilkins was stunned because he had not openly criticized White, and he immediately recognized that he was caught in the middle of a "squeeze play." Wilkins and his supporters tried to counter the charges but to no avail. Although Roosevelt could not prove her allegations, she still questioned Wilkins's leadership abilities and political savvy, and the rest of the Board, afraid to lose its most valued member, finally capitulated. In May 1950, White again assumed the leadership of the NAACP while Wilkins was reassigned to the position of chief administrator.[20]

18. Wilkins to Patterson, November 22, 1949, ibid.; Marshall to Wilkins, memo, November 16, 1949, ibid.
19. Benjamin Mandel to Wilkins, December 6, 1949, ibid.
20. Alfred A. Duckett, "Top NAACP Executive Faces Possible Dismissal for Interracial Marriage," August 6, 1949, found in Box 610, File "Staff: Walter White Marriage, 1949," ibid.; Eleanor Roosevelt to Carl Murphy, August 30, 1949, Box 3336, File "Murphy: A–Z," *Roosevelt Papers*; Wilkins to Board of Directors, memo, September 12, 1949, Box 611, File "Staff: Roy Wilkins Appointed Acting Secretary, 1949," *Papers of the NAACP*; White to Eleanor [Roosevelt], October 28, 1949, Box 3389, File "White, Walter, 1947–50," *Roosevelt Papers*; Eleanor Roosevelt to Wilkins, December 9, 1949, Box 3338, File "NAACP, 1949," ibid.; Eleanor Roosevelt to Walter [White], December 15, 1949, Box 3389, File "White, Walter, 1947–1950," ibid.; White to Eleanor [Roosevelt], February 27, 1950, ibid.; Wilkins to White, March 16, 1950, Box 30, File "Eleanor Roosevelt, 1949–50," *Wilkins Papers*; Minutes of the Meeting of the Board of Directors, March 1950, Part 1, Reel 3, *NAACP*; Minutes of the Meeting of the Board of Directors, March 3, 1950, Reel 3, *NAACP/LC*; Eleanor Roosevelt to Walter [White], March 29, 1950, Box 3389, File "White, Walter, 1947–50," *Roosevelt Papers*; Eleanor Roosevelt to Roy Wilkins, April 4, 1950, Box 3338, File "NAACP, 1950," ibid.; A. Maceo Smith to Wilkins, April 21, 1950, Box 616, File "Staff: Roy Wilkins, Statement Concerning Role of Executive Secretary, 1950," *Papers of the NAACP*; Eleanor Roosevelt to Mrs. [Roy] Wilkins, April 24, 1950, Box 3500, File "Wile-Will," *Roosevelt Papers*; Channing H. Tobias to Louis T. Wright, May 2,

The timing could not have been worse for W. E. B. Du Bois, who had just been charged by the Justice Department with being an agent of a foreign government. Following the April 1949 World Peace Congress, Du Bois had thrown himself into the "peace offensive." He was convinced that atomic weapons were morally wrong, aggravated Cold War tensions, and encouraged a dangerous arrogance and swagger in U.S. foreign policy.[21] If the people only understood the deadly implications of America's atomic superiority, he reasoned, they would demand that all atomic materials come under UN control. The fact that Du Bois' beliefs aligned with Soviet attempts to neutralize America's primary area of military dominance set him on a collision course with the State and Justice Departments.

The Soviet Union's "phony" peace offensive, according to State Department officials, was little more than an attempt to make the United States look as if it were "afraid that peace will break out."[22] And those who supported this Soviet "stunt" deserved to be "attack[ed] as Communist inspired and controlled."[23] For Secretary of State Dean Acheson, the Stockholm Peace Appeal was the Soviets' most malevolent ploy. The Appeal, which emerged from the 1949 World Peace Congress, had already been signed by millions. It called for international control of atomic weapons, denounced as a war criminal any nation that would use atomic weapons first, and, as a result, put the United States in a difficult position. After all, the Americans had dropped atomic bombs on Japan and had

1950, Box 34, File "Walter White Return to Duty, 1949–50," *Wilkins Papers*; Wilkins to A. Maceo Smith, May 2, 1950, Box 616, File "Staff: Roy Wilkins, Statement Concerning Role of Executive Secretary, 1950," *Papers of the NAACP*; Wilkins to Branch Officers, memo, May 8, 1950, Box 34, File "Walter White Return to Duty, 1949–50," *Wilkins Papers*; Fred A. Jones to Arthur Spingarn, May 5, 1950, ibid.; William Lloyd Imes to Board of Directors NAACP, memo, May 5, 1950, ibid.; Clotild S. Ferguson et al. to Arthur Spingarn, telegram, May 4, 1950, ibid.; Presley S. Winfield to Arthur Spingarn, telegram, May 3, 1950, ibid.; Digest of News Releases, April 16–May 15, 1950, "Secretary's Return," Box 610, File "Staff: Walter White Leave of Absence, 1950," *Papers of the NAACP;* Minutes of the Meeting of the Board of Directors, May 8, 1950, ibid.; Walter White to Eleanor [Roosevelt], May 11, 1950, Box 3389, File "White Walter, 1947–50," *Roosevelt Papers*; "Recalled to Office, White Asks Support for NAACP Program," Box 610, File "Staff: Walter White Leave of Absence, 1950," *Papers of the NAACP*.

21. Du Bois, "I Speak for Peace," speech, September 24, 1950, Reel 65, *Du Bois*.
22. The Acting Secretary of State to the United States Representative at the United Nations (Austin), telegram, September 14, 1950, *FRUS* (1950), 2: fn. 1, 396; United States Delegation Working Paper: Tentative Staff Views on Tactics for Dealing with Vishinsky Resolution, September 30, 1950, ibid., 401.
23. The Ambassador of the Soviet Union (Kirk) to the Department of State, March 31, 1951, *FRUS* (1951), 2:464.

also repelled Soviet attempts to place their atomic arsenal under the UN's aegis.[24]

Du Bois walked into this superpower struggle when he and a small coterie of leftist friends launched the Peace Information Center (PIC) in New York City.[25] The Center disseminated the Stockholm Peace Appeal throughout the United States, publicized the location and results of worldwide peace conventions, and helped provide the pro-peace plank for Du Bois' U.S. Senate candidacy. The Justice Department, trying to clamp down on suspected Communists, demanded that the PIC officers, including Du Bois, who was in Prague at the time, register as agents of a foreign government.[26]

Denouncing the Justice Department's request as "absurd," Du Bois and his colleagues refused to comply. On the contrary, they tried to convince William E. Foley, chief of the foreign agents registration section, that the financially troubled PIC was simply a group of American citizens terrified that the Cold War could unleash an atomic holocaust and "snuff out civilization as we know it."[27] But the stalling tactic and Du Bois' attorney's insistence that the Department identify the Center's alleged foreign

24. The Acting Secretary of State to the United States Representative at the United Nations (Austin), telegram, September 14, 1950, *FRUS* (1950), 2:396–97; The Acting Secretary of State to the United States Representative at the United Nations (Austin), telegram, September 21, 1950, ibid., 397–98; United States Delegation Working Paper: Tentative Staff Views on Tactics for Dealing with Vishinsky Resolution, September 30, 1950, ibid., 398–403; The United States Representative at the United Nations (Austin) to the Secretary of State, telegram, October 14, 1950, ibid., 404–05; United States Delegation Working Paper: Staff Views on Substitute Resolution on Soviet Item, October 17, 1950, ibid., 407; Extract from Daily Secret Summary of Decisions Taken at United States Delegation Meeting, October 18, 1950, ibid., 408; United States Delegation Working Paper: Alternate Substitute for Soviet "Peace" Declaration, October 19, 1950, ibid., 408–09; The Secretary of State to the United States Representative at the United Nations (Austin), October 19, 1950, ibid., 409–10; Secret Daily Summary of Decisions Taken at United States Delegation Meeting, New York, October 20, 1950, ibid., 410–11; The United States Representative at the United Nations (Austin) to the Secretary of State, October 21, 1950, ibid., 413–14; The Secretary of State to the United States Representative at the United Nations (Austin), October 23, 1950, ibid., 415–16; The Secretary of State to Certain Diplomatic and Consular Offices, February 17, 1951, *FRUS* (1951), 2:455–56; The Acting United States Representative at the United Nations (Gross) to the Secretary of State, March 15, 1951, ibid., 463–64; The Secretary of State to Certain Diplomatic and Consular Offices, April 28, 1951, ibid., 472–76.
25. Minutes—Provisional Committee Americans for World Peace, April 3, 1950, Reel 64, *Du Bois*.
26. William E. Foley to Gentlemen, August 11, 1950, Reel 65, ibid.; Du Bois to State Department Passport Division, August 1, 1950, ibid.; Du Bois to Anson Phelps-Stokes, September 18, 1950, ibid.
27. Peace Information Center News Release, August 24, 1950, ibid.; Gloria Agrin to William E. Foley, September 14, 1950, ibid.; Foley to Agrin, October 3, 1950, ibid.

sponsor only served to infuriate Justice Department officials. It was obvious to everyone, Foley contended, that the PIC was in "direct support of Soviet foreign policy," and he insisted that Du Bois and his colleagues register as foreign agents. When they refused, the government indicted them.[28] Du Bois was stunned. At his arraignment, he defiantly questioned how the same government that was consistently unable to find even one statute to protect African Americans from lynching could have absolutely no problem in "contorting" legislation to go after an 83-year-old man who just wanted peace.[29]

At news of the indictment, NAACP members voted overwhelmingly to support the co-founder of their organization, but the leadership felt very differently.[30] Walter White, still carrying out his vendetta against Du Bois, decided that the peace offensive was "Communist-inspired propaganda," and he did not want the NAACP anywhere near it – especially if that meant he could withhold the considerable legal resources and prestige of the NAACP from his bitter enemy.[31] White quickly convinced his Board that the Justice Department had solid proof that "money from Russia was behind the Peace Information Center" and that the House Un-American Activities Committee would question the NAACP's patriotism if it jumped into this fight. Channing Tobias echoed White's warning and asserted that if the Association became "embroiled in this case," it would "run the risk of being . . . tied to the issue" of communism. Duly frightened, several Board members urged the Association to confine itself to racial discrimination cases and avoid the Du Bois issue at all costs. After all, Tobias noted, Du Bois was a smart man. He got himself into this mess without consulting the NAACP, he could get himself out the same way.[32] White was more than willing to follow the Board's directive and approved a policy statement that the NAACP would not provide legal, financial, or moral resources to aid the aging and recently widowed Du Bois.[33]

28. Gloria Agrin to Abbott Simon, August 31, 1950, ibid.; William E. Foley to Gloria Agrin, September 19, 1950, ibid.; Minutes Executive Board Meeting Peace Information Center, September 14, 1950, ibid.; Executive Board Meeting, October 12, 1950, ibid.
29. Statement of Dr. Du Bois at Time of Arraignment, n.d., Reel 66, ibid.
30. A Statement to the President and Attorney General of the United States, n.d., found in Reel 2, *Robeson*.
31. Ruby Hurley to White, memo, September 7, 1950, Box 201, File "Communism: General, 1949–50," *Papers of the NAACP*.
32. Minutes of the Meetings of the Board of Directors, February 13, 1951, Reel 3, *NAACP/LC*; Minutes of the Meetings of the Board of Directors, March 12, 1951, ibid.; Minutes of the NAACP Legal Defense and Educational Fund, Inc.: Meeting of the Board of Directors, May 14, 1951, Box 400, File "Legal Defense and Educational Fund: Minutes of the Board and Other Meetings, 1940–55," *Papers of the NAACP*.
33. Gloster Current to NAACP Branches, memo, October 29, 1951, Box 241, File "William E. B. Du Bois: General, 1949–55," ibid.

Yet, for all of the bluster, there was no money trail, no interlocking secretariat, no formal agreements to link the PIC to the Soviet Union. Even the government's main witness, O. John Rogge, former fellow traveler and now born-again American, could produce no documentation of a connection between the Center and the USSR. The Justice Department tried to prove that the literature from the PIC sounded just like the propaganda of other Soviet-inspired peace advocates, but Judge James McGuire, a political conservative, refused to accept the government's arguments and dismissed the case even before the defense could call its first witness.[34] Worn out by the "bitter experience" and distraught by the NAACP's "malignant behavior," Du Bois had "bowed before the storm," but, as he put it, "I did not break."[35]

Instead, it was the NAACP that broke, a fact that was not lost on the black community. Shirley Graham was visibly outraged that the "'top Negroes'... were quite willing to see W. E. B. Du Bois go to jail on a ridiculous, trumped up charge which they *knew to be false*." *Pittsburgh Courier* editor Percival Prattis declared that it should have been obvious to even the most myopic observer that the indictment was designed to intimidate the black leadership into silence and, given the NAACP's behavior, it was clear that the government had succeeded. It was also clear, as one man put it, that the "big Negroes took cover" and allowed Du Bois to twist in the wind. Even more difficult for many African Americans to tolerate was Walter White's repeated brash statements that the PIC, and by inference, Du Bois, were bought and paid for by "soviet (sic) money." As far as many African Americans were concerned, the "so-called leaders" had shown their "craven cowardice" and were more attuned to befriending the McCarthyites than protecting one of their own from an obvious injustice.[36]

34. Manning Marable, *W. E. B. Du Bois: Black Radical Democrat*, Twayne's Twentieth-Century American Biography Series, ed. John Milton Cooper, Jr. (Boston: Twayne Publishers, 1986), 187.

35. Ibid., 187, 189.

36. Otis W. Merriweather to Editor of the *Courier*, March 11, 1950, Box 144-5, Folder 9, *Prattis Papers*; Shirley Graham to Percival Prattis, September 27, 1952, Box 144-5, Folder 6, ibid.; Marcus H. Ray to [Percival] Prattis, Box 144-5, Folder 9, ibid.; Hubert T. Delany to E. Franklin Frazier, February 16, 1951, Reel 66, *Du Bois*; Percival Prattis, "Handcuffs on Dr. Du Bois is Evidence of the 'The Terror' Used to Victimize Us," Reprint from the *Pittsburgh Courier*, found in Reel 67, ibid.; Jose Garcia to the Editor, March 11, 1951, Box 144-5, Folder 9, *Prattis Papers*; Mrs. Alma Illery to P. L. Prattis, March 14, 1951, ibid.; Albert George to Percival Prattis, March 14, 1951, ibid.; Roy C. Anderson to Dear Sirs, October 23, 1951, Reel 66, *Du Bois*; Hubert T. Delany to Du Bois, November 27, 1951, ibid.; Harry Roberts to Du Bois, n.d. (ca. November 1951), Reel 67, ibid.; Du Bois to Lawrence Hautz, December 3, 1951, Reel 66, ibid.; Lawrence A. Hautz to Du Bois, December 4, 1951, ibid.

Sadly, this was an accurate assessment of the NAACP, whose abandonment of Du Bois was just one in a long string of dubious choices. As Roy Wilkins demonstrated in the Rosa Ingram case, the Association leadership had decided that, instead of using international pressure to force the American government to end the repression of blacks, the NAACP determined that there was much more to be gained by aligning with the Truman administration to beat back Soviet charges of racial discrimination in the United States. In fact, Walter White believed that the government had not been aggressive enough in countering Soviet taunts about American racism. He blasted members of the Senate for allowing the Kremlin to pump the Third World with "tragic distortions" about the Roman holiday lynchings and terror-filled elections in the United States.[37] And, on multiple occasions, White made sure that the Truman administration knew that he was ready, willing, and able to refute "Soviet propaganda" about the oppressive conditions under which black Americans lived.[38]

Dazzled by an "all day off-the-record meeting at the State Department" about the need "to tell the story of America, particularly on the race issue, more accurately and fully to the rest of the world," White eagerly published a "Progress Report" on civil rights, which he encouraged Eleanor Roosevelt to use whenever the Soviets launched into their standard harangue about American racism.[39] As Roosevelt and others knew, White, as head of the NAACP, was an unimpeachable source. Unlike the "racial progress" releases coming out of the Voice of America and the State Department, the Soviet Union could not so easily dismiss the leader of the largest civil rights organization in the United States. More importantly, White had the credentials to persuade non-Communist nations to disregard the Soviet bloc's stories of American atrocities. In his "Progress

37. White to Senator Albert Thomas, July 6, 1950, Box H1, File "Agreements with Foreign Governments, 1948–1953," *Papers of the NAACP Washington Bureau.*

38. White to Eleanor Roosevelt, November 11, 1949, Box 3389, File "White, Walter, 1947–50," *Roosevelt Papers*; White to David Niles, July 13, 1950, ibid.; White to Matthew J. Connelly, Box 27, File "Civil Rights/Negro Affairs, 1949–52," *Niles Papers*; White to Harry S Truman, September 7, 1950, ibid.; White to Truman, telegram/cross reference sheet, December 11, 1950, Box 545, File, "OF 93 Miscellaneous—1950," *Truman: OF*; Remarks by Walter White at Dinner to Dr. Ralph J. Bunche, January 24, 1951, Box 3338, File "NAACP, 1951," *Roosevelt Papers*; "Equal Justice Under the Law: On the occasion of the dinner in honor of Ralph J. Bunche, 1950 Nobel Peace Laureate, launching the 1951 Appeal of the N.A.A.C.P. Legal Defense and Educational Fund," January 24, 1951, Box 161, File "Ralph Bunche Dinner, 1950–51," *Papers of the NAACP*; "White Cites Gains in U.S. Race Relations," press release, September 13, 1951, Part 2, Reel 17, *CRC*; White to Eleanor Roosevelt, September 27, 1951, Box 3389, File "White, Walter, 1951–52," *Roosevelt Papers*; Francis J. McConnell to Eleanor Roosevelt, October 15, 1951, ibid.

39. White to Fay E. DeFrantz, March 12, 1951, File "D, 1951–52," *Papers of the NAACP.*

Report," the executive secretary of the NAACP, therefore, contended that the quality of life for blacks, especially in such key areas as voting, housing, employment, and education, was quickly approaching that of white Americans. And while he acknowledged that there was still work to be done, he whitewashed a string of atrocities in Illinois, Florida, Texas, and Alabama, and he understated the South's successful efforts to circumvent the U.S. Supreme Court's decision on white primaries. He even applauded Hollywood for its positive portrayal of African Americans at a time when the NAACP had launched a boycott of the Amos 'n Andy television show. In short, while White saw "positive gains," there were some bitter truths that he refused to acknowledge.[40]

Indeed, shortly after the publication of White's "Progress Report," there was yet another brutal killing in a small Southern town. The stage had been set two years earlier in 1949 when whites in Groveland, Florida, had rampaged through the black sections of town burning African American children alive, yet, the only screams authorities heard were those of a white woman shouting "rape." The charge was dubious. Although she claimed to have just been gang raped, witnesses at the hospital described her as "quite calm and self-possessed" with no wounds that matched those she said her assailants had inflicted upon her. Her husband, who had supposedly ran to get help during the attack, actually hung out with the sheriff's detectives for several hours before mentioning that his wife was being gang raped in a ditch by the side of the road. In other words, the charge simply did not ring true. Nonetheless, the manhunt was on,

40. Francis J. McConnell to Eleanor Roosevelt, October 15, 1951, Box 3389, File "White, Walter, 1951–52," *Roosevelt Papers*; White to Eleanor Roosevelt, September 27, 1951, ibid.; Walter White, "Time for a Progress Report," *The Saturday Review of Literature* (September 1951), found in ibid.; General Debate: Draft international covenant on human rights and measures of implementation, December 20, 1951, A/C.3/SR.371, Third Committee 371st Meeting, General Assembly Sixth Session, *UN*; "Voter Registration Stymied by Lack of Board in Alabama," December 18, 1947, *Washington Post* found in Box 485, File "Negroes (Politics)–Voting Alabama," *RNC*; "South Carolina Democrats Chart Resistance to Negro," June 10, 1948, *Christian Science Monitor* found in Box 485, File "Negroes (Politics)–Voting South Carolina," ibid.; "Alabama Law Voided as Bar to Negro Vote," January 8, 1949, *New York Herald Tribune* found in Box 485, File "Negroes (Politics)–Voting Alabama," ibid.; "Negro Vote Reined in South Carolina: New Law Requires Literacy or Property Ownership—Thurmond Forces Win," April 14, 1950, *New York Times* found in Box 485, File "Negroes (Politics)–Voting South Carolina," ibid.; James A. Dombrowski to Harry Truman, letter/cross reference sheet, October 24, 1950, Box 545, File " OF 93 Miscellaneous–1950," *Truman:OF*; "Alabama Election to Weigh Proposed Voting Restrictions," October 10, 1951, *Christian Science Monitor* found in Box 485, File "Negroes (Politics)–Voting Alabama," *RNC*; "Alabama Due to Ballot on Amendment to Put Race Curbs on Voting," December 9, 1951, *Washington Star* found in ibid.; "Tighter Election Law Amendment Leading in Alabama Balloting," December 12, 1951, *Washington Star* found in ibid.

Photo 4.1. Reign of terror in Groveland, Florida. African Americans are burned out of their homes as part of the wave of anti-black violence that seized Florida for several years, 1949.
Visual Materials from the NAACP Records, Library of Congress.

and four black men were quickly arrested, one of whom was killed by the police even before he made it to the jail. In this hostile atmosphere, justice, in the words of the NAACP attorney, had "all the earmarks of a dime store criminal novel." Two years later, in 1951, the U.S. Supreme Court agreed, overturned the convictions, and demanded a change of venue to retry the defendants. Samuel Shepherd, one of the accused, would never make it to a second trial. While transporting two of the defendants, Sheriff Willis McCall, obviously convinced that justice had been denied, stopped the car, opened the door, told Shepherd and Walter Irvin to get out, and unloaded his guns in their backs. Although images of their sprawled, bloodied bodies spread across the wire service as fast as the fire that had consumed Groveland, McCall was fully exonerated.[41]

41. NAACP, "Groveland U.S.A.: Riots, Hate, Terror, Lynch Law, Ku Klux Klan, Night Riding, Home Burning," pamphlet, found in Part 2, Reel 19, *CRC*; "Report of Miss L. B. DeForest in interview of Thomas Virgil Ferguson," July 27, 1950, Box 1101, Folder 1, *ACLU Papers*. (Emphasis in original.); "Bullet Backs Charge Against Fla. Sheriff," December 16, 1951, *New York Post* found in ibid.; Thurgood Marshall to Patrick Malin, December 20, 1951, ibid.

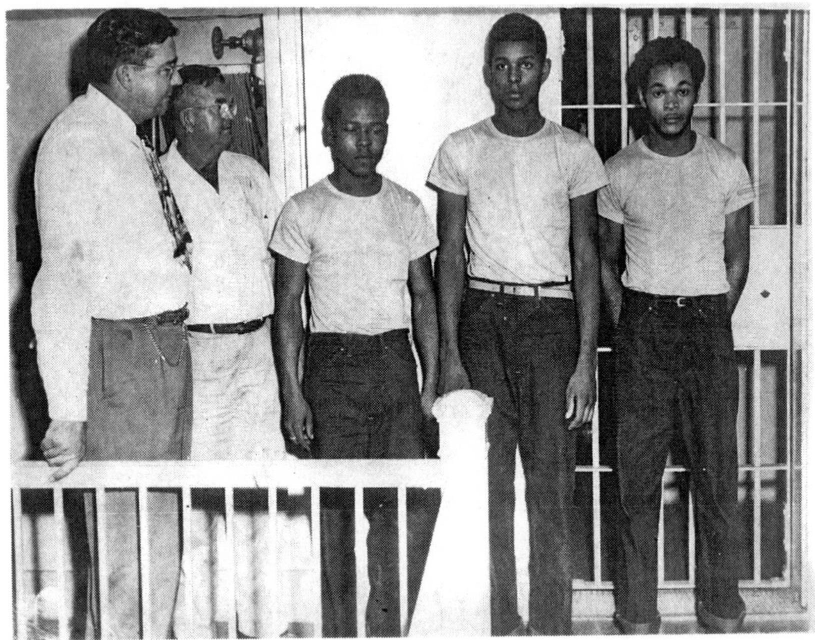

Photo 4.2. Three of the four men charged with raping a white woman in Groveland, Florida. Police killed one of the "suspects" before he made it to the jail and, after the Supreme Court ordered a new trial, Sheriff Willis McCall would eventually kill Samuel Shepherd, right, and seriously wound Walter Irvin, left, for trying to "escape."
Visual Materials from the NAACP Records, Library of Congress.

Soviet Foreign Minister Andrei Vishinsky pounced. Was it really progress, he asked, when U.S. courts condoned the murder and near fatal wounding of handcuffed black men by a Southern sheriff? The NAACP leadership was incensed by the crime, as well, but was even more concerned that this latest example of Southern Justice would further tarnish America's image. Therefore, even though the bullet-riddled prisoners had been NAACP clients, Association board member Channing Tobias blithely ignored the lynch mob atmosphere that had surrounded the case, and instead, dismissed the incident as tragic, but not indicative of anything important.[42]

42. "What Dr. Tobias Replied to Russia's Andrei Bishinsky (sic)," November 21, 1951, Folder 42, "United Nations 1951–1952,"*Papers of the YMCA: Biographical File: Channing H. Tobias Collection*, University of Minnesota, Minneapolis, Minnesota, (hereafter *Tobias Papers*).

Photo 4.3. NAACP Board member and alternate member to the U.S. delegation to the UN, Channing Tobias.
Visual Materials from the NAACP Records, Library of Congress.

Describing Tobias' response as "disgraceful," the African American Left, led by William Patterson and the CRC, chose a different method for dealing with Soviet charges of racial violence in the United States.[43] With encouragement and support from the Communist Party, U.S.A., Patterson and the CRC decided to document the violence and present it to the UN.[44] Unlike the NNC, however, or the NAACP, both of which had accused the United States of violating African Americans' human rights, the Civil Rights Congress decided to charge the United States with genocide.[45] With this goal in mind, Patterson and a small team of writers, including author Howard Fast and scholar Oakley Johnson, painstakingly and shrewdly compiled data from *To Secure These Rights*, NAACP publications, Census Bureau reports, and from other non-Communist sources. To be sure, the facts on lynching, segregation, and unequal education, housing, and

43. William Z. Foster to Patterson, November 23, 1951, Part 2, Reel 2, *CRC*.
44. Patterson to Jefferson Hurley, October 25, 1948, Part 2, Reel 1, ibid.
45. Patterson to Oakley C. Johnson, May 6, 1952, Part 2, Reel 3, ibid.

health care had already been told in *An Appeal to the World*; but, in this case, the CRC set out to prove governmental intent.

Patterson argued forcefully that Jim Crow was the result of a deliberate government policy to destroy African Americans. In direct contrast to White's "Progress Report," Patterson contended that 32,000 African Americans died each year because they did not enjoy the same quality health care, jobs, education, and housing as whites. Those deprivations, he maintained, cut the average life expectancy of blacks by eight years. Patterson wrote:

> Out of the inhuman black ghettos of American cities, out of the cotton plantations of the South, comes this record of mass slayings on the basis of race, of lives deliberately warped and distorted by the willful creation of conditions making for premature death, poverty, and disease. It is a record that calls aloud for condemnation, for an end to ... the ever-increasing violation of United Nations Convention on the Prevention and Punishment of the Crime of Genocide.[46]

The State Department, of course, claimed that the UN Convention on Genocide was not applicable to the American situation. The Department argued that the United States had not signed the Convention and, more importantly, not enough blacks had been lynched to constitute genocide.[47] Patterson retorted that the Convention did not require the complete annihilation of a group, only governmental intent to destroy "in whole or in part" a racial minority. As he surveyed the American landscape, he saw very little that suggested otherwise and even suspected that the United States had refused to sign the Genocide Convention because of the intense international scrutiny that would certainly result. On that point, he was right. The State Department acknowledged that there was an overwhelming fear that the Genocide Convention would allow the UN to prosecute lynchers who, despite "convincing evidence of guilt," had been acquitted in America's courts. Southern senators in particular "were afraid" that the Genocide Convention was a "back-door method of enacting federal anti-lynching legislation" and, for that reason, Senators Tom Connally and Walter George (D-GA) refused to even put the treaty on the Senate Foreign Relations Committee's calendar for debate.[48]

46. Civil Rights Congress, *We Charge Genocide*, xi; "We Charge Genocide," pamphlet, February 7, 1952, Part 2, Reel 14, ibid.; Aubrey Grossman to Friend, July 15, 1951, Part 2, Reel 8, ibid.
47. "Questions and Answers on Genocide Convention," n.d., Box 8, File "Genocide (folder 1 of 2)," Lot File 55D429, *RG 59*.
48. "We Charge Genocide: Speech Delivered by William L. Patterson ... to Launch the Publication of the Book," November 12, 1951, Box 5, Folder 27, *Papers of William Patterson*, Moorland-Spingarn Research Center, Howard University, Washington, DC (hereafter *Patterson Papers*); *Blaisdell*; Sandifer to Gross, memo, April 14, 1948, Box 8,

This looked like governmental complicity to Patterson. The Southern bloc had consistently torpedoed anti-lynching legislation and scuttled other civil rights bills.[49] "If the government could not apprehend a single lyncher in the years during which some six thousand lynchings had been perpetrated," Patterson wrote, "then the question of government endorsement might logically be raised."[50]

The CRC's petition, by design, attacked the United States in its most vulnerable area. Jim Crow's reputation was known worldwide and had caused the State Department an endless amount of embarrassment as diplomats from Ethiopia, India, and Liberia were denied housing, thrown out of "whites only" theaters, and frequently harassed by the police. These first-hand experiences with the day-to-day brutality of Jim Crow, coupled with the steady surge of reports about executions, Klan-directed bombings, and race riots raised a healthy dose of international skepticism about America's democracy.[51] Adding to this brush fire of doubt was *We Charge Genocide.*

File "Genocide (folder 1 of 2)," Lot File 55D429, *RG 59*; "Position on Genocide Convention in ECOSOC Drafting Committee: Through Gross and Sandifer," 2 April 1948, ibid.; *Sandifer*; Brien McMahon to Harry Truman, July 13, 1950, Box 1699, File "2352," *Truman:OF*; Fisher to Rusk, memo, January 19, 1950, Box 8, File "Genocide (folder 1 of 2)," Lot File 55D429, *RG 59*; "Text of UN Convention Outlawing Genocide," found in Box 3249, File "American Association for the UN, 1948–49," *Roosevelt Papers*.

49. "We Charge Genocide: Speech Delivered by William Patterson ... to Launch the Publication of the Book," November 12, 1951, Box 5, Folder 27, *Patterson Papers*.
50. Patterson to Robert Cushman, April 23, 1952, Part 2, Reel 1, *CRC*.
51. K. L. Rankin to the Secretary of State, memo, July 22, 1948, Box 4685, Decimal File, 811.4016/7-2248, *RG 59*; "Comment Paper: Report of Third Session of Commission on Human Rights," October 9, 1948, Box 45, File "US(P)/A/C.3/1-106," *RG 84*; Howard Donovan to the Secretary of State, memo, December 28, 1948, Box 4685, Decimal File, 811.4016/4-1449, *RG 59*; Felix Cole to Secretary of State, memo, December 31, 1948, Box 4685, Decimal File, 811.4016/12-3148, ibid.; Bancroft to Raynor et al., memo, March 25, 1949, Box 8, File "Human Rights: Suppression in Hungary & Bulgaria," Lot File 55D429, ibid.; J. F. Huddleston to the Secretary of State, memo, April 14, 1949, Box 4685, Decimal File, 811.4016/4-1449, ibid.; Popper to Sandifer, memo, July 27, 1949, Box 89, File "Rights: Human (1946–49)," *RG 84*; Kotschnig to Sandifer, memo, October 10, 1949, Box 5048, Decimal File, 811.4016/10-1049, *RG 59*; Sandifer to Mrs. Roosevelt, memo, October 12, 1949, Box 4685, Decimal File, 811.4016/10-1041, ibid.; Durward Sandifer to George Washington, October 14, 1949, Box 5048, Decimal File, 811.4016/10-1041, ibid.; Green to Sandifer, memo, January 5, 1950, Box 16, File "Discrimination and Protection of Minorities, Subcommittee on Prevention," Lot File 55D429, ibid.; Pete to Jack, November 15, 1950, Box 11, File "General Assembly-Fifth Session, Miscellaneous Memoranda," Lot File 55D429, ibid.; Eleanor Roosevelt to Truman, December 14, 1950, Box 4560, File "Harry S Truman, 1949–1952," *Roosevelt Papers*; "Another Negro Executed in America," May 9, 1951, Box 10, Folder 224, *Edith Spurlock Sampson Papers*, Schlesinger Library, Radcliffe College, Cambridge, Massachusetts (hereafter *Sampson Papers*).

Patterson had consulted extensively with William Z. Foster, chairman of the CP, to make sure that the CRC created a "remarkably effective weapon" that would have enormous "ideological . . . and organizational value." He was aware, however, that to serve its true purpose, the petition would have to look as politically neutral as possible. *We Charge Genocide* would lose its impact if it was seen as just another propaganda blast from the Soviet Union or its allies, which is why Patterson decided that he would downplay the party's involvement.[52]

Yet, while Patterson wanted his strategy to evoke the greatest "ideological . . . and organizational value" for the party, he was slow to craft a similar method to gain the greatest impact for African Americans. This oversight reflected the low priority that he initially placed on having the petition reviewed by the UN. In fact, he told labor leader Ben Gold that it did not matter "whether" the petition was "placed on the [UN's] agenda . . or not." If it had mattered, he would have tried to work out a strategy for maneuvering the petition through the UN and have consulted with Du Bois about the intricacies of the UN agenda and committee structure. But, instead, he waited until he was at the UN meeting in Paris before the notion of which delegations to target even crossed his mind, and only then because some comrades in the French Communist party finally raised the question. To be sure, Patterson had planned for Paul Robeson and W. E. B. Du Bois to submit *We Charge Genocide* to the UN, but this tactic was to give the petition a certain cachet. Yet, the idea to actually place the petition on the UN's agenda was late in coming. On the other hand, he had devised a plan to publicize this "bitter book . . . [of] horrors," well before he left the United States, and to distribute it to his Communist allies in Eastern Europe, Britain, and France.[53]

52. Patterson to William Z. Foster, November 16, 1951, Part 2, Reel 1, *CRC*; Patterson to John Green, November 28, 1951, Part 2, Reel 2, ibid.; Patterson to Pettis Perry, November 26, 1951, Part 2, Reel 1, ibid.; Draft I Go to the United Nations, Box 7, Folder 47, *Patterson Papers*; Foster to Patterson, November 23, 1951, Part 2, Reel 2, *CRC*.

53. Patterson to Ben Gold, November 20, 1951, ibid.; Patterson to John Adams Kingsbury, November 28, 1951, Reel 66, *Du Bois*; Patterson to Ferdinand C. Smith, September 6, 1951, Part 2, Reel 2, *CRC*; Patterson to Ferdinand C. Smith, November 2, 1951, ibid.; Patterson to Harry Pollitt, November 9, 1951, ibid.; Patterson to Joseph Starobin, November 26, 1951, ibid.; Elizabeth to Patterson, n.d., Part 2, Reel 33, ibid.; Patterson to Darling (Louise Patterson), n.d., Box 9, Folder 87, *Patterson Papers*; Draft Chapter XVIII: At the Palais Chaillot in Paris, n.d., Box 7, Folder 56, ibid.; Patterson to Eleanor Roosevelt, December 18, 1951, Part 2, Reel 2, *CRC*; Patterson to All Delegates to the General Assembly of the United Nations, December 18, 1951, Box 5, Folder 70, *Patterson Papers*.

Patterson's actions make it clear that *We Charge Genocide* was not about the needs of black people, but about those of the CP. Anti-Communist hysteria had taken its toll on the political Left, including the CRC, which was in desperate need of funds to pay its staff, its utility bills, and, most importantly, to finance the legal defense needs of the jailed American Communist party leadership.[54] Potential allies, especially blacks and organized labor, however, had closed their wallets and their organizations to the CRC, and Patterson hoped that *We Charge Genocide* would overcome their distrust.[55]

To accomplish that feat, however, the CRC had to erase the suspicions left by the sellout during World War II and recreate the glory days of the Great Depression. With that goal in mind, the CRC looked for some kind of Jim Crow "stunt" to demonstrate that it was a defender of everyone's rights, not just those of the CP.[56] What Patterson and his colleagues really wanted was another case as shocking as Scottsboro, a case of such obvious and brutal racism that organized labor and African Americans would overcome their declared aversion to working with a communist organization and join the CRC in the struggle against both racism and anti-Communism. This well-financed, united front, the CRC believed, would then become the battering ram to free the CP leadership.[57]

54. Report to the National Committee, February 7, 1949, Box 9, Folder 51, ibid.; Muriel to Leon, May 13, 1949, Box 9, Folder 43, ibid.; Patterson to Friend, August 27, 1948, Part 2, Reel 8, *CRC*; Len Goldsmith to Pat (Patterson), September 22, 1948, Part 2, Reel 2, ibid.; Kevin Mullen to Frank Marshall Davis, November 15, 1948, Part 2, Reel 1, ibid.; Patterson to Elizabeth Gurley Flynn, May 17, 1949, Part 2, Reel 4, ibid.; Patterson to A. S. Houghton, December 14, 1949, Box 9, Folder 43, *Patterson Papers*, Patterson to Anne Shore, January 6, 1950, Part 2, Reel 22, *CRC*; Patterson to Anderson, January 25, 1950, Part 2, Reel 1, ibid.; "Introductory Remarks Concerning The Following Organizational Plans," May 17, 1949, Part 2, Reel 8, ibid.; Resume Report: Major CRC Campaigns, Chicago Conference of the CRC Chapters Secretaries, June 21, 1949, Part 2, Reel 18, ibid.; "Summary of Findings and Decisions of the Conference for Civil and Human Rights," June 25, 1949, Part 2, Reel 29, ibid.; "Major CRC Campaigns," July 16, 1949, Part 2, Reel 11, ibid.; Minutes: Resident Board Meeting July 1949, July 16, 1949, Part 2, Reel 12, ibid.; Paul Robeson form letter, July 26, 1949, Part 4, Reel 2, ibid.; Patterson to George Marshall, August 12, 1949, Box 9, Folder 43, *Patterson Papers*; George Marshall to Patterson et al., November 2, 1949, Box 9, Folder 51, ibid.; "Some Suggestions for the Baltimore Conference," n.d., Part 2, Reel 26, *CRC*.
55. Patterson to Margie Robinson, November 17, 1949, Part 2, Reel 22, ibid.; Patterson to Jack Raskin, November 25, 1949, Part 2, Reel 27, ibid.
56. Len Goldsmith to William Patterson and George Marshall, memo, February 7, 1949, Box 9, Folder 51, *Patterson Papers*.
57. Patterson to Raskin, November 4, 1948, Part 2, Reel 27, *CRC*; Patterson to Benjamin J. Davis, Jr., March 11, 1949, Part 2, Reel 1, ibid.; Patterson to Mrs. Franklin D. Roosevelt, April 27, 1949, Box 3270, File "Civic-Clap," *Roosevelt Papers*; Trenton Six Appeal to Be Argued May 16, news release, May 10, 1949, Part 2, Reel 13, *CRC*; Marcia Friedman

Finding another Scottsboro was not easy, however. As horrific as were the cases of Rosa Ingram, the Martinsville Seven, and Willie McGee, as consistent as the racist and brutal pattern of Southern Justice had become, there still was nothing of the magnitude of the Scottsboro trials. Even after Patterson asked Benjamin Davis, vice president of the Communist party, to have their "parent organization" promote the case of the Trenton Six, there was still no overwhelming surge of outrage over this "Northern Scottsboro." Patterson complained bitterly that white Americans had become "complacent about the brutalization" of African Americans and could therefore expect to be "piped into hell," just like the Germans, who had acquiesced in the destruction of the Jews.[58]

The CRC's charge that the American government was fully engaged in the systematic, long-term destruction of 15 million people solely because of their race was shocking and contained just enough truth to resonate. With *We Charge Genocide*, the CRC believed that it had found its new Scottsboro. The document was a damning indictment that had the potential emotive and moral power to move the black churches as well as organized labor into action. It would also show, as Patterson declared, that America had "plumbed to the lowest depths" of its Nazi "German counterpart."[59] Just as Munich and Auschwitz had revealed the vile nature

to Friend, May 13, 1949, ibid.; Patterson to Phil Frankfeld, October 19, 1949, Part 2, Reel 26, *CRC*; "Why CRC Should Continue as a General Civil Rights Organization," January 2, 1950, Box 9, Folder 51, *Patterson Papers*; Patterson to Percival Prattis, March 27, 1950, Part 2, Reel 33, *CRC*; Patterson to Nancy Kleinbord, May 1, 1950, Part 2, Reel 24, ibid.; Patterson to Ida Rothstein, January 5, 1951, Part 2, Reel 23, ibid.; "The First Line of Defense: Statement by Negro Americans to the President and Attorney General of the United States," July 28, 1948, Box 167-7, Folder 6, *Strong Papers*; Sale of "We Charge Genocide" Vital: Plan of Work, ca. November 1951, Part 2, Reel 14, *CRC*.

58. Charles H. Martin, "The Civil Rights Congress and Southern Black Defendants," *The Georgia Historical Quarterly* 71:1 (Spring 1987), 25–52; Patterson to Benjamin J. Davis, Jr., March 11, 1949, Part 2, Reel 1, ibid.; Patterson to Eleanor Roosevelt, April 27, 1949 [includes pamphlet "Lynching Northern Style"], Box 3270, File "Civil-Clap," *Roosevelt Papers*; "Trenton Six Appeal To Be Argued May 16: Death Sentences in Northern Scottsboro Case Have Been Widely Protested Here and Abroad," news release, May 10, 1949, Part 2, Reel 13, *CRC*; Patterson to C. C. Dejoie, Jr., July 11, 1949, Box 9, Folder 43, *Patterson Papers*; Patterson to Mrs. Whitelaw Reid, February 1, 1951, Part 2, Reel 1, *CRC*; Patterson to T. O. Thackery, November 12, 1951, Part 2, Reel 19, ibid.

59. Patterson to Jack Raskin, November 4, 1948, Part 2, Reel 27, ibid.; Patterson to Nancy Kleinbord, May 1, 1950, Part 2, Reel 24, ibid.; Patterson to Ida Rothstein, January 5, 1951, Part 2, Reel 23, ibid.; Patterson to Darling (Louise Patterson), n.d., Box 9, Folder 87, *Patterson Papers*; Patterson to C. L. Crum, August 21, 1951, Part 2, Reel 1, *CRC*; Patterson to Holland Roberts, November 26, 1951, Part 2, Reel 5, ibid.; Patterson to Rev. J. C. Olden, July 17, 1951, ibid.; Patterson to Carl Murphy, August 10, 1951, Part 2, Reel 1, ibid.; Patterson to J. Finley Wilson, August 24, 1951, ibid.; Patterson

Photo 4.4. William Patterson, national secretary of the Civil Rights Congress, at a rally for the Communist 12.
© *Julius Lazarus/Special Collections, Rutgers University Libraries.*

of the Nazi regime, the petition, according to Patterson, would unmask the barbaric nature of the American government, including the racism in its foreign policy.[60] He hoped that the superbly crafted *Genocide* petition would so "pollute" the air with the "stink" of America's horrendous crimes that the Europeans, who were under considerable pressure from the U.S. government to rearm West Germany and build the North American Treaty Organization (NATO), would have no choice but to "cry 'Americans . . . go home.'"[61]

In the final analysis, *We Charge Genocide* was a deftly crafted CP document that skillfully used the plight of African Americans to meet the major

to Carl Murphy, November 20, 1951, Part 2, Reel 19, ibid. (similar letters were also sent to the editors of the *Chicago Defender*, the *Oklahoma Black Dispatch*, and the *Amsterdam News*).

60. "We Charge Genocide: Speech Delivered by William Patterson . . . to Launch the Publication of the Book," November 12, 1951, Box 5, Folder 27, *Patterson Papers*.

61. Patterson to Daniel Hughes, August 27, 1951, Part 2, Reel 2, *CRC*; Patterson to D. N. Pritt, August 28, 1951, ibid.; Patterson to Joseph Starobin, November 26, 1951, ibid.; Draft I Go to the United Nations, n.d., Box 7, Folder 48, *Patterson Papers*; Patterson to William Rutherford, January 28, 1952, Part 2, Reel 2, *CRC*.

legal and financial objectives on the CRC's "Free the Communist 11" agenda. As a result, the CRC was not fully prepared to use the *Genocide* petition to directly advance the cause of black equality. Patterson confessed to an ally that there was a fight beyond Negro rights that was "of infinitely greater importance." Yet, he was shrewd enough to recognize that no other "feature of the American scene" called into question "more sharply . . . the morality and political integrity of the U.S.A.," and he was determined to find some way to "develop that issue to the advantage and interest of labor."[62]

The NAACP, however, had other plans. As columnist Drew Pearson noted, "Walter White, the patriotic Negro leader," was furious and determined to issue a "scathing blast" at the CRC for "publishing Communist propaganda . . . that the south is massacring Negroes."[63] At the behest of the State Department, White resolved that the NAACP had an obligation to aid the United States in its anti-Communist crusade and eagerly penned a stinging rebuttal.[64] He sought first to undermine the credibility of the CRC by defining *We Charge Genocide* as "a gross and subversive conspiracy" by "prominent American Communists." He also impugned the research itself, describing the 50 pages of lynching and racist incidents as "alleged instances" designed to "suborn the allegiance of Negro citizens . . . to their foremost loyalty—loyalty to the United States of America."[65]

After it became clear that the CRC had meticulously verified each incident, White tried another tactic. The "facts are true," he lamented, but "like all indictments drafted by a prosecutor," *We Charge Genocide* "paints only the gloomiest picture of American democracy and the race question." White, therefore, countered with his own, rosier version of life in the United States. He saw "phenomenal gains in civil rights" and heralded the "marked reduction" in segregation in the military, the lessening of disfranchisement in the South, and the measurable reduction in racial bigotry in the United States. Of course, the disgracefully large number of black soldiers convicted of cowardice during the Korean War, the killing of Macio Snipes for voting in a Georgia election, the reign of

62. Patterson draft memo on "The Negro and Some Phases of His Development," n.d., Box 9, Folder 51, *Patterson Papers*; Patterson to George Marshall, August 12, 1949, Box 9, Folder 43, ibid.
63. Drew Pearson script, November 23, 1951, Box 636, File "United Nations: Genocide, 1947–51," *Papers of the NAACP*.
64. Wilkins to Committee on Administration, memo, November 20, 1951, ibid.; White to Wilkins, memo, November 23, 1951, ibid.
65. Mr. Seamans to Mr. Devine, reference slip, 12/26/51, Box 60, File "Genocide Against the Negroes, 1951–52," Entry 1587, *RG 59;* Untitled statement to John Pauker—Voice of America, November 16, 1951, Box 636, File "United Nations: Genocide, 1947–51," *Papers of the NAACP*.

terror in Cicero, Illinois, where a handful of blacks dared to move into a white neighborhood and barely got out with their lives, and the murders and executions in Groveland, Florida, told another tale; but, "Patriotic Negro" White attributed these and similar incidents to the "unfinished business of democracy."[66]

This was too much even for Roy Wilkins, who was perhaps the staunchest anti-Communist in the NAACP. Although Wilkins despised the CRC, he nonetheless wondered how the Association could "'blast' a book that uses [NAACP] records as source material." Wilkins asserted that the entire array of NAACP initiatives, including a federal ban on lynching, equal employment legislation, and an end to Jim Crow in education, had as its initial starting point the government's "mistreatment of Negroes in America." On that point, the CRC was right. In fact, just a few months earlier, Wilkins had been in exactly the same position as Patterson when the editors of the *Atlanta Constitution* accused the NAACP of "distorting the picture" of race relations "for the propaganda effect." Wilkins's retort was simple. The picture "is bad enough .... Why try to paint blacker the inside of a cave?" He then went on to recount the horrors of lynching "at the rate of 2, 3, and sometimes 4 a week," the horrors of peonage "that [held] thousands of families in virtual slavery," the horrors of "the rotten court system which has sent thousands of us to jail and death for the 'crime' of being black," and the horrors of a segregated school system that "shameless[ly] rob our children of their futures." Given these brutal realities, and the government's reluctance to break the Southern filibuster and pass corrective legislation, Wilkins was adamant that this was not the NAACP's fight. The "State Department cannot expect that we will ... assume the role of 'blaster'" of this petition.[67]

Board Member Judge Hubert T. Delany was even more blunt. Let the State Department do its own dirty work, he said; defending the U.S. government was not the NAACP's job. As Delany saw it, the CRC's petition accused the U.S. government of the very atrocities that the NAACP had detailed in *An Appeal to the World* four years earlier, and those conditions, he added, still existed. Thus, while White raved about the "marked reduction" in segregation in the military, 98 percent of the army was still Jim Crow. While he glowed about the ebb tide of segregation in the South, Washington, D.C., still proudly maintained separate cemeteries for "colored pets." Although he heralded the increase in black voters in the

66. Statement by Walter White Made upon Request of the U.S. State Department, n.d. (November 1951), ibid.

67. Wilkins to White, memo, November 21, 1951, ibid.; Addenda to Address by Roy Wilkins ... in Answer to Editorial Appearing in the Atlanta *Constitution*, June 26, 1951, found in Part 2, Reel 17, *CRC*.

South, less than 1,500 African Americans in Alabama and "barely 5,000 black citizens" in Mississippi were registered to vote. Under these circumstances, Delany felt compelled to level his own blast. "If we issue the statement," he said, "it means that instead of our being a militant organization fighting for first-class citizenship for the Negro, we are saying to the very people who are denying us [our] rights... that we are in effect satisfied." Nothing, he told White, could be further from the truth.[68]

Wilkins' and Delany's dissension angered White. Their doubts about the wisdom of challenging the CRC's petition meant that he could not respond as quickly to the State Department as he wanted and that *We Charge Genocide* might gain momentum before the NAACP could stop it. Determined to circumvent Wilkins' and Delany's criticism, White worked feverishly to get his rebuttal to the U.S. delegation, and he found an ally in NAACP Board member Dr. Channing Tobias, who was an alternate member of the U.S. delegation at the UN meeting in Paris.[69] Tobias was, in the words of one State Department official, "an outstanding colored man" who could help the U.S. counter Soviet "propaganda" about the brutal treatment of African Americans.[70]

First, however, Tobias had to get through a Senate confirmation hearing which, because of his previous affiliation with the CAA, promised to be grueling and vicious. Indeed, the moment Tobias' name surfaced as a possible delegate, journalist Westbrook Pegler launched an unrelenting assault on the NAACP Board member as a fellow traveler and Communist stooge. During the hearings, Tobias professed his unswerving loyalty to the United States. He admitted that he had foolishly attached his name to ad hoc organizations that were, unbeknown to him, Communist fronts,

68. Hubert T. Delany to White, November 23, 1951, Box 636, File "United Nations: Genocide, 1947–51," *Papers of the NAACP*; "Report on Korea: The Shameful Story of the Courts Martial of Negro GIs by Thurgood Marshall," found in Part 2, Reel 19, *CRC*; "The use of the poll tax as a restriction on suffrage..." n.d., Box 27, File "Civil Rights/Negro Affairs, 1949–52," *Niles Papers*; Frederickson, *The Dixiecrat Revolt*, 48; Stephen Greene, "The Negro in Democracy's Showcase," *American Unity*, February–March 1949 found in Box 3274, File "Council A–Z," *Roosevelt Papers*.
69. John Devine, Memorandum of Telephone Conversation with Mr. Drew Pearson, November 17, 1951, Box 60, File "Genocide Against the Negroes, 1951–52," Entry 1587, *RG 59*.
70. Mr. Wainhouse to Mr. Hickerson, memo, April 24, 1951, Box 11, File "General Assembly Sixth Session, U.S. Delegation, Paris, 1951," Lot File 55D429, ibid; John D. Hickerson "Memorandum for File," Box 2, File "6th General Assembly," Lot File 58D33, ibid.; "Dr. Tobias Named Alternate U.S.–UN Delegate," September 20, 1951, Folder 42, "United Nations 1951–1952," *Tobias Papers;* "Remarks by Channing H. Tobias at testimonial dinner in honor of Ralph J. Bunche," January 24, 1951, Box 3338, File "NAACP, 1951," *Roosevelt Papers.*

but he also denounced the Communists and recalled his battles to oust them from the CAA. Meanwhile, Walter White and the White House staff mobilized to undercut Pegler and paint Tobias as a "strong supporter of the President" who had helped "thwart" the "communist plan to use 15,000,000 American Negroes as shock troops of revolution." The counteroffensive worked. Despite the rampant anti-Communist hysteria gripping the nation, Tobias's appointment was confirmed. Outraged, Westbrook Pegler vowed to expose Tobias and all of the sinister machinations going on at the UN. Thus, just as *We Charge Genocide* was ready to be unleashed in Paris, Channing Tobias was under enormous pressure to prove his anti-Communist/pro-America mettle. He would not disappoint.[71]

Tobias's and the NAACP's efforts were so important because the United States did not want to be distracted from its well-laid plans to expose the "sham" of human rights in the Soviet bloc. In plotting its strategy for the UN meeting in Paris, the State Department crowed that "one of the weakest [and] most sensitive... points in the armor of the Soviets... is the denial of human rights... This weakness should be fully exploited." Thus, after carefully laying the groundwork over a three-year period, the United States had maneuvered a full General Assembly debate on the violations of human rights in Hungary, Rumania, and Bulgaria.[72] The State Department accused the Soviet bloc of "pervert[ing]" the judicial

71. Clarence Mitchell to Walter White, memo, October 17, 1951, Box H126, File "Loyalty Review Board Cases, 1947–1951," *Papers of the NAACP Washington Bureau*; Walter White to Harry S Truman, September 21, 1951, Box 15, File " 'W,'" *HST:Nash Files*; Philleo Nash to Martin Friedman, memo, November 14, 1951, Box 14, File " 'T' (folder 1)," ibid.; Alvin E. White, "Attack on Dr. Tobias Another Pegler Anti-Negro Action," September 26, 1951, Folder 42, "United Nations 1951–1952," *Tobias Papers*; Westbrook Pegler, "As Pegler Sees It: List Un-American Committee Citations of Channing Tobias," October 16, 1951, ibid.; Westbrook Pegler, "Dr. Tobias Leanings to Reds are Cited," October 16, 1951, ibid.; "Nomination of Channing H. Tobias: Hearing before a Subcommittee of the Committee on Foreign Relations United States Senate: Eighty Second Congress, First Session," October 18, 1951, found in ibid.; "Senate Approved Dr. Tobias After Testimony Before House Committee," October 22, 1951, ibid.; Westbrook Pegler, "Dr. Tobias Served a Pro-Red Magazine," October 23, 1951, ibid.; "Sub-Committee Approves Dr. Tobias Despite Pegler's Smear Campaign," October 24, 1951, ibid., *Tobias Papers*; "Tobias Sails for Paris, While Controversy Still Rages in Newspapers," October 31, 1951, ibid.

72. United States Program in the General Assembly, August 15, 1951, Box 2, File "6th General Assembly," Lot File 58D33, *RG 59*; (Secretary-General) to Chairman of the United States Delegation, November 19, 1951, Box 1, File "UN Letters from GA Held in Paris (1951)," *RG 84*; "Black and White," Voice of America Special Projects Howard Maier Commentary #97, November 19, 1951, found in Reel 67, *Du Bois*; DELGA, Paris (U.S. Delegation to the UN) to Department of State, November 21, 1951, Box 1, File "UN Letters from GA Held in Paris (1951)," *RG 84*.

process to the point where "equality before the law no longer existed," and of resorting to "cold-blooded murder" and "intimidation of voters" to "thwart the attainment of [a] representative government."[73]

Of course, as *We Charge Genocide* made so clear, similar charges could be leveled against the United States. In South Carolina, after applying an alchemy of poll taxes, "understanding clauses," and election-day terrorism, only 14.1 percent of all adults voted in the 1948 election. The same could be said of Georgia, where officials managed to pervert the judicial process and intimidate black voters in one decisive move. In 1948, black businessmen Robert Mallard was murdered for voting. During his killer's trial, in a move that defied every notion of jurisprudence, "[t]wo jurors entered the witness" box, testified on "behalf of the defendant," and then returned to the jury to render a "not guilty" verdict.[74] Given these and other abuses, the State Department had to acknowledge that the United States could "not claim perfection in human rights." But it still saw an "enormous propaganda advantage" to be gained from "continued prosecution" of the Communist record on human rights, so long as the Department could also stop a full UN investigation into the human rights abuses in the United States.[75]

With that goal in mind, the State Department argued that the UN had jurisdiction when it came to violations of human rights in the Communist bloc, because these rights were guaranteed by the peace treaties signed by

73. "Draft Statement on Hungary," August 27, 1948, SD/A/C.1/143, Box 20, File "SD/A/C.1/130-167," Lot File 82D211, *RG 59*; "Draft Statement on Bulgaria," SD/A/C.1/142, August 27, 1948, ibid.; "Draft Statement on Rumania," SD/A/C.1/141, August 27, 1948, ibid.; Position Paper: United States Position on the General Assembly Items Relating to Suppression of Human Rights in Hungary and Bulgaria, SD/A/C.1/206/Rev.1, April 6, 1949, Box 21, File "SD/A/C.1/200-225," ibid.; Proceeding in the Fourth Regular Session of the General Assembly on the Agenda Item 'Observance in Bulgaria, Hungary and Rumania of Human Rights and Fundamental Freedoms," October 13, 1949, ibid.

74. "The use of the poll tax as a restriction on suffrage...," n.d., Box 27, File "Civil Rights/Negro Affairs 1949–52," *Niles Papers*; "Mrs. Amy Mallard," *Providence (RI) Chronicle*, March 5, 1949, found in Box 59, File "Civil Rights and Southern Splits: Desk Corresp. Clippings–Senatorial," *Sen. McGrath Papers*; Paul H. Van Ness to Truman, January 30, 1949, Box 548, File "OF 93a," *Truman:OF*.

75. "The Negotiation of the Human Rights Articles in the Treaties of Peace with Italy, Rumania, Bulgaria, and Hungary: Research Project No. 126," August 1949, Box 24, File "SD/A/C.1/410-457," Lot File 82D211, *RG 59*; "Hungary," February 7, 1949, Box 8, File "Human Rights: Suppression in Hungary & Bulgaria," Lot File 55D429, ibid.; Acheson to Certain American Diplomatic Officers, memo, August 4, 1950, Box 14, File "SD/A/220-242," Lot File 82D211, ibid.; Background Paper "Observance of Human Rights and Fundamental Freedoms in Bulgaria, Hungary, and Rumania: History of the Problem, April 1949–September 1950," n.d., SD/A/C.1/324, Box 20, File "SD/A/C.1/300-349," Lot File 82D211, ibid.

governments in Hungary, Rumania, and Bulgaria after World War II. By emphasizing treaty rights, rather than the UN's human rights instruments, the United States had established a principle by which it could attack the Communists while shielding its "Negro problem" from UN scrutiny.[76]

Armed with this principle, the United States ripped into Czechoslovakia for jailing American journalist, William Oatis, as a spy. Denouncing the incident as an assault on freedom of the press, the State Department asked Channing Tobias to lead the charge, which he did with a vengeance. As a black man born in Georgia, Tobias used those credentials to claim that he recognized the denial of human rights when he saw it, and that when it came to such abuses, Communist-controlled Czechoslovakia was even worse than the American South.[77]

In short, the United States had taken the human rights offensive against the Soviet bloc and did not want to be distracted by troubling charges about the treatment of it own black citizens. Under these circumstances, silencing the *Genocide* petition took on even greater importance, especially after the State Department's internal review determined that the petition was "well documented [and] carefully presented." One delegate warned Patterson that *We Charge Genocide* had "deeply annoyed" Mrs. Roosevelt, "upset" the U.S. delegation, and led to "sharp" internal

76. "Hungary," February 7, 1949, Box 8, File "Human Rights: Suppression in Hungary & Bulgaria," Lot File 55D429, ibid.; Acheson to Certain American Diplomatic Officers, August 4, 1950, Box 14, File "SD/A/220-242," Lot File 82D211, ibid.; "Observance of Human Rights and Fundamental Freedoms in Bulgaria, Hungary, and Rumania," Status Paper, September 2, 1950, SD/A/C.1/333, Box 20, File "SD/A/C.1/300-349," Lot File 82D211, ibid.; "Observance of Human Rights and Fundamental Freedoms in Bulgaria, Hungary, and Rumania: History of the Problem, April 1949–September 1950," n.d., SD/A/C.1/324, Box 20, File "SD/A/C.1/300-349," Lot File 82D211, ibid.

77. "United States Program in the General Assembly," August 15, 1951, Box 2, File "6th General Assembly," Lot File 58D33, ibid.; Hickerson to The Secretary, memo, October 24, 1951, Box 2, File "6th General Assembly," Lot File 58D33, ibid.; Walter White to Channing Tobias, February 11, 1952, Box 147, File "Board of Directors: Channing Tobias—General, 1950–53," *Papers of the NAACP*; Report of the Economic and Social Council, January 30, 1952, A/C.3/SR.413, Third Committee 413th Meeting, UN General Assembly Sixth Session, *UN*; United States Delegation to the Sixth General Assembly: "Statement by the Honorable Channing Tobias... On violation of Freedom of Information in the Case of William Oatis," press release 1407, January 30, 1952, Folder 42, "United Nations 1951–52," *Tobias Papers*; "Free Nations Back U.S. on Oatis in UN," January 31, 1952, *New York World-Telegram* found in ibid.; United States Delegation to the United Nations: "Statement by the Honorable Channing H. Tobias,... in Committee III on Freedom of Information," press release 1424, February 2, 1952, found in Box 147, File "Board of Directors: Channing Tobias—General, 1950–53," *Papers of the NAACP*; Albert Anderson, "Dr. Tobias Was Well-Prepared for Oatis Statement Before UN," February 11, 1952, found in Folder 42, "United Nations 1951–52," *Tobias Papers.*

debates. The State Department therefore told Walter White that "it would be most desirable for some outstanding Negro leaders to be present in Paris" to discredit the CRC and refute the charge of genocide.[78]

The NAACP obliged. With Tobias's help, White's rebuttal was approved by the Board of Directors, phoned into the State Department, and then wired to Paris.[79] Moreover, in addition to White patrolling the domestic front, the Paris line-up read like a Who's Who of black America: Nobel Peace Prize winner, Dr. Ralph Bunche; director of the Phelps-Stokes Fund and YMCA executive, Dr. Channing Tobias; executive director of the Association for the Study of Negro Life and History as well as NAACP foreign policy consultant, Professor Rayford Logan; and attorney Edith Sampson, a black Chicagoan who had served on the U.S. delegation during the previous UN session. Sampson, who was not originally scheduled to be in Paris, was called in specifically to undertake a whirlwind tour of Scandinavia to undo any damage caused by the *Genocide* petition.[80] Patterson was disgusted. "For money and a title," he said, "these Negro hirelings will travel the ... world ... preaching the glories of this bloodthirsty dollar-democracy."[81]

In the tradition of the fiery evangelist, White used his syndicated column as a bloody pulpit to preach the blessings of American democracy, vilify the CRC, and ridicule the charges of genocide. He proposed to write a book extolling the enormous progress African Americans had made in attaining equality in the United States and, in line with the State Department's latest thrust, he challenged the CRC to detail Soviet atrocities as well.[82] Tobias also took up the battle cry. In an abrupt about-face from the NAACP's own *An Appeal to the World*, Tobias now contended that the UN had no authority to demand internal changes in the way a state treated

78. Walter White to Paul Hoffman, November 29, 1951, Box 636, File "United Nations: Genocide, 1947–51," *Papers of the NAACP*.
79. Minutes of Thirty-Sixth Meeting of the United States Delegation to the General Assembly, Paris, December 21, 1951, *FRUS* (1951), 2:856–59.
80. Chester S. Williams to Michael Weyl, December 19, 1951, Box 11, Folder 231, *Sampson Papers*. For a brief review of Sampson's work as a UN delegate see, Hanes Walton, Jr., *Black Women at the United Nations: The Politics, a Theoretical Model, and the Documents*, eds. Paul David Seldis and Mary A. Burgess (San Bernadino, California: The Borgo Press, 1995), 54–66.
81. "*We Charge Genocide*: Speech Delivered by William L. Patterson ... to Launch the Publication of the Book," November 12, 1951, Box 5, Folder 27, *Patterson Papers*.
82. White to Paul Hoffman, November 27, 1951, Box 636, File "United Nations: Genocide, 1947–51," *Papers of the NAACP*; White to Lessing J. Rosenwald, November 30, 1951, Box 161, File "Ralph Bunche Dinner, 1950–51," ibid.; White to Tobias, December 12, 1951, Box 636, File "United Nations, 1947–51," ibid.; White to Harry W. Seamans, December 14, 1951, ibid.; White to George Cornish, December 17, 1951, ibid.; White to George Cornish, December 20, 1951, ibid.

its citizens. He denounced the *Genocide* petition as "traitorous" and blasted Patterson for trying to "discredit" the American government.[83] In a heated encounter with the CRC's leader, he slammed the CRC for resorting to hyperbole and treating "isolated" incidents as if they represented a deliberate, governmental attempt to destroy African Americans. He also launched into a recital of Soviet atrocities, wanted to know why Patterson did not love America enough "to write about genocide in the Soviet Union," and demanded to know where Patterson "expects to get with" this petition. When Patterson replied that the answer depended "in part upon your courage," a disgusted Tobias turned his back and walked away. The encounter was typical of the exchanges between Patterson and the "outstanding Negroes," who, in his view, "ran interference for the American government" so well that it was clear that the United States "has done a good job in seducing" them.[84]

Patterson had anticipated that the U.S. government would bring out the big names to discredit the CRC, but he still believed, wrongly as it turned out, that "neither the State Department, nor its hired apologists" could stop the petition.[85] Indeed, he made the U.S. delegation pay for its copies of *We Charge Genocide*, boldly sent White and Roger Baldwin of the American Civil Liberties Union a personal copy so that they could do a "hatchet job" on it, and he also began to line up Du Bois, Paul Robeson, and other black celebrities to support his efforts in Paris.[86] As it turned out, however, the State Department, which initially suspected Robeson of writing *We Charge Genocide*, would not allow the singer to get to France, where he would have yet another opportunity to humiliate

83. Minutes of Thirty-Sixth Meeting of the United States Delegation to the General Assembly, Paris, December 21, 1951, *FRUS* (1951), 2:856–59; Marginalia from Patterson to Darling (Louise Patterson) written on "*We Charge Genocide*: A Speech Prepared by William L. Patterson for the . . . United Nations," December 1951, Box 9, Folder 87, *Patterson*.

84. Pat [William Patterson] to Angie, December 1951, Part 2, Reel 3, *CRC*; Pat [William Patterson] to [Louise Patterson], n.d., ibid.; "*We Charge Genocide*: A Speech Prepared by William L. Patterson for the General Assembly of the United Nations, Paris France," December 1951, Box 9, Folder 87, *Patterson Papers*; Pat [William Patterson] to Darling [Louise Patterson], December 7, 1951, ibid.; Pat [William Patterson] to Darling [Louise Patterson], n.d., ibid.; Patterson to Darling [Louise Patterson], n.d., ibid.; Draft Chapter XVIII At the Palais Chaillot in Paris, Box 7, Folder 56, ibid.; Patterson to H. H. Robnett, February 1, 1952, Part 2, Reel 24, *CRC*.

85. Civil Rights Congress news release, November 20, 1951, Box 636, File "United Nations: Genocide, 1952–53," *Papers of the NAACP*.

86. Charles V. Mantione to Miss Block, November 30, 1951, Part 2, Reel 5, *CRC*; Patterson to Roger Baldwin, November 21, 1951, Part 2, Reel 1, ibid.; Patterson to White, November 10, 1951, Box 369, File "Leagues: Civil Rights Congress, 1951," *Papers of the NAACP*; Patterson to Ben Gold, November 20, 1951, Part 2, Reel 2, *CRC*.

the United States. As Walter White knew well in advance and apparently condoned, the State Department denied Robeson a passport, which then forced him to deliver a copy of the petition to a "subordinate subordinate in the Secretariat's office" in New York.[87]

Government pressure also took its toll on Du Bois. Convinced that it was time to "stand and be counted," rather than "grin and bow" or "run and hide when somebody whispers 'Communist'," Du Bois was eager to lead the CRC contingent to Paris.[88] He anticipated the inevitable passport problems with the State Department, but he did not foresee the warnings from his attorney, his physicians, and from his new wife, Shirley Graham, all of whom warned that his health could not withstand the trip, and that it would be foolish to provoke another indictment so soon after winning a bitter and expensive legal battle against the Justice Department. Guided by this advice, Du Bois reluctantly informed Patterson that he had "decided not to go to Paris," even though, as Patterson pointed out, he was the only black leader of sufficient stature to "expose the machinations" of Tobias, Bunche, and the other State Department blacks.[89]

In Paris, alone, Patterson's frustration almost reached the breaking point. Hundreds of petitions, which the CRC had mailed to London and Paris, just vanished although those sent to Hungary managed to arrive with no problem. What is more, when Patterson finally realized that he had to do more than just present the petition, he approached the Indian, then the Ethiopian, Egyptian, Haitian, Dominican, and Liberian delegations, only to be told, their own sympathies notwithstanding, how they could not help the CRC without risking Point IV dollars or development aid from the United States. Nor were the Soviet Union or Communist bloc countries an option, given their ties to the CP in the United States, not to mention the American government's relentless pursuit of the human rights cases against Hungary, Rumania, and Bulgaria, which forced the Soviet bloc to argue that such internal matters were beyond the UN's jurisdiction.[90] Still worse, no sooner had Patterson secured an interview with a

87. To Mr. Kohler, unsigned [John Hickerson?], November 15, 1951, Box 60, File "Genocide Against the Negroes, 1951–52," Entry 1587, *RG 59*; Logan to White, November 19, 1951, Box 404, File "Rayford Logan, 1950–51," *Papers of the NAACP*; Aubrey Grossman to Patterson, December 17, 1951, Part 2, Reel 3, *CRC*.

88. Quoted in, "Address by Paul Robeson to be Delivered at National Council of American Soviet Friendship," November 10, 1949, Part 2, Reel 7, ibid.

89. Du Bois to Patterson, memo, November 27, 1951, Part 2, Reel 1, ibid.; Patterson to John Adams Kingsbury, November 28, 1951, Part 2, Reel 3, ibid.; Patterson to Du Bois, memo, November 28, 1951, Part 2, Reel 1, ibid.; Patterson to Du Bois, November 28, 1951, Reel 66, *Du Bois*; Du Bois to John Adams Kingsbury, November 30, 1951, ibid.; Du Bois to Patterson, November 30, 1951, Part 2, Reel 1, *CRC*.

90. William A. Rutherford to William Patterson, February 19, 1952, Part 2, Reel 2, ibid.; Draft I Go to the United Nations: Contemplating the Project, n.d., Box 7, Folder

reporter from the *New York Times*, than the U.S. Embassy attempted to seize his passport and deport him because his presence in Paris was "not in the best interest of the United States."[91] Ever defiant, Patterson told the embassy to "go to hell," threw his always-packed suitcases in a taxi, rushed to the airport, and fled to Eastern Europe on a "grey card" given to him by colleagues in the French Communist party.[92]

It appeared that the CRC's attempts to have *We Charge Genocide* discussed were all but finished when they were suddenly reinvigorated by another shocking blow out of the American South. The cold-blooded murder of Samuel Shepherd and near fatal wounding of Walter Irvin had been just the latest tragedy in a two-year reign of terror in Truman's vacation paradise of Florida. Throughout 1949, 1950, and 1951, Jewish synagogues, Catholic churches, and black homes in white neighborhoods were bombed at will. Indeed, Florida experienced an average of one bombing every two months during this period, and there was also rampant antiblack violence in the form of murders, vicious beatings, and other acts of terrorism. The Florida authorities could never find the perpetrators, and the Justice Department claimed to have little authority to stop the bloodletting. "We had only . . . two small statutes to work with," recalled one Justice Department official, and because the civil rights division was not quite sure "what . . . rights *[were]* protected by the Constitution," there was very little that it could do. Besides, the Justice Department attorney concluded, the "victims . . . were either too frightened to testify, or . . . so ignorant that they couldn't."[93]

Sheriff McCall's cold-blooded murder of Samuel Shepherd was the last straw for Harry T. Moore, State Director of Florida's NAACP, who publically challenged the government to rein in the Klan and bring the cowards to justice. With that last act of courage, Harry T. Moore signed his death warrant. On Christmas night, as Moore and his wife slept, the Klan detonated a bomb directly underneath his bedroom. Moore died almost instantly, while his wife, who suffered horrendous burns, lingered in agony for days until, mercifully, death finally put her out of her misery.

The incident outraged the African American community, which viewed Moore and his wife as the latest victims of Klan violence and government

48, *Patterson Papers*. A good sample of the Soviet bloc's positions can be found in "Proceedings in the Fourth Regular Session of the General Assembly on the Agenda Item 'Observance in Bulgaria, Hungary and Rumania of Human Rights and Fundamental Freedoms," October 13, 1949, Box 21, File "SD/A/C.1/200-225," Lot File 82D211, *RG* 59.

91. Walter Winchell broadcast, transcript, December 30, 1951, Box 9, Folder 37, *Patterson Papers*.

92. Draft Chapter XVIII At the Palais Chaillot in Paris, n.d., Box 7, Folder 56, ibid.

93. *Bontecou*.

Photo 4.5. An obviously weary Walter White speaking before a crowd of 9,000 at the Oakland (California) Arena concerning the wave of violence in Florida, including the killing of Samuel Shepherd, the wounding of Walter Irvin, and the Christmas assassinations of Harry T. and Harriet Moore, January 1952.
E. F. Joseph, African American Museum and Library at Oakland.

indifference.[94] They and others wanted to know how the American government could marshal the financial and moral resources to defend the "oppressed" in Eastern Europe and Korea, but declare bankruptcy when it came to protecting the lives of black citizens in the United States. "If you can intervene in a civil war in far off Korea," one group wrote to Truman, surely "you can intervene in the war against the ... Negro people in the United States." One man observed that something was wrong when black men had a better chance on the front lines in Korea than they

94. For a representative sample of the outcry see, Peter Robertson to Truman, telegram, December 27, 1951, Box 547, File "OF 93 Misc.-Moore Bombing 'R,'" *Truman:OF*; Ann Lloyd to Truman, telegram, December 28, 1951, Box 547, File "OF 93 Misc.-Moore Bombing 'L,'" ibid.; Leo Linder to Truman, telegram, December 28, 1951, Box 547, File "OF 93 Misc.-Moore Bombing 'K,'" ibid.; "Acid Test for FBI," n.d. (*Cleveland Call and Post*, January 12, 1952), found in Part 2, Reel 14, *CRC*.

had in Truman's vacation paradise of Florida.[95] Even the venerable and staid National Baptist Convention asked Truman how he could cross an ocean to defend democracy when he was unable "to reach across state lines" to protect African Americans from being lynched, bombed, and tortured.[96] Fed up with all of the government's excuses, another woman simply "demand[ed]" that Truman "get off [his] rear end and do the right thing – NOW!"[97]

Just like the outrage provoked by Monroe, Georgia, many wanted to know how the FBI could catch every notorious criminal in the United States, from gangsters to Communists spies, but had yet to find one shred of evidence against any lyncher or bomber. And the answer seemed obvious to them. The Truman administration had allowed the violence in Florida to escalate, it had let arsonists, bombers, and murderers escape justice, and had condoned Florida's murderous and inept authorities for years. By tolerating such savagery, it had assured the Klan that it could act with impunity, and was, thus, just as responsible for the Moores' assassination.[98]

The stark reality of that disturbing fact evoked a crisis of confidence in one of Truman's most ardent supporters, the NAACP. When news of the bombing reached Channing Tobias in Paris, he bowed his head in shame. The NAACP had worked hard to protect America's honor against the CRC, he said, afraid Moore's death was a body blow from which the NAACP and the Truman administration might not recover. State-condoned murders of civil rights workers – on Christmas – seemed to confirm what Patterson and the CRC had spelled out in *Genocide*. Maybe one or two murders could be explained away as "isolated" incidents, but the assassination of Moore and his wife was clearly the capstone on years of state-sanctioned persecution. After the killings, Tobias bemoaned, "the American delegation [was] . . . confronted daily" with "a recital of racial violence," not only from the Soviets, but also "from the non-white

95. Joe Jacobs to Truman, telegram, December 29, 1951, Box 547, File "OF 93 Misc.-Moore Bombing 'J,'" *Truman:OF*.
96. The Teen Age Club of Elizabeth to Truman, telegram, January 6, 1952, Box 547, File "OF 93 Misc.-Moore Bombing 'T,'" ibid.; Mrs. Gloria Rosenfeld to Truman, June 17, 1952, Box 544, File "OF 93 February 1952–53," ibid.; Sandy F. Ray and D. V. Jemison to Truman, telegram, December 29, 1951, Box 547, File "OF 93 Misc-Moore Bombing 'S,'" ibid.
97. S. Rosenblatt to Truman, December 28, 1951, Box 547, File "OF Misc.-Moore Bombing 'R,'" ibid. (Emphasis in original.)
98. For a representative sampling of this viewpoint see, Carl Stellato et al. to Truman, telegram, December 26, 1951, Box 547, File "OF 93 Misc.-Moore Bombing 'U,'" ibid.; Rev. Harold S. Williamson to Truman, telegram, December 27, 1951, Box 547, File "OF 93 Misc.-Moore Bombing 'W,'" ibid.

nations."[99] Tobias, himself, was also "closely questioned" by the French, Swedes, Italians, and Germans "as to the validity of [Walter White's] thesis that substantial progress has been made" in the "treatment of Negroes in the United States."[100] White had to ask himself the same question. Temporarily shaken out of his "enormous progress" realm, he told Edith Sampson that "of the more than forty lynchings and more than twenty race riots" he had investigated, "this was by long odds the most cold-blooded, unjustified, and heinous one of them all."[101] In a letter drafted by Wilkins, Arthur B. Spingarn, and Louis Wright made a similar point to President Truman. Harry T. Moore, they wrote, "believed in the American Declaration of Independence" and "in the Constitution." Moore protested the brutal murder of Samuel Shepherd "in the American way, with the American weapons of law and order." Yet, for believing in America, he was murdered by a group of cowards that had been allowed to terrorize blacks, Jews, and Catholics for years. "If Harry T. Moore was wrong," they concluded, "then there is no America ... and all the dreams we preach have no meaning."[102]

Although Truman apparently believed that most of the howling was just more of the same, shrill Communist wailing, Philleo Nash, his assistant in the minority affairs office, tried to set the record straight. He explained that, in just one week, the White House had been deluged with hundreds of angry telegrams, and while there were clearly some Communists who complained, "as indicated by their use of the word 'genocide,'" there were many telegrams "from sincere and loyal Americans who are shocked by the crime and feel that [the President] should do something about it personally." Indeed, by March, the White House had more than 6,000 telegrams protesting both the murders and, by this time, the administration's apparent unwillingness to track down the killers. Even Walter White was pleading in vain for the administration to act. He tried to impress upon Attorney General J. Howard McGrath how crucial it was to have a strong federal presence in the investigation and to help calm the "seriously grave" situation in Florida. But McGrath, who had engineered

99. White to Thurgood Marshall et al., memo, January 25, 1952, Box 147, File "Board of Directors: Channing Tobias—General, 1950–53," *Papers of the NAACP*; Channing H. Tobias, "Not for the Negro Alone," speech, March 15, 1952, Box 148, File "Board of Directors: Channing Tobias, Reaction to His Broadcast—1952," ibid.

100. "Draft of Suggestions for Mr. Walter White for His Testimony on the McCarran-Walter Act," by Rayford W. Logan, in Logan to White, September 21, 1952, Box 117, File, "Bills: McCarran Bill—General—1950–52," ibid.

101. White to Edith Sampson, January 3, 1952, Box 3, Folder 72, *Sampson Papers*.

102. David Singer to Honorable Fuller Warren et al., January 4, 1952, Box 547, File "OF 93 Misc.-Moore Bombing 'S,'" *Truman:OF*; Arthur B. Spingarn and Louis T. Wright to Truman, December 27, 1951, Box 10, File "Miami Bombings," *HST:Nash Files*.

the Democratic party's reconciliation with the Dixiecrats, decided that it was best if the administration maintained a low profile and kept out of Florida.[103]

On the other hand, the CRC was not about to let the murders just fade away. As Angie Dickerson, assistant executive secretary of the CRC, remarked, "the bomb that sent Mr. and Mrs. Harry Moore to eternity was exploding for all the world to hear."[104] CRC branches immediately pointed to the Moores' charred remains as "Genocide: Exhibit A." They linked the American Embassy's attempt to seize Patterson's passport with the administration's need to keep the slaughter of African Americans hidden "behind the cotton curtain."[105] The Moores' deaths simply rejuvenated William Patterson, the Civil Rights Congress, and the CRC's sagging *Genocide* petition efforts. *We Charge Genocide* now had more than cachet, it had credence. The CRC reported that "two 'very important

103. Truman to Philleo Nash, telegram, December 29, 1951, ibid.; Philleo Nash to Truman, memo, January 3, 1952, ibid.; R. G. Moore to Philleo Nash, memo, March 12, 1952, ibid.; Charles Walker to Truman, January 25, 1952, Box 547, File "OF 93 Misc.-Moore Bombing 'W,'" *Truman:OF*; White to J. Howard McGrath, telegram, January 3, 1951 (sic), Box 113, File "National A," *Papers of J. Howard McGrath*, Harry S Truman Presidential Library, Independence, Missouri (hereafter *McGrath Papers*); "Report of the Secretary," May 9, 1949, Part 1, Reel 7, *NAACP*; "The Dixiecrat Purge," November 15, 1949, Box 59, File "Civil Rights and Southern Splits: Desk Corresp. Clippings–Senatorial," *Sen. McGrath Papers*; J. Howard McGrath to Walter White, telegram, January 11, 1952, Box 113, File "National A," *McGrath Papers*.

104. Angie Dickerson to Roscoe Dunjee, January 14, 1952, Part 2, Reel 1, *CRC*.

105. S. L. Pullman to Truman, telegram, December 28, 1951, Box 547, File "OF 93 Misc.-Moore Bombing 'P,'" *Truman:OF*; Ben Henlock et al. to Truman, telegram December 26, 1951, Box 547, File "OF 93 Misc.-Moore Bombing 'X-Y-Z' [1 of 2]," ibid.; New York State Communist party to Truman, telegram, December 26, 1951, Box 547, File "OF 93 Misc.-Moore Bombing 'N,'" ibid.; Rockaway Citizens to Truman, telegram, December 26, 1951, Box 547, File "OF 93 Misc.-Moore Bombing 'R,'" ibid.; Mr. and Mrs. Thomas Leavy to Truman, telegram, December 26, 1951, Box 547, File "OF 93 Misc.-Moore Bombing 'L,'" ibid.; Joseph Marzell to Truman, telegram, December 26, 1951, Box 547, File "OF 93 Misc.-Moore Bombing 'M,'" ibid.; Mr. and Mrs. Fred Kotter to Truman, telegram, December 26, 1951, Box 547, File "OF 93 Misc.-Moore Bombing 'K,'" ibid.; Civil Rights Congress San Francisco Chapter to Truman, telegram, December 26, 1951, Box 547, File "OF 93 Misc.-Moore Bombing 'S,'" ibid.; Lester Davis and Chapman Wells to Truman, telegram, December 31, 1951, Box 547, File "OF 93 Misc.-Moore Bombing 'X-Y-Z' [1 of 2]," ibid.; Mrs. Odessa Cox to Truman, telegram, December 30, 1951, Box 547, File "OF 93 Misc.-Moore Bombing 'P,'" ibid.; Miriam Kahn to Truman, telegram, December 28, 1951, Box 547, File "OF 93 Misc.-Moore Bombing 'K,'" ibid.; Frances Leon to Truman, telegram, December 28, 1951, Box 547, File "OF 93 Misc.-Moore Bombing 'L,'" ibid.; J. Bradley et al. to Truman, telegram, December 27, 1951, Box 547, File "OF 93 Misc.-Moore Bombing 'X-Y-Z' [1 of 2]," ibid. The reference to the "cotton curtain," was earlier but appropriate in this context, see Patterson to Albert E. Hart, May 11, 1950, Part 2, Reel 1, *CRC*.

countries'" from outside the Soviet bloc had agreed to place the *Genocide* petition on the agenda of the Commission on Human Rights. Shortly after this announcement, Patterson triumphantly returned to Paris.[106] The American government moved in.

Eleanor Roosevelt had already alerted Truman that the *Genocide* petition had "hurt [the U.S.] in so many little ways."[107] For example, the debates on the draft Covenant on Human Rights were already tense, and the *Genocide* petition made it difficult for the United States to impose its limited vision of human rights on the rest of the delegates. The American delegation had tried desperately to keep economic and social rights out of the Covenant and, failing that, to have a federal–state clause inserted that would allow the American South to ignore the Covenant on Human Rights with the same brashness that it ignored the Bill of Rights.[108]

Amazingly, given his wretched performance in the *Genocide* affair, Walter White exploded when he saw the American government's severely constricted interpretation of human rights. White blasted the State Department for being "timorous," for "pussyfoot[ing]" around with the

106. "Two Non-'East Bloc' Countries to Seek Action by United Nations on Petition Charging U.S. Government with Anti-Negro Genocide," press release, January 6, 1952, Part 2, Reel 19, ibid.; William A. Rutherford, "Patterson Defies Ban Returns to Paris," press release, January 12, 1952, Box 9, Folder 88, *Patterson Papers*.

107. Eleanor Roosevelt to Truman [fragment], December 29, 1951, Box 2, File "Mrs. Eleanor Roosevelt, 1949 to 1951," Lot File 58D33, *RG 59*; Eleanor Roosevelt to Truman, December 21, 1951, Box 4560, File "Harry S Truman, 1949–1952," *Roosevelt Papers*.

108. "Minutes of the Meeting of the Board of Directors of the American Association for the United Nations," June 22, 1949, Box 3249, File "American Association for the UN, 1948–49," *Roosevelt Papers*; Gilbert W. Stewart to Eleanor Roosevelt [including attachment: Suggested Statement for January 3 Press Conference on the Covenant on Human Rights], December 29, 1949, Box 4588, File "Human Rights Commission, 1949," ibid.; Robert M. MacIver to Eleanor Roosevelt, March 28, 1950, Box 3250, File "American Civil Liberties Union, 1949–52," ibid.; Durward Sandifer to Mr. Cates, memo, May 11, 1950, Box 8, File "Human Rights: Miscellaneous, January 1, 1950–October 18, 1951," Lot File 55D429, *RG 59*; Eleanor Roosevelt to Truman, May 28, 1950, Box 11, File "I," [2 of 2], *HST:Nash Files*; John M. Cates, Jr., to Durward V. Sandifer, August 16, 1950, Box 8, File "Human Rights: Miscellaneous, January 1, 1950–October 18, 1951," Lot File 55D429, *RG 59*; Eleanor Roosevelt to Sandy [Durward Sandifer], March 31, 1951, Box 3362, File "Sandifer, Durward, 1947–51," *Roosevelt Papers*; Durward Sandifer to Eleanor Roosevelt, April 4, 1951, Box 8, File "Human Rights: Miscellaneous, January 1, 1950–October 18, 1951," Lot File 55D429, *RG 59*; Eleanor Roosevelt to Durward Sandifer, May 15, 1951, Box 3362, File "Sandifer, Durward, 1947–51," *Roosevelt Papers*; Memorandum of Conversation concerning Position of United States Concerning Draft Covenant on Human Rights in ECOSOC and General Assembly, May 29, 1951, Box 8, File "Human Rights: Miscellaneous, January 1, 1950–October 18, 1951," Lot File 55D429, *RG 59*; John D. Hickerson to Mr. Rusk, May 30, 1951, Box 2, File "Mrs. Eleanor Roosevelt, 1949 to 1951," Lot File 58D33, ibid.

basic principles of human rights, and for stooping so low as to craft a Covenant that even the most vile Dixiecrat would approve. His harangue, however, occurred before the *Genocide* petition had emerged. After that bombshell landed in Paris, White's disdain for America's version of the Covenant was tragically muted and remained so even after the American delegation unveiled its latest version of the federal–state clause. At that time, Eleanor Roosevelt emphasized three key, important areas in which the current balance of federal–state power would be sacredly preserved. The federal government, she promised, would never interfere in "murder cases," investigate concerns over "fair trials," or insist on "the right to education." In essence, Eleanor Roosevelt had just assured the Dixiecrats that the sacred troika of lynching, Southern Justice, and Jim Crow schools would remain untouched, even with a Covenant on Human Rights. Given that the pronouncement came from Mrs. Roosevelt, Walter White said nothing.[109]

The Soviets were not so quiet. America's aversion to economic and social rights, as well as its insistence on inserting the doctrine of states' rights into an international treaty was, according to the Soviets, the only way that the United States could continue to abuse its black population. Roosevelt bristled at this interpretation. She shot back with Walter White's "Progress Report," but she did not have such an easy retort for the delegates from the Middle East, South Asia, and the Caribbean. The nations in the developing world, already angry when the United States tried to suspend the work of the UN's Subcommission on the Prevention of Discrimination and Protection of Minorities, were even more disturbed when the U.S. delegation decided to treat economic and social rights as, at best, unattainable goals. These rights, they declared, offered the only "true hope" for their countries to emerge from the shackles of poverty and economic exploitation. They would not accept a Covenant that did not incorporate these rights on an equal footing with political and legal rights. Their position raised the question of whether there would be one covenant that incorporated all rights, which is what the developing nations and the Soviet Union had desired, or two covenants, with political and legal rights in one and economic and social rights in the other, which is what the Americans wanted. Thus, as the Sixth Session closed

109. White to Rayford Logan, September 25, 1951, Box 181-8, Folder 3, *Logan-MSRC*; White to Rayford Logan, October 24, 1951, ibid.; "Statement to the Press by Mrs. Franklin D. Roosevelt on the 'Federal State' Clause of the Covenant on Human Rights," press release, June 6, 1952, Box 4588, File "Human Rights Commission, undated," *Roosevelt Papers*; Lowell Limpus, "UN Pact Won't Clash with States' Rights, Says Mrs. Roosevelt," June 9, 1952, found in Box 626, File "UN Secur. Council 'Commission on Human Rt. of the Econ. & Soc. Coun.,'" *RNC*; White to Jacob Javits, March 6, 1952, Box 117, File "Bills: McCarran Bill—General—1950–52," *Papers of the NAACP*.

for a holiday recess, the tendentious arguing had left Roosevelt frustrated and exhausted, and the prospects for the next session, especially with the Moores' ghosts and William Patterson's *Genocide* petition stalking the corridors of the UN, seemed equally dismal.[110]

Patterson's reemergence on the Paris scene could now only portend more difficulties for the U.S. delegation. It was clear that Patterson had to be removed and the damage undone. Earlier in 1951, he had dodged a "contempt of Congress" conviction because of a mistrial. Apparently, the lone African American juror was outraged that the Georgia congressman who had called Patterson "a black son-of-a-bitch" was not the one cited for "contempt," and she simply refused to find the national secretary of the CRC guilty of any wrongdoing. Because of her resolve, Patterson was free, but only temporarily as his international exploits had prompted the U.S. government to set a new trial date for January 28, 1952. With the new court date looming, government officials moved in, threw Patterson on a plane back to New York, confiscated his passport, and strip searched him almost the moment his feet touched American soil. Shortly thereafter, he learned that his case had been postponed. With no passport, however, he was unable to return to Paris because, he said, the U.S. government "was afraid to face the . . . 'charges of genocide.'"[111]

110. Summary Record, December 12, 1951, A/C.3/SR.367, Third Committee 367th Meeting, General Assembly Sixth Session, *UN*; Summary Record, December 12, 1951, A/C.3/SR.366, Third Committee 366th Meeting, General Assembly Sixth Session, ibid.; Summary Record, December 13, 1951, A/C.3/SR.368, Third Committee 368th Meeting, General Assembly Sixth Session, ibid.; Summary Record, December 19, 1951, A/C.3/SR.370, Third Committee 370th Meeting, General Assembly Sixth Session, ibid.; Summary Record, December 20, 1951, A/C.3/SR.371, Third Committee 371st Meeting, General Assembly Sixth Session, ibid.; Eleanor Roosevelt to Marjorie Whiteman, n.d., Box 4570, (no file), *Roosevelt Papers*; Summary Record, November 29, 1951, E/CN.4/Sub.2/SR.83, Commission on Human Rights, Sub-Commission on Prevention of Discrimination and Protection of Minorities, Fourth Session, *UN*; Summary Record, November 28, 1951, E/CN.4/Sub.2/SR.82, Commission on Human Rights, Sub-Commission on Prevention of Discrimination and Protection of Minorities, Fourth Session, ibid.; Summary Record, January 21, 1952, A/C.3/SR.396, Third Committee 396th Meeting, General Assembly Sixth Session, ibid.; Summary Record, January 25, 1952, A/C.3/SR.403, Third Committee 403rd Meeting, General Assembly Sixth Session, ibid.; Report of the Economic and Social Council (Chapter V) Agenda Item 11, January 30, 1952, A/C.3/L.237, Third Committee, General Assembly Sixth Session, ibid.; Summary Record, February 1, 1952, A/C.2&3/SR.66, Joint Second and Third Committee 66th Meeting, General Assembly Sixth Session, ibid.

111. "Patterson, CRC Head, Faces Second Trial Jan. 28 in Washington, D.C.," press release, January 21, 1952, found in Box 636, File "United Nations: Genocide, 1952–53," *Papers of the NAACP*; no title, press release, January 24, 1951, Part 2, Reel 42, *CRC*; Ferdinand Smith to William Patterson, January 28, 1952, Part 2, Reel 2, ibid.; Draft My Return from Paris, n.d., Box 7, Folder 57, *Patterson Papers*.

There was another "truth" the State Department wanted the world to hear, and the U.S. government wanted Edith Sampson – not William Patterson – to tell it. Sampson was tailor-made for the State Department. She would rhapsodize about the beauty of America, the land of opportunity, and then declare that all of the horror stories about lynching and segregation were just a pack of Soviet lies. Sampson seemed so believable that most members in her audience would acquiesce to her apparent first-hand knowledge about the real conditions in the United States. Indeed, with her friendly, down-home style and sanitized version of life in America, she had proven her worth to the State Department, where officials knew they had a winner when Sampson vowed to "link arms with the worst Dixicrat (sic)...to save [her] country." Indeed, at a meeting with a group from India, Sampson prattled on and on about the wonderful "benefits of slavery," such as "never hav[ing] to worry about unemployment.... food, clothing, and shelter." Such a performance made her the perfect kind of American Negro for the State Department, especially at a time when the *Genocide* petition and the Moore bombing were undercutting all of the hard work done to portray the Soviet bloc as the *bétè noir* of human rights.[112]

Sampson, of course, shared the State Department's fears. She was greatly concerned that *We Charge Genocide* would be accepted as gospel by the Scandinavians, who had already been sensitized to the horrors of Jim Crow by Gunnar Myrdal's landmark study, *An American Dilemma*. As far as Sampson was concerned, Myrdal's 1944 study was hopelessly "obsolete" and the *Genocide* petition was nothing but the "Communists...spreading misinformation about the Negro." She swore to do a "stepped-up, hard-hitting job...to offset the damage which has already been done [by America's] enemies."[113]

True to her word, she told an audience in Helsinki that the U.S. judicial system had driven the Klan out of business. She boasted to the Finns that "the KKK has disappeared" from the American scene and that its leaders had been "sent to the penitentiary." She scoffed at the idea of Jim Crow and assured her audience that she had never attended a racially segregated school, did not live in a black neighborhood, or worship at an all-black church. She claimed that African Americans had attained a higher level

112. Edith Sampson to Mrs. Eugenia Anderson, March 16, 1952, Box 11, Folder 229, *Sampson Papers*; "Mrs. Edith Sampson's Record of Performance at the Fifth General Assembly," n.d., Box 10, Folder 210, ibid.; "Address by Mrs. Edith S. Sampson, Alternate U.S. Representative to the General Assembly at the Meeting of the India League Celebrating Gandhi's Birthday," press release, October 1, 1950, Part 14, Reel 17, *NAACP Int'l*; Chester S. Williams to Michael Weyl, December 19, 1951, Box 11, Folder 231, *Sampson Papers*.

113. Sampson to Eleanor Roosevelt, January 26, 1952, Box 11, Folder 234, ibid.

of education than the residents of Great Britain, and she allayed concerns about the franchise. "Negroes did not exercise their right to vote," she said, but there was nothing stopping them, including the poll tax, which was a relic of the past. Job discrimination had been eliminated, as well, which meant that African Americans were not consigned to low-paying positions and, as such, the majority of black women no longer worked as domestics. In the United States today, Sampson said triumphantly, African Americans were an integral part of labor unions, management, and professional guilds. In fact, Sampson intoned, the Negroes she knew all had big shiny, black Cadillacs, lived in $100,000 homes, and sent their children to schools that made most whites envious. As for the rest, they did not live in slums, but, in fact, owned homes that were the envy of the world, including the Soviet Union. Nor were African Americans in the rural areas excluded from this bountiful life. They were not trapped in debt slavery or in a brutal sharecropping system from which there was no escape, but owned hundreds of thousands of acres of farmland and were quite prosperous. Sampson concluded this amazing speech by arguing that both Sheriff McCall's execution of Shepherd and the Moores' assassination were just "the last-ditch acts . . . of a small group of pathological people." Sampson repeated these assertions in her whirlwind tour of Norway, Sweden, and Denmark. As she took her final bows, she would swear that she had "not attempted to paint a prettier picture" than that which actually existed in the United States, but had "simply given the truth, the whole truth, and nothing but the truth."[114]

In fact, what Edith Sampson had really done was to betray the cause of black equality. The bane of African Americans' existence was not the CP or the Soviet Union. As Henry L. Moon noted in 1948, "Communism is not regarded by the Negro as the enemy. The black folk of America know the enemy, the *real* enemy. They have looked into his hard white face. It is the fiendish face of reaction."[115] Communists did not kill

114. "Mrs. Sampson's Speech (auspices Finnish American Society)," January 14, 1952, Box 11, Folder 231, ibid.; "Summary of Address delivered by Mrs. Edith Sampson in Stockholm, Sweden . . . on 'The Negro in America,'" January 18, 1952, Part 14, Reel 17, *NAACP Int'l*; From Ernie Johnson, News Unit, Department of State, new release, February 1952, ibid.; "State Department Charged with Hiding Its 'Overseas Propaganda' on Negroes from U.S.," press release, February 11, 1952, Part 2, Reel 40, *CRC*; "Statement Made in Copenhagen by Mrs. Edith Sampson . . . while visiting Mrs. Eugenia Anderson, American Ambassador to Denmark," January 26, 1952, Part 2, Reel 5, ibid.

115. Henry Lee Moon, "Balance of Power–The Negro Vote," found in William L. Batt, Jr., to Philleo Nash, Box 59, File "WH Files-Minorities-Negro Publications-Balance of Power of the Negro Vote by H. L. Moon–Review, June 1948," *Nash Papers*. (Emphasis in original.)

the Moores, Samuel Shepherd, Robert Mallard, Willie McGee, or the Martinsville Seven, nor did they invent the white primary, understanding clauses, literacy tests, and the poll tax. Communists did not work hand-in-hand with the Federal Housing Administration and mortgage lenders to ensure that African Americans would not be able to own decent homes, and they were not responsible for underfunded black colleges and public schools that robbed African American children of their future. It was the United States that had managed to do all of that and more. Sampson's Scandinavian performance fully absolved the American government of its responsibility. Indeed, her beautiful soliloquy on the remarkable attainment of African American economic and political equality clearly implied that all demands for civil rights were illegitimate, a scandalous attempt to achieve "preferential treatment," or Communist-inspired propaganda. The public relations director for the *Toledo Blade* therefore felt wholly comfortable in conversing with Sampson about the "*alleged* economic and social hardships imposed upon the American Negro."[116]

State Department officials, of course, congratulated themselves on their brilliant strategy and raved about what "an unqualified success" Sampson's "carefully-planned Scandinavian speaking tour" had been. One report asserted that "there is no question whatever that Mrs. Sampson's visit did a great deal to open the eyes of a good many Swedes to the fact that the days of Uncle Tom's Cabin belong to the past." That phrase, which was one of Sampson's favorite, was difficult to reconcile with a Justice Department attorney's analysis that "Southern Negroes... were treated... as if there had never been a Reconstruction. They lived in fear just as they had many years ago."[117]

Because of that reality, not everyone in Sampson's audience was as gullible as the State Department hoped. One Danish woman, who had just returned from Harlem, blasted Sampson for distorting the horrendous living conditions of blacks in the United States. At another meeting, despite his continuously raised hand, Sampson refused to recognize a young black man whom she thought might contradict her rosy view. Nor did Sampson's speeches go unnoticed by the African American leadership. One reporter for the NAACP's *Crisis* declared that Sampson's Copenhagen performance was "dishonest and... revolting." Sampson, he wrote, "created an observable shudder of revulsion... by boasting about the 'expensive black

116. Harry R. Roberts to Edith Sampson, December 27, 1951, Box 3, Folder 70, *Sampson Papers*. (Emphasis added.) For an alternate, more favorable interpretation of Sampson see, Helen Laville and Scott Lucas, "Edith Sampson, the NAACP, and African American Identity," *Diplomatic History* 20:4 (Fall 1996), 565–80, 588–90.

117. State Department memo [fragment], February 5, 1952, Box 11, Folder 231, *Sampson Papers*; *Bontecou*.

cars' and the $100,000...homes which a few wealthy Negroes own." Although she tried to illustrate black equality in the United States by pointing to a handful of African Americans who enjoyed some success, Sampson, "failed to explain...how the appointment of a Negro judge improves the living conditions of 14,999,999 other Negroes." In short, the reporter concluded, Sampson's "propaganda with a capital 'P'.. was sheer fantasy" straight out of "Cloud-Cuckoo Land." Of course, Eleanor Roosevelt "did not like the report in *Crisis* on Mrs. Sampson's speech," and made sure that Walter White knew it. Yet, a Swedish woman who had heard the speech implored White to set the record straight. It was "a betrayal of the Negro people" and "demonstrates its venality" by totally misrepresenting the power and influence of the KKK. The impact of the "damage" Sampson did would be hard to assess. But one thing was very clear. Sampson, the Swede declared, was so caught up in the Truman administration's cynical policy of "brazenly denying" the deplorable condition of blacks in the United States that she failed to use America's vulnerability in the area of civil rights to "wring from [the United States] greater justice for the Negro." The CRC also lambasted Sampson and predicted that, after the extent of her "State Department-inspired lies" became known, she would be "so ridiculed by the masses of the Negro people that she could never again be advertised as a so-called spokesman for Negro Americans."[118]

That honor the CRC wanted for itself. Patterson had come out hard against Sampson, he had denounced the U.S. government for its sins of omission in allowing the slaughter to occur in Florida, and he had backed up that fiery defense of "Negro rights" with a petition submitted to the UN. Was this enough for the CRC to position itself more favorably in the African American community? Patterson certainly hoped so because the legal and financial needs of the CP leadership were becoming desperate. In June 1951, the Supreme Court upheld the Smith Act convictions of the Communist Eleven, and, the remaining leadership, sensing that it was "'five minutes to midnight,'...disappeared into an elaborate underground apparatus." The CRC was also teetering on the brink. Its

118. American Embassy Copenhagen, "News of the Day (Danish Press)," January 30, 1952, Box 11, Folder 229, *Sampson Papers*; Rea Stanton to Walter White, February 3, 1952, Part 14, Reel 17, *NAACP Int'l*; William Worthy, "In Cloud-Cuckoo Land," *Crisis* (April 1952), 226–30, found in ibid.; Eleanor Roosevelt to Walter White, May 12, 1952, Box 3389, File "White, Walter, 1951–52," *Roosevelt Papers*; "State Dep't Charged with Hiding Its 'Overseas Propaganda' on Negroes from U.S.," press release, February 11, 1952, Part 2, Reel 40, *CRC*; "Statements Made in Copenhagen by Mrs. Edith Sampson...while visiting Mrs. Eugenia Anderson, American Ambassador to Denmark," Part 2, Reel 5, ibid.

"organizational weaknesses" had left it in a "very dangerous position," which only a massive infusion of money and members could solve.[119]

Now was the time to form the united front. "I think our main fight now is for unity," Patterson explained to a CRC colleague. He was confident that the *Genocide* petition provided "great possibilities for unifying elements who hitherto were sympathetic but would not move in concert with us." Now, however, Patterson saw "equally great possibilities for moving the trade unions in support of our fight and getting these two basic social forces in America, the Negro people and the trade unions, together in struggle." Patterson especially targeted the black church, confiding to a colleague at the National Council of American-Soviet Friendship, that the CRC had decided through the skillful use of the *Genocide* petition to undertake a "systematic and persistent effort... to raise the thinking of the Negro clergy." The church had to become "a fighting church," he said, that would not acquiesce to the annihilation of a people, trade unions, or minority political parties. In wooing the church, he offered D. V. Jemison, the head of the National Baptist Convention, the role of chair of the National Committee to End Genocide. He also tried to persuade the largest black Baptist organization in the United States to issue a massive reprint of the *Genocide* petition and distribute it at the upcoming national convention of ministers.[120]

Clearly, the issue of African Americans' rights was the moral hook that Patterson hoped would bring the church's membership and financial resources to bear on the CRC's "A-1 civil rights case," the imprisonment and ongoing persecution of the CP leadership. "Every effort," Patterson directed, "should be made to use Negro History Week for memorial services around the question of the apprehension of Moore's murderers and their punishment. We should use it also to publicize Genocide, ... and of course, in all of these actions, must be injected the fight against the Smith and McCarran acts, and for the rights of minority political parties."[121] That, Patterson believed, would be the CRC's and the CP's only salvation. Thus, in a fund-raising letter to religious and fraternal organizations, Patterson, evoking the name of *We Charge Genocide,* declared that the

119. Johanningsmeier, *Forging American Communism*, 324–29; Patterson to John Daschbach, February 18, 1952, Part 2, Reel 31, *CRC*; D. Quailey to Miss Block, February 15, 1952, Part 2, Reel 2, ibid.; George Marshall to Milt Wolff, n.d., Box 9, Folder 36, *Patterson Papers*; Frederick V. Field to Aubrey Grossman, May 28, 1952, Part 2, Reel 2, *CRC*; Aubrey Grossman to Frederick V. Field, June 9, 1952, ibid.

120. Patterson to Bishop J. H. Clayborn, January 30, 1952, Part 2, Reel 1, ibid.; Patterson to H. H. Robnett, February 1, 1952, Part 2, Reel 24, ibid.; Patterson to Rev. Richard Morford, February 21, 1952, Part 2, Reel 1, ibid.; Angie Dickerson to Dr. D. V. Jemison, May 2, 1952, ibid.

121. Patterson to H. H. Robnett, February 1, 1952, Part 2, Reel 24, ibid.

petition had firmly established the CRC's civil rights credentials and insisted that the "offensive" begun for the "rights and human dignity of the Negroes" could now "be enlarged," with the financial support of the churches and the unions, "in defense of minority political parties, and, as well, those elements which can go so very far to destroy the Smith and McCarran Acts and the Taft-Hartley law."[122]

The national secretary of the CRC fully realized, however, that to have the united front he so desperately craved, he would have to either neutralize the NAACP or bring the Association around to his point of view. Even though Patterson's previous attempts to forge some type of rapprochement with the NAACP were answered "with as rotten a statement as [Patterson] has ever seen in all [his] life," he was willing to try again.[123] Of course, the NAACP's vehement denunciation of the *Genocide* petition had not gone unnoticed. In fact, Patterson bitterly recalled, Tobias was "the main stooge for the American government in preventing the whole question of the genocidal policy of this government from getting an airing before the people of the world."[124] But clearly, the Moores' brutal assassination had chastened even the NAACP. Was it not about time, Patterson offered in yet another open letter to the NAACP leadership, that we "end once and for all the pitting of Negro against Negro?"[125] The problem, however, was that Negro was not pitted against Negro. Rather, Red Negro was pitted against American Negro so that no one articulated the comprehensive needs of African Americans.

The CRC's priorities were decidedly skewed. Although its Marxist analysis sometimes provided rapier insight into the economic conditions of black America, the CRC's devotion to the CP hobbled the organization's effectiveness and severely crippled the CRC's credibility. As long as the CRC continued to maintain that the "A-1 civil rights case in America" was that of the Communist Eleven, it was in no position to launch a full frontal assault on American racism and black inequality.[126] Indeed, the CRC leadership openly acknowledged that its efforts to defend blacks who had been rushed to the executioner's chair were "spotty and weak."[127]

122. Patterson to Dear Friend, February 1952, Part 2, Reel 40, ibid.

123. Patterson to Anne Shore, June 14, 1950, Part 2, Reel 27, ibid.

124. Patterson to Roscoe Dunjee, January 14, 1952, Part 2, Reel 1, ibid.; Patterson to Christopher Bates, February 1, 1952, Part 2, Reel 2, ibid.

125. "Let us end once and for all the pitting of Negro against Negro...," *Washington Afro-American*, February 23, 1952, found in Box 636, File "United Nations—Genocide, 1952–53," *Papers of the NAACP*; Patterson to all district leaders, boards and organizers, memo, February 19, 1952, Part 2, Reel 5, *CRC*.

126. George Marshall to Milton Wolff, memo, November 2, 1949, Box 9, Folder 51, *Patterson Papers*.

127. George Marshall to Milton Wolff, memo, December 28, 1949, ibid.

This admission had to be painfully obvious to Willie McGee. In the final quarter of 1948, the CRC allocated only $67 for his legal fund, but spent well over $26,000 on the defense of the Communist Twelve.[128] Even in cases such as the Groveland massacre in 1949, the CRC's performance was sluggish. Although the case epitomized the flaws in America's political and legal system, the CRC was "tied up with a multiplicity of cases" and "had no funds" or staff available to help the victims at Groveland. Patterson, of course, wailed when the NAACP's defense team swooped in to aid Samuel Shepherd and the other defendants, but he did acknowledge that the CRC had "move[d] far too slowly, ... show[ed] tremendous timidity, and ... did not immediately get someone to Groveland when the matter broke."[129] In the end, however, Patterson was unapologetic. After all, he insisted, the CRC had "not sought to become an organization of Negro liberation struggles." The only reason why the CRC was involved in this endless stream of legal lynching cases in the first place was because of the "limitless potential" they held for rallying supporters "[a]round all other activities of a democratic character." Specifically, "the fight to save ... the rights of all oppositional political parties and especially the Communist Party." Thus, even while finalizing the *Genocide* petition, Patterson confided to a colleague that of all the human rights struggles in United States, he "put *first* ... the fight against the Smith Act and *then* the fight for Negro rights."[130]

As is evident by its vicious, misguided attack on the *Genocide* petition, the NAACP clearly had its own problems. To borrow from and paraphrase Du Bois, the NAACP had bleached its soul in a flood of white Americanism and, in doing so, the Association undermined its own, larger agenda.[131] Indeed, it is clear that, as the Cold War intensified, the NAACP's once coherent quest for human rights was rapidly dissolving and would not be able to withstand the formidable challenges that lurked just beyond the 1952 presidential election.

128. Civil Rights Congress: Statement of Financial Condition, December 31, 1948, Part 2, Reel 14, *CRC*.
129. Patterson to Ewart Guinier, July 23, 1949, Part 2, Reel 38, ibid.; Patterson to Mrs. Bobby Graff, August 13, 1949, Part 2, Reel 24, ibid.
130. "Report of National Executive Secretary for the Meeting of the National Executive Board—Civil Rights Congress," July 7, 1952, Part 2, Reel 10, ibid.; Patterson to D. Pritt, August 28, 1951, Part 2, Reel 2, ibid. (Emphasis added.)
131. Du Bois, *Souls of Black Folks*, 45.

5

The Mirage of Victory

The attitude of using only the legal approach had something of the Booker T. Washington in it. The NAACP leadership did not understand the gravity of the situation.

William Patterson[1]

After he finished a distant second to the coonskin-capped Estes Kefauver in the 1952 New Hampshire primary, Truman had clearly and finally run out of options.[2] Yet, despite all the signs that he was in trouble politically, his abdication completely "startled" and dismayed the NAACP leadership.[3] Thurgood Marshall just could not believe it. He lamented that Truman was the only "real president"; the only one who was willing to make a "fearless stand" for civil rights when others were "running to cover."[4] Walter White bemoaned that, although the president had "appeared to soft-pedal the civil rights issue during recent months, no occupant of the White House since the nation was born has taken so frontal or consistent a stand against racial and religious discrimination as has Mr. Truman."[5]

Now, with the president out of the running, White looked over the field of remaining candidates and could only envision one dismal civil rights disaster after the next. The Democrats, in a move clearly designed to heal the breach of 1948, appeared to be toying with some ticket configuration that would grant either the presidency or vice-presidency to a dyed-in-the-wool segregationist.[6] Walter White exploded. "If the Democrats want

1. William Patterson, n.d., Box 6, Folder 212, *Patterson Papers*.
2. McCullough, *Truman*, 891–94.
3. Walter White, press release, April 3, 1952, Box 1235, File "413 (1950–53)," *Truman:OF*.
4. Thurgood Marshall to Harry S. Trumen (sic), telegram, n.d., Box 13, File "'M' [3 of 6]," *HST:Nash Files*; Thurgood Marshall to Philleo Nash, July 16, 1952, ibid.
5. Walter White, press release, April 3, 1952, Box 1235, File "413 (1950–53)," *Truman:OF*.
6. In fact, the Democrats nominated Alabaman John Sparkman as the vice presidential candidate on the ticket with Adlai Stevenson.

to commit political hari-kari," he warned, "let them nominate Richard Russell, Robert Kerr or any other anti-civil rights candidate . . . or" for that matter, "pussyfoot" around with the civil rights plank. If they did so, he thundered, "they can kiss the Negro vote goodbye."[7]

While the Democrats' actions were, to say the least, disturbing, the Republicans, from White's perspective, were just as unsavory. The Republican front-runner, World War II hero Dwight David Eisenhower, had a reputation as a "timorous," "reluctant" warrior for civil rights, whose "views on . . . FEPC and segregation . . . place him to the right of even Taft and Russell."[8]

Although that last characterization was a bit of an overstatement, it was true, however, that in the "most delicate" realm of civil rights, as Eisenhower liked to call it, he was an ardent believer in the power of "local control," education, "persuasion," and, most importantly, time. Lots and lots of time.[9] White, therefore, blasted Eisenhower's so-called plan for civil rights as no plan at all, because America had already had plenty of time and plenty of education – "343 years" worth "since [the] first Negro slaves were brought to Virginia in 1609 (sic)" – to come to grips with the basic idea of African American equality.[10]

Roy Wilkins was equally disturbed by Eisenhower's weak-kneed stance on civil rights. When they met in August, the general "was tense," "knew very little about racial matters in the United States," and had to turn to the "squadron of aides at his side" to answer Wilkins' questions.[11] Just as unsettling was Eisenhower's "comment . . . that civil rights is a political football" that needed to be "remov[ed] . . . from politics." A dumbfounded Wilkins retorted that Eisenhower's statement just "smacks of ducking on a matter of fundamental Americanism – equality of citizens."[12]

7. Address by Walter White at the 43rd Annual Convention of the NAACP, June 29, 1952, Box 48, File "Annual Convention Speeches, 1952," *Papers of the NAACP*.
8. Walter White, press release, April 3, 1952, Box 1235, File "413 (1950–53)," *Truman:OF*; Address by Walter White at the 43rd Annual Convention of the NAACP, June 29, 1952, Box 48, File "Annual Convention Speeches, 1952," *Papers of the NAACP*.
9. Draft for section of State of the Union Message, M. S. Pitzele, n.d., Box 9, File "Civil Rights (S.O.U. 1953), *Records of Bryce N. Harlow*, Dwight David Eisenhower Presidential Library, Abilene, Kansas (hereafter *Harlow Records*); Eisenhower, diary entry, July 24, 1953, Box 9, File "Diary-Copies of DDE Personal 1953–54," Diary Series, *Papers of Dwight David Eisenhower: Ann Whitman File*, Dwight David Eisenhower Presidential Library, Abilene, Kansas (hereafter *Eisenhower-AWF*).
10. White to Roderick Stevens and Irving Ives, telegram, June 20, 1952, Box 248, File "Dwight D. Eisenhower, 1952," *Papers of the NAACP*.
11. Wilkins, *Standing Fast*, 212.
12. Items for Eisenhower interview, August 26, 1952, Box 23, File "Dwight D. Eisenhower Interview, 1952," *Wilkins Papers*.

Concerns among the black leadership about Eisenhower's commitment to civil rights grew even stronger after South Carolina Governor James F. Byrnes broke Democratic ranks and threw his support behind the general.[13] Byrnes, Truman's former secretary of state, was an "aging... embittered,"[14] "unreconstructed rebel"[15] who "charged that 'during the past four years the national Democratic administration has been more antagonistic toward the South than any Republican administration since... Reconstruction." Yet, while Truman was knuckling under to blacks' incessant demands, Byrnes intoned, the GOP had faithfully worked with the Southern Democrats to stop Truman's scorched earth rampage through the South.[16] For Byrnes, however, it was more than the GOP that seemed to be in sync with Southern norms and values, it was Eisenhower, as well. While on the campaign trail in South Carolina, Eisenhower played "political music to Jimmy Byrnes' ears," when, on hearing the band strike up "Dixie," the general rose from his chair and told the crowd, "'I always stand up when they play that song.'" Eisenhower was clearly someone who understood the "South's way of life," and Byrnes, as a "presidential kingmaker," gladly delivered four of the eleven states of the "old Confederacy" – of the Solid Democratic South – to the GOP.[17]

This realignment was decidedly more threatening than the Dixiecrat revolt of 1948 because instead of isolating the Southerners in a powerless, ultra-right wing third party, it cemented that "evil combination" of Dixiecrats and the GOP that had consistently "blockade[d]" and "lynched" civil rights legislation. That realignment, in effect, pulled the racist, fanatical fringe into the wholly acceptable mainstream.[18] Naturally, the NAACP leadership was worried and became convinced that there had to be some type of "'secret understanding'" between Byrnes and Eisenhower. U.S. Senator William Benton (D-CT) thought otherwise. "They don't have to" have any kind of secret pact, Benton explained to Clarence Mitchell. "Governor Byrnes is one of the shrewdest politicians in the South. He knows where Eisenhower stands," and he "knows he can

13. David Robertson, *Sly and Able: A Political Biography of James F. Byrnes* (New York: W. W. Norton, 1994) 502, 510–12.
14. Address by Walter White at the 43rd Annual Convention of the NAACP, June 29, 1952, Box 48, File "Annual Convention Speeches, 1952," *Papers of the NAACP*.
15. Fletcher Knebel, "Byrnes and Byrd Lead Civil War," *Minneapolis Tribune*, July 24, 1952, found in Box H18, File "James Byrnes (South Carolina)," *NAACP-Washington Bureau*.
16. John N. Popham, "Byrnes Asks Bloc of South's Whites," *New York Times*, May 16, 1952, found in ibid.
17. Quoted in Robertson, *Sly and Able*, 512.
18. Address by Walter White at the 43rd Annual Convention of the NAACP, June 29, 1952, Box 48, File "Annual Convention Speeches, 1952," *Papers of the NAACP*.

count on the Republican party with Eisenhower... in the White House" to ensure that there will "be no chance of civil rights legislation" ever darkening Congress's doorstep. "It is just as simple as that."[19]

Not surprisingly then, after Eisenhower handily won the election, the black leadership could only wonder aloud "Where do we go from here"?[20] Wilkins explained to White that the NAACP could either "writ[e] off" the Republican Congressional "leadership as hostile," which meant relying on a fractured Democratic party that had not been able, even during Truman's heyday, to muster one single piece of civil rights legislation. Or, the NAACP could try to find some way to work with the GOP, which Walter White had already derisively labeled "the 'Gone Old Party.'"[21] Regardless of how "gone" the GOP may have been, Wilkins counseled, "I think if we give the impression that we regard... the Republican leadership as completely hostile to our objectives we either will be shut out completely, or they will ignore us and proceed to enact the kind of program they desire, leaving us in the frustrating role of mere opposition."[22]

Frustration and political exile was exactly what Byrnes had in mind for the black leadership. In a memo to the White House, Byrnes emphasized that when it came to African Americans, the president "owes them nothing." Byrnes noted that nearly all of the black leadership's speeches and editorials – before and after the election – were decidedly anti-Eisenhower. Moreover, "approximately 90 percent of the Negro votes were cast against President Eisenhower," which only "proved that a candidate can win with the Negroes voting 10 to 1 against him." Therefore, as far as Byrnes was concerned, Eisenhower had no moral obligation to listen to African Americans nor did the president have to worry about any political fallout for ignoring their bothersome demands.[23]

At the top of those demands, of course, was the destruction of Jim Crow via the integration of public schools, which Byrnes had sworn to fight with every resource at his command.[24] Black South Carolinians, in fact, had already identified their governor as "'our sworn enemy,'" because he had "'damned our children for the next generation' by advocating continued

19. William Benton to Clarence Mitchell, October 14, 1952, Box 163, File "Byrnes, James F., General 1950–55," ibid.
20. Wilkins to White, memo, January 16, 1953, Box 248, File "Dwight D. Eisenhower, 1953–1955," ibid.
21. Wilkins, *Standing Fast*, 203.
22. Wilkins to White, memo, January 16, 1953, Box 248, File "Dwight D. Eisenhower, 1953–1955," *Papers of the NAACP*.
23. Memorandum from James Byrnes, n.d., Box 3, File "Byrnes, James F. (2)," Name Series, *Eisenhower:AWF*.
24. "Byrnes Won't Kill Jim Crow," n.d., newsclipping attached to Grace Plater to Truman, April 9, 1951, Box 545, File "OF 93 Misc.—1951 [2 of 2]," *Truman:OF*.

racial segregation in the public schools."[25] Byrnes added to that reputation when he vowed to shut down the entire public school system in South Carolina if the Supreme Court ruled that state-supported Jim Crow education was unconstitutional.[26] He also tried to make the entire issue moot by pulling together enough funds to finally equalize the deplorable facilities that passed themselves off as schools for black children.[27] Of course, the NAACP immediately recognized what this last-ditch effort to equalize schools was all about and scoffed at the state's frantic attempts to construct "guilded (sic) citadels of segregation." Byrnes's $75 million program was "too little, too late," because the time for equalization had long since passed. "We shall not," the NAACP declared, "be misled or . . . diverted from our determined efforts to destroy segregation." The "handwriting is on the wall," the end of Jim Crow was drawing near, and although the "professional southerners, including some old-line politicians are crying, 'Never!'," their defiance, the NAACP noted with just a hint of glee, was voiced "with more bravado than assurance."[28]

The shrewd Byrnes, however, did not need bravado. He had the president's ear and seized the moment to warn Eisenhower that "Negroes," despite their complete repudiation of the president, "will use every available means to cause the Republican Administration to enter into the school cases before the Supreme Court, and urge the Court to overrule the . . . doctrine of separate but equal." He advised the president to withstand the pressure and "adhere," as Eisenhower had done throughout the campaign, "to his conviction that . . . the States have the right to control matters that are purely local."[29]

Eisenhower quickly assured Byrnes, his "great friend," that he did not envision or condone the federal government meddling in this states' rights issue. In fact, he commiserated with Byrnes about the Court's steady erosion of *Plessy.* "Two or three court decisions of recent years," Eisenhower complained, "have . . . tended to becloud the original decision of 'equal but

25. "NAACP Attack on Byrnes Deeply Resented, Is Claim," *Greenville (South Carolina) News*, October 22, 1952, found in Box H18, File "James Byrnes (South Carolina)," *NAACP-Washington Bureau.*
26. "Byrnes Urges End of Public Schools," *Oklahoma Black Dispatch*, October 25, 1952, found in ibid.; "Segregation Vote Urged: South Carolina Governor Backs Amendment on School System," *New York Times*, October 17, 1952, found in ibid.
27. Robertson, *Sly and Able*, 512–13; Brown, *James F. Byrnes*, 390–92; James F. Byrnes to John Foster Dulles, March 12, 1952, Box 58, File "Byrnes, James F., 1952," *JFD-Princeton.*
28. "NAACP 44th Annual Conference Resolutions," June 23–28, 1953, Box 47, File "Annual Conventions: Resolutions Voted 1953," *Papers of the NAACP.*
29. Memorandum from James Byrnes, n.d., Box 3, File "Byrnes, James F. (2)," Name Series, *Eisenhower:AWF.*

separate' facilities." One case in particular, *McLaurin v. Oklahoma State Regents*, stood out above all others. The president expressed his absolute amazement that the Court could somehow rule that a "Negro in graduate school attending exactly the same classes as whites, but separated from them by some kind of railing was . . . the victim of discrimination." To Eisenhower, that just seemed so absurd. The president was, therefore, very supportive when Byrnes voiced fears about "riots" and especially the dangers of "putting the children together" if the Supreme Court overturned *Plessy*. Eisenhower reaffirmed his "belief that improvement in race relations is one of those things that will be healthy and sound only if it starts locally." The intervention of the federal government in such an instance would only "bring about conflict" and "set back the cause of progress in race relations for a long, long time." He, therefore, promised Byrnes that, "no matter what[,] . . . the principle of local operation and authority would be emphasized to the maximum degree consistent with [the attorney general's] legal opinions."[30]

Unfortunately, Eisenhower's handling of the UN and human rights issues were guided by the same retrograde philosophy he used to mishandle the civil rights crisis brewing in America.[31] One of his first actions was to insist on the resignation of Eleanor Roosevelt from the U.S. delegation to the UN, and, as a consequence, from the CHR. Of course, the call for resignations from those whom Truman had appointed was to be expected. And, frankly, Mrs. Roosevelt had no intention of serving in the Eisenhower administration anyway. She was adamant that, "if General Eisenhower is elected, I do not want to work under him in the United Nations or elsewhere."[32]

Yet, Mrs. Roosevelt's removal, coming so fast on the heels of Eisenhower's election day victory, sent a strong signal to the party faithful. She, more than anyone else, symbolized so much of what the

30. Eisenhower, diary entry, July 24, 1953, Box 9, File "Diary-Copies of DDE Personal 1953–54 (2)," Diary Series, ibid.; Memorandum for the Record, August 19, 1953, Box 8, File "Brownell, Herbert, Jr., 1952–54 (6)," Administration Series, ibid.; *McLaurin v. Oklahoma State Regents*, 339 U.S. 637; 70 S. Ct. 851; 96 L. Ed. 1149 (1950); Eisenhower to James F. Byrnes, December 1, 1953, Box 4, File "DDE Diary December 1953 (2)," Diary Series, *Eisenhower:AWF.*

31. Kenneth O'Reilly, "Racial Integration: The Battle General Eisenhower Chose Not to Fight," *Journal of Blacks in Higher Education* 0:18 (Winter 1997–1998), 110–19; Michael S. Mayer, "With Much Deliberation and Some Speed: Eisenhower and the Brown Decision," *The Journal of Southern History*, 52:1 (February, 1986), 43–76.

32. Carlisle H. Humelsine to Eleanor Roosevelt, November 18, 1952, Box 3283, File "Eisenhower, Dwight D., 1947–1952," *Roosevelt Papers*; Eleanor Roosevelt to Dwight D. Eisenhower, December 4, 1952, ibid.; Eleanor Roosevelt to Mrs. Archie W. Naylor, October 13, 1952, Box 63, File "Eleanor Roosevelt, 1952," *JFD-Princeton.*

Dixiecrats and isolationist Republicans despised. One detractor blasted Roosevelt as a "pernicious ... meddling" woman who had no business nosing around in international affairs.[33] Another critic bitterly denounced "that ... Roosevelt woman [as] ... a menace to our liberties."[34] The instrument for her betrayal, of course, was the UN, its specialized agencies such as the International Labor Organization (ILO), and most importantly, the variety of human rights declarations and treaties, regardless of how effectively she had neutered them, emerging out of the CHR.[35]

The critique of Roosevelt was, in reality, just the tip of a bitter iceberg of resentment against the UN and a belief that American values, especially the Constitution, were being subverted by socialistic, even communistic, ideas about freedom and democracy. The Daughters of the American Revolution (DAR) repeatedly denounced the UN as "'that Socialist organization'" that "'has caused unrest adn (sic) discontent by preaching equality'" to unequal people.[36] The vice president of another patriotic organization, Mrs. Enid H. Griswold, echoed that assessment and derided the UN's initiatives as "absurd ... international giveaway programs." She recounted a story in which the UN gave medical treatment – financed by the United States – to some African children, and instead of being grateful, the African mother then expected "her children be served breakfast by the United Nations staff." Honestly, Griswold said incredulously, "[w]e are being called upon to serve breakfast to the children in darkest Africa."[37] Equality, medical care, and food, however, were only the beginning of the UN's socialistic crimes. One man was "particularly concerned ... that the United Nations made a secret of those sections of the Covenant which guaranteed all citizens ... adequate housing." He just could not believe that the United States was going to sit idly by and let the UN dictate "a

33. Warren Jefferson Davis to John Foster Dulles, January 28, 1949, Box 46, File "United Nations Correspondence Includes: Genocide, Declaration of Human Rights," ibid.

34. Dennis J. Dooley to Mrs. Oswald Bates Lord, May 5, 1953, Box 1, File "1953 Correspondence," *Papers of Mary Pillsbury Lord*, Dwight David Eisenhower Presidential Library, Abilene, Kansas (hereafter *Lord Papers*).

35. Durward Sandifer to Eleanor Roosevelt, August 6, 1951, Box 3362, File "Sandifer, Durward, 1947–51," *Roosevelt Papers*; Jack K. McFall to Senator Blair Moody, Box 3306, File "Human Rights, 1949–1952," ibid.; Herzel H. E. Plaine to Mrs. Franklin D. Roosevelt, May 23, 1952, ibid.; Dean Acheson to Eleanor Roosevelt, June 20, 1952, Box 3247, File "Acheson, Dean, 1946–1952," ibid.

36. Bess Furman, "D.A.R. Intensifies War Against U.N.," *New York Times*, April 23, 1953, found in Box 113, File "Bills: Bricker Amendment Press Releases, 1953–54," *Papers of the NAACP*.

37. "Statement of Mrs. Enid H. Griswold, Vice President of the National Economic Council, Inc., New York, New York," Congress, Senate, Subcommittee of the Committee on the Judiciary, *Treaties and Executive Agreements*, 83rd Congress, 1st sess., February 19, 1953, 176.

nation wide program of government built low cost housing."[38] For many, the specialized agencies were equally suspect. One Chicagoan was greatly concerned about the possibility that a series of ILO agreements and covenants would "impose" on the United States "programs embracing compulsory health insurance, hospitalization, federalization of workmen's compensation and other similar plans, all of which tend strongly toward the Socialist philosophy."[39] The UN's insistence on these "so-called social and economic rights," suggested to some that the UN was "engaged in setting up in every nation completely socialistic forms of government."[40]

The UN, however, was not only portrayed as socialistic, but also as a direct threat to U.S. power and sovereignty. From across the nation, a disgruntled section of the American population vented their rage. A Missouri man was convinced that the UN had already become "the Supreme judicial body of the U.S." and was now "seeking" the "Legislative powers" of Congress.[41] A Colorado woman railed that, "When the U.S. Congress and president ten years ago signed the treaty making the United States a Member of the United Nations they surrendered our sovereignty as a nation. As long as we remain a Member," she contended, "we are not the captains of our own souls, the makers of our own destiny. We are at the absolute mercy of a conglomeration of other nations, including a darn good-sized Communist vote. How members of Congress salved their consciences when they fell for that," she bristled, "I can't imagine."[42] A Miami resident charged that, "[s]ince the founding of the United Nations in 1945, we have seen repeated efforts made by this international body to supplant the purpose of the Constitution itself with various international schemes," such as the "so-called Covenant of Human Rights, the Genocide Convention," and other efforts that would "teach our children to be world citizens rather than good Americans."[43]

38. Alexander Summer to Walter D. Head, September 5, 1952, Box 3306, File "Human Rights, 1949–52," *Roosevelt Papers*; Roosevelt to Walter Head, October 12, 1952, ibid.
39. Neville Pilling to Sir [Thomas Hennings, Jr.], April 2, 1953, Folder 4776B, *Hennings Papers*.
40. "Statement of Frank E. Holman, Seattle, Wash., Past President, American Bar Association," Congress, Senate, Subcommittee of the Committee on the Judiciary, *Treaties and Executive Agreements*, 83rd Congress, 1st sess., February 18, 1953, 143; "Memorandum Re: Japanese Peace Treaty by Frank E. Holman, March 20, 1952," attachment to Frank Holman to John W. Bricker, March 19, 1952, Box 160, File "1," *Papers of John W. Bricker*, Ohio Historical Society, Columbus, Ohio (hereafter *Bricker Papers*).
41. L. Jameton to Senator [Thomas] Henning (sic), April 19, 1956, Folder 2968, *Hennings Papers*.
42. Mrs. G. N. Eklund to Mr. Hennings, April 13, 1956, ibid.
43. Robert LeFevre to Mrs. Oswald Bates Lord, April 18, 1953, Box 1, File "1953 Correspondence," *Lord Papers*.

To rescue America and its children from the clutches of the UN, Republican Senator John W. Bricker of Ohio led the charge of the right brigade. As one journalist noted, Bricker, who had been on this isolationist crusade long before most had even noticed, launched his campaign "during that halcyon era for conservative nationalist like himself when anything seemed desirable and legal to Congress provided it was sure to annoy Harry Truman."[44] By late 1952, Bricker was joined by Frank Holman, former president of the ABA, who spent more than $30,000 of his "own money" stumping around the country and testifying before Congress that "the [UN] charter, Universal Declaration, and future 'blank check' human rights treaties" were Soviet "Trojan horses" mounted by "internationalists" who wanted to transform the United States "'from a republic to a socialistic and centralized state.'"[45]

The United States had to protect itself, Holman admonished, because it would be easy for a nation like this – one committed to justice and democracy – to be seduced by the Sirens' song of human rights and end up shipwrecked on the jagged rocks of communism. Just look at the Genocide Convention, Holman exclaimed. It was an illusion, "a 'trick' document" that, despite all of the hoopla, did "not outlaw the kind of genocide that... is now occurring in Russia and in Russian satellite countries." Yet, he asserted, it was typical of all of the other treaties coming out of a Commission on Human Rights that has "'responded for the most part more to Soviet than to western promptings.'"[46] Senator Bricker reinforced Holman's characterization with the "shocking" truth that the "Human Rights Commission" had turned its back on the supposedly "unimaginative" west and had been irreparably tainted "by 'the increasing impact of Marx.'" This had made it difficult, if not impossible, for the United States to "get... our point of view ever accepted." Thus, as far as he was concerned, any definition of political, civil, and economic rights would be dictated by the Soviet Union, which made the vaunted human rights treaty nothing more than a "'Covenant on Human Slavery.'"[47]

44. Doris Fleeson, "Democrats Move to Save Ike Policy," n.d., found in Box 113, File "Bills: Bricker Amendment Press Releases, 1953–54," *Papers of the NAACP*.

45. Congress, Senate, Subcommittee of the Committee on the Judiciary, *Treaties and Executive Agreements*, 83rd Congress, 1st sess., February 18, 1953, 13; Frank Holman, *The Life and Career of a Western Lawyer, 1886–1961* (Baltimore, Maryland: Port City Press, Inc., 1963), 565; Quoted in Brucken, "A Most Uncertain Crusade," 233.

46. Congress, Senate, Subcommittee of the Committee on the Judiciary, *Treaties and Executive Agreements*, 83rd Congress, 1st sess., February 18, 1953, 10, 144.

47. "Statement of Hon. John W. Bricker, A United States Senator from Ohio," ibid., 153; Quoted in Brucken, "A Most Uncertain Crusade," 247.

"United Nations delegate, huh? Flighty, crackpot, radical One-Worlder, huh?"

MAULDIN 6-12

Illustration 5.1. Cartoon that summarizes best the contempt that Bricker Amendment supporters had for the UN and its representatives.

Holman, therefore, carefully laid out to a group of senators that what looked so innocent and benign on the surface was actually an "insidious process."[48] He explained how the human rights treaties were like kudzu creeping and crawling into every crevice of American life strangling

48. Statement of Frank E. Holman, Seattle, Wash., Past President, American Bar Association, Congress, Senate, Subcommittee of the Committee of the Judiciary, *Treaties and Executive Agreements*, 83rd Congress, 1st sess., February 18, 1953, 144.

basic rights and freedoms and replacing everything that the United States held dear with the weed of foreign regimes, foreign laws, and foreign diktats. To illustrate his point, Holman contended, for example, that if a white person, while driving, just happened to "run over a Negro child running out into the street in front of him, what would have been a local offense under a charge of gross negligence or involuntary manslaughter would, under the Genocide Convention, because of the racial differential, not be a local crime but an international crime" and, worse yet, the white driver "would be transported some place overseas for trial where he would not have any of the protections of our own Bill of Rights, to wit: presumption of innocence, trial by jury, etc."[49] The United States, he thus warned, was in "imminent danger."[50] "It is not an overstatement," Holman somberly concluded, "to say that the Republic is threatened to its very foundations."[51]

In this epic battle to save the Republic, Bricker and Holman proposed the ultimate weapon – a constitutional amendment to alter the treaty approval process. As it stood, treaties, to take effect, required ratification by two-thirds of the Senate, but executive agreements did not. The Bricker Amendment, however, would have changed all of that and more. The amendment would require all treaties and executive agreements first to be ratified by two-thirds of the U.S. Senate, *then* by both houses of Congress with enabling legislation, and finally, as the proposal mutated, by *all* 48 state legislatures before becoming "the law of the land." This amendment, Bricker crowed, would rein in the "eager beavers in the UN," "erect a safeguard against treaty law drafted in faraway places by the non-elected representatives of socialist, communist, and fascist" regimes, and prevent "some Americans" from using UN treaties "as a substitute for national legislation on purely domestic matters."[52]

Therefore, the much-heralded Bricker Amendment, under the banner of strengthening the Constitution, was designed to reduce the president to a "figurehead," and assert the supreme role of Congress and state legislatures in international relations. This "radical" change to the Constitution enjoyed the support of a number of conservative, "patriotic" organizations such as the DAR and the Veterans of Foreign Wars, as

49. Holman, *The Life and Career*, 569–70.
50. "Statement of Hon. John W. Bricker, A United States Senator from Ohio," Congress, Senate, Subcommittee of the Committee on the Judiciary, *Treaties and Executive Agreements*, 83rd Congress, 1st sess., January 18, 1953, 2.
51. Brucken, "A Most Uncertain Crusade," 300.
52. "Bringing the Constitution Up-To-Date: Address by Senator John W. Bricker before the Annual Convention of the Ohio State Bar Association at Cincinnati, Ohio," April 22, 1953, Box 160, File "2," *Bricker Papers*.

well as the ABA, the U.S. Chamber of Commerce, the National Association of Manufacturers, and the American Medical Association, which feared that the human rights treaties would inevitably bring about "socialized medicine."[53] All of that support, however, while impressive, would have been relatively unimportant except that every Senate Republican, but three, and 18 Democrats (mostly from the South) – just enough to achieve ratification – had lined up behind the Bricker Amendment. Thus, as historian Rowland Brucken observed, "Eisenhower's first foreign policy crisis occurred" not in some far-off land, but "just down Pennsylvania Avenue."[54]

During the Senate hearings, which began in earnest shortly after Eisenhower's inauguration, Bricker advocates hauled up the Genocide Convention as proof of the way that the humanitarians and do-gooders had tried to sneak an "anti-lynching" bill past Congress.[55] They ridiculed the "impractical idealists, unthinking humanitarians, and others whose motives were less honorable" as being so intent on world government that the "preservation of our constitutional republic" became expendable.[56] They generated alarm among the Southern Democrats that the UN Charter "has already conferred on ... Congress ... the power to take over the whole field of human rights and push ... the States out of the way."[57] They chastised the U.S. delegation to the UN for going too "far ... in the negotiation" of the Covenant on Human Rights, because that treaty "would be destructive of the existing division of authority between States and Nation," it would "enlarge Federal power at the expense of the States," and it would allow "some foreign nation" to tell us "how we would treat our own people."[58] They especially blasted the "internationalists" for trying

53. Thomas Hennings, Jr., to Mr. President [Eisenhower], May 8, 1956, Folder 2968, *Hennings Papers*.

54. "Bricker Says Taft Backs Curb on President's Treaty Powers," *New York Post*, June 16, 1953, found in Box 113, File "Bills: Bricker Amendment Press Releases, 1953–54," *Papers of the NAACP*; Stephen E. Ambrose, *Eisenhower: The President*, Vol. II (New York: Simon and Schuster, 1984), 68; Brucken, "A Most Uncertain Crusade," 368.

55. Fisher to Rusk, memo, January 19, 1950, Box 8, File "Genocide (folder 1 of 2)," Lot File 55D429, *RG 59*; Phleger to Dulles, memo, March 30, 1953, Box 70, File "Re: Genocide Convention, 1953," *JFD-Princeton*.

56. "Statement of Mrs. James C. Lucas, Executive Secretary, National Society, Daughters of the American Revolution," Congress, Senate, Subcommittee of the Committee on the Judiciary, *Treaties and Executive Agreements*, 83rd Congress, 1st sess., February 19, 1953, 172.

57. "Statement of Alfred J. Schweppe—Resumed," ibid., February 18, 1953, 62.

58. "Excerpts from Report on Proposed Constitutional Amendments Relating to the Making of Treaties and Their Effect, Presented June 1952," quoted in, "Statement of Alfred J. Schweppe, Seattle, Wash., Chairman, Committee on Peace and Law Through the United Nations of the American Bar Association," ibid., 49.

to foist socialism on the United States through a series of "international agreements" that would "regulate labor, education, social security and other human rights."[59]

Senator Bricker began the cavalcade of patriots when he insisted that the UN and its specialized agencies respected no boundaries and, thus had made the vaunted domestic jurisdiction clause about as effective as the Maginot Line in stopping an enemy invasion. To illustrate his point, he regaled his Senate colleagues with a tale about a proposed ILO treaty where "[m]otherhood would become a subject of international concern," and the "babies of working mothers would be financed by Government benefits." Bricker was even more appalled that the "Government would provide nurseries at the factory so that mothers could nurse their offspring on company time."[60]

Frank Holman expounded on this theme when he explained that the UN's overreach was a direct result of some "grandiose theory that world peace may be achieved if somehow economic, social, humanitarian, educational, cultural, and health conditions are by treaties put on an expressed equality throughout the world, even though to do so may bring the more advanced nations down to the level of the backward nations – in rights – in legal concepts, and in form of government." He urged the Senate to now see why the Declaration of Human Rights was a "complete blueprint for socializing the world," for dragging down the standard of living in the United States, and for "liquidat[ing] our individual enterprise system." Article 24 of the Declaration, Holman exclaimed, was so infused with socialism that it tried to convince people that they had the right to "'just and favorable remuneration'" for their labor and a right to expect "'protection against unemployment.'" The language in Article 25 was even more troubling. The UN, Holman asserted, insisted that "everyone has 'the right to food, clothing, housing, and medical care, and necessary social services, and the right to security in the event of unemployment sickness, disability, widowhood, old age.'" Yet, there was absolutely nothing in Article 25, Holman complained, that required people to "work for it or help establish a fund to pay for it." With no acknowledgment of individual responsibility, he continued, the Declaration essentially put the onus directly, squarely, and fully on government. Thus, if the United States tried to meet the diktat of this human rights "Tower of Babel," Holman

59. Brucken, "A Most Uncertain Crusade," 358; Doris Fleeson, "Democrats Move to Save Ike Policy," n.d., found in Box 113, File "Bills: Bricker Amendment Press Releases, 1953–54," *Papers of the NAACP*.

60. "Statement of Hon. John W. Bricker, a United States Senator from Ohio," Congress, Senate, Subcommittee of the Committee on the Judiciary, *Treaties and Executive Agreements*, 83rd Congress, 1st sess., February 18, 1953, 9–11.

warned, it would "transform . . . the United States from a republic into a completely socialistic state." Then, still mesmerizing the audience with his gift for "questionable legal accuracy," Holman claimed that the UN's human rights initiatives would also "open . . . up" America's immigration laws and "eliminate all screening processes of this country"; and it "could mean that, in times of revolution in Cuba, or Mexico or India or elsewhere, thousands of aliens might legally claim the right of asylum here."[61]

For the Bricker contingent, the flood of additional brown people into the United States was bad enough, but then there was also the issue of the black people who were already in the United States. Holman was unequivocal. In his opinion, "it would have been better for this country, better for the world, [and] better for civilization if the South had won the Civil War."[62] Thus, when ABA member Frank Ober informed the Senate that in one year alone the UN had received more than 25,000 "communications alleging violations of human rights," he asked the senators to "Just think of this Pandora's box of poisonous political propaganda that will be presented on a silver platter to our enemies by this idea of making complaints before an international body."[63] Mrs. Griswold reinforced that apocalyptic vision when she named the plagues and pestilence that the UN had already let loose on the world, namely, the National Negro Congress, the NAACP, and the Civil Rights Congress. All of these Negro organizations, she intoned, had petitioned the UN and "sought to make our domestic affairs the subject of international debate and jurisdiction." This, as nothing else, she enjoined, sent "a clear warning to us of the uses to which this international body will be put, if not checked by a constitutional amendment."[64]

Bricker and Holman concluded their presentation with a "hair-raising" speech that Dulles had made prior to the election and his appointment as secretary of state.[65] In April 1952, Citizen Dulles, in a talk in Louisville, Kentucky, declared that the "'treatymaking power is an extraordinary power, liable to abuse. . . . treaty law can override the Constitution.

61. "Statement of Frank E. Holman, Seattle, Wash., Past President, American Bar Association," ibid., 136–37; Brucken, "A Most Uncertain Crusade," 296.
62. Holman, *The Life and Career*, 348.
63. "Statement of Frank B. Ober, on Behalf of the Committee on Peace and Law, American Bar Association, Baltimore," Congress, Senate, Subcommittee of the Committee on the Judiciary, *Treaties and Executive Agreements*, 83rd Congress, 1st sess., February 19, 1953, 168.
64. "Statement of Mrs. Enid H. Griswold, Vice President of the National Economic Council, Inc., New York, New York," ibid., 175.
65. "Bringing the Constitution Up-to-Date: Address by Senator John W. Bricker before the Annual Convention of the Ohio State Bar Association at Cincinnati Ohio," April 22, 1953, Box 160, File "2," *Bricker Papers*.

Photo 5.2. Senator John Bricker and Mrs. Robert Murray stand behind a mound of petitions supporting the constitutional amendment to make it nearly impossible for any treaty to be ratified, especially one from the UN dealing with human rights, 1954.
Corbis.

Treaties... can take powers away from Congress and give them to the President; they can take powers from the States and give them to the Federal Government, or to some international body, and they can cut across the rights given the people by the... Bill of Rights.'"[66] Dulles' 1952 clarion call – given his instrumental role in drafting the UN Charter, especially the domestic jurisdiction clause, his participation in virtually every UN meeting, and his current position as the secretary of state – added credibility to Holman's and Bricker's charges and undercut the sentiment that "the ABA had 'fallen into the hands of a lot of crotchety old men approaching senility.'"[67]

There were dissenters, however, crying like voices in the wilderness. The American Jewish Congress (AJC) registered strong concern among its

66. Quoted in, "Statement of Hon. John W. Bricker, A United States Senator From Ohio," Congress, Senate, Subcommittee of the Committee on the Judiciary, *Treaties and Executive Agreements*, 83rd Congress, 1st sess., February 18, 1953, 3.
67. Quoted in Brucken, "A Most Uncertain Crusade," 220.

members and affiliated organizations that the Bricker Amendment "would seriously cripple, if not make impossible, all attempts at international cooperation to protect and safeguard human rights."[68] In a January 1953 press release, the NAACP further characterized the Bricker Amendment as motivated by fear that the United States might actually "find itself committed to anti-lynching or other civil rights legislation because of some treaty agreed upon with foreign Governments."[69]

The National Lawyers Guild, which "was founded in 1937 as an alternative to the conservative and racially segregated American Bar Association,"fully explored the links between the Bricker Amendment, international human rights, and civil rights in the United States.[70] The conservatives' attempt to rewrite the Constitution, the Guild asserted, had very little to do with preserving rights or protecting the Constitution and everything to do with "specific expressed fears over the potential consequences of American participation in the UN Genocide Convention . . . , the proposed Covenant on Human Rights, [and] the barely consideered (sic) international court for the trial of genocide." The Guild understood the implications of Bricker's motives and feared that if the amendment passed, it would have a disastrous effect on the struggle for black equality. "The civil rights of Negroes are now widely curtailed [in] . . . the United States by government policy, legislation and otherwise." The passage of the Bricker Amendment would maintain that status quo, "create a favorable climate . . . to cut the United States off from effective international cooperation with other nations in the pursuit of international" human rights treaties, and thereby "impede the improvement of our civil rights which may be encouraged by the development of international law." The Guild argued that this was neither a transitory nor minor issue. "Given the permanent quality of constitutional amendments and the complexity of the amending process," the Bricker Amendment could cripple the development of human and civil rights for "our generation, and undoubtedly for future generations."[71] As much as the NAACP, the American Jewish Congress, and the National Lawyers Guild detested the Bricker Amendment, however, the big question was what was Eisenhower going to do.

68. Leo Pfeffer to Community Relations Councils Group Relations Agencies, February 26, 1953, Box 113, File "Bills: Bricker Amendment Press Releases, 1953–54," *Papers of the NAACP.*
69. Clarence Mitchell to Senator, January 9, 1953, Box H157, File "Press Releases, 1953–1954," *NAACP-Washington Bureau.*
70. "Highlights from NLG's History," http://www.nlg.org/admin/history.html. Accessed July 21, 2001.
71. National Lawyers Guild: Report of the Committee on International Law and Relations on Senate Joint Resolution One, February 24, 1953, Folder 4770, *Hennings Papers.*

With more than 60 senators sponsoring the amendment and the Republican party firmly behind Bricker, the president realized that he had a fight on his hands.[72] The "real crux of the matter" in his mind, however, was not the UN, human rights, civil rights, or even Bricker's determination "'to save the United States from Eleanor Roosevelt,'" but, rather, the amendment's suffocating, paralyzing effect on the president's ability to conduct foreign policy.[73] Dulles, too, finally came to recognize the danger inherent in the Bricker Amendment. Thus, despite his 1952 speech and the fact that he was still somewhat "sympathetic to the point of view reflected in Senate Joint Resolution 1,"—the Bricker Amendment—Dulles alerted Governor Sherman Adams, Eisenhower's right-hand man at the White House, that Bricker's hypothetical fears had resulted in a proposed constitutional amendment that would "seriously impair the... ability of the President to deal with current matters, notably U.S. troops abroad," which was critical given the ongoing Korean War and the extensive commitments the United States had made to NATO. He also "warned" the president's Cabinet that the "amendment would seriously limit Executive authority and make impossible effective conduct of foreign affairs." Clearly, Dulles concluded, the administration and Bricker were en route to a "head-on collision."[74]

Eisenhower hoped against all hope that Dulles was wrong. The president truly wanted to avoid an open and, what promised to be, a bloody brawl with his fellow Republicans. Internecine warfare, coming so early in his term, with a Senate that held only a one vote Republican majority, would be disastrous. Therefore, Eisenhower's initial opposition to the Bricker Amendment was somewhat "'fuzzy'" and not nearly as implacable as it would eventually come to be. Thus, at the beginning of 1953, instead of taking the Brickerites head-on, he desperately searched for some sort of compromise.[75] Although Dulles floated the suggestion that U.S.

72. Ambrose, *Eisenhower*, 155.

73. Eisenhower to J. Earl Schaefer, January 22, 1954, Box 5, File "DDE Diary January 1954 (1)," Diary Series, *Eisenhower:AWF*; quoted in Ambrose, *Eisenhower*, 70.

74. "Statement of Hon. John Foster Dulles, Secretary of State of the United States," Congress, Senate, Subcommittee of the Committee on the Judiciary, *Treaties and Executive Agreements*, 83rd Congress, 1st sess., March 31, 1953, 826, 829; Dulles to Governor Adams, memo, January 2, 1953, Box 8, File "Memoranda of Meetings from November 1952," Subject Series, *Papers of John Foster Dulles*, Dwight Eisenhower Presidential Library, Abilene, Kansas (hereafter *Dulles Papers*); Minutes of Cabinet Meeting, February 20, 1953, Box 1, File "Cabinet Meeting of February 20, 1953," Cabinet Series, *Eisenhower:AWF*; Minutes of Cabinet Meeting, March 13, 1953, Box 1, File "Cabinet Meeting of March 13, 1953," Cabinet Series, ibid.

75. Ambrose, *Eisenhower*, 69; Notes on the Bricker Amendment from Donovan's book, *Eisenhower, The Inside Story*, n.d., Box 7, File "Bricker Amendment-Draft Talk (1)," Administration Series, *Eisenhower:AWF*.

withdrawal from the UN might serve that purpose, Eisenhower apparently dismissed that idea as too extreme. Yes, he was "impatient" with the "meanderings of the UN," but still, he seriously "doubt[ed] . . . the wisdom" of making "a kind of American declaration of independence" from that international body.[76] Nevertheless, something had to be done, something had to give.

As a result, in early February 1953, the State Department, recognizing that it was the human rights initiatives that had sent Bricker supporters into a feeding frenzy on the president's powers, laid out for Dulles three options concerning America's continuing involvement in the development of human rights treaties and the impact each alternative would have on the Bricker sharks circling in the water. In weighing the pros and cons of each option, the foreign policy analysts wanted to "accomplish . . . a change in United States policy with the least damage to our public position at home and abroad."[77] They would not succeed.

The first option, crafted in hauntingly familiar language, recommended that the United States end its support for the Covenants on Human Rights because "progress can best be made not through the imposition of legal obligations, but through means of public discussion and persuasion." The analysts went on to explain that "[c]ontinued United States effort in support of the Human Rights Covenants might appear, at least to some observers and critics in this country, as inconsistent with the Administration's policy on civil rights . . . where the emphasis is now on persuasion as against any new federal civil rights legislation." The State Department analysts also argued that continued work on the Covenants was futile, because the Senate would never ratify either treaty, "even the Covenant on Civil and Political Rights." Moreover, the Covenants "could work to the disadvantage of [the] United States" because "given the conditions within this country," those treaties were sure to "be a source of propaganda attack." Finally, and this was the whole point of the exercise, if the Eisenhower administration "press[ed] ahead with the Covenants," it "would tend to keep alive and strengthen support for the Bricker amendments to the Constitution."[78]

76. Emmet J. Hughes to The Secretary of State (Dulles), memo, March 5, 1953, Box 99, File "United Nations (2)," Subject Series, *Papers of Dwight David Eisenhower: White House Central File* (hereafter *Eisenhower: WHCF*).

77. Durward Sandifer to Hickerson, February 9, 1953, Box 8, File "Human Rights: Miscellaneous, October 19, 1951–February 19, 1953," Lot File 55D429, *RG 59*; Phleger and Hickerson to The Secretary (Dulles), memo, February 18, 1953, ibid.; "United States Policy Regarding Draft International Covenants on Human Rights," February 17, 1953, ibid.

78. Ibid.

The policy paper then went on to suggest additional options, such as continuing to work solely on the Covenant on Political and Civil Rights, which, by design and strenuous negotiations, was a virtual mirror image of the Bill of Rights. There was also the option that the United States could pretend to support the drafting of the Covenants but, in reality, play the role of an obstructionist until all of the other nations were so frustrated by the nitpicking ordeal that they would throw their hands up in despair, recognize the futility of the effort, and walk away from both Covenants.[79]

The solution that Dulles and the president seized on was the first – the complete abandonment of both Covenants. There was no "agonizing reappraisal" here. Indeed, as historian Caroline Pruden observed, the "final decision to withhold support from the Human Rights Covenants was not difficult."[80] In fact, only three days passed from the time the State Department completed its report until the Cabinet meeting in which the Covenants' fate was sealed for the next 40 years.[81]

In the process, Eisenhower also withdrew support for the Genocide Convention because, as Vice President Richard Nixon noted, that treaty was the primary catalyst for the Bricker Amendment.[82] Earlier, to try to overcome the Southern Democrats' resistance, the State Department and Ralph Lemkin, the scholar who was the intellectual guide behind the convention, had argued that the United States actually had nothing to fear because "genocide occurred only when an intent existed to destroy an entire group, and those who committed lynchings lacked this requisite motivation." Lemkin further explained that lynching was not really genocide because "'the basic policy of the South is not to destroy the Negro but to preserve that race on a different level of existence.'"[83] Dulles, in 1949, had also tried to persuade the Genocide Convention's opponents that it was incomprehensible, especially in wake of the Holocaust, not to support publicly this baseline standard for human decency and civilization. At that time, he was "greatly disappointed" with the ABA for its

79. Ibid.
80. Caroline Pruden, *Conditional Partners: Eisenhower, the United Nations, and the Search for a Permanent Peace* (Baton Rouge: Louisiana State University Press, 1998), 202.
81. John Foster Dulles to Mr. Phleger et al., memo, February 20, 1953, Box 1, File "Chronological—John Foster Dulles February, 1953 (2)," Chronological Series, *Dulles Papers*. The U.S. would eventually ratify the Genocide Convention on November 25, 1988 and the Covenant on Civil and Political Rights on June 8, 1992. The Covenant on Economic, Social, and Cultural Rights, although signed by the president in 1977, is still awaiting ratification.
82. Minutes of Cabinet Meeting, February 20, 1953, Box 1, File "Cabinet Meeting of February 20, 1953," Cabinet Series, *Eisenhower:AWF*.
83. Quoted in Brucken, "A Most Uncertain Crusade," 309.

denunciation of the Genocide Convention and asserted that it was "hard to see how a beginning can ever be made in developing international law if the nations are not willing to ban effectively the crime of genocide." Dulles had also argued that "it would be lamentable if the United States, which has always been at the forefront in developing international law, should now take the lead in repudiating this first great Convention on human rights."[84] Four years later, however, that is exactly what the United States planned to do. And, for good measure, Secretary of State Dulles added the Convention on the Political Rights of Women to the list because he had a "grave question as to whether this Convention deals with a proper subject for international treaties." In the secretary of state's opinion, whether "women of some other country can vote on equal terms with men" was absolutely irrelevant to the United States. After all, he continued, it was "debatable whether under our Constitution a woman can be President," so why fret about what happens in some other country?[85] Perhaps that viewpoint also made it easy to jettison the Convention on the Abolition of Slavery, as well.[86]

In place of all of the human rights treaties dealing with genocide, women, slavery, political, civil, social, economic, and cultural rights, the United States planned to urge the UN to adopt, instead, a three-pronged "Action Program" that focused on each nation simply reporting on the status of human rights in their respective countries, having an official rapporteur at the UN to receive the reports, and creating a pool of human rights experts at the UN to provide advice when and if they were asked. As milquetoast as those suggestions were, however, Dulles still feared that the sheer act of reporting to the UN carried a distinct threat. He, therefore, stressed to his staff that this Action Program had "to avoid any new mechanisms which might give the Soviets an opportunity for prying around in human rights conditions in the United States."[87]

Thus, as Dulles prepared to testify before the Senate, he hoped that this "change in United States policy," with its total repudiation of human

84. "Statement by John Foster Dulles," September 9, 1949, Box 46, File "United Nations Correspondence Includes Genocide, Declaration of Human Rights," *JFD-Princeton*.
85. Dulles to the Legal Adviser, memo, March 5, 1953, Box 1, File "Chronological-John Foster Dulles March 1–17, 1953 (4)," Chronological Series, *Dulles Papers*.
86. Pruden, *Conditional Partners*, 203.
87. Phleger and Hickerson to The Secretary (Dulles), memo, February 18, 1953, Box 8, File, "Human Rights: Miscellaneous, October 19, 1951–February 19, 1953," Lot File 55D429, *RG 59*; "Statement of Background on, and Issues Involved in, Certain Provisions of the Proposed Covenant on Human Rights, Particularly Those Relating to Freedom of Information," n.d., Box 3306, File "Human Rights, 1949–52," *Roosevelt Papers*; Durward Sandifer to Kotschnig, memo, February 19, 1953, Box 8, File "Human Rights: Miscellaneous, October 19, 1951–February 19, 1953," Lot File 55D429, *RG 59*.

rights treaties and elevation of self-congratulatory human rights reports, would be "helpful in combating the Bricker Amendment."[88] That hope evaporated the moment Dulles opened his mouth to testify because, amazingly enough, he "began the fight by frantically retreating."[89] Instead of hammering home how not one treaty in the history of the United States had violated the Bill of Rights, and how infeasible it was that the president would sign, the Senate would ratify, and the Supreme Court would uphold an unconstitutional treaty, the secretary of state immediately conceded that the Bricker Amendment's supporters had a "legitimate" concern. He sympathetically admitted that their "widespread" fears had been fueled by a "tendency" during the Truman administration "to consider treatymaking as a way to effectuate reforms, particularly in relation to social matters, and to impose upon our Republic conceptions regarding human rights which . . . were alien to our traditional concepts." He promised that, with this new administration, the nightmare of social engineering was over. Eisenhower, he emphasized, had "revers[ed] . . . the trend" so prevalent in the Truman administration of using those treaties "to effect internal social changes." Then, as if trying to still a volcano by sacrificing virgins, Dulles lined up each one of the covenants and threw them in. He promised Bricker and the amendment's sponsors that the "present administration" would not "become a party to any . . . covenant" on human rights, nor would "this administration . . . sign the Convention on Political Rights of Women." Rather, Dulles asserted, the Eisenhower Administration would "encourage the promotion everywhere of human rights and individual freedoms" through "persuasion, education, and example rather than formal undertakings which commit one part of the world to impose its particular social and moral standards upon another part of the world community." Dulles ended with a solemn vow that the "era of . . . domestic, social, and economic 'reforms' through international treaties is at an end."[90]

Much to the administration's chagrin, however, Dulles's testimony and the Action Program only served to convince the amendment's advocates that they had been right all along. The *Wall Street Journal* wrote that,

88. Minutes of Cabinet Meeting, February 20, 1953, Box 1, File "Cabinet Meeting of February 20, 1953," Cabinet Series, *Eisenhower:AWF*.

89. "Treaties and Rights," ca. April 1953, found in Box 2, File "1953 Magazine and Newspaper Clippings," *Lord Papers*.

90. "Statement of Hon. John Foster Dulles, Secretary of State of the United States," Congress, Senate, Subcommittee of the Committee on the Judiciary, *Treaties and Executive Agreements*, 83rd Congress, 1st sess., March 31, 1953, 824; "Won't Let U.S. be 'Reformed' by UN Pacts: Ike Wipes Out Work of Mrs. Roosevelt," *Des Moines Sunday Register* April 12, 1953, found in Box 144, File "Board of Directors: Eleanor Roosevelt, 1946–55," *Papers of the NAACP*.

although it was not his intention, Dulles was "the most convincing witness of all for the need to safeguard the Constitution from encroachment by treaty." The essence of Dulles' argument, the *Journal* explained, was that Eisenhower would not do what Truman did. But what about the next administration? What guarantees were there that Eisenhower's successor would not revert to old form and use the UN to reorganize America's domestic policies? Without the Bricker Amendment, the *Journal* asserted, there were no guarantees.[91] In a similar vein, a California businessman declared that it was "not sufficient to say that *this* President and *this* administration will not negotiate treaties which will restrict or infringe upon our domestic rights and freedom. Future Presidents *may* do so, as they have done in the past."[92] An Ohio newspaper editorial also seemed equally bemused and unimpressed by Dulles' "curious argument" and "brilliant... volte-face." No matter how well Dulles executed his "Flip-Flop," the editorial observed, "by the time he finished his performance, he had greatly strengthened the position of the proponents of the Constitutional change." Dulles's candid admission about Truman's "full support" for these "social welfare" Covenants was more than sufficient to make the Bricker Amendment's case, but the secretary of state removed all doubt when he, without prodding, abandoned the human rights treaties. The paper asserted that there could only be "one reason" for the Eisenhower Administration to make this "noble" but "startling pledge" and that was because those covenants had to be as "inherently dangerous" as Senator Bricker warned. Dulles' "pledge, recognizing as it does the ease with which the Constitutional rights of Americans could be abridged, is an admission of the need for the restraints the Bricker Amendment would put on the Administration – any Administration, even Mr. Eisenhower's."[93]

While Bricker proponents all but thanked Dulles for proving their point, his "faint-hearted" testimony that was so obviously "studded with bouquets for the amendment's sponsors," riled the NAACP and others.[94] The *New York Times* and the *Washington Post* branded the Bricker Amendment a "strait jacket" and an ill-conceived attempt to drag the United States back to the 18th century and the old, unworkable days of the

91. "Review and Outlook: Mr. Dulles and the Treaty Power," *Wall Street Journal*, April 9, 1953, found in Box 2, File "1953 Magazine and Newspaper Clippings," *Lord Papers*.
92. Leslie E. Gehres to Senator Hennings, April 13, 1953, Folder 4776B, *Hennings Papers*. (Emphasis in original.)
93. "Mr. Dulles and His Flip-Flop," Reprint of Editorial in the *Toledo Times*, April 9, 1953, ibid.
94. "Treaties and Rights," n.d., found in Box 2, File "1953 Magazine and Newspaper Clippings," *Lord Papers*; Doris Fleeson, "Democrats Move to Save Ike Policy," n.d., found in Box 113, File "Bills: Bricker Amendment Press Releases, 1953–54," *Papers of the NAACP*.

Articles of Confederation. In trying to time-travel back to some isolationist utopia, the editorials asserted, the Ohio senator had provoked a constitutional crisis as "momentous" as the one when "President Roosevelt attempted to pack the Supreme Court." Just like that bit of folly, the Bricker Amendment was equally "unnecessary, unwise, and dangerous." The senator's proposal was a "narrow-visioned" "product of fear" that tried to "erect a sort of voodoo wall" around the United States by creating an "aura of illusions" that this was "a benevolent effort to safeguard our liberties against potential tyrants conspiring with other countries." The truth of the matter, however, was that Bricker and his supporters could "not point to a single treaty in all our history that represents an abuse of power." Thus, in the final analysis, "what Mr. Bricker is really doing is striking a blow for the isolationists against full American participation in the United Nations," "the International Monetary Fund, the International Telecommunications Union, the World Health Organization, and . . . the North Atlantic Treaty Organization." The Bricker Amendment was like Frankenstein's monster, the papers warned, for in "these days of cold war and perpetual crises," this "backward-looking resolution . . . ought to send cold chills up the spine of any responsible statesman."[95]

Dulles added greatly to that sense of distress when, shortly after his Senate testimony, he spoke before Roosevelt's American Association for the United Nations and confirmed the administration's determination to toss the Covenants on the scrap heap of history. Dulles asserted that human rights could not be achieved "by a stroke of the pen," and that it was unrealistic to think that a mere Covenant could create a world of justice and democracy. Rather, he asserted, it would take "campaigns of education, publicity," and "a long time," "to create a foundation for what may ultimately be a law that stems from the will of the community itself."[96]

As could be expected, the former first lady was "none too happy."[97] Not only had everything that she "stood for . . . been erased by one stroke of the Eisenhower administration,"[98] but Dulles and Eisenhower had also just "sold out to the Brickers and McCarthys" and did so for the astronomical

95. "Undercutting American Leadership," *Washington Post*, March 23, 1953, found in Folder 8239, *Hennings Papers*; "Pathway to Chaos," *New York Times*, April 8, 1953, found in ibid.; Merlo J. Pusey (Associate Editor, the *Washington Post*), "Bricker's Treaty Straitjacket," *St. Louis Post Dispatch*, April 2, 1953, found in ibid.

96. John Foster Dulles to the President [Eisenhower], memo, April 7, 1953, Box 1, File "Dulles, John Foster April, 1953," Dulles-Herter Series, *Eisenhower:AWF*.

97. Eleanor Roosevelt to Sandy [Durward Sandifer], March 20, 1953, Box 3479, File "Sandifer, Durward and Irene, 1953–56," *Roosevelt Papers*.

98. "Won't Let U.S. be 'Reformed' by UN Pacts: Ike Wipes Out Work of Mrs. Roosevelt," *Des Moines Sunday Register*, April 12, 1953, found in Box 144, File "Board of Directors: Eleanor Roosevelt, 1946–55," *Papers of the NAACP*.

"price" of "not supporting either Covenant." Mrs. Roosevelt knew that there was not "the slightest chance of getting the Covenant on Economic and Social Rights so worded that it would be possible for the Senate to ratify it," but there was a way, she believed, to make "more palatable . . . the one on Civil and Political Rights." But instead of taking on that most important battle—a battle that could have provided another legal foundation on which to base the struggle for justice in the United States and elsewhere, the Administration just raised the white flag and surrendered. "[U]nder this administration," she sadly and angrily concluded, "[t]he U.S. is going backward."[99]

It was also clear to the AJC how regressive Eisenhower's human rights policy stance actually was. The AJC noted disdainfully that those who were complaining the loudest that the UN's treaties would "water . . . down rights presently enjoyed by residents of the United States under the . . . Constitution . . . have hardly been in the forefront of the fight to preserve existing rights." After all, the DAR, which had blocked African American contralto Marian Anderson from performing in Constitution Hall, could never be described as a civil rights organization. Even a cursory look at the other pro-Bricker groups – such as the virtually lily-white and segregationist ABA and the American Medical Association – suggested "that they are inspired more by hostility towards the United Nations than by any danger to the rights of American citizens."[100]

After spotlighting the sheer hypocrisy of the Bricker proponents, the AJC then focused on the fallout from Dulles's horrific Senate performance. All he had managed to do, the AJC explained to its members, was to compel the Senate Subcommittee to "report . . . out a revised version of the Bricker proposal which . . . represents a more extreme limitation on the treaty-making power than that initially proposed."[101]

99. Eleanor Roosevelt to Sandy [Durward Sandifer], March 20, 1953, Box 3479, File "Sandifer, Durward and Irene, 1953–56," *Roosevelt Papers*; Eleanor Roosevelt, "The Human Rights Issue," *The Nashville Tennessean*, April 4, 1953 found in Box 113, File "Bills: Bricker Amendment Press Releases, 1953–54," *Papers of the NAACP*.

100. Commission on Law and Social Action Reports: Memorandum on the Bricker Resolution, July 2, 1953, attachment to Will Maslow to Jewish Community Relations Councils Group Relations Agencies, July 7, 1953, Box 113, File "Bills: Bricker Amendment Correspondence, 1952–55," ibid. For the conservative, segregationist composition of the ABA see, Duane Tananbaum, *The Bricker Amendment Controversy: A Test of Eisenhower's Political Leadership* (Ithaca, New York: Cornell University Press, 1988), 8.

101. Commission on Law and Social Action Reports: Memorandum on the Bricker Resolution, July 2, 1953, attachment to Will Maslow to Jewish Community Relations Council Group Relations Agencies, July 7, 1953, Box 113, File "Bills: Bricker Amendment Correspondence, 1952–55," *Papers of the NAACP*.

The additional and even more threatening problem was the "which clause" or as it would become known, the "witch clause." This infamous initiative, added by Senator Arthur Watkins (R-UT), asserted that even if the Senate ratified a treaty, it would be meaningless unless Congress already had the explicit authority to pass legislation on that area or subject.[102] Senator Thomas Hennings, Jr. (D-MO), who slowly but surely became one of the chief and most decisive critics of the Bricker Amendment, explained the destructive and tourniquet-like effect that the "which clause," alone, would have on the United States' ability to enter into any kind of international agreement:

> This means, first of all, that a treaty would be ineffective unless and until the matter... was introduced in the form of legislation in both the House of Representatives and the Senate, had gone through the process of committee hearings and floor debate, had been approved by majorities of each House, and signed by the President. A bill, of course, may take months or even years to go through the Congress, and there are, moreover, many legislative devices... to postpone action indefinitely.... [Yet] even the cumbersome legislative procedure which I have just described would not make a treaty valid... [The "which clause"] would prevent the President from negotiating treaties relating to such matters as the control of narcotics, the conservation of wildlife, the collection of debts, and the status of troops and international organizations, *unless* treaties relating to these subjects were ratified by the legislatures of the 48 states.[103]

Given those strangling parameters, the AJC had no recourse but to conclude that the Bricker Amendment was a "straitjacket" designed to make it impossible for the United States to ever participate in "negotiating and enforcing international agreements" dealing with genocide, human rights, and "the elimination of international threats to health and safety such as atomic warfare and traffic in narcotics."[104]

Walter White was even more unequivocal. In a no-holds barred radio broadcast, White "refuse[d] to believe that last November's election can in any wise be interpreted as a mandate to fight and oppose human rights at home or abroad." He asserted that the Bricker Amendment,

102. Notes on the Bricker Amendment from Donovan's Book, *Eisenhower, The Inside Story*, Box 7, File "Bricker Amendment-Draft Talk (1)," Administration Series, *Eisenhower:AWF*.

103. Tananbaum, *The Bricker Amendment*, 184; "From the Office of Senator Thomas C. Hennings, Jr.," press release, January 27, 1954, Folder 4766, *Hennings Papers*.

104. Commission on Law and Social Action Reports: Memorandum on the Bricker Resolution, July 2, 1953, attachment to Will Maslow to Jewish Community Relations Council Group Relations Agencies, July 7, 1953, Box 113, File "Bills: Bricker Amendment Correspondence, 1952–55," *Papers of the NAACP*.

with its proviso that all 48 state legislatures had to approve any treaty, would drag the United States down to the "moral and intellectual level of the most backward state of the nation." That frightening scenario, he exclaimed, meant "that as a nation we could take no higher moral ground than that permitted by states like Mississippi or South Carolina." But, of course, he added, that was the whole point. The NAACP chieftain stated that it was no accident that Senator Bricker's crusade gained momentum only after a California court ruled that a racially discriminatory law violated the Declaration of Human Rights. That ruling, White explained, caused "consternation in conservative circles lest our international moral commitments require us to live up to those commitments here at home." Now was the time, White pleaded, for "those who really believe in freedom" to confront "Senator Bricker and the other sixty-three senators who have joined with him" and let them know that we "do not want to stand in shame before the world preaching one doctrine and practicing another."[105] The "more we study this amendment," he noted in an address to congressional leaders, "the more dangerous we believe it to be."[106]

This fierce denunciation was echoed by the NAACP Board of Directors who "deplore[d]" the Bricker Amendment and the fact that it was "'[m]otivated, at least in part by a sectional desire to impede progress in human relations,... bolster the anti-civil rights filibuster and set up an additional roadblock to civil rights." Yet "it is not only civil rights that is endangered by this attack," the Board declared, "but also progress towards... international labor, welfare and human rights standars (sic)."[107] The NAACP, therefore, mobilized its branches, launched a major lobbying campaign in the Senate, and called on the "52 national church, labor, civic, fraternal, and minority group organizations which have cooperated with the NAACP on civil rights issues" in the past, to "work for the defeat of" the Bricker Amendment.[108]

The Senate, however, would not budge.[109] Thus, the threat of that amendment hovered over everything and added immeasurably to the difficulties of the U.S. delegation at the spring 1953 meeting of the UN. Here,

105. Broadcast WLIB and Affiliated Stations: Walter White, April 9, 1953, Box 113, File "Bricker Amendment Press Releases, 1953–54," ibid.

106. Walter White to Senator, April 16, 1953, Box 113, File "Bills: Bricker Amendment Correspondence, 1952–55,: ibid.

107. Minutes of the Board of Directors Meeting, April 13, 1953, Reel 3 *NAACP/LC*.

108. Gloster B. Current to NAACP Branch Officers, April 21, 1953, Box 113, File "Bills: Bricker Amendment Press Releases, 1953–54," *Papers of the NAACP*.

109. Robert C. Hendrickson to White, April 17, 1953, Box 113, File "Bills: Bricker Amendment Correspondence, 1952–55," ibid.; Ralph E. Flanders to White, April 16, 1953, ibid.; Everett McKinley Dirksen to White, April 17, 1953, ibid.

in complete deference to Senator Bricker, the administration unveiled the faintest outlines of its Action Program and hailed the "new approach to human rights." Eisenhower's message at the opening ceremonies, while peppered with platitudes about freedom and liberty, focused on letting the UN know that "there were better ways of achieving respect for human rights than by drafting formal treaties on the subject." Then, just as choreographed, Dulles, through an emissary, informed the UN Commission on Human Rights that the United States had decided that "no good would come" from trying to draft and ratify any document that spoke to issues of universal human rights. But, instead of laying the blame for this abandonment of the Covenants at the feet of the South, where it appropriately belonged, the administration decided to put the responsibility for this moral collapse on the Soviets. Dulles and the president, in a concerted, deliberate attempt to divert international attention away from the Covenants and channel the UN's focus on human rights violations in the Soviet Union, asserted that it was an exercise in futility to try to codify human rights standards as long as totalitarian regimes continued to "have no respect for the dignity of the human person." Any covenant, they insisted, "could not be as good as the actual practice in advanced democracies. It could not have any effect in countries where people have few or none of the traditional human rights. And it would not be applied in totalitarian states." Until there was "wider general acceptance of human rights goals," Dulles concluded, it was impractical and senseless to continue down the path of drafting covenants.[110]

This message of hopelessness and futility was bad enough, but complicating the problem for the delegation was Eisenhower's replacement for Eleanor Roosevelt – flour-mill heiress Mary Pillsbury Lord. No matter how the administration tried to dress it up, Lord's most important, if not sole, credential for the position was that she co-chaired the Citizens for Eisenhower-Nixon Committee during the campaign. Thus, the White House's only viable way to market Lord to the Senate and the public was to put an "emphasis . . . on the fact that Mrs. Lord is a Republican – her Republican background" had to "be spelled out."[111] Granted, this

110. "Ike Urges New Approach to Human Rights," *Washington Post*, April 8, 1953, found in Box 2, File "1953 Magazine and Newspaper Clippings," *Lord Papers*; "U.S. Asks Realism on Human Rights," *New York Times*, April 7, 1953, found in ibid.; "Eisenhower for Human Rights Gain," *New York Herald Tribune*, April 7, 1953, found in ibid.; Thomas E. Stephens (Secretary to the President) to David Kulok, August 28, 1953, Box 584, File "116-H-5 Genocide Convention," *Eisenhower:WHCF*.

111. "Two Appointments," *Herald Tribune* January 1953, found in Box 2, File "1953 Magazine and Newspaper Clippings," *Lord Papers*; Charles F. Willis, Jr. to Sherman Adams, memo, January 16, 1953, Box 2, File "Lord, Mrs. Oswald," Name Series, *Eisenhower:WHCF*.

differentiated Lord from her much vilified predecessor, but still, it hardly seemed adequate. That inadequacy was especially revealing when Lord, the appointee to the UN Commission on Human Rights, told a reporter "'Ask me anything about the children's fund . . . but I can't make a comment on civil rights – I've got a lot of homework to do first.'" Or when she erroneously declared that the United States had not endorsed the Declaration of Human Rights because "its emphasis on the guarantee of social and economic rights like work and free medical care was at variance with U.S. ideals."[112] That kind of careless attention to detail reinforced the aura of a lightweight socialite and "Housewife First," who was poorly suited for the rough and tumble world of international diplomacy. That perception was so pervasive that about the only one who had any confidence in her at all was Eisenhower.[113]

The doubts about Lord's ability were, of course, compounded by the tough assignment she was supposed to carry out. One State Department official, in looking back, observed that "Mary Lord came into a very, very difficult position," because the first "thing that Mrs. Lord had to do, on instructions from Washington, was to announce in the Human Rights Commission that the United States would *not* sign the Human Rights convention."[114] Although Dulles had already indicated that decision, Lord would be the person in the CHR meetings who would have to deliver that message officially and then persuade all of the other delegations to drop the Covenants and sign on to the Action Program. "Good luck to you," James Hendrick wrote to her, "God knows you'll need it."[115]

Mrs. Roosevelt sent her condolences. "Good luck to you in Switzerland!" the letter began, "I can't say I envy you," especially, Roosevelt implied, now that the United States regarded the Commission's efforts to draft the Covenants as irrelevant. "I am sure," given the circumstances, that it "will be hard for you to get along with the other representatives and to do any worthwhile work."[116] To Sandifer, Roosevelt confided that she felt "sorry for Mrs. Lord. Anything emptier than to go to

112. "Mrs. Lord to Spotlight 'Everyday' Deeds of UN," *The Houston Post*, January 18, 1953, found in Box 2, File "1953 Magazine and Newspaper Clippings," *Lord Papers*.
113. Sidney Fields, "Only Human—Mary Lord: The Road to Human Rights," n.d., found in ibid.; D. [Eisenhower] to Sherman Adams, memo, January 10, 1953, Box 1, File "Adams, Sherman (7)," Administration Series, *Eisenhower:AWF*.
114. *Blaisdell*. (Emphasis in original.)
115. James P. Hendrick to Mrs. Oswald Lord, February 24, 1953, Box 2, File "Human Rights: JP Hendrick Personal," *Hendrick Papers*.
116. Eleanor Roosevelt to Mary Lord, April 4, 1953, Box 1, File "1953 Correspondence," *Lord Papers*.

Geneva with these positions, I can not imagine." What "a terrible waste of time."[117]

The UN meeting in April and May 1953 did indeed deliver one embarrassing moment after the next for the U.S. delegation. Mary Lord's State Department adviser, James Green, reported that the "first week of the session was pretty grim," and we "all felt that, during the first week, we had fallen off a very high cliff." Several factors, however, converged to transform what promised to be an unmitigated disaster into merely the "most difficult circumstances." First, Green noted, the "fact that this session [was] held in Geneva, ... instead of in New York, where we would have been the center of far too much attraction ... saved" the U.S. delegation. Second, the recent death of Joseph Stalin and the tenuous peace feelers the new triumvirate sent out to the United States meant that "the Soviet bloc [was] all milk and honey at the moment."[118] Thus, the Soviet critique of the U.S.'s new human rights policy, much to everyone's amazement, was the "mildest" of all.[119] On the other hand, the "UK and Western European Governments took rather strenuous exception to the [U.S.'s] proposals."[120]

The fact that the United States stood alone, without even its most reliable allies, made the simplest procedure impossible. Green observed that, in one case, as the United States tried to figure out how to "cut-off ... debate on the Covenants in order to allow ample time for the introduction and discussion of our new action programs," it soon became apparent that this was going to "be a difficult manoeuvre because our usual friends, the western powers, are hostile to our new program ... and the under-developed countries ... are devoted to the Covenants and want to see that their favorite proposals are incorporated in them."[121] The Indian delegate was suspicious of American motives and asserted that the "U.S. Government's decision to refuse ratification of the covenants ... long before their preparation had been completed was calculated as an

117. Eleanor Roosevelt to Sandy [Durward Sandifer], March 20, 1953, Box 3479, File "Sandifer, Durward and Irene, 1953–56," *Roosevelt Papers*.

118. James Green to Durward Sandifer, April 22, 1953, Box 8, File "Ninth Session of the Commission," Lot File 55D429, *RG 59*; James Green to Durward Sandifer, May 21, 1953, ibid.

119. "Geneva Commission is Hard Hit by U.S. Human Rights Stand," *The [Washington, D.C.] Evening Star*, April 8, 1953, found in Box 2, File "1953 Magazine and Newspaper Clippings," *Lord Papers*.

120. Sandy [Durward Sandifer] to Eleanor Roosevelt, July 3, 1953, Box 3479, File "Sandifer, Durward and Irene, 1953–56," *Roosevelt Papers*.

121. James Green to Durward Sandifer, April 22, 1953, Box 8, File "Ninth Session of the Commission," Lot File 55D429, *RG 59*.

attempt ... to render valueless the work of the Commission" and to "'take the bottom out' of the group's work." The delegates from the "small countries" were determined, however, that with or without the United States, the work on the Covenants would continue. Those treaties, they agreed, were "essential."[122]

Getting a sense of how unsplendid splendid isolationism was, the U.S. delegation decided to hold off on a full exploration of the Action Program until later in the session and move onto its next, yet equally provocative, agenda item. Continuing a policy started during the Truman administration, the United States tried once again to subvert the Sub-commission on the Prevention of Discrimination and Protection of Minorities. To date, the United States had attempted to "eliminate the Sub-Commission, postpone its meetings, and – at this session – to restrict its agenda and change its membership." Both Green and Mrs. Lord "were very skeptical" about the wisdom of this maneuver and their instincts were right. In "some ways," Green confided to Sandifer, the attempt to neutralize and ostracize MINDIS was "the most painful of the whole session." The "situation in which we found ourselves was absolutely hopeless. From every quarter we learned that we had no support whatever ... and that we had aroused widespread suspicion and resentment." The day of reckoning came with the "arrival of Sub-Commission Chairman, Mr. Roy" from Haiti who was one of the "most eloquent, ruthless, and effective opponents" Green had "ever encountered in the United Nations." Green remembered that, when the United States had previously attempted to disband MINDIS, Roy "attacked the ... decision ... so violently" that he even caused the nearly unflappable Mrs. Roosevelt to "disregard her instructions and abstain on the vote." Now, with the rookie Lord sitting there, Roy "was obviously on the point of another vituperative attack," and the heiress had no choice but to beat a hasty retreat and withdraw the U.S. plan from the table.[123]

When the United States circled back around to finally launch the "good ship 'Action,'" as Green called it, the send-off was equally rocky and unspectacular.[124] Mrs. Lord naively underestimated the savvy and

122. "Geneva Commission is Hard Hit by U.S. Human Rights Stand," *The [Washington, D.C.] Evening Star*, April 8, 1953, found in Box 2, File "1953 Magazine and Newspaper Clippings," *Lord Papers*; "Opening of Ninth Session of UN Commission of Human Rights," *Pravda*, April 8, 1953, found in ibid.; "Rights Pact Drafters Shaken by U.S. Bolt," *New York World-Telegram and Sun*, April 8, 1953, found in Box 636, File "United Nations Declaration on Human Rights, 1952–53," *Papers of the NAACP*.

123. James Green to Durward Sandifer, May 21, 1953, Box 8, File "Ninth Session of the Commission," Lot File 55D429, *RG 59*.

124. James Green to Durward Sandifer, May 21, 1953, ibid.

intelligence of her Commission colleagues and, therefore, tried to pawn off Eisenhower's surrender to the right wing in American politics as an international breakthrough in human rights. She asserted, for example, that the Action Program was "the product of earnest and careful consideration" and had "been framed in the sincere belief that [its] adoption will make more significant and meaningful the work of the United Nations in the field of human rights." She also said that it was conceived as a way to redirect the considerable talents and energies of the Commission from its "preoccupation" with drafting the Covenants "to the practical problems of helping all governments and peoples to move ahead in the advancement of their well-being."[125] Of course, none of this was true.

With barely three months between Eisenhower's inauguration, the Bricker crisis, and the UN meeting, the "good ship Action" had to be rushed into service well before it was ready to sail into a major international conference. Thus, whereas Lord described a program that had been thoroughly scrutinized and given "careful and deliberate consideration," Green explained to Sandifer that "owing to the lateness of the decision to shift our policy," the State Department simply did not have the time to explore fully all of the issues and "do a lot of the basic thinking and drafting that is usually done in the Department weeks ahead of a meeting." And because "no one had time to think through all their implications," the position papers that were supposed to guide Lord through her maiden voyage on the Commission were "skeletal" and did "not cover the details of our new action program." As a consequence, Green suggested, "our Government has merely jumped from the frying pan into the fire."[126] He did hold out hope, nonetheless, that with the ongoing intense debates over the inclusion of various "unacceptable" articles in the human rights treaties, that "the Covenants . . . will eventually collapse of their own weight, with resulting concentration of attention on our new action program." That hope would be dashed, however, when late in the session the Commission finally heard Mary Lord describe the framework for the Action Program. The response, to put it mildly, was less than enthusiastic. In fact, "the reaction by UNCHR members, even U.S. allies, was harsher than the State Department had predicted." As reality quickly set in, Green informed Sandifer that it would be impractical to push for adoption of the Action Program at this meeting, because a "vote under present circumstances with the Western Powers abstaining, might be worse than no

125. "A New Human Rights Action Program," *Department of State Bulletin*, June 15, 1953, found in Box 1, File "1953 Human Rights—Reprints from Department of State Bulletin," *Lord Papers*.

126. James F. Green to Durward Sandifer, April 22, 1953, Box 8, File "Ninth Session of the Commission," Lot File 55D429, *RG 59*.

vote at all."[127] Instead, the administration decided to submit the Action Program again at the next UN meeting in the fall.

The prelude to that meeting carried with it even more rancor and discontent than ever before as the liberal coalition, which was already on edge because of the Bricker Amendment and the denunciation of the Covenants, watched in disbelief as Eisenhower nominated the"apostle of uncompromising white supremacy," James Francis Byrnes, to the U.S. delegation to the UN.[128] One New York paper noted that "Jimmy Byrnes is perhaps the nation's outstanding apostle of race supremacy. Jimmy Byrnes stands out like a sore mind even among the more moth-eaten statesmen of the Old South. Jimmy Byrnes is the monotonous voice of plantation times." Just how, the editorial asked, was "Jimmy Byrnes going to be able to sit down in the General Assembly," with its multiracial membership,"and talk about a world he won't live in unless it's lily-white?"[129] The NAACP could not have agreed more and mounted an all-out campaign to "Block Byrnes."[130]

For Walter White, the fact that Byrnes was even considered for the position was "'shocking.'"[131] White blasted the nomination as one of incredible "ineptitude" where, at first sight, "it appeared that only Gov. Herman Talmadge of Georgia could be a worse choice."[132] He just could not believe that Byrnes, with his "47-year record of implacable hostility to Negroes," could be nominated when "one of the gravest issues faced by the American Delegation to the UN is that of human rights and racial

127. James F. Green to Durward Sandifer, May 21, 1953, ibid.

128. John W. Hanes, Jr., to Murray Snyder, memo, July 27, 1953, Box 3, File "Chronological O'Connor & Hanes July-1953 (2)," Special Assistants Chronological Series, *Dulles Papers*; "What Qualifies One to be a UN Delegate?" *The Courier-Journal*, July 29, 1953, found in Box 162, File "James F. Byrnes, Appointment to United Nations—General, 1953," *Papers of the NAACP*.

129. "Comment on Byrnes from Daily Press: Wrong Man, Wrong Job," *New York Post*, reprinted in *St. Paul Recorder*, August 7, 1953, found in Box H18, File "James Byrnes (South Carolina)," *NAACP-Washington Bureau*.

130. Eisenhower to Strom Thurmond, telegram, April 16, 1955, Box 3, File "Byrnes, James F. (1)," Name Series, *Eisenhower:AWF*; Walter White to Eisenhower, telegram, July 27, 1953, Box 162, File "James F. Byrnes Appointment to UN: Branch Protests, 1953–54," *Papers of the NAACP*; "Byrnes Appointment a Blunder," *Minneapolis Spokesman*, July 31, 1953, found in Box H18, File "James Byrnes (South Carolina)," *NAACP-Washington Bureau*; "Nation Moves To: Block Byrnes," *St. Louis Argus*, July 31, 1953, found in Box 162, File "James F. Byrnes, Appointment to United Nations—General, 1953," *Papers of the NAACP*.

131. "President Names 4 UN Delegates: Walter White Calls Nomination of Gov. Byrnes to Session of Assembly 'Shocking,'" *New York Times*, July 28, 1953, found in Box H18, File "James Byrnes (South Carolina)," *NAACP-Washington Bureau*.

132. "From Walter White for release to subscribing newspapers," press release, July 30, 1953, Box 162, File "James F. Byrnes, Appointment to United Nations—General, 1953," *Papers of the NAACP*.

equality." White contended that "'Governor Byrnes' lifelong career of intransigent opposition to the rights of Negroes, immigrants, labor and other minorities makes him the worst possible spokesman for American democracy in the United Nations at this crucial period of world history.'" Byrnes's "'record is so bad,'" White continued, "that he will become the immediate and exceedingly vulnerable target of Communist and other critics of American democracy.'"[133]

White buttressed that argument when he asserted that during Byrnes' previous incarnation as a diplomat, the South Carolinian had "ridicule heaped upon him by Soviet spokesmen" who were stunned that Byrnes had the audacity to lecture them about the need for democracy in, of all places, Bulgaria. "'Practice what you preach,' said Mr. Molotov."[134] Then, White noted, "the Communist spokesmen brought out the detailed record of disfranchisement in South Carolina by the poll tax and the 'white primary' and challenged Mr. Byrnes to clean up his own back yard before dictating to the rest of the world how it should manage its affairs." After that, White recalled, Byrnes "was forced to retreat in humiliation."[135]

Surely, one editorial remarked, there "must be another spot, free of color lines, where the President can install his new-found friend."[136] Perhaps, one journalist noted, Eisenhower could "find a more appropriate appointment for the Governor's talents, such as Ambassador to Siberia or better still, the North Pole."[137]

Under no circumstances, however, was the UN an appropriate payoff for a "renegade Democrat who rode the 'I Like Ike' bandwagon in the last campaign."[138] "If Governor Byrnes cannot uphold in its entirety the

133. Walter White to The Editor *New York Times*, August 3, 1953, Box 675 File "Max Yergan, 1941–53," ibid.; "NAACP Deplores Byrnes Approval by Senate Foreign Affairs Unit," press release, July 30, 1953, Box 162, File "James F. Byrnes, Appointment to United Nations—General, 1953," ibid.

134. "From Walter White for release to subscribing newspapers," press release, July 30, 1953, ibid.; "Byrnes Appointment a Blunder," *Minneapolis Spokesman*, July 31, 1953, found in Box H18, File "James Byrnes (South Carolina)," *NAACP-Washington Bureau*.

135. "From Walter White for release to subscribing newspapers," press release, July 30, 1953, Box 162, File "James F. Byrnes, Appointment to United Nations—General, 1953," *Papers of the NAACP*.

136. "Comment on Byrnes from Daily Press: Wrong Man, Wrong Job," *New York Post*, reprinted in *St. Paul Recorder*, August 7, 1953, found in Box H18, File "James Byrnes (South Carolina)," *NAACP-Washington Bureau*.

137. Soren A. Toroian, Letter to the Editor: "Byrnes in UN," *St. Louis Post-Dispatch*, July 31, 1953, found in Box 162, File "James F. Byrnes, Appointment to United Nations—General, 1953," *Papers of the NAACP*.

138. "Comment on Byrnes from Daily Press: Wrong Man Wrong Job," *New York Post*, reprinted in *St. Paul Recorder*, August 7, 1953, found in Box H18, File "James Byrnes (South Carolina)," *NAACP-Washington Bureau*.

Constitution of the United States," the *Carolina Times* asserted, "we are wondering by what stretch of imagination the president of the United States thought he would uphold the Declaration of Human Rights of the United Nations."[139] Byrnes's plan to shut down the public schools, while providing state funding for white children to attend private, "whites only" schools led one man to insist that this scheme only proved that Byrnes was "'gonna keep these blacks ignorant and poor, the Supreme Court and United Nations notwithstanding.'"[140]

The Association, therefore, demanded that it have the opportunity during the Senate confirmation hearings "to express its vigorous and uncompromising opposition to [the] appointment of Governor James Byrnes... as a member of [the] United Nations' delegation."[141] Hit with this "avalanche of protests," the Senate Foreign Relations staff immediately relayed to Dulles that "a number of the colored groups wished to be heard in opposition to Governor Byrnes' appointment." Although certain that "this 'left-wing negro' opposition" would not have much, if any, influence on the Senate vote, the chair of the Foreign Relations Committee, Senator Alexander Wiley (R-WI), was reluctant to hold any hearings that would allow African Americans to "embarrass... Governor Byrnes at this late date."[142]

The right wing, instead, went on the offensive. North Carolina Senator Clyde R. Hoey denounced Byrnes's critics as "'left wing groups'" who were trying to destroy "'a real American.'"[143] The *Arkansas Gazette* kept up the Communist drumbeat and declared that Byrnes' views on racial matters were irrelevant, and all that the NAACP had really done was to "'pave... the way for'" the "'Kremlin propagandists'" to stir up trouble.[144] A Virginia newspaper slammed White's protests as "resentful, ill-timed, and irritating," but about the most that could be expected from the Communist-tainted NAACP. "The Red bloc trumps up every lie it can

139. "That Byrnes Appointment to the United Nations," *Carolina Times*, August 15, 1953, found in ibid.

140. "A Dissertation about Views of Max Yergan," *Pittsburgh Courier*, October 31, 1953, found in Box 675, File "Max Yergan, 1941–53," *Papers of the NAACP*.

141. Clarence Mitchell to Alexander Wiley, telegram, July 28, 1953, Box 162, File "James F. Byrnes Appointment to UN: Branch Protests, 1953–54," *Papers of the NAACP*.

142. "Ignoring Minorities' Protest: Senate Confirms Byrnes as New Delegate to UN," *Afro-American*, August 4, 1953, found in Box H18, File "James Byrnes (South Carolina)," *NAACP-Washington Bureau*; John W. Hanes, Jr., to Dulles, memo, July 29, 1953, Box 3, File "Chronological O'Connor & Hanes July–1953 (1)," Special Assistants Chronological Series, *Dulles Papers*.

143. "Jimmy Byrnes 'Great American': Senator Labels Byrnes' Critics 'Left Wingers,'" *Carolina Times*, August 8, 1953, found in Box H18, File "James Byrnes (South Carolina)," *NAACP-Washington Bureau*.

144. "How Stupid Can We Get?" n.d., found in ibid. (Emphasis in original.)

Photo 5.3. FBI informant and former head of the National Negro Congress and the Council on African Affairs, Max Yergan.
Visual Materials from the NAACP Records, Library of Congress.

about American 'mistreatment' of minorities. Perhaps if Judge Byrnes were not there the Reds would find somebody else to lie about."[145] An even more pointed attack came in an anonymous letter to White. "You bastard!" the missive began, "you are a communist bitch who doesn't appreciate the good life you are too fortunate to have here in the U.S . . . why don't you go to Africa where you belong." The writer warned that White's "traitorous statement" against the "wonderful Mr. Byrnes" would be the death of the NAACP leader. White obviously did not understand, the writer railed, that a "stinking, ugly, thick-lipped, black negro is not an American. He is not now and never will be an American. He is nothing," whereas, on the other hand, "Mr. Byrnes. He is an American."[146] Of course, all of those denunciations, threats, and smears coming from remnants of the old Confederacy were to be expected, but when Max Yergan joined the chorus, the NAACP and black leadership looked on in disbelief.

145. "Byrnes to the UN" (Newport News-Hampton Road, Virginia), *Daily Press*, July 30, 1953, found in Box 162, File "James F. Byrnes Appointment to United Nations—General, 1953," *Papers of the NAACP*.

146. Anonymous to Walter White, August 17, 1953, Box 162, File "James F. Byrnes Appointment to UN: Branch Protests 1953–54," ibid.

In a stinging letter to the *New York Times* and other papers, Yergan denounced Walter White as a has-been race man and Communist propagandist who did not understand that, given the Soviet threat, Byrnes' nomination was to be "commended."[147] The executive secretary of the NAACP was "twenty-five years out of date," Yergan insisted. The "time has long since passed for dealing with race issues in our country in terms of American foreign relations." Jim Crow was a domestic issue that could only be dealt with "within the United States." To "inject" race "into our foreign relations," the way Walter White had done, only furthered the Communist cause. White and others of his ilk, Yergan railed, were nothing but "professional racists" whose "stock in trade" was keeping the racial pot boiling and ignoring the fact that "'America is committed'" to the "'principle of first class citizenship for all its citizens.'"[148]

This, of course, was not the first time Yergan had swung wildly at White and landed a low blow. In addition to the altercation at the San Francisco Conference, they had tangled earlier in 1953 when Yergan, the former Communist, now evangelical American, came back from South Africa singing the praises of *apartheid*.[149] In an article in *U.S. News and World Report* and in conversations with the FBI, Yergan warned that the brewing insurrection in South Africa was not about *apartheid* at all, which, as he saw it, was necessary to meet the labor and security demands of white South Africans. Rather, the protests movements were Communist-directed and financed.[150]

In his office in New York, White immediately received word from his contacts that Yergan's pro-*apartheid* article was "being used more and

147. Max Yergan, Letter to the Editor: Byrnes Selection Discussed, His Appointment as a Delegate to the United Nations Commended, *New York Times*, August 3, 1953, found in Box 675, File "Max Yergan, 1941–53," *Papers of the NAACP*; Max Yergan, Letter to the Editor: Byrnes and UN, *New York Herald Tribune*, August 2, 1953, found in ibid.

148. Max Yergan, Letter to the Editor: Byrnes Selection Discussed, His Appointment as a Delegate to the United Nations Commended, *New York Times*, August 3, 1953, found in ibid.; Max Yergan, Letter to the Editor: Byrnes and UN," *New York Herald Tribune*, August 2, 1953, found in ibid.; W. O. Walker, "Down the Big Road," *Cleveland Call-Post*, August 29, 1953, found in ibid.

149. Yergan, "Africa: Next Goal of Communists," *U.S. News and World Report*, May 1, 1953, 53–54, 57, 63.

150. Ibid., 52; Boardman to Bureau, teletype, November 6, 1953, *FBI File on Max Yergan*; "Interview of Max Yergan," November 5, 1948, 100-26603, ibid. For an excellent analysis of Yergan's deep-seated need for creature comforts and status above all else and how that may have been part of his motivation for becoming an FBI informant see, David H. Anthony, "Max Yergan and South Africa: A Transatlantic Interaction," in Sidney Lemelle and Robin D. G. Kelley, *Imagining Home: Class, Culture, and Nationalism in the African Diaspora* (London and New York: Verso, 1994), 196–200.

more in Washington as justification of the actions of Malan." White complained to the media and his colleagues that to have a black man, a man who had spent so many years in South Africa to now come running to the defense of the most racially repressive regime since Adolf Hitler, was "Uncle Tomism" at its worst and at its most "exceedingly dangerous."[151] Yergan, of course, countered that the only reason Walter White was on the attack was because the head of the NAACP openly consorted with Fifth Amendment Communists.[152]

That charge was so absurd – as was the defense of *apartheid* – that the black leadership was sure that something had "happened" to Max Yergan.[153] Thus, when barely two months later, Yergan took up the defense of James Byrnes, the black leadership knew that the South Africa apologia was no aberration; Yergan had obviously defected to the ultra-right wing's corner.[154] Of course, this was a very dangerous place for a black man to be. "Governor Byrnes has been looking a long time for some Negro he could present as approving him and his views. It seems that Dr. Yergan comes pretty close to being that man."[155] *Cleveland Call Post* editor William Walker further declared that Yergan, "in leveling charges of disloyalty against members of the Board of the NAACP, . . . is only helping our enemies" and, what is even more unforgivable, he knows full well "the potential damage his charges can do."[156]

White, of course, went after Yergan with a mudslinging, red-baiting counterattack that while stinging, was misdirected and missed the point.[157] Charles Howard, an Association member, explained. By

151. Max Yergan to Ralph Bunche, April 29, 1936, Reel 2, *Bunche*; "Max Yergan Replies to Walter White," n.d., Part 14, Reel 5, *NAACP-Int'l*; Walter White to Carl Murphy, May 6, 1953, Box 675, File "Max Yergan, 1941–53," *Papers of the NAACP*; Minutes of the Meetings of the Board of Directors, June 8, 1953, Reel 3, *NAACP/LC*.
152. "Max Yergan Replies to Walter White," n.d., Part 14, Reel 5, *NAACP-Intl*.
153. Walter White to W. O. [Bill] Walker, September 17, 1953, Box 675, File "Max Yergan, 1941–53," *Papers of the NAACP*; Channing Tobias to Claude Barnett, August 18, 1953, ibid.; Martin Fann, Letter to the Editor, Reader Calls Max Yergan "Uncle Tom," n.d., Part 2, Reel 6, *CRC*; Claude Barnett to Channing Tobias, August 10, 1953, Box 675, File "Max Yergan, 1941–53," *Papers of the NAACP*; "Max Yergan Back From Africa—Mum," n.d., Part 2, Reel 6, *CRC*; SAC, New York, memo, March 14, 1955, *FBI File on Max Yergan*; SAC, New York to Director, memo, June 12, 1957, ibid.
154. Emmett Walker, Letter to the Editor: "A Dissertation About Views of Max Yergan," *Pittsburgh Courier*, October 31, 1953, Box 675, File "Max Yergan, 1941–53," *Papers of the NAACP*.
155. W. O. Walker, "Down the Big Road," *Cleveland Call Post*, August 29, 1953, found in ibid.
156. Ibid.
157. Walter White, Letter to the Editor: Opposition to Byrnes Stated, *New York Times*, August 10, 1953, found in Box 675, File "Max Yergan, 1941–53," *Papers of the NAACP*.

wrapping the denunciation of Yergan (and Byrnes for that matter) in anti-Communist rhetoric, White had placed the weight of his objections to these men on either their association with the Soviets or how the Soviets would react. Yet, where was the impact that these men have had and would have on the struggle for black equality in that objection? Howard recognized what was at stake, and although he did not condone it, he even understood the rationale behind the red-baiting. After all, he told White, it was "perfectly obvious that Max Yergan, speaking for some higher power than himself, is trying to catalog you as a 'fellow traveler' and the NAACP as 'subversive.'" It was also apparent, Howard noted sympathetically, that "leaders of Negro mass organizations... have had to so conduct themselves that they would save their organizations from being placed on the subversive list, and I take it that many of the stands you have taken have been in light of this thinking." However, he continued, "I have always thought that the leaders of the NAACP would one day regret making war on the Communists a major activity," because it "shackled" the organization to an anti-Communist rhetoric and rationale that twisted the NAACP's focus. "For example," Howard noted, "you take the position that the great tragedy of an experience like Cicero, Illinois is that it is grist to the mill for Russia." Not so. "The point is not Russia, the tragedy of Cicero is the Negro people" and their inability to live in peace in some place other than a teeming, dilapidated, over-priced slum. Similarly, "the reason for opposing Byrnes is not what Russia thinks about it – but what the Negro people of the United States think about it and what a tragedy it is to the Negro people of the United States and colored peoples everywhere to have a man like Byrnes deciding the fate of the black people of South Africa, or any other question for that matter." In other words, "Walter," the major "criterion of judgment on any issue is whether or not it *advances the rights of colored people*. When this criterion... is subordinated to, or replaced by, any other criterion, such as how anti-Communist or anti-Russia an individual or policy is," the civil rights leadership and the struggle itself is compromised.[158] White was taken aback by the criticism, but, to his credit, did not dismiss it out of hand. Instead, he decided to rethink his strategy and tone down his public red-baiting brawl with Yergan.[159]

While the NAACP was engulfed in charges and countercharges about the Association's loyalty to the United States and about its focused commitment to the struggle for black equality, Byrnes' nomination rolled through Washington. Eisenhower, of course, had no intention of

158. Charles P. Howard to Walter White, August 27, 1953, ibid. (Emphasis in original.)
159. Walter White to Channing H. Tobias, September 30, 1953, ibid.

abandoning his "great friend" Byrnes, certainly not for the likes of the NAACP and organized labor. As the *Afro-American* noted, the "White House... turned a deaf ear to the protests probably because many of them came from organizations and individuals who did not support Mr. Eisenhower in his campaign for the presidency last year."[160] The Senate, meanwhile, quietly, without hearings, confirmed the entire slate of UN delegates. Officially, the rationale for not "holding extended hearings" was that "so little time remained before the anticipated adjournment" and that there was no need because, "the group as a whole was a good one." One senator explained that it was not that his colleagues were not fully aware of Byrnes' views regarding equality, civil rights, and segregation, it was just that "it was the consensus opinion that these views would not militate against his value and experience" at the UN.[161] A disappointed Clarence Mitchell complained to an NAACP branch president that "the fact that he was confirmed illustrates the many cross currents that operate against civil rights. I am sorry to say that many of the stalwarts who should have been opposed to Byrnes felt that their opposition would help the Communists in the war of ideas. For this reason, they privately expressed themselves as disgusted with the Byrnes appointment, but publicly did nothing about it."[162] To balance the scale, the NAACP's supporters in the Senate hoped that the approval of black Republican and Chicago Alderman, Reverend Archibald Carey, Jr., to the delegation would eventually soften the blow and counteract the white supremacist message that Byrnes' confirmation suggested. Initially, it did not. But then Carey had a surprise for everyone.

At the fall UN meeting, the General Assembly had proposed a resolution urging all nations that had not yet ratified the Genocide Convention to "accelerate their ratification" and "to take measures designed to create publicity in favor of such ratification." Of course, given the pending vote on the Bricker Amendment and what the Genocide Convention meant to the Southern Democrats, Carey's instructions from the State Department were clear. Abstain. He refused. Carey informed U.S. Ambassador to the UN Henry Cabot Lodge in no uncertain terms that he was going to vote "'yes.'" Lodge was stunned and complained to Dulles that "Carey was becoming difficult." Lodge had tried to persuade Carey to take the "easiest way out" and "drop the item." Once again, Carey refused. The

160. "Ignoring Minorities' Protest: Senate Confirms Byrnes as new Delegate to UN," *Afro-American*, August 4, 1953, found in Box H18, File "James Byrnes (South Carolina)," *NAACP-Washington Bureau*.

161. Guy Gillette to Walter White, August 1, 1953, Box 162, File "James F. Byrnes Appointment to UN: Branch Protest, 1953–54," *Papers of the NAACP*; Homer Ferguson to Walter White, August 3, 1953, ibid.

162. Clarence Mitchell to Lionel O. Lindsay, August 7, 1953, ibid.

most that he would agree to was to not make a speech in the UN about the importance of outlawing genocide. But, nevertheless, he was going to vote yes. Reverend Carey explained that, as a member of the U.S. delegation, he understood his instructions perfectly. But as a black man from Chicago, he could face neither his conscience nor his community "if he didn't vote on" the genocide resolution. After that piece of not-so-good news, Lodge then dropped the second bombshell on Dulles. What had made the situation even more untenable for the beleaguered ambassador, he explained, was that Durward Sandifer, the State Department's director for UN Affairs, had "sided with Carey." Unbelievably, Lodge railed, Sandifer had also assigned Carey to oversee the other human rights issues during this session. Dulles exploded. He was convinced "that it was probably deliberate [because] no one could be so stupid as to put a colored man on two such explosive items." Sandifer would get his, of that Lodge and Dulles would make sure. Shortly after the meeting, in fact, Dulles took "a personal interest in the case of Durward Sandifer and . . . directed the Office of Personnel to find an assignment for him at a Foreign Service post."[163] Within a month, Sandifer was banished to Argentina.[164] In the meantime, however, Lodge and Dulles had a problem. How could the official U.S. representative vote "yes" on a resolution encouraging nations to ratify the Genocide Convention when Dulles and Eisenhower had made a solemn vow to the Senate that the administration had abandoned all human rights treaties? Carey had "got them into a terrible situation," and they were "on the spot."[165]

After much ranting, phone calls, and policy swings, Dulles ordered Lodge to "'absorb' this 'problem'" and explain away the impending and inexplicable "yes" vote. Lodge angrily but reluctantly obeyed. As Rowland Brucken described, "[d]espite Lodge's extraordinary efforts to delay a vote by trying to cancel the Sixth Committee's meeting, the body

163. Telephone Conversation with Ambassador Lodge, October 7, 1953, Box 5, File "John Foster Dulles Chronological October 1953 [telephone conversations]," Chronological Series, *Dulles Papers*; George F. Wilson to Charles F. Willis, Jr., memo, February 5, 1954, Box 2, File "Kotschnig, Walter M.," Name Series, *Eisenhower:WHCF*.

164. *Sandifer*.

165. Dulles to Lodge, telegram, October 8, 1953, Box 5, File "John Foster Dulles Chronological October 1953," Chronological Series, *Dulles Papers*; Telephone Conversation with Ambassador Lodge, October 7, 1953, Box 5, File "John Foster Dulles Chronological October 1953 [telephone conversations]," Chronological Series, ibid.; Telephone Conversation with David Wainhouse from NYC, October 8, 1953, ibid.; Report of the Sixth Committee, "Appeal to States to Accelerate Their Ratification of, or Accessions to, the Convention on the Prevention and Punishment of the Crime of Genocide," October 13, 1953, A/2507, found in Box 7, File "UN Matters 1953–54," Subject Series, ibid.; Telephone Conversation with Ambassador Lodge, October 21, 1953, Box 5, File "John Foster Dulles Chronological October 1953 [telephone conversations]," ibid.

unanimously approved the resolution on 8 October with Carey voting as part of the majority. After the General Assembly passed the resolution on 3 November, again with American support, Lodge had to issue an awkward press release."[166] The meandering, conflicting statement said that the vote merely reflected America's revulsion at the crime of genocide but nothing more than that. It certainly did not commit the United States to any timetable for ratification. Nor, for that matter, did it commit the United States to ratification at all. And, for that reason, the United States would look askance at any attempt by the UN or the secretary general to influence Senate deliberations, generate propaganda supporting the Convention, or any other activities that did not respect the U.S.'s determination that there were "other and better ways to achieve the desired ends."[167] After hearing this "curioser and curioser" speech, Senator Herbert Lehman (D-NY) mocked the Eisenhower administration for botching something as simple as taking a stand against the crime of genocide. The senator pounded Lodge's statement as "a distressing concession to the backward-looking elements in the Congress and to the hysterical elements outside the Congress."[168]

Those "backward-looking elements in the Congress," however, were gearing up to vote on the Bricker Amendment and at that moment, Eisenhower's human rights policies, which were created to deflect Bricker's attack, were in shambles. Thus, by the start of the new year, the Bricker forces were very confident that they would prevail. So far, there had been no defections from their camp, which meant that they still had enough votes in the Senate to pass the amendment. They were further emboldened by the fact that Eisenhower had remained publicly mute on the issue and sent his emissaries, including Attorney General Herbert Brownell and Dulles, to find some compromise that would leave his presidency intact. The most objectionable component for Eisenhower was, of course, the "which clause." He wanted it gone. After intense negotiations in early January 1954, Bricker finally agreed to jettison the "which clause" as long as certain executive agreements would still come under the purview

166. Brucken, "A Most Uncertain Crusade," 318.

167. Telephone Conversation with David Wainhouse from NYC, October 8, 1953, Box 5, File "John Foster Dulles Chronological October 1953 [telephone conversations]," Chronological Series, *Dulles Papers*; Draft on Government's position on the Genocide Convention, November 9, 1953, Box 70, File "Re: Genocide Convention, 1953," *JFD-Princeton;* Mary Alice Baldinger to Organizations Associated through the National Civil Liberties Clearing House, November 11, 1953, Box 636, File "United Nations: Genocide, 1952–53," *Papers of the NAACP*.

168. Senator Lehman Shocked at Ambassador Lodge's Genocide Statement, press release, November 4, 1953, ibid.

of the Senate and the Bricker Amendment. Eisenhower breathed a sigh of relief and believed that he had now avoided a public cat fight among the Republican leaders and still provided the senator with enough substance to claim a victory. Yet, when Bricker informed Holman about the deal, the former ABA president exploded and before Eisenhower knew what hit him, "Bricker repudiated the compromise the very next day" and reinserted the "which clause" into the amendment.[169]

That repudiation was like a declaration of war. "At long last, and none too soon," one columnist wrote, "the counteroffensive against the Bricker Amendment has begun on all fronts." Eisenhower took the safety off his trigger and "let go a heavy-caliber salvo against it."[170] Just like the well-known battle at Little Rock in 1957, what the president could not and would not tolerate was a challenge to federal/presidential authority and a public official reneging on a deal with the White House. Even though he knew that he would antagonize the Southern Democrats and GOP stalwarts, Eisenhower decided to mobilize his forces to bring the press, public opinion, and key senators around to his way of thinking. In other words, when Eisenhower wanted to lead, he could. The president made it clear to the Republican Senate leadership that he was "unalterably opposed" to the Bricker Amendment, in any form. He declared that if this amendment passed, it would "shackle the Federal Government so that it is no longer sovereign in foreign affairs."[171] It would, he asserted, throw the United States back to the "agonizing experiences in the days of the [Articles of] Confederation" when "each of the states simply passed their own laws[,] . . . ignored treaties" and made "our nation . . . a laughing stock in the world."[172] Eisenhower expressed particular concerns that if "each state had a right to repudiate treaties," it would "saddle" him and Dulles "with the impossible task of representing 48 governments."[173]

Eisenhower's long-delayed counteroffensive started to turn the tide of battle. One by one, Bricker's supporters began to defect. Bricker opponents, girded by the president's willingness to take on the Senate Republicans, demanded to see the constitutional vampires that were giving Bricker adherents "difficulty in sleeping at night." They "questioned

169. Tananbaum, *The Bricker Amendment*, 133–38; Ambrose, *Eisenhower*, 68–69.

170. Edward A. Conway, "'Darling Daughter' Amendment," *America*, January 23, 1954, found in Folder 4772, *Hennings Papers*.

171. Eisenhower to Senator William F. Knowland, January 25, 1954, Box 5, File "DDE Diary January 1954 (1)," Diary Series, *Eisenhower:AWF*.

172. Eisenhower to Earl Schaefer, January 22, 1954, ibid.

173. Notes on the Bricker Amendment from Donovan's book, *Eisenhower, The Inside Story*, Box 7, File "Bricker Amendment—Draft Talk (1)," Administration Series, ibid.

rather sharply" the likelihood that any public official would "turn . . . the Constitution over to lunatics."[174] They "point[ed] out the . . . sheer absurdity of the arguments made by Senator Bricker and his supporters during the debate."[175] They mocked Bricker's forces as being "shrouded in the fog of isolationist schemes" and creating a "judicial monster" out of harmless court decisions. And they scolded the Bricker proponents for proposing "fatal medicine for a hypothetical disease."[176] If the issue was a lack of faith in the president, they chided, tampering with the Constitution was not the way to deal with it. "A vote of no confidence in our Chief Executive is a matter to be decided at the polls every four years; it is not a matter which should be resolved by rewriting the Constitution." The tongue lashing and incisive rebuttals were finally having some effect. Sponsors began to fall by the wayside and one version of the Bricker amendment after the next failed to receive the requisite number of votes. As proposal after proposal flooded the chambers, the opponents derided the "thoroughly confused" attempt to "rewrite the Constitution on the Floor of the Senate." This whole affair, Senator Hennings asserted, simply "does violence to good sense." It was, he contended, highly irresponsible to make "drastic constitutional changes" when no substantial opportunity had been given to examine closely the wording and implications of each of the "so-called perfecting amendments." Because of the parliamentary confusion over exactly what version of the amendment the Senate was voting on, and because clauses were added, removed, and changed on the floor without much scrutiny, columnist Walter Lippman denounced all of the substitute proposals as being "'unwashed, unpeeled, uncooked, and not yet fit to be eaten by the Senate of the United States.'"[177]

Into the breach, however, stepped Senator Walter George, who, as everyone knew, was one of the "key people" in Congress. George, for a

174. Congress, Senate, Senator Fulbright of Arkansas against the Amendment to the Constitution Relating to Treaties and Executive Agreements, S. J. Res. 1, 83rd Congress, 2nd sess., *Congressional Record* (February 1, 1954), Vol. 100, Pt. 1, 1074; Congress, Senate, Senator Stennis of Mississippi recapping the debates on the Amendment to the Constitution Relating to the Treaties and Executive Agreements, S. J. Res. 1, 83rd Congress, 2nd sess., *Congressional Record* (February 1, 1954), Vol. 100, Pt. 1, 1073.

175. "Address by U.S. Senator Thomas C. Hennings, Jr., Before the Missouri State Rural Electrification Association at Jefferson City, Missouri," February 25, 1954, Folder 4767, *Hennings Papers*.

176. "Statement by U.S. Senator Thomas C. Hennings, Jr., (D-MO.) On Senate Floor in Opposition to Substitute Proposals of Bricker Amendment," February 11, 1954, Folder 4766, ibid.

177. Quoted in, ibid.

variety of reasons, "commanded attention and got respect from members of the Senate."[178] That influence combined with his Southern Democrat values portended disaster. George made no secret of the fact that he was greatly concerned that the UN's human rights treaties "might affect the Colored question."[179] He was particularly concerned that the Genocide Convention "would bring within the area of Congressional power anti-lynching legislation." Issues of lynching, in the senator's opinion, were appropriately handled by the states. As a result, George wanted the Bricker Amendment to succeed at all costs. He, therefore, introduced his own substitute proposal and, with his cachet and clout, immediately breathed new life into the amendment's sagging chances.[180]

As historian Duane Tananbaum noted, this was the "showdown." The moment of truth. Hennings knew it, too. He had "no fear that the Senate [would] adopt the extreme proposal in any of its variations urged by the Senior Senator from Ohio," but he was afraid that the "brilliance and prestige of the great Senator from Georgia" would be more than enough to persuade his "colleagues [to] adopt" the amended resolution. Therefore, although he "was genuinely reluctant to take issue with the venerable 'master' of Senatorial eloquence," Hennings openly challenged George's constitutional assumptions and systematically dismantled the Georgian's interpretations of the court decisions that supposedly allowed the UN and the president to wreak havoc on the Bill of Rights. The Missouri senator also belittled the attempt to find some compromise amendment just so Bricker could "save face." A constitutional amendment, he insisted, was not a consolation prize for disgruntled lawmakers who did not want to walk away from a legislative session empty-handed. The Senate, he scolded, needed to treat the Constitution with just a little bit more respect than that. After the intense debates, the voting began. "As the clerk began calling the roll that evening for the final vote . . . , the outcome remained uncertain." At one point, it "looked bleak," especially after several Eisenhower Republicans jumped ship and "voted with Bricker and George." But then, several Democrats, who had previously supported the amendment, swung to other side. Back and forth it went until "as the vote

178. Francis O. Wilcox, Chief of Staff, Senate Foreign Relations Committee, 1947–55, Oral History, Interview #3, Congress and the Cold War, March 21, 1984, http://www.senate.gov/learning/learn_history_oralhist_wilcox3.html, 133, 148–49. Accessed July 15, 2001 (hereafter *Wilcox Oral History*).

179. Ralph E. Becker to Thomas Hennings, Jr., memo, January 22, 1954, Folder 4772, *Hennings Papers*.

180. Mr. Phleger to Dulles, memo, March 30, 1953, Box 70, File "Re: Genocide Convention, 1953," *JFD-Princeton*.

was ending, 60 senators had voted for the amendment and only 30 had voted against it." Bricker had his two-thirds! But then out of the blue, or more accurately, out of the tavern, "staggered into the Senate chamber" Harley Kilgore, "a liberal Democrat from West Virginia." The drunken lawmaker was "propped up by various aides and colleagues," and when the clerk "asked for the senator's vote . . . a 'nay' was heard—whether from Kilgore or one of the others is uncertain." What was certain, however, was that the George resolution had just gone down to defeat—by one drunken vote.[181] Although ghostly variations of the amendment would continue to haunt the Senate chambers for years, the real threat of the Bricker Amendment had finally passed.[182]

Although Eisenhower clearly felt vindicated, it was a pyrrhic victory for African Americans. The fact that the president chose to confront the Bricker forces only at the very last minute and instead, attempted, at least initially, to appease the right wing by auctioning off the human rights treaties, cost African Americans dearly. The administration's sacrifice of the Covenants and Genocide Convention, the loss of real American involvement in the development of international human rights protocols, and the pervasive notion that there was something un-American and foreign, if not totally communistic, about human rights converged to severely constrict the agenda for real black equality.

As the NAACP well knew, because of the tendency to "link the advocacy of full equality for Negroes . . . to subversion or 'un-Americanism,'" it was difficult enough to fight for civil rights. Of course, in the battle for civil rights, the NAACP could at least run for cover, as it often did, behind the shield of the Constitution. The Association leadership consistently asserted that the NAACP, "based upon the Constitution, the Bill of Rights, and orderly court procedure," was "perfecting democracy through [the] United States Supreme Court," "through democratic means, and within

181. "Statement by U.S. Senator Thomas C. Hennings, Jr. (D-MO.) On Senate Floor in Opposition to Substitute Proposals of Bricker Amendment," February 15, 1954, Folder 4767, *Hennings Papers*; Thomas Hennings, Jr., to Dick [Rep. Richard Bollings], March 3, 1954, Folder 2964, ibid.; "Statement by U.S. Senator Thomas C. Hennings, Jr. (D-MO.) On Senate Floor in Opposition to Substitute Proposals of Bricker Amendment," February 11, 1954, Folder 4766, ibid.; Senator Thomas C. Hennings, Jr., "Separation of Powers, Anent Bricker Amendment," [draft], for *Virginia Law Weekly Series*, n.d., Folder 4768, ibid.; "Statement by Senator Thos. C. Hennings, Jr. (D-MO.) On Senate Floor in Opposition to Bricker Amendment," February 3, 1954, Folder 4766, ibid.; Thomas Hennings, Jr. to Bill [William P. Gruner], February 19, 1954, Folder 2964, ibid.; Amendment to Constitution Relative to Treaties and Executive Agreements, roll call votes, *Journal of the Senate of the United States of America*, 83rd Congress, 2nd sess., 159; Tananbaum, *The Bricker Amendment*, 179–80.

182. Ibid., 191–215.

the American system of government."[183] In an article entitled "Stalin's Greatest Defeat," Roy Wilkins declared that the Communists had never been able to recruit African Americans, because "[t]hey had sadly misjudged the Negro, his aims, aspirations, and loyalties. They thought he wanted mere social recognition, when, in truth, he wanted solid, first-class American citizenship, including jobs, education, and the privileges and responsibilities inherent in the Constitution and the Bill of Rights."[184] As American as the NAACP proclaimed to be, the Association still ran afoul of the anti-Communist witch hunts. NAACP members had great difficulty getting through loyalty hearings. Walter White's book, *Rising Wind*, had been pulled from the shelves of the overseas USIS (United States Information Service) libraries by McCarthy's henchmen and Rayford Logan's *What the Negro Wants* suffered a similar fate.[185]

Thus, on a battlefield where loyalty to America was the ultimate armor, the supposedly un-American human rights treaties could offer no protection at all. As the clash over the Bricker Amendment made clear, the UN's human rights initiatives – maligned, characterized, and portrayed by even the administration as "alien" – provided zero sanctuary against forces that were powerful enough to come within a whiskey-soaked breath of rewriting the Constitution and emasculating the presidency of a World War II hero. Roscoe Dunjee of the *Oklahoma Black Dispatch* observed that the Bricker Amendment exposed just how far the South was ready to go to make sure that the UN's treaties would never cross the Mason-Dixon line. Dunjee declared that, "Never before have we had an opportunity to see so clearly what conformity to narrow sectional sanctions will do to halt progress and advancement." But, there it was. To "preserve... peonage, illiteracy, ill health and half dozen other appendages to second class citizenship in Dixie, the South would amend the constitution and stop the clock of human advancement."[186] The closeness of the vote, however, showed that the South was not alone.

The Amendment's defeat, to be clear, was not about a triumph for human rights, it was about the hard core protection of presidential power.

183. Roy Wilkins to A. T. Whayne, October 25, 1955, Box 202, File "Communism: General, 1955," *Papers of the NAACP*; Walter White to Eleanor Roosevelt, May 26, 1952, Box 3338, File "NAACP, 1952," *Roosevelt Papers*; Channing H. Tobias to Whom It May Concern, February 5, 1954, Reel 3, *Bunche*.
184. Roy Wilkins, "Stalin's Greatest Defeat," *American Magazine* December 1951, 110.
185. AMCONGEN, Calcutta (USIS) to Department of State, telegram, May 7, 1953, Box 1, File "Book Burning (1)," Subject Series, *Dulles Papers*.
186. "Background to the Bricker Amendment Exposed," *Oklahoma Black Dispatch*, February 13, 1954, found in Box 113, File "Bills: Bricker Amendment Press Releases, 1953–54," *Papers of the NAACP*.

Even the liberal Democrats who "led the opposition throughout the debate" stressed that they were "opposed [to] Bricker's resolution and all the so-called harmless substitutes," because it was an "attempt 'to paralyze the traditional powers of the Presidency in our foreign relations.'"[187] Thus, although the Bricker Amendment was defeated, the xenophobic, racist, and anti-liberal sentiment that fostered it, was not repudiated. Most telling was that the defeat of the Bricker Amendment did not result in the United States rejoining the world's efforts to develop the Covenants on Human Rights or to even ratify the Genocide Convention. Instead, the United States continued to cling to the Action Program, which, much to the administration's distress, was given "only 40 minutes" of discussion "out of $7^1/_2$ weeks of substantive debate" at the Spring 1954 UN meeting. And when the Soviets "ciritcized (sic) it as being disguised to block completion of the Covenants," that only reinforced the widespread belief that internationally defined human rights were anti-American, pro-Soviet, and, therefore, communistic.[188]

That is why as difficult as the civil rights struggle was, the struggle for human rights was even more perilous. An NAACP report noted, for example, that "advocates of low-cost public housing were already branded as Socialists, while those advocating non-segregated housing are now being called Communists."[189] The Association's leaders, however, took comfort in believing that another portal for equality existed. Victory through the courts in the school desegregation cases, the NAACP leadership assured itself , was a panacea that would, in the words of the *Amsterdam News*, "'alleviate troubles in many other fields.'"[190] Roy Wilkins asserted that once "housing and school segregation passes, other separations will melt away and Negroes will be able to live . . . on a plane of equality and dignity."[191] Moreover, if the Bricker Amendment and the NAACP's near-death experience with *An Appeal to the World* were not enough to send the signal about how truly dangerous it was to be associated with the UN and human rights, the attack on the State Department, the United Nations, and Ralph Bunche removed all doubt.

187. Tananbaum, *The Bricker Amendment*, 185.
188. Mrs. Oswald B. Lord, *Report on the Tenth Session of the United Nations Commission on Human Rights*, April 26, 1954, Box 3493, File "United Nations," *Roosevelt Papers*.
189. "NAACP 44th Annual Conference Resolutions," June 28, 1953, Box 47, File "Annual Conventions: Resolutions Voted 1953," *Papers of the NAACP*.
190. James T. Patterson, *Brown v. Board of Education: A Civil Rights Milestone and Its Troubled Legacy*, Pivotal Moments in American History, eds. David Hackett Fischer and James M. McPherson (New York: Oxford University Press, 2001), xiv.
191. Roy Wilkins to William Gordon, August 20, 1953, attached manuscript, Box 83, File "Articles, Roy Wilkins, 1948–55," *Papers of the NAACP*.

McCarthyism hit the foreign policy bureaucracy with the ferocity, "proportions and destructiveness of a tornado."[192] The survivors were truly the walking wounded. "I have never seen the morale of the State Department people, both at home and abroad, so shattered," reported Philip Reed, a friend of Eisenhower's who had just returned from a three-week business trip in Europe. He bemoaned that "dedicated and hard working anti-communists" were resigning en masse and "dropping off the vine." Even "worse," Reed relayed, was that "there [was] a very evident hesitation on the part of responsible people in our Missions to report the true situation and the reasons for it because all official communications are thought to reach" McCarthy henchman and State Department security chief Scott "McLeod or his people."[193] Francis O. Wilcox, chief of staff, for the Senate Foreign Relations Committee, similarly recalled that it "was a terrible period when all kinds of improper things were done in the State Department and on Capitol Hill, when few people had the courage to stand up and speak the truth." A major part of the problem was that Joseph McCarthy "was able to get into the State Department some people on the security side who were sympathetic to his position and who took a very damaging position in the Department in persecuting people who were considered a little too liberal for his way of thinking." Wilcox remembered, for example, how when he transferred over to the State Department, he was warned to watch closely "a bunch of One Worlders" on the staff of the Department's Bureau of International Organization Affairs, which, not surprisingly, was the division responsible for the UN.[194] One of those staffers, Donald Blaisdell, recalled that era as "a nasty thing." There were all kinds of allegations that the "State Department hadn't been zealous and resolute enough in checking on the credentials of *Americans* who were in the [UN] secretariat" and those insinuations made his work with the UN "just a hell of a job." It was just so "nasty," Blaisdell kept repeating. The right wing, "mostly Republicans – rode this hobby horse of theirs that the Communists were infiltrating the United States through the United Nations, and that they were using their membership in the UN to infiltrate Communists into the Secretariat of the United Nations."[195]

Thus, not only was the State Department supposedly honeycombed with Communists, but so, too, now was the UN. In an "unbridled

192. "NAACP 44th Annual Conference Resolutions," June 28, 1953, Box 47, File "Annual Conventions: Resolutions Voted 1953," ibid.
193. Philip D. Reed to Eisenhower, June 8, 1953, attached to Dulles to Philip D. Reed, July 1, 1953, Box 1, File "White House Correspondence 1953 (3)," White House Memoranda Series, *Dulles Papers*.
194. *Wilcox Oral History*, 102–04.
195. *Blaisdell*. (Emphasis in original.)

attack," Mississippi Senator James O. Eastland charged that "'the United Nations has become a nesting place for American subversives .... a hotbed of American Reds'" and that in "'the United Nations among the American employés (sic) there is the greatest concentration of Communists that this [Senate] committee has ever encountered.'"[196] One Senate committee report "declared, incredibly, that evidence had established the participation of UN officials in 'a full-scale operation of subversive activities directed against the security of this nation.'"[197] The Soviets were even accused of using the UN as an "underground railroad" to ferry Communist spies into the United States, thereby deliberately linking an icon of the African American fight for freedom with the growing Red menace.[198] The witch hunt was on and regardless of how bitterly Trygve Lie and his successor, Dag Hammarskjöld, protested, and regardless of the toll – in lives, in jobs, in reputations – there was nothing they could do to stop it.

John Foster Dulles met with Senator Alexander Wiley, chair of the Foreign Relations Committee, to discuss "at some length" the issue of "Communist inflitration (sic) in the UN." Wiley's aide "stated that of the 375 U.S. nationals on the professional staff, 50 to 75 ... were recognized by cursory FBI check as known Communists." Dulles was floored and demanded to know "who was the U.S. person chiefly responsible for channeling these subversives into the UN." Although "[t]here was no answer forthcoming to this question," there "was some discussion about Mr. Bunche."[199]

Serious rumblings against Bunche, in fact, began in the fall of 1953 when columnist Walter Winchell, "a dedicated hitman for the extreme right,"

196. "UN Won't Use 'Lynch Law' Against U.S. Reds, Lie Says," *Baltimore Sun*, October 25, 1952, found in Box 621, File "UN 'Forg. Agts' #2: Investigations, Jan. 1950–Nov. 1952," *RNC*.
197. Urquhart, *Ralph Bunche*, 247.
198. Frank Holman to John W. Bricker, March 19, 1952, Box 160, File "1," *Bricker Papers*; Glenn Green, "Spy Smuggling Traced to UN: Agents Brought Here by 'Underground [Railroad],'" August 2, 1949, *New York Times*, found in Box 621, File "UN 'Forg. Agt': Investigations, July 1948–December 1949," *RNC*; James E. Warner, "Senators Reveal New Testimony Against UN as Red Spy Center," July 31, 1949, *New York Herald Tribune*, found in ibid.; "Witness Charges Red 'Terror' in UN," July 24, 1949, *New York Times*, found in ibid.; Westbrook Pegler, "Dr. Tobias Served a Pro-Red Magazine," October 23, 1951, found in Folder 42, "United Nations 1951–1952," *Tobias Papers*; Craig Thompson, "The Sinister Doings at the UN," November 17, 1951, *Saturday Evening Post*, found in Box 621, File "UN Foreign Agents (miscl.) Investigations," *RNC*; Chesly Manly, "Mrs. Roosevelt Makes UN Move for Socialism," April 29, 1952, *Chicago Tribune* found in Box 626, File "UN Secur. Council 'Commission on Human Rt. of the Econ. & Soc. Coun.,'"ibid.
199. Memorandum of Conversation #2, November 25, 1952, Box 8, File "Memoranda of Meetings from November 1952," Subject Series, *Dulles Papers*.

published an article that implied that the Nobel Peace Prize winner would soon be "'charged as a meeting-attending commie.'"[200] Although Dulles had quipped earlier "that there was practically no negro, even Ralph Bunch, (sic) who could come through an FBI check lily white, because all of their organizations had been infiltrated," toward the end of the year, the secretary of state meant every word of it and voiced "serious reservations" about the man scheduled to become the second-highest ranking official at the United Nations.[201] Thus, by the time Bunche received the call from the White House in January 1954 that he was under investigation for multiple counts of disloyalty to the United States, he was already presumed guilty. The Loyalty Board had compiled a lengthy list of allegations and, just as Winchell had intimated, two eyewitnesses claimed that Bunche had "attended a 'meeting of the Communist Party in John P. Davis' office in May 1935 ... allegedly to ensure Communist Party control of the National Negro Congress."[202]

Although the charges all suggested disloyalty based on his affiliation with the CP, in truth, Bunche's crimes stemmed from his blackness, his elevation of the UN as a viable, important player in international affairs, and his unwillingness to bow down to Jim Crow. This explains, in part, how someone like Yergan, who was knee-deep in Communist activities, but who had rolled over and become an apologist for Jim Crow, could escape the loyalty hearings while Bunche could not. Even when it was clear that Yergan had perjured himself about the depth of his affiliation with the Communist party, he was still shielded from prosecution.[203] Unlike so many others who were persecuted and demonized during this era, however, many of Bunche's allies, especially the leadership of the NAACP, refused to abandon him. The NAACP realized that if someone like Bunche

200. Urquhart, *Ralph Bunche*, 248.

201. Telephone Conversation with Leonard Hall, May 6, 1953, Box 3, File "Chronological—John Foster Dulles May 1–31, 1953 [telephone calls]," Chronological Series, *Dulles Papers*; Telephone Conversation with Dean Rusk, November 16, 1953, Box 5, File "John Foster Dulles Chronological November 1953 (2) [telephone calls]," ibid.

202. Urquhart, *Ralph Bunche*, 249; Ralph Bunche to William R. Jenner, 16 March 1953, Reel 3, *Bunche*.

203. Boardman to Bureau, teletype, November 16, 1953, *FBI File on Max Yergan*; SA to SAC, New York, memo, December 17, 1953, ibid.; SAC, New York to Director, FBI, memo, July 15, 1954, ibid.; SAC, New York to SAC, Philadelphia, memo, May 18, 1955, ibid.; SA to SAC, New York, memo, June 27, 1955, ibid.; SA to SAC, New York, August 29, 1955, ibid.; Kelly to Bureau, airtel, January 19, 1956, ibid.; SAC, Newark from SAC, New York, memo, May 8, 1956, ibid.; Memo, August 16, 1956, ibid.; Kelly, memo, October 24, 1956, ibid.; SAC New York to Director, FBI, memo, June 12, 1957, ibid.

could be dragged through the mud on the dubious word of "professional ex-communists," no black man or woman was safe in America. Walter White, in fact, was willing to "stake whatever reputation" he had "on Dr. Bunche's unqualified loyalty and integrity."[204]

In mounting his defense, Bunche and the NAACP developed a two-pronged attack. The first element emphasized that Bunche was "a symbol of Americanism" – the ultimate embodiment of equal opportunity.[205] Bunche was, in the words of Eslande Goode Robeson, "Exhibit A in the showcase of American democracy."[206] The second element in the attack called for the complete denunciation of his accusers and their allegations. The charges, Bunche and his allies railed, were "tenuous and distorted." His accusers were "professional informers" and "renegades who profess to have known nearly everybody everywhere ... and remember what each one has said, and under what circumstances they said it, as far back as 20 years ago."[207] Although Yergan was not one of the official accusers, his claim that during the San Francisco Conference, Bunche was under his control and willing to do the CP's bidding, resurfaced with brute force. And, when two black ex-Communists, Manning Johnson and Leonard Patterson, took the stand to testify against Bunche, the Nobel prize winner's word was not enough to discredit these men. In the end, as biographer Brian Urquhart described, Bunche "soon realized that only John P. Davis ... could convincingly give the lie to the most damaging charge." Bunche and Davis, however, had not spoken since the tumultuous NNC meeting where Davis engineered the ouster of A. Philip Randolph and the coronation of Max Yergan. Since that time, however, Davis, had broken away from his former colleagues and started a whole new, quiet life. Bunche, nonetheless "was extremely reluctant to resume contact with" Davis, but with his career, reputation, and life's work dangling by a thread, he had run out of options. As much as he wanted help, though, during their conversation, "Bunche pointed out that the revelation of Davis'

204. Walter White to Pierce J. Gerety, May 28, 1954, Box 161, File "Ralph Bunche: General, 1950–55," *Papers of the NAACP*; Urquhart, *Ralph Bunche*, 249; "NAACP Hails Bunche as Symbol of Americanism," press release, May 27, 1954, Box 161, File "Ralph Bunche: General, 1950–55, "*Papers of the NAACP*.

205. Ibid.

206. Eslande Goode Robeson, "The Ralph Bunche-United Nations-Loyalty Board Story: Exhibit A was in Danger," May 28, 1954, Reel 3, *Bunche*.

207. [Reply to Loyalty Allegations begins "YES 1. Commonwealth College: ...]," n.d., Reel 1, ibid.; Eslanda Robeson, "Ralph Bunche and the United Nations: Second Thoughts," *Freedom* June 1954, Reel 3, ibid.; Article to *Chicago Defender* and *New York Age*, attached to Walter White to Ralph Bunche, June 14, 1954, ibid.; Henry S. Villard to Ralph Bunche, January 28, 1954, ibid.

membership in the Communist Party in the 1930s might" prove damaging if it came out. Nonetheless, "Davis insisted on taking the stand. Appearing on the last day of the hearings, he testified under oath that Bunche had never attended any such meeting as alleged" and that he "had taken the risk... of testifying and thus revealing his communist past because he believed Bunche was innocent of the charges against him."[208] With that, the Loyalty Board finally cleared Bunche of all charges. It is indicative of the times that despite his accusers' questionable credibility, his professions of innocence, and his allies' unstinting support, in the final analysis, it took an ex-Communist and sworn enemy to rescue him. In this "Kafkaesque" world, Walter White could only wonder "how much of the attack on Dr. Bunche was motivated by isolationist attacks on the United Nation [sic]... and a determination to destroy or at least weaken all those who speak out on the issue of human and civil rights."[209]

Yet, although Bunche had escaped the gallows, there would be no stay of execution for either the Council on African Affairs or the CRC. Not surprisingly, Max Yergan was instrumental in destroying both of those organizations. He told the FBI that he was "glad to be of service." He volunteered that he was "in possession of considerable information concerning communist control and domination of... the Civil Rights Congress, [the] National Negro Congress, [and the] Council on African Affairs and that... it [was] his intention to expose them at every opportunity."[210] He then "'advised'" the FBI that "'Paul Robeson, Doxie Wilkerson, and Alphaeus Hunton, were the guiding body of the Communist dominated group within the Council on African Affairs.'"[211] He also claimed that Hunton and Robeson met repeatedly with the CP leadership and members of the Soviet Consulate in New York to determine how best to funnel money into the anti-apartheid movement in South Africa. He further offered that, under direct Soviet guidance and supervision, Hunton prepared reports "regarding the treatment of the Negro both in the U.S. and Africa," which were then used by "the Russian delegation at the United Nations... to attack British and American imperialism and discrimination against Negroes." This collaboration was no one-time occurrence, Yergan made clear. Hunton "appeared to be on close terms with

208. Urquhart, *Ralph Bunche*, 253–54.

209. Ibid., 249; Article to *Chicago Defender* and *New York Age*, attached to Walter White to Ralph Bunche, June 14, 1954, Reel 3, *Bunche*.

210. "Interview of Max Yergan," memo, November 5, 1948, *FBI File on Max Yergan*; Boardman to Bureau, teletype, November 6, 1953, ibid.; Scheidt to Bureau, December 1, 1948, ibid.

211. Edward Scheidt to Director, FBI, memo, September 15, 1948, ibid.

Vice-Consul . . . Fedosimov." He had also "established contact" with a number of Communists in the UN, several of whom "always came to see Hunton and . . . there [was] a man . . . who was always calling Hunton from the UN."[212] Yergan, in short, had provided all of the materials needed to construct the perfect hangman's noose.

Thus, when the attorney general's office demanded that the Council register under the McCarran Act as a Communist-front organization and appear before the Subversive Activities Control Board (SACB), the charges read like a verbatim transcript from Yergan's interviews with the FBI. This is despite the fact that, early in the investigation, Yergan's credibility had come under serious fire when it became clear that he had tried to extort money from a former lover unless she paid him several thousand dollars to return the "indiscreet" letters that she had written. Although the blackmail letter was supposedly anonymous, and Yergan categorically denied any involvement, his distinctive handwriting was immediately identified by the forensics experts in the Post Office Department. The former lover, who had paid the "hard-up for money" Yergan thousands of dollars already, refused to pay anymore and demanded that he be prosecuted. The FBI, however, immediately intervened and explained to the Post Office investigators and to the assistant United States attorney in New York that, although there was incontrovertible proof that Yergan was the extortionist, he was also a key witness in several cases regarding the Communist party and, therefore, it was important "to stall on any action against Yergan until it became more clear as to whether" he would be called to testify.[213] While the FBI protected Yergan, a man who had blatantly lied to federal agents about his involvement in a blackmail plot, the American government threw everything that it had at the CAA.

The U.S. attorney general charged that the CAA had to register under the McCarran Act, because "[t]hroughout its existence, the Council has been and is substantially directed, dominated and controlled by the Communist Party." That control included an interlocking directorate that allowed the Council to "receive support, financial and otherwise, from and at the direction of the Communist Party." One of the key activities that the CP financed, according to the indictment, was for "the Council . . . to create and further hostility among the negroes in this country to the United States for the purpose of rendering this segment of the

212. SAC, New York, memo, March 14, 1955, ibid.; "Interview of Max Yergan," memo, March 5, 1948, ibid.; Scheidt teletype message, August 23, 1948, ibid.

213. A. H. Belmont, memo, December 2, 1948, ibid.; A. H. Belmont, memo, December 3, 1948, ibid.; A. H. Belmont, memo, December 3, 1948 (a different memo on the same day), ibid.; A. H. Belmont, January 10, 1949, ibid.; SA, memo, February 27, 1950, ibid.

population susceptible to Communist indoctrination." Not content to foment discord at home, "representatives of the Council have met with, and given assistance to, representatives of the Soviet Union to further the positions of representatives of the Soviet Union with respect to matters relating to Negroes and to the African colonies."[214]

The Council, of course, tried to defend itself.[215] Yet, despite all of its bravado, the Council did not have much to fight back with. The CAA was in major financial trouble. In a desperate fund-raising appeal, Hunton wrote, "We are confronted with the necessity of raising at once a minimum of $2,000 for immediate legal and other expenses incidental to the conduct of our case before the SACB."[216] Within a year's time, contributions to the CAA had declined by 62 percent, and overall net income fell by 46 percent. By early January 1954, the Council could not meet its rental payments and was "unable financially . . . to reestablish the Council in new quarters," and therefore had to put its library in storage and "share office space" with another organization. The February meeting of the Executive Committee was like a scene out of Thomas Mann's "Death in Venice," with beautiful, sweet, sickening despair everywhere. Hunton's report "made clear the financial handicaps" under which the Council was trying to operate and Robeson acknowledged that the organization was trying to accomplish its work "under extreme difficulties." But, even as Robeson vowed "not to retreat 'a single inch,'" membership and resources were steadily ebbing away. The Council leadership, nevertheless, unrealistically projected a 210 percent increase in revenue and the hiring of "a second executive staff officer" based on "an enlarged program of work."[217]

How this "enlarged program" was actually going to be achieved (i.e., who was going to do the work, and how it was going to be financed)

214. "In the Subversive Activities Control Board: Herbert Brownell Jr., Attorney General of the United States, *Petitioner v. Council on African Affairs, Inc.* Respondent, April 20, 1953," Reel 69, *Du Bois*.

215. Statement issued by Paul Robeson on behalf of the Council on African Affairs, concerning the Justice Department's order for that organization to register under the McCarran Act, press release, April 24, 1953, ibid.; "Prosecution Threatened for Aid to Africans," *Spotlight on Africa*, October 16, 1954, found in Reel 70, ibid.; [Draft of Response to Charges:] handwritten document begins "The C is a non-partisan, non-profit org. devoted to objective . . . " n.d., Reel 1, *Hunton*; "Here Are the Facts . . . You be the Judge!: The Council on African Affairs Answers Attorney General Brownell," October 23, 1953, Reel 69, *Du Bois*.

216. Du Bois to Mr. X, draft, June 18, 1953, ibid.

217. W. A. Hunton to Du Bois, January 14, 1954, Reel 70, ibid.; Council on African Affairs, *Summary of Income and Disbursements for 1952 and 1953 and Budget for 10 Months, March–December 1954*, ibid.; Minutes of the Meeting of the Executive Committee and Invited Guests, February 17, 1954, ibid.

was never practically determined. Robeson was under enormous pressure from the government as his passport had been seized, thus cutting off his access to income from overseas concerts. He was virtually banned from major concert venues in the United States, and smaller halls were even reluctant to book his shows.[218] There clearly was no money to be had there. And, in terms of staffing, Hunton's wife recalled that "[f]ew volunteers were available for the many pressing office tasks, and Alphaeus found himself practically a one-man organization, persevering under the most trying conditions and working late into the night without pay."[219]

Sensing an organization in the middle of its death throes, the United States tightened its grip. The attorney general and the SACB were already applying pressure. In April 1954, the IRS came after the Council with one of its unrelenting audits and demands for records. Then, the U.S. District Court in Washington, D.C., issued a subpoena demanding that the Council bring all correspondence and communication between the CAA and the African National Congress, the South African Indian Congress, all individuals outside the United States affiliated with a foreign government, all foreign political parties, all organizations located in a foreign country, all political parties in general, all financial records, and "all materials published and/or disseminated by the Council on African Affairs" from January 1, 1946 to the present. Despite this overwhelming demand, the Court essentially gave the Council one week to pull all of those materials together – in an age with no Xerox machines – or be held in contempt. A few months later, a New York legislative committee subpoenaed the Council's financial records. Then the IRS came back and went after Robeson directly, charging that he owed $10,000 in back taxes. Thus, when the SACB issued a hearing notice for July 1955, Hunton and the Council had already sustained too many punishing body blows in the earlier rounds to come out of the corner again.[220]

On June 14, 1955, the Council held it last meeting. Hunton argued that "the Council was no longer needed to stimulate American interest in Africa as in the earlier period of its work and it should accordingly be dissolved." Hunton further noted, more accurately and more to the point, that "continuing Government harassment of the organization made it difficult if not impossible for it to function." The "various investigations" had sapped the "organization's finances," and the hearing of the SACB

218. Duberman, *Robeson*, 381–428.

219. Dorothy Hunton, "The Unsung Valiant: Biography of W. A. Hunton," draft manuscript, Reel 3, *Hunton*.

220. W. Alphaeus Hunton, "Review of Work of Council: Refer to *Here are the Facts*," handwritten notes, Reel 1, ibid.; United States District Court subpoena, September 27, 1954, ibid.

"scheduled to start July 11" would put an "intolerable strain" on the CAA. Robeson and the other members, although expressing their regrets, "voiced their general endorsement of [Hunton's] views and agreed that the Council should be dissolved."[221] The "extended funeral rites of so worthy an organization" included the important business of submitting a motion to the SACB to stop all proceedings against the Council because the CAA "has ceased to exist." Motion granted.[222]

The CRC was also dealt a death sentence. Its trip through the anti-Communist gauntlet, however, was intensified because of the organization's financial support to the CP leadership. As Frederick Vanderbilt Field, a trustee for the CRC bail fund, recalled, when four convicted members of the Communist party jumped bail, "all hell broke loose."[223] "We are facing a period of trial compared to which the attacks of the past will seem Lilliputian," Patterson prophesied in 1952. Federal and state authorities prosecuted, subpoenaed, imprisoned, harassed, infiltrated, and tormented the CRC at will. The organization was hit with a $75,000 bill for back taxes. With that enormous lien weighing on the CRC like an incubus, there "was no money" to mount a planned mobilization effectively. There was no money to even pay the attorneys who then threatened to "drop the case" unless they were paid within five days. The National Office held a series of meetings to determine how to "substantially reduc[e] ... expenses," including "cut[ting] the staff, ... cut[ting] salaries," and combining several office functions with the New York branch of the CRC. Nothing worked. By spring 1954, Patterson issued an urgent plea to the CRC branches for money. "The entire work of the national office ... is in danger of being stopped by forces who are prepared to use governmental powers for that purpose." Already, Patterson had been "keel-hauled by governmental inquisitions" and jailed twice for contempt because he refused to turn over a list of contributors. Patterson, of course, remained defiant. Nevertheless, the CRC had a date with destiny and had to face the "threat of the Subversive Activities Control Board."[224]

221. Minutes of the Meeting of the Executive Board, June 14, 1955, ibid.

222. Albert Maltz to W. Alphaeus Hunton, July 15, 1955, ibid.; Affidavit in Support of Motion for Leave to Intervene, June 29, 1955, ibid.; Council on African Affairs, Inc. (Docket No. 110–53), Reel 45, *Records of the Subversive Activities Control Board* (Frederick, Maryland: University Publications of America, 1988). Hereafter *SACB*.

223. Frederick Vanderbilt Field, *From Right to Left: An Autobiography* (Westport, Connecticut: Lawrence Hill & Co., 1983), 219, 223–30.

224. Abridged Report of National Organizational Secretary for meeting of National Board, July 7, 1952, Part 2, Reel 10, *CRC*; Sylvia Brown to William Patterson, February 1, 1955, Box 9, Folder 39, *Patterson Papers*; William Patterson to David O. McKay, February 2, 1955, Box 9, Folder 47, ibid.; Milton H. Friedman to William Patterson, December 7, 1956, Box 9, Folder 40, ibid.; Aubrey Grossman to William Patterson,

For a brief moment, Patterson's continuing incarceration for contempt, oddly enough, gave the CRC a reprieve. The Congress' attorney, Ralph Powe, was able to postpone the SACB hearing for several months arguing that with the organization's key executive imprisoned, there was no opportunity to mount an effective defense. Trying to defend the CRC without Patterson's help in answering the charges, Powe asserted, might "very well be . . . the death knell of the organization." Although that rationale worked initially, the third attempt to postpone the SACB hearing only provoked a sharp rebuke from the Board about a "boy crying 'Wolf,'" and a command to appear within a matter of days and answer the charge of being a Communist-front. From then on, witness after witness took the stand, asserting by innuendo and rumor, that the CRC was "a grateful and fanatic servant of the Communist Party" – a black Igor doing its Red master's evil bidding.[225]

The CRC tried to hang on. "Those who created [the CRC] envisioned stormy weather in the realm of civil rights," Patterson insisted. Therefore, McCarthyism was simply a hurricane that "a strong people's organization" like the CRC had to withstand, because the Congress, Patterson intoned, was the only "defense organization" that did not "place full dependence upon the courts." Patterson then begged the CRC membership that "all thought, talk, and most of all, those steps which lead to liquidation or suggest liquidation of the CRC must be stopped."[226]

The U.S. government, however, did not stop. Its determination to drive a stake through the heart of the CRC was unrelenting. Patterson finally recognized it, too. At the CRC's last meeting on January 6, 1956, Patterson noted that "reactionary forces in government have intensified their legal

memo, July 25, 1952, Part 2, Reel 3, *CRC*; Lib to Aubrey, July 9, 1952, ibid.; William Patterson, Milton Wolff and Aubrey Grossman to the Staff, memo, n.d., ibid.; William Patterson to Friend, March 26, 1954, Part 2, Reel 2, ibid.; Facts of the Case, n.d., Reel 69, *Du Bois*; Muriel Symington to Walter White, November 12, 1954, Box 4, Folder 6, *Patterson Papers*; "Patterson, CRC Head, Jailed," press release, July 1, 1954, Box 369, File "Leagues: Civil Rights Congress, 1952–55," *Papers of the NAACP*; United States Court of Appeals Second Circuit, United States of America, Plaintiff-Respondent, against, William L. Patterson, Defendant-Appellant: Brief for Defendant, 1954, Box 4, Folder 1, *Patterson Papers*; William Patterson, handwritten notes, begins "Czechoslovakia and Hungary—Meeting with Steins . . . " n.d., Box 6, Folder 212, ibid.; William Patterson to Anita Whitney, October 9, 1954, Box 9, Folder 46, ibid.; Memo to Patterson, Aubrey Grossman, Ralph Powe et al., July 23, 1953, Part 2, Reel 3, *CRC*.

225. Official Report of Proceedings before the Subversive Activities Control Board, Herbert Brownell, Jr., Attorney General of the United States, *Petitioner v. Civil Rights Congress*, Respondent, November 15, 1954, November 29, 1954, November 30, 1954, December 1, 1954, Reel 22, *SACB*.

226. *Report of the National Executive Secretary to the Leadership Conference of the Civil Rights Congress*, n.d., Part 2, Reel 10, *CRC*.

persecution of [the] Civil Rights Congress" and were "continuing to conduct a series of pseudo-legal assaults," ranging from federal and state grand juries, to the IRS, to New York's Banking Department, to the SACB, and the attorney general. At this point, the CRC no longer had the resources or the strength to fight back. On that winter evening, the Civil Rights Congress "dissolved."[227]

While the black Left was slowly but surely being crushed, the NAACP was savoring the sweet smell of success. The Supreme Court's landmark *Brown* decision in May 1954, which overturned *Plessy* and ruled that Jim Crow was unconstitutional, seemed to validate the Association's faith in American democracy and the court-based strategy to black equality. Walter White, less than a year before his death, proclaimed that the "fact that [the decision] was both unanimous and unequivocal is one of the most encouraging affirmations of democracy in our time."[228]

That blue sky prediction, however, quickly gave way to major storm clouds on the horizon. The decision, while unequivocal about *de jure* segregation, thoroughly equivocated on implementation and ignored any ameliorative steps to undo what more than three centuries of slavery, Jim Crow, and racism had done. Moreover, President Eisenhower steadfastly refused to lead his nation out of the land of Jim Crow and hoped, instead, that the "segregation issue" would "die out" if only the Court's implementation decision, scheduled for the next year, would "be very moderate and accord a maximum initiative to local courts."[229] Even as there were clear, distinct signs that the South would defy *Brown*, Eisenhower adamantly refused to meet with the African American leadership. Blacks, his administration paternalistically believed, ought to be "grateful" for all the progress that has happened during Eisenhower's presidency. There was no need to meet.[230]

The Northern Democrats were equally reluctant to provide that landmark decision with a solid foundation. Although Senator Lehman wanted to push for civil rights legislation in the upcoming session, Senator Hubert Humphrey, who had made the rousing human rights address at the 1948 Democratic Convention, now deemed it "'impractical'" to put civil

227. Minutes of the National Convention of Civil Rights Congress, January 6, 1956, Part 2, Reel 17, ibid.

228. Walter White to Alan, June 8, 1954, Box 1103, Folder 33, *ACLU Papers*.

229. Eisenhower to E. E. [Swede] Hazlett, Jr., October 23, 1954, Box 18, File "Hazlett, Swede 1954," Name Series, *Eisenhower:AWF*.

230. A. Philip Randolph to Roy Wilkins, August 31, 1955, Box 507, File "A. Philip Randolph, 1942–55," *Papers of the NAACP*; A. Philip Randolph to Eisenhower, ibid.; E. Frederic Morrow to Governor Adams, memo, December 16, 1955, Box 10, File "Civil Rights Official Memoranda 1955–56," *Morrow Records*.

rights issues on the legislative agenda. "'Why should we do this just to please these civil liberties groups?' Humphrey asked the assembled Democrats.... 'We have to remember,'" he said, "'that we were united on many issues in the last session, Southern and Northern Democrats alike.'" There was no reason to jeopardize that unity now.[231] Humphrey's strategy, which of course would appear again at the 1964 Democratic Convention, showcased, as Clarence Mitchell noted, that "fatal tendency to sacrifice civil rights in the interest of party harmony."[232]

As expected, the South fought the *Brown* decision with a vengeance. "The Georgia legislature considered bills to abolish the Supreme Court and remove all Negroes from the state."[233] Just as Byrnes warned, entire public school systems shut down across the South, and black children were left with few or no educational options for years.[234]

Massive Resistance also entailed trying to shut down the NAACP itself. In Louisiana, the legislature invoked a law "forcing [the NAACP] to suspend" its "activities in the State." In South Carolina, "[t]hey... passed a statute... denying public employment to NAACP members. In Mississippi, teachers [were] required to sign an oath that they [were] not members of" the NAACP.[235]

As could be expected, resistance to black equality moved beyond the legislature and straight into the lynch mob. In Money, Mississippi, a 14-year-old black boy was tortured and killed for allegedly saying "bye baby" to a white woman. To underscore how something so simple but so symbolic threatened a "way of life," one of Emmett Till's killers, J. W. Milam, justified the murder of a 14-year-old in words that evoked the spirit of Monroe, Georgia. "'Well, when he [Till] told me about this white girl he had,'" something just snapped because "'that's what this war's about down here now. That's what we got to fight to protect.'" From there, Milam "'just looked at [Till] and said, 'Boy, you ain't never going to see

231. Robert G. Spivack, "Party Liberals Rebuff Lehman on Civil Rights," *New York Post*, January 6, 1955, found in Box 353, File "Leadership Conference on Civil Rights, 1955: Correspondence," *Papers of the NAACP*; Marquis Childs, "Lehman-Humphrey," *New York Post*, January 7, 1955, found in ibid.

232. *1954 Annual Report of the Washington Bureau of the National Association...*, n.d., Box 163, File "Washington Bureau Annual Reports, 1950–57," ibid.

233. Bob Smith, *They Closed Their Schools: Prince Edward County, Virginia, 1951–1964* (Chapel Hill: University of North Carolina Press, 1965), 83.

234. Ibid., 151–259; Alexander Leidholdt, *Standing Before the Shouting Mob: Lenoir Chambers and Virginia's Massive Resistance to Public-School Integration* (Tuscaloosa and London: The University of Alabama Press, 1997).

235. Roy Wilkins, "The NAACP: An American Organization," n.d., Box 68, File "Articles: Communism, on—1950–55," *Papers of the NAACP*.

the sun come up again.'"[236] Despite eyewitness testimony and undeniable evidence of their guilt, Emmett Till's killers were exonerated after only 67 minutes of deliberation – and it "wouldn't have taken that long" except the sheriff-elect told the jurors to "make it 'look good'" so they "stopped to drink pop."[237] As the European press denounced the verdict as "'scandalous,' 'monstrous,' and 'abominable,'" the American Civil Liberties Union reflected that the "Emmett Till murder trial has become a symbol of an important part of the unfinished business of American Democracy."[238] White House staffer and black Republican Frederic Morrow tried to explain to his colleagues what Till's murder and the administration's nonchalant attitude really meant. The "failure of any prominent member of the Administration to speak out against, and deplore, the present condition of terrorism and economic sanction against the Negroes in Mississippi" had led many African Americans to "feel that . . . the Eisenhower Administration has completely abandoned the Negro in the South and left him to the mercy of state governments that have manifested their intention to violate all laws, human and divine, as long as it results in 'keeping the Negro in his place.'"[239]

African Americans, of course, refused to stay in their "place." Unfortunately, because of the destructive power of the Cold War and McCarthyism, even as the Civil Rights Movement began – launched by the insurgency borne of World War II, the horror of Emmett Till's murder, the joy over the *Brown* decision, and the galvanized communities that were determined to destroy Jim Crow – it was, in the end, only a *civil rights*, not a human rights, movement.[240] As such, it could only scratch the surface of black inequality. Thus, as hard as African Americans fought, as much

236. Henry Hampton and Steve Fayer, eds., *Voices of Freedom: An Oral History of the Civil Rights Movement from the 1950s through the 1980s* (New York: Bantam Books, 1990), 13–14.
237. Stephen J. Whitfield, *A Death in the Delta: The Story of Emmett Till* (New York: The Free Press, 1988), 33–42.
238. American Jewish Committee, "Strengthen Justice Department's Civil Rights Power to Repair Damage to American Prestige Abroad Because of Till Case . . . ," press release, October 22, 1955, Box 1105, Folder 2, *ACLU Papers*; "ACLU Statement on Till Case," press release, October 5, 1955, ibid.
239. E. Frederic Morrow to Governor Adams, memo, December 16, 1955, Box 10, File "Civil Rights Official Memoranda 1955–56," *Morrow Records*.
240. Clenora Hudson-Weems, *Emmett Till: The Sacrificial Lamb in the Modern Civil Rights Movement*, 2nd ed., with a Foreword by Robert E. Weems, Jr. (New York: Bedford Publishers, Inc., 1996); Aldon D. Morris, *Origins of the Civil Rights Movement: Black Communities Organizing for Change* (New York: The Free Press, 1986); Hampton and Fayer, *Voices of Freedom*, xxiii–xxviii.

courage as they displayed, William Patterson, perhaps, summarized it best when he looked at the phantom victory of *Brown* and the intense, violent backlash it entailed. "Let us bear in mind that not a single advance, not a single step forward, not a single achievement won by the Negro people is . . . safe."[241]

241. William Patterson, "Some Probelems (sic) of Theory, Ideology, and Tactics in Negro Work," May 1954, Box 8, Folder 36, *Patterson Papers*.

Epilogue
The Prize

Black people have no permanent friends, no permanent enemies... just permanent interests.

William L. Clay[1]

Almost fifty years after the *Brown* decision – and more than three decades after the Civil Rights Movement—the reality of stunted opportunities and abridged human rights continues to haunt the daily lives of African Americans and the United States. The substandard housing, inadequate health care, limited employment opportunities, and abysmal education systems that dominated the lives of African Americans before the Civil Rights Movement still exist, especially if we refuse to be consoled by the balm that "'things are far better than they used to be.'"[2] Sociologist Dalton Conley distills this idea best when he notes that in the 1990s:

> we find that over half of all African American children under the age of six live in poverty, three times greater than the proportion in the white community.... When we move... into the labor market, the situation deteriorates.... The black unemployment rate has only rarely dipped below double digits since the dawn of the civil rights era, and it surpassed 20 percent during the 1982–83 recession.... In 1997, the median income for black families was 55 percent that of white families.... Educational differences do not explain these income gaps.... African American male high school graduates earned 73 cents to the dollar earned by white male high school graduates. For more educated groups, wage ratios are not much better.[3]

1. William L. Clay, *Just Permanent Interests: Black Americans in Congress, 1870–1991*, with a foreword by Governor L. Douglas Wilder (New York: Amistad, 1992), ix.
2. King, *Where Do We Go From Here*, 8; Mary Barnett Gilson, *What's Past is Prologue: Reflections on My Industrial Experience* (New York and London: Harper & Brothers, 1940), 292.
3. Dalton Conley, *Being Black, Living in the Red: Race, Wealth, and Social Policy in America* (Berkeley: University of California Press, 1999), 10–11.

After also noting how more than 135 years since the Emancipation Proclamation, African Americans' ownership of the total wealth of the United States has only increased from .05 to 1 percent, Conley could only conclude that, "Race, family, and life chances seem to be inextricably linked in a vicious circle of inequality over the life course."[4]

This cycle of inequality is directly related to the widespread, continuing violation of African Americans' human rights. While egregious civil rights abuses – such as the lynching of James Byrd, voting rights irregularities in the 2000 presidential election, and the New York Police Department's killing of Amadou Diallo and torture of Abner Louima – still carry some capacity to stun the nation, the less obvious, but even more deadly, human rights violations in education, health care, and housing have just become part of the accepted day-to-day grind for black America. And, while these are often conceived as phenomenon reserved for poor, inner-city residents, that is a fallacy. As the recent reports on discrimination in health care and in mortgage lending make clear, those violations transcend class.[5]

Thus, even the rise of the black middle class, which is often heralded as a testament to the success of the Civil Rights Movement, cannot balance the growing poverty and hopelessness that permeates so much of black America.[6] As Melvin Oliver and Thomas Shapiro noted, "it is entirely premature to celebrate the rise of the black middle-class," because it is "middle-class" by the sheer grace of income alone, which in volatile economic times can disappear in a moment's notice. "From 1979 to 1984," for example, "one-half of black males in durable-goods manufacturing in five Great Lakes cities lost their jobs."[7] Or, to put it another way, "[i]n cases where minority workers made up only 10 to 12 percent of the work force in their area, they accounted from 60 to 70 percent of those laid off in 1974."[8] The lack of job security was exacerbated by the lack of assets, especially home ownership and all of the benefits that accrue to those who own property. To understand how this could happen is to understand that, within a 30-year span, while the Federal Housing Administration helped support the dream of home ownership for millions of Americans, "'fewer than one percent of all mortgages in the nation were

4. Conley, *Being Black*, 12, 25.
5. Sheryl Gay Stolberg, "Minorities Get Inferior Care, Even if Insured, Study Finds," *New York Times*, March 21, 2002; Melvin L. Oliver and Thomas M. Shapiro, *Black Wealth/White Wealth: A New Perspective on Racial Inequality* (New York and London: Routledge, 1997), 19–20.
6. Cornel West, *Race Matters* (New York: Vintage Books, 1994), 19.
7. Oliver and Shapiro, *Black Wealth*, 7, 26.
8. George Lipsitz, *The Possessive Investment in Whiteness: How White People Profit from Identity Politics* (Philadelphia, Pennsylvania: Temple University Press, 1998), 12.

issued to African Americans.'"[9] With no assets to act as a safety net, "the economic foundation of the black middle class lacks one of the pillars that provide stability and security to middle-class whites – assets." As a result, not only does the black middle class "earn seventy cents for every dollar earned by middle-class whites but they possess only fifteen cents for every dollar of wealth held by middle-class whites."[10]

These inequalities, caused by centuries of closed opportunities, obviously did not, as Wilkins hoped, just "melt away" after the *Brown* decision. Nor were they destroyed within the five-year time frame that Thurgood Marshall predicted. They also proved impervious to boycotts, sit-ins, marches, jail-ins, and Freedom Rides, which, although important, were targeted solely at the attainment of civil rights objectives. Civil rights, however, did not then and does not now have the language, the tools, nor the means to address the systemic issues that haunt black America. To "go beyond the establishment of legal equality," to go beyond *Brown*, human rights had to be defined and fought for as the ultimate goal for black equality.[11]

Toward the end of World War II, the NAACP tried to do just that. Even as it continued its civil rights mission, the Association, recognizing the opportunity that the founding of the United Nations and the moral revulsion that the Holocaust presented, expanded its vision and its program to include human rights. It was clear to most in the NAACP leadership that without economic rights, civil liberties rested, at best, on quicksand. Thus, the NAACP, working in concert with other organizations at the San Francisco Conference, applied an enormous amount of pressure to force the United States to agree to the inclusion of human rights in the UN Charter. Then, sickened by the wave of postwar lynching that gripped the nation, fearful of the impending economic collapse that threatened the black community, and dismayed with the federal government's sluggish response to the plight of African Americans, the NAACP, doing what it believed the too-small and too-compromised NNC could not, took black America's case before the United Nations. Yet, the tendency of "friends" and foes alike to depict human rights as communistic, Soviet-inspired, and treasonous – especially during the McCarthy era – threatened to expose the NAACP to the same inquisition that was destroying the black Left. The barely veiled threat of extinction compelled the NAACP leadership to retreat to the haven of civil rights, wrap itself in the flag, and distance the Association from the now-tainted struggle for human rights. Bolstered by

9. Conley, *Being Black*, 37.
10. Oliver and Shapiro, *Black Wealth*, 7, 11–52.
11. Patterson, *Brown v. Board of Education*, 205.

the hope of *Brown*, the Association tried unsuccessfully to subsume the curses of housing, education, health care, and employment inequalities under an ill-defined, ill-fitting civil rights banner.

The black Left was in an even greater bind. It had aligned and theorized itself into an ideological corner that left it estranged from the black community. The problem, of course, was that the black Left was so enamored with the Communist Party, U.S.A. that it failed to discern the limits inherent in that alliance. As a result, while the black Left could analyze the contradictions and flaws in American democracy with razor-sharp precision, it could not provide that same penetrating analysis to the CP or the Soviet Union to determine when to follow party initiatives and when to ignore them. Not only did this cost the NNC and the CRC greatly in terms of credibility, but it also dulled their capacity to understand that the issue was never about red, or even red, white, and blue. The issue was black. That is to say, just as Charles Howard explained to Walter White that the true measure of any policy has to be "will this advance the rights of colored people," the same advice held true for the black Left. For example, would centralizing operations and leaving branches to wither help the NNC advance the rights of colored people? Would focusing a tremendous amount of finite resources on securing the release of the CP leadership, even while the Willie McGees of this world faced the executioner's chair, advance the rights of colored people? Would charging the United States with genocide to raise funds for the Communist party advance the rights of colored people? While the black Left believed it would, the black community answered with a resounding no. It is no wonder then that the CRC had to resort to some type of Jim Crow "stunt" to woo the black community. But that wooing was in vain because the CRC's message that the fight for the Communist party was the "A1 civil rights case" facing the nation was a message that would not and could not resonate in a community that had endured the worst that America had to offer. In this struggle, the needs of black people had to come first. And because of its inability to see that, the black Left, whose courage and intellect could have made a lasting, significant contribution, was pushed to the margins by a movement that refused to take a back seat to anyone, especially the Communist Party, U.S.A.

While the nuisance of the CP was easily contained, the battle against powerful forces within the United States, who were determined to keep the "Negro in his place," was another matter altogether. As the groundswell for the Bricker Amendment made clear, those who loathed the UN's human rights initiatives were incensed that the covenants threatened an American "way of life" created and perpetuated on racial inequality and white privilege. For the right wing in American politics, that way of life had to be preserved at all costs. If that meant rewriting the Constitution, reducing the president to a figurehead, and jettisoning every international human rights treaty under consideration – even at the risk of scorn and derision from some of America's staunchest allies – then so be it. In 1955, even after the UN finally accepted the mislabeled Action Program, the United States was still not satisfied and maneuvered to strip its own program of any potential that it may have held for improving the observance of human rights. Mary Pillsbury Lord proudly conveyed to Senator George how the United States, in a move that would "augur well for the future," was able to keep the scope of the Action Program's self-studies restricted to a few, discrete areas despite the fact that the "Soviet bloc pressed hard for the addition of a long list of other subjects, including... many economic and social rights and... a reference to the rights enumerated in the Universal Declaration of Human Rights and in the Draft Covenants on Human Rights."[12]

Meanwhile, "friends of the Negro" played an equally important role in trying to keep the UN and human rights away from the struggle for black equality. The motivation behind Truman's order to "'kill the Covenant'" was clear enough. Eleanor Roosevelt's efforts also spoke volumes about her priorities. Thus although, theoretically, the liberal Roosevelt and the staunchly segregationist State Department should have approached the issue of black equality from different perspectives, for the most part, they did not. There was a difference in tone, to be sure, but in substance, where it really counted, it was obvious that in those critical moments when issues of racial discrimination came to the fore – such as the NAACP's petition and the complaint lodged against South Africa – Roosevelt was in complete agreement with the State Department. She worked diligently, even to the point of using her influence on the Board of Directors, to blackmail the NAACP into submission. The federal–state clause and other artifacts of America's Jim Crow democracy were also important tools Roosevelt touted to erect a formidable barrier between the oversight abilities of the UN and the horrific conditions in the African American community. One scholar commented that "there was no disagreement between her and the Department on the fundamentals of what a UN human rights program should be. This compatibility of outlook applied to matters of substance," as well as "a similar basic compatibility on tactical

12. Walter F. George to Mrs. Oswald B. Lord, July 23, 1955, Box 1, File "1955 Correspondence," *Lord Papers*; Mrs. Oswald B. Lord, "A New Approach to Human Rights: Eleventh Session of the United Nations Commission on Human Rights, April 5–29," *State Department Bulletin*, August 15, 1955, found in Box 2, File "Article 'A New Approach to Human Rights' by Mrs. Lord (*The Department of State Bulletin*)," ibid.

questions."[13] Roosevelt's actions, of course, were rationalized as "pragmatic" and necessary because of the power of the Southern Democrats and the need to not air America's "dirty laundry" during the Cold War.

The Cold War had obviously transformed human rights into an ideological battlefield between the Soviet Union and the United States and engulfed the struggle for black equality. The Cold War identified in stark, pejorative terms entire categories of rights as antithetical to basic American freedoms. It punished mercilessly those who advocated a more expansive definition and a more concrete commitment to those rights. And it demanded unconditional loyalty. Historian Kenneth O'Reilly rightfully concluded that when "America fought the cold war at home and abroad, African Americans lost on both fronts."[14]

The resulting inability to articulate the struggle for black equality as a human rights issue doomed the subsequent Civil Rights Movement to "'a series of glorious defeats.'"[15] And even as the limits of the movement became obvious, as an unemployment rate reminiscent of the Great Depression fueled the rage that burned Watts to the ground and as the housing conditions in inner-city Chicago drained the life out of its inhabitants, the African American leadership was simply incapable of embracing the now tainted human rights platform. This explains why, in part, it was so easy to dismiss the calls from Malcolm X and Martin Luther King, Jr., when each pleaded to transform the Civil Rights Movement into a human rights movement. Those exhortations must be understood as coming at a time when both men were, in one sense or another, civil rights outcasts and government renegades. They were marginalized. The stigma against human rights clearly held, and large segments of the black community, demoralized by the oversold but now evaporated promises and hope of the Civil Rights Movement, dissolved into a self-destructive vat of "nihilism" and "bling-bling."[16]

The opportunity that World War II presented has long since passed. Nevertheless, it is important to remember what was lost and why so that when the *Third* Reconstruction begins, and it must, the unresolved work of the First and Second Reconstructions can finally be completed and a nation will arise with a true commitment to equality and human rights. That is the prize.

13. Mower, *The United States*, 39.
14. O'Reilly, "Racial Integration," 111.
15. Patterson, *Brown v. Board of Education*, 204. Quote is from Kenneth Clark reflecting on his own work in the struggle for civil rights.
16. West, *Race Matters*, 17–31; Robert E. Weems, Jr., "'Bling-Bling' and Other Recent Trends in African American Consumerism," conference paper, Missouri Black Expo, August 17, 2002.

Bibliography

Primary Sources

Archival Material

Cleveland Public Library, Cleveland, Ohio
Papers of the United Nations

Dwight D. Eisenhower Presidential Library, Abilene, Kansas
Dwight D. Eisenhower Papers as President, Ann Whitman File, 1953–61
Dwight D. Eisenhower Records as President, White House Central Files, 1953–61
Papers of John Foster Dulles
Papers of E. Frederic Morrow
Papers of Mary Pillsbury Lord
Republican National Committee Newspaper Clippings
Records of Bryce N. Harlow
Records of E. Frederic Morrow

Federal Bureau of Investigation, Washington, D.C.
FBI Files on Max Yergan

Library of Congress, Washington, D.C.
Papers of Rayford Whittingham Logan
Papers of the NAACP, Group II, Series A, General Office File, 1940–55
Papers of the NAACP, Group II, Series B, Legal File, 1940–55
Papers of the NAACP, Group II, Series C, Branch File, 1940–55
Papers of the NAACP, Group II, Series H, Washington Bureau, 1940–55
Papers of the NAACP, Group II, Series L, Addendum, 1910–43
Papers of A. Philip Randolph
Papers of Roy Wilkins
NAACP Minutes of the Board of Directors Meeting, 1944–53. Microfilm.

Moorland-Spingarn Research Center, Howard University, Washington, D.C.
Papers of Rayford Whittingham Logan
Papers of William Patterson
Papers of Percival Prattis
Papers of Arthur B. Spingarn

Papers of Edward Strong
Papers of Louis T. Wright

National Archives II, College Park, Maryland
Record Group 59, General Records of the Department of State
Record Group 84, Records of the U.S. Mission to the United Nations

Ohio Historical Society, Columbus, Ohio
Papers of John W. Bricker

Franklin Delano Roosevelt Presidential Library, Hyde Park, New York
Papers of Eleanor Roosevelt
FBI File on Eleanor Roosevelt. Microfilm.

Schlesinger Library, Radcliffe College, Boston, Massachusetts
Edith Spurlock Sampson Papers

Schomburg Center for the Study of Black Culture, New York, New York
Papers of W. Alphaeus Hunton. Microfilm.

Seeley Mudd Manuscript Collection, Princeton University, Princeton, New Jersey
Papers of the American Civil Liberties Union
Papers of Hamilton Fish Armstrong
Papers of John Foster Dulles

Harry S Truman Presidential Library, Independence, Missouri
Papers of Harry S Truman: Official File
Papers of Harry S Truman: Philleo Nash Files
Papers of Clark M. Clifford
Papers of James Hendrick
Papers of J. Howard McGrath
Papers of Senator J. Howard McGrath
Papers of David K. Niles
Papers of Philleo Nash
Papers of the President's Committee on Civil Rights
Papers of Stephen J. Spingarn
Donald C. Blaisdell Oral History
Eleanor Bontecou Oral History
William H. Hastie Oral History
Isador Lubin Oral History
Durward Sandifer Oral History

University of Minnesota, Minneapolis, Minnesota
Papers of the YMCA
Biographical File: Channing H. Tobias Collection

University of North Carolina, Chapel Hill, North Carolina
Papers of Jonathan Daniels

Western Historical Manuscript Collection, University of Missouri–Columbia, Columbia, Missouri

Papers of Thomas C. Hennings, Jr., 1934–60

Interview

Theodore Berry, Sr.

Published Papers

Papers of Mary McLeod Bethune, 1923–1942. New Orleans: Amistad Research Center. Microfilm. 1976.

Papers of Ralph Bunche. Los Angeles, California: University of California, Los Angeles. Microfilm. 1980.

Papers of the Civil Rights Congress. Washington, D.C.: University Publications of America. Microfilm. 1989.

W. E. B. Du Bois Papers. Sanford, North Carolina: Microfilming Corporation of America. Microfilm. 1980.

Papers of the NAACP: 1909–1950. Parts 1, 7-Series B, and 14, Washington, D.C.: University Publications of America. Microfilm. 1982.

Papers of the National Negro Congress. Washington, D.C.: University Publications of America. Microfilm. 1988.

The Paul Robeson Collection. Washington, D.C.: University Publications of America. Microfilm. 1989.

The Papers of Eleanor Roosevelt, 1933–1945. Frederick, Maryland: University Publications of America. Microfilm. 1986.

Published Government Papers

FBI File on the National Negro Congress. Wilmington, Delaware: Scholarly Resources. Microfilm. 1987.

FBI File on Paul Robeson. Wilmington, Delaware: Scholarly Resources. Microfilm. 1987.

Records of the Subversive Activities Control Board. Frederick, Maryland: University Publications of America. Microfilm. 1988.

To Secure These Rights: The Report of the President's Committee on Civil Rights. With a foreword by Charles E. Wilson. New York: Simon and Schuster, 1947.

United Nations Information Organization. *Documents of the United Nations Conference on International Organization.* 22 vols. Vol. 3, *Dumbarton Oaks Proposals: Comments on Proposed Amendments.* New York: United Nations, 1945.

——. *Yearbook of the United Nations: 1946–47.* Lake Success, New York: United Nations, 1947.

U.S. Congress. House. Committee on House Un-American Activities. *Hearings Regarding Communist Infiltration of Minority Groups.* 81st Congress, 1st sess., July 13, 1949.

U.S. Congress. Senate. Subcommittee of the Committee on the Judiciary. *Treaties and Executive Agreements*, 83rd Congress, 1st sess., February 18, 1953.

U.S. Congress. Senate. *Congressional Record* (August 11, 1937), Vol. 81, Pt. 8.

U.S. Congress. Senate. *Congressional Record* (January 11, 1938), Vol. 83, Pt. 1.

U.S. Congress. Senate. *Congressional Record* (February 1, 1954), Vol. 100, Pt. 1.

U.S. Congress. Senate. *Journal of the Senate of the United States of America*, 83rd Congress, 2nd sess., 1954.

U.S. Congress. Senate. "Francis O. Wilcox, Chief of Staff, Senate Foreign Relations Committee, 1947–55, Oral History Interview, #3," *Congress and the Cold War* (March 1984).

U.S. Department of Commerce, *Bureau of Labor Statistics Data: Consumer Price Index, All Urban Consumers,* http://wwwstats.bls.gov/top20.html. Accessed September 28, 1998.

U.S. Department of State. *Foreign Relations of the United States, 1945.* Vol. 1, *General: The United Nations.* Washington, D.C.: Government Printing Office, 1967.

——. *Foreign Relations of the United States, 1950.* Vol. 2, *The United Nations: The Western Hemisphere.* Washington, D.C.: Government Printing Office, 1976.

——. *Foreign Relations of the United States, 1951.* Vol. 2, *The United Nations: The Western Hemisphere.* Washington, D.C.: Government Printing Office, 1979.

U.S. Supreme Court. *Screws v. United States*, 325 U.S. 91 (S. Ct. 1945).

——. *McLaurin v. Oklahoma State Regents*, 339 U.S. 637; 70 S. Ct. 851; 96 Led. 1149 (1950).

Diaries and Memoirs

Clifford, Clark. *Counsel to the President: A Memoir.* New York: Random House, 1991.

Byrnes, James F. *Speaking Frankly.* New York and London: Harper & Brothers Publishers, 1947.

Field, Frederick Vanderbilt. *From Right to Left: An Autobiography.* Westport, Connecticut: Lawrence Hill & Co., 1983.

Holman, Frank. *The Life and Career of a Western Lawyer, 1886–1961.* Baltimore, Maryland: Port City Press, Inc., 1963.

White, Walter. *A Man Called White: The Autobiography of Walter White.* New York: The Viking Press, 1948.

Wilkins, Roy. *Standing Fast: The Autobiography of Roy Wilkins.* With an introduction by Julian Bond. New York: The Viking Press, 1982.

Recordings

Asch, Moses, *W. E. B. Du Bois: A Recorded Autobiography.* Recording, 1961.

Decision: The Conflicts of Harry S Truman. Episode 16, "Give'em Hell Harry." Produced by Independence Productions, Inc., Screen Gems, Inc., 1964.

Eyes on the Prize: America's Civil Rights Years, 1954–1965. Volume 4. *No Easy Walk (1961–1963).* Produced and directed by James DeVinney and Callie Crossely. Boston, Massachusetts: Blackside, Inc., 1987.

Paul Robeson: Here I Stand. Produced by Chiz Schultz and directed by St. Clair Bourne. American Masters Series. Public Broadcasting System, 1999.

Contemporary Periodicals

Baltimore Afro-American
Chicago Defender
Chicago Herald Tribune
Congress View
Detroit News
New Africa
New York Age
New York Amsterdam News
New York Times
P.M.
People's Voice

Secondary Sources

Books and Articles

Alpha Kappa Alpha Sorority, Inc., "National History," http://www.uca.edu/org/aka/nationalhistory.htm. Accessed May 18, 2002.

Ambrose, Stephen E. *Eisenhower: The President.* Vol. II. New York: Simon and Schuster, 1984.

Anthony, David H. III. "Max Yergan and South Africa: A Transatlantic Interaction," in *Imagining Home: Class Culture, and Nationalism in the African Diaspora*, eds. Sidney Lemelle and Robin D. G. Kelley. London and New York: Verso, 1994.

Asher, Robert E. et al., eds. *The United Nations and Promotion of the General Welfare.* Washington, D.C.: Brookings Institution, 1957.

Ashmore, Harry S. *Civil Rights and Wrongs: A Memoir of Race and Politics, 1944–1994.* New York: Pantheon Books, 1994.

Baldwin, James. *The Fire Next Time.* New York: The Dial Press, 1963.

Berger, Jason. *A New Deal for the World: Eleanor Roosevelt and American Foreign Policy.* Social Science Monographs. New York: Columbia University Press, 1981.

Berman, William C. *The Politics of Civil Rights in the Truman Administration.* Columbus: The Ohio State University Press, 1970.

Black, Allida. M. *Casting Her Own Shadow: Eleanor Roosevelt and the Shaping of Postwar Liberalism.* New York: Columbia University Press, 1996.

Borstlemann, Thomas. *Apartheid's Reluctant Uncle: The United States and Southern Africa in the Early Cold War.* New York: Oxford University Press, 1993.

——. *The Cold War and the Color Line: American Race Relations in the Global Arena.* Cambridge and London: Harvard University Press, 2001.

Brown, Walter J. *James F. Byrnes of South Carolina: A Remembrance.* Macon, Georgia: Published for the Watson-Brown Foundation by Mercer University Press, 1992.

Brucken, Rowland. "A Most Uncertain Crusade: The United States, Human Rights and the United Nations, 1941–1954," Ph.D. diss., The Ohio State University, 1999.

Capeci, Dominic, Jr. *The Lynching of Cleo Wright.* Lexington: University of Kentucky Press, 1998.

Carson, Clayborne, Vincent Harding et al., eds. *The Eyes on the Prize Civil Rights Reader: Documents, Speeches and Firsthand Accounts from the Black Freedom Struggle.* New York: Viking Penguin, 1991.

Carter, Dan T. *Scottsboro: A Tragedy of the American South.* Baton Rouge: Louisiana State University Press, 1969.

Civil Rights Congress. *We Charge Genocide: The Historic Petition to the United Nations for Relief From a Crime of the United States Government Against the Negro People.* New York: Civil Rights Congress, 1951.

Clay, William L. *Just Permanent Interests: Black Americans in Congress, 1870–1991.* New York: Amistad Press, Inc., 1992.

Cohen, Deborah L. "Half of Black, Hispanic Children May Be Poor by 2010," *Education Week* November 3, 1993.

Cohodas, Nadine. *Strom Thurmond & the Politics of Southern Change.* New York: Simon & Schuster, 1993.

Conley, Dalton. *Being Black, Living in the Red: Race, Wealth, and Social Policy in America.* Berkeley and Los Angeles: University of California Press, 1999.

Council on African Affairs. *The San Francisco Conference and the Colonial Issue: Memorandum Prepared for Consideration in Relation to the Establishment of the Charter of a World Organization at the San Francisco Conference of the United Nations.* New York: Council on African Affairs, 1945.

——. *United Nations Charter: Text and Analysis of the Colonial Provisions.* New York: Council on African Affairs, 1945.

——. *What Does San Francisco Mean for the Negro?* New York: Council on African Affairs, 1945.

Dalfiume, Richard M. *Desegregation in the United States Armed Forces: Fighting on Two Fronts, 1939–1953.* Columbia: University of Missouri Press, 1969.

——. "The 'Forgotten Years' of the Negro Revolution," *Journal of American History* Vol. 55, no. 1 (June 1968): 90–106.

"Death of a Demagogue." *American Heritage* (July/August 1997): 99–100.

Divine, Robert A. *Foreign Policy and U.S. Presidential Elections: 1940, 1948.* New York: New Viewpoints, 1974.

Douglass, Frederick. *Two Speeches by Frederick Douglass: One on West India Emancipation Delivered at Canandaigua, Aug. 4th, and the Other on the Dred Scott Decision, Delivered in New York, on the Occasion of the Anniversary of the American Abolition Society, May 1857.* Rochester, New York: C. P. Dewey [1857].

Du Bois, William E. B. *Color and Democracy: Colonies and Peace.* New York: Harcourt Brace, 1945.

——. *I Take My Stand for Peace.* New York: Masses & Mainstream, 1951.

——. *The Souls of Black Folks.* Introduction by Nathan Hare and Alvin Poussaint. New York: New American Library, 1969.

Duberman, Martin Bauml. *Paul Robeson.* New York: Alfred A. Knopf, 1988.

Dudziak, Mary L. *Cold War Civil Rights: Race and the Image of American Democracy.* Politics and Society in Twentieth Century America Series, eds. William Chafe, Gary Gerstle, and Linda Gordon. Princeton, New Jersey and Oxford: Princeton University Press, 2000.

——. "Desegregation as a Cold War Imperative," *Stanford Law Review* Vol. 41, no. 1 (November 1988): 61–120.

Ellison, Ralph. *Shadow and Act.* New York: Random House, 1964.

Fanon, Frantz. *Black Skins White Mask.* New York: Grove Press, Inc. 1967.

Forsythe, David P. "Human Rights in U.S. Foreign Policy: Retrospect and Prospect," *Political Science Quarterly* Vol. 105, no. 3 (Autumn 1990), 435–54.

Foster, William Z. *The Negro People in American History.* New York: International Publishers, 1954.

Frederickson, George. *Black Liberation: A Comparative History of Black Ideologies in the United States and South Africa.* New York: Oxford University Press, 1995.

Frederickson, Kari. *The Dixiecrat Revolt & the End of the Solid South, 1952–1968.* Chapel Hill and London: University of North Carolina Press, 2001.

Gilson, Mary Barnett. *What's Past Is Prologue: Reflections on My Industrial Experience.* New York and London: Harper & Brothers, 1940.

Green, A. Wigfall. *The Man Bilbo.* Baton Rouge: Louisiana State University Press, 1963.

Greenberg, Cheryl. "The Black/Jewish Dilemma in the Early Cold War," conference paper. American Historical Association-Pacific Coast Branch, August 8, 1998.

Greene, Lorenzo J., Gary R. Kremer, and Antonio F. Holland. *Missouri's Black Heritage*, 2nd ed., revised by Gary R. Kremer and Antonio F. Holland. Columbia: University of Missouri Press, 1993.

Grill, Johnpeter Horst and Robert L. Jenkins. "The Nazis and the American South in the 1930s: A Mirror Image?" *Journal of Southern History* Vol. 58, no. 4 (November 1992): 667–94.

Guzman, Jason Parkhurst, ed. *Negro Year Book: A Review of Events Affecting Negro Life, 1941–1946*. Tuskegee, Alabama: Department of Records and Research, Tuskegee Institute, 1947.

Hale, Grace Elizabeth. *Making Whiteness: The Culture of Segregation in the South, 1890–1940*. New York: Pantheon Books, 1998.

Hampton, Henry and Steve Fayer, with Sarah Flynn. *Voices of Freedom: An Oral History of the Civil Rights Movement from the 1950s through the 1980s*. New York: Bantam Books, 1991.

Harris, Robert L., Jr. "Racial Equality and the United Nations Charter," in *New Directions in Civil Rights Studies*, Carter G. Woodson Institute Series in Black Studies, eds. Armstead L. Robinson and Patricia Sullivan. Charlottesville: University Press of Virginia, 1991.

Hendrix, Jerry A. "Theodore G. Bilbo: Evangelist of Racial Purity," in *The Oratory of Southern Demagogues*, eds. Cal M. Logue and Howard Dorgan. Baton Rouge and London: Louisiana State University Press, 1981.

Henkin, Louis. "U.S. Ratification of Human Rights Conventions: The Ghost of Senator Bricker," *American Journal of International Law* 89, no. 2 (April 1995), 341–50.

Hilderbrand, Robert C. *Dumbarton Oaks: The Origins of the United Nations and the Search for Postwar Security.* Chapel Hill and London: The University of North Carolina Press, 1990.

Horne, Gerald. *Black and Red: W. E. B. Du Bois and the Afro-American Response to the Cold War, 1944–1963*. SUNY Series in Afro-American Society Series, eds. John Howard and Robert C. Smith. Albany, New York: State University of New York Press, 1986.

———. *Black Liberation/Red Scare: Ben Davis and the Communist Party*. London and Toronto: Associated University Presses, 1994.

———. *Communist Front? The Civil Rights Congress, 1946–1956*. London and Toronto: Associated University Presses, 1988.

Hudson-Weems, Clenora. *Emmett Till: The Sacrificial Lamb in the Modern Civil Rights Movement*. 2nd ed. With a foreword by Robert E. Weems, Jr. New York: Bedford Publishers, Inc., 1996.

Hughes, Cicero Alvin. "Toward a Black United Front: The National Negro Congress Movement." Ph.D. diss., Ohio University, 1982.

Hunt, Michael H. *Ideology and U.S. Foreign Policy*. New Haven, Connecticut: Yale University Press, 1987.

Inge, M. Thomas, ed. *Dark Laughter: The Satiric Art of Oliver W. Harrington.* Jackson: University Press of Mississippi, 1993.

Janken, Kenneth Robert. *Rayford W. Logan and the Dilemma of the African-American Intellectual.* Amherst: University of Massachusetts Press, 1993.

Johanningsmeier, Edward P. *Forging American Communism: The Life of William Z. Foster*. Princeton, New Jersey: Princeton University Press, 1994.

Jones, James H. *Bad Blood: The Tuskegee Syphilis Experiment*. New York: Free Press, 1981.

Karabell, Zachary. *The Last Campaign: How Harry Truman Won the 1948 Election*. New York: Alfred A. Knopf, 2000.

Kelley, Robin Davis Gibran. *Hammer 'n' Hoe: Alabama Communists During the Great Depression*. Chapel Hill: University of North Carolina Press, 1990.

Kèuhl, Stefan. *The Nazi Connection: Eugenics, American Racism, and German National Socialism*. New York: Oxford University Press, 1994.

King, Martin Luther, Jr. *Where Do We Go From Here: Chaos or Community?* New York: Harper & Row, 1967.

Kluger, Richard. *Simple Justice*. New York: Vintage Books, 1977.

Kozol, Jonathan. *Savage Inequalities: Children in America's Schools*. New York: Harper Perennial, 1991.

Krenn, Michael L. *Black Diplomacy: African Americans and the State Department, 1945–1969*. Armonk, New York: M. E. Sharpe, 1999.

——. "Unfinished Business: Segregation and U.S. Diplomacy at the 1958 World's Fair," *Diplomatic History* Vol. 20, no. 4 (Fall 1996): 591–612.

Lash, Joseph P. *Eleanor: The Years Alone*. With a foreword by Franklin D. Roosevelt, Jr. New York: W. W. Norton & Company, 1972.

Laville, Helen and Scott Lucas. "The American Way: Edith Sampson, the NAACP, and African American Identity in the Cold War," *Diplomatic History* Vol. 20, no. 4 (Fall 1996): 565–90.

Lauren, Paul Gordon. *The Evolution of International Human Rights: Visions Seen*. Pennsylvania Studies in Human Rights, ed. Bert Lockwood, Jr. Philadelphia: University of Pennsylvania Press, 1998.

Leidholdt, Alexander. *Standing Before the Shouting Mob: Lenoir Chambers and Virginia's Massive Resistance to Public-School Integration*. Tuscaloosa and London: The University of Alabama Press, 1997.

Lewis, David Levering. *W. E. B. Du Bois: Biography of a Race, 1868–1919*. New York: Holt, 1993.

——. *W. E. B. Du Bois: The Fight for Equality and the American Century, 1919–1963*. New York: Holt, 2000.

Lipsitz, George. *The Possessive Investment in Whiteness: How White People Profit from Identity Politics*. Philadelphia: Temple University Press, 1998.

Lockwood, Bert B., Jr. "The United Nations Charter and United States Civil Rights Litigation: 1946–1955," *Iowa Law Review* Vol. 69 (1984): 901–49.

Logan, Rayford W. *The African Mandates in World Politics*. Washington, D.C.: Public Affairs Press, 1948.

——. "Charter Will Not Prevent Wars," *Pittsburgh Courier*, July 21, 1945.

——. *The Negro and the Post-War World: A Primer*. Washington, D.C.: The Minorities Publishers, 1945.

——. *The Operation of the Mandate System in Africa, 1919–1927 with an Introduction on the Problem of the Mandates in the Post-War World*. Washington, D.C.: The Foundation Publishers, Inc., 1942.

——. Series on the founding of the United Nations and an analysis of the UN Charter. *Pittsburgh Courier*, April 28; May 5, 12, 19, and 26; and June 2, 9, and 16, 1945.

——. "The System of International Trusteeship." *The Journal of Negro History* Vol. 18 (1933): 33–38.

——, ed. *W. E. B. Du Bois: A Profile*. New York: Hill and Wang, 1971.
——, ed. *What the Negro Wants*. Chapel Hill: The University of North Carolina Press, 1944.
——with P. L. Prattis. "Race Equality at Conference." *Pittsburgh Courier*, May 5, 1945.
Lynch, Hollis R. *Black American Radicals and the Liberation of Africa: The Council on African Affairs, 1937–1955*. Introduction by St. Clair Drake. Africana Studies and Research Center Monograph Series, No. 5. Ithaca, New York: Cornell University Press, 1978.
Malcolm X and Alex Haley. *The Autobiography of Malcolm X*. New York: Ballantine, 1972.
Marable, Manning. *W. E. B. Du Bois, Black Radical Democrat*. Twayne's Twentieth-Century American Biography Series, no. 3. Boston: Twayne, 1986.
Martin, Charles H. "The Civil Rights Congress and Southern Black Defendants," *The Georgia Historical Quarterly* Vol. 71, no. 1 (Spring 1987): 25–52.
Massey, Douglas S. and Nancy A. Denton. *American Apartheid: Segregation and the Making of the Underclass*. Cambridge: Harvard University Press, 1993.
Mayer, Michael S. "With Much Deliberation and Some Speed: Eisenhower and the Brown Decision," *The Journal of Southern History* Vol. 52, no. 1 (February 1986): 43–76.
McAuliffe, Mary Sperling. *Crisis on the Left: Cold War Politics and American Liberals, 1947–1954*. Amherst: The University of Massachusetts Press, 1978.
McCoy, Donald R. and Richard Ruetten. *Quest and Response: Minority Rights and the Truman Administration*. Lawrence: University Press of Kansas, 1973.
McCullough, David. *Truman*. New York: Simon & Schuster, 1992.
Meier, August and John H. Bracey, Jr. "The NAACP as a Reform Movement, 1909–1965: 'To Reach the Conscience of America,'" *The Journal of Southern History* Vol. 59, no. 1 (February 1993): 3–30.
Mezerik, A. G. "Negroes at UN's Door," *The Nation* Vol. 165 (December 13, 1947): 644–46.
Morris, Aldon D. *Origins of the Civil Rights Movement: Black Communities Organizing for Change*. New York: The Free Press, 1986.
Morrow, E. Frederic. *Black Man in the White House*. New York: Macfadden-Bartell, 1963.
Mower, A. Glenn, Jr. *The United States, the United Nations, and Human Rights: The Eleanor Roosevelt and Jimmy Carter Eras*. Studies in Human Rights, no. 4, ed. George W. Shepherd, Jr. Westport, Connecticut: Greenwood Press, 1979.
Myrdal, Gunnar. *An American Dilemma: The Negro Problem and Modern Democracy*. Twenty-Fifth Anniversary Edition. New York: Harper & Row, 1962.
National Association for the Advancement of Colored People. *An Appeal to the World! A Statement on the Denial of Human Rights to Minorities in the Case of Citizens of Negro Descent in the United States of America and an Appeal to the United Nations for Redress*. New York: NAACP, 1947.
National Lawyers Guild. "Highlights from NLG's History," http://www.nlg.org/admin/history.html. Accessed July 21, 2001.

National Negro Congress. *A Petition to the United Nations on Behalf of 13 Million Oppressed Negro Citizens of the United States of America*. New York: National Negro Congress, 1946.

Oliver, Melvin L. and Thomas M. Shapiro. *Black Wealth/White Wealth: A New Perspective on Racial Inequality*. New York and London: Routledge, 1997.

O'Reilly, Kenneth. "Racial Integration: The Battle General Eisenhower Chose Not to Fight," *Journal of Blacks in Higher Education* no. 18 (Winter, 1997–1998): 110.

Orfield, Gary, Susan E. Eaton et al. *Dismantling Desegregation: The Quiet Reversal of Brown v. Board of Education*. New York: New Press, 1996.

Oshinsky, David. M. "*Worse Than Slavery: Parchman Farm and the Ordeal of Jim Crow Justice*." New York: Simon & Schuster, 1996.

Ottley, Roi. *New World-A-Coming*. The American Negro: His History and Life Series, ed. William Loren Katz. Cambridge: Riverside Press, 1943; reprint New York: Arno Press and the *New York Times*, 1968.

Patterson, James T. *Brown v. Board of Education: A Civil Rights Milestone and Its Troubled Legacy*. Pivotal Moments in American History Series, eds. David Hackett Fischer and James M. McPherson. New York: Oxford University Press, 2001.

Perry, Earnest L., Jr. "Voice of Consciousness: The Negro Newspaper Publishers Association During World War II." Ph.D. diss., University of Missouri–Columbia, 1998.

Pintzuk, Edward C. *Reds, Racial Justice, and Civil Liberties: Michigan Communists during the Cold War*. Minneapolis: MEP Publications/University of Minnesota, 1997.

Plummer, Brenda Gayle. *Rising Wind: Black Americans and U.S. Foreign Affairs, 1935–1960*. Chapel Hill: University of North Carolina Press, 1996.

Post, Hyde, Andy Miller, and Peter Scott. "Murder at Moore's Ford," *Atlanta Journal-Constitution*, May 31, 1992.

Pruden, Caroline. *Conditional Partners: Eisenhower, the United Nations, and the Search for a Permanent Peace*. Baton Rouge: Louisiana State University Press, 1998.

Record, Jane Cassels. "The Red-Tagging of Negro Protest," *The American Scholar* Vol. 26, no. 3 (Summer 1957): 325–33.

Record, Wilson. *Race and Radicalism: The NAACP and the Communist Party in Conflict*. Communism in American Life Series, ed. Clinton Rossiter. Ithaca, New York: Cornell University Press, 1964.

Reilly, Phillip. *The Surgical Solution: A History of Involuntary Sterilization in the United States*. Baltimore, Maryland: Johns Hopkins University Press, 1991.

Riggs, Robert E. "Overselling the UN Charter—Fact and Myth."*International Organization* Vol. 14 (1960): 277–90.

Roark, James L. "American Black Leaders: The Response to Colonialism and the Cold War, 1943–1953," *African Historical Studies* Vol. 4, no. 2 (1971): 253–70.

Robertson, David. *Sly and Able: A Political Biography of James F. Byrnes*. New York: W. W. Norton, 1994.

Robins, Dorothy B. *Experiment in Democracy: The Story of U.S. Citizen Organizations in Forging the Charter of the United Nations*. New York: The Parkside Press, 1971.

Ruchames, Louis. *Race, Jobs, & Politics: The Story of FEPC*. Westport, Connecticut: Negro Universities Press, 1971 (reprinted).

Sitkoff, Harvard. "The Detroit Race Riot of 1943," *Michigan History* Vol. 53, no. 3 (Fall 1969): 183–206.

——. *A New Deal for Blacks: The Emergence of Civil Rights as a National Issue*. Vol. 1, *The Depression Decade*. New York: Oxford University Press, 1978.

——. "Racial Militancy and Interracial Violence in the Second World War," *Journal of American History* Vol. 58 (December 1971): 667–81.

——. "Harry Truman and the Election of 1948: The Coming of Age of Civil Rights in American Politics," *Journal of Southern History* Vol. 38, no. 4 (November 1971): 597–616.

——. *The Struggle for Black Equality: 1954–1992*. American Century Series, ed. Eric Foner. New York: Hill and Wang, 1993.

Skretny, John David. "The Effect of the Cold War on African-American Civil Rights: America and the World Audience, 1945–1968," *Theory and Society* Vol. 27 (April 1998): 237–85.

Smith, Bob. *They Closed Their Schools: Prince Edward County, Virginia, 1951–1964*. Chapel Hill: University of North Carolina Press, 1965.

Smith, J. David. *The Eugenic Assault on America: Scenes in Red, White, and Black*. Fairfax, Virginia: George Mason University Press, 1993.

Smith, Jessie Carney and Robert L. Johns, eds. *Statistical Record of Black America*. New York: Gale Research, Inc., 1995.

Southard, Jo L. "Human Rights Provisions of the UN Charter: The History in U.S. Courts," *Iowa Law Students Association Journal of International & Comparative Law* Vol. 1 (1995): 41–65.

Stolberg, Sheryl Gay. "Minorities Get Inferior Care, Even If Insured, Study Finds," *New York Times*, March 21, 2002.

Streater, John Baxter, Jr. "The National Negro Congress, 1936–1947." Ph.D. diss., University of Cincinnati, 1981.

Strong, Edward E. "On the 40th Anniversary of the NAACP," *Political Affairs* Vol. 29 (1950): 23–32.

Sugrue, Thomas J. *The Origins of the Urban Crisis: Race and Inequality in Postwar Detroit*. Princeton Studies in American Politics: Historical, International, and Comparative Perspectives, eds. Ira Katznelson, Martin Shefter, and Theda Skocpol. Princeton, New Jersey: Princeton University Press, 1996.

Tananbaum, Duane. *The Bricker Amendment Controversy: A Test of Eisenhower's Political Leadership*. Ithaca, New York: Cornell University Press, 1988.

Thomas, Dorothy Q. "We Are Not the World: U.S. Activism and Human Rights in the Twenty-First Century," *Signs: Journal of Women in Culture and Society* Vol. 25, no. 4 (2000): 1121–24.

Tolley, Howard, Jr. *The UN Commission on Human Rights*. Boulder, Colorado, and London: Westview Press, 1987.

Truman, Harry S. "The Truman Doctrine," *The Annals of America*, Vol. 16, *1940–1949: The Second World War and After*. Chicago: Encyclopedia Britannica, Inc., 1968.

"Tuberculosis Survey in Harlem: Three Groups Join in Two-Month X-Ray Campaign Among New York Negroes," *National Negro Health News* Vol. 14, no. 1 (January–March), 1946.

Tucker, William H. *The Science and Politics of Racial Research*. Urbana: University of Illinois Press, 1994.

Urquhart, Brian. *Ralph Bunche: An American Life*. New York: W. W. Norton & Co. 1993.

Vogelgesang, Sandy. "Diplomacy of Human Rights," *International Studies Quarterly* Vol. 23, no. 2 (June 1979): 230–35.

Von Eschen, Penny M. *Race Against Empire: Black Americans and Anticolonialism, 1937–1957*. Ithaca, New York: Cornell University Press, 1997.

Walton, Hanes. *Black Women at the United Nations: The Politics, A Theoretical Model, and the Documents*, eds. Paul David Seldis and Mary A. Burgess. San Bernadino, California: Borgo Press, 1995.

Watson, Denton L. *Lion in the Lobby: Clarence Mitchell, Jr.'s Struggle for the Passage of Civil Rights Laws*. New York: William Morrow and Company, Inc., 1990.

Weems, Robert Jr. *Desegregating the Dollar: African American Consumerism in the Twentieth Century*. New York: New York University Press, 1998.

——. "'Bling-Bling' and Other Recent Trends in African American Consumerism." Conference paper, Missouri Black Expo, August 2002.

West, Cornel. *Race Matters*. New York: Vintage Books, 1993.

White, Walter. "Behind the Harlem Riot," *The New Republic* Vol. 109 (August 16, 1943): 220–22.

——. *How Far the Promised Land?* New York: Viking Press, 1955.

Whitfield, Stephen. *A Death in the Delta: The Story of Emmett Till*. New York: The Free Press, 1988.

Wilkins, Roy. "Stalin's Greatest Defeat," *American Magazine*, December 1951.

Williams, Charles. "Harlem at War," *The Nation* Vol. 156 (January 16, 1943): 86–88.

Williams, Juan. *Eyes on the Prize: America's Civil Rights Years, 1954–1965*. With an introduction by Julian Bond. New York: Viking Penguin, 1987.

Wilson, Sondra Kathryn, ed. *In Search of Democracy: The NAACP Writings of James Weldon Johnson, Walter White, and Roy Wilkins (1920–1977)*. New York: Oxford University Press, 1999.

Wilson, William Julius. *When Work Disappears: The World of the New Urban Poor*. New York: Knopf, 1997.

——. *The Truly Disadvantaged: The Inner City, the Underclass, and Public Policy*. Chicago: University of Chicago Press, 1990.

Wittner, Lawrence S. *American Intervention in Greece, 1943–1949*. New York: Columbia University Press, 1982.

Yergan, Max. "Africa: Next Goal of Communism," *U.S. News and World Report*, May 1, 1953.

——. "The Status of the Natives in South Africa," *Journal of Negro History* Vol. 24, no. 1 (January 1939): 44–56.

Yergin, Daniel. *Shattered Peace: The Origins of the Cold War and the National Security State*. Boston: Houghton Mifflin Company, 1977.

Zangrando, Robert L. *NAACP Crusade Against Lynching, 1909–1950*. Philadelphia, Pennsylvania: Temple University Press, 1980.

Acronyms

ABA	American Bar Association
AJC	American Jewish Congress
CAA	Council on African Affairs
CHR	Commission on Human Rights
CIO	Congress of Industrial Organizations
CP	Communist Party
CRC	Civil Rights Congress
DAR	Daughters of the American Revolution
DNC	Democratic National Committee
FBI	Federal Bureau of Investigation
FDR	Franklin Delano Roosevelt
FEPC	Fair Employment Practices Committee
GOP	Grand Old Party
HST	Harry S Truman
ILO	International Labor Organization
IRS	Internal Revenue Service
MINDIS	UN Sub-Commission on Prevention of Discrimination and Protection of Minorities
NAACP	National Association for the Advancement of Colored People
NATO	North Atlantic Treaty Organization
NLG	National Lawyers Guild
NNC	National Negro Congress
PCCR	President's Committee on Civil Rights
PIC	Peace Information Center
SACB	Subversive Activities Control Board
UN	United Nations
UNCIO	UN Conference on International Organization
USIS	United States Information Service

Index

CPSIA information can be obtained
at www.ICGtesting.com
Printed in the USA
FFOW03n1628070115
10158FF

9 780521 531580